THIRD EDITION

MAKING
A
DIFFERENCE
COLLEGE GUIDE

OUTSTANDING COLLEGES
TO HELP YOU MAKE
A BETTER WORLD

MIRIAM WEINSTEIN

SAGE PRESS
San Anselmo, California

Publisher: Miriam Weinstein
Cover Design: Miriam Weinstein   Cover Art Production: E Arts
SAGE PRESS
524 San Anselmo Ave #225
San Anselmo, CA 94960
(415) 258-9924   (800) 218-4242

Publisher's Cataloging in Publication
(Prepared by Quality Books Inc.)

Weinstein, Miriam H.
    Making a difference college guide : outstanding colleges
    to help you make a better world / Miriam Weinstein. -- 3rd ed.
    p. cm.
    Includes bibliographical references and index
    ISBN 0-9634618-2-6

    1. Universities and colleges--United States--Directories. 2.
Universities and colleges--United States--Moral and ethical
aspects. 3. Environmental sciences--Study and teaching (Higher)--
United States. 4. Vocational guidance.   I. Title.

L901.W45 1994   378.73
                                      QB194-1283

Printed on recycled paper.

Printed in the United States of America

Individual copies: $12.95 plus $2.50 postage and handling. Discounts available
for quantity orders. We encourage orders by schools, non-profits, grassroots and
religious groups working to make a better world. For information please write to
SAGE PRESS, 524 San Anselmo Ave. #225   San Anselmo, CA 94960
Phone / Fax (415) 258-9924

For my children,

Radha, Elam, Pascal, Mira

and to native peoples and their struggles

ACKNOWLEDGMENTS

First, this edition would not be complete without the sincerest appreciation to Marty Nemko, who has freely and generously given me of his time, his mentoring and continuing support. Thanks to my mother Jill Weinstein, to my childhood neighborhood - The Amalgamated - a hotbed of social consciousness, and to my friend Joanne Lukomnik who dragged me along on many picket lines. Thanks to the people who have made a difference in my life: to Mike and Susie McConneloug, Stuart Kutchins, Barry Gordon, Jenna Jackson and Aftab. I would like to thank the gracious educators who gave of their time to write the introductory essays - often on very short notice. I am greatful for the enthusiastic reception and cooperation I've received from the colleges. Thanks to my kids for bearing with me and the terrible cooking. My apologies to my lovely dog Brindle for still not getting her walk. Lastly, heartfelt appreciation to our Mother Earth.

CONTENTS

PREFACE
WALTER H. CORSON
GLOBAL TOMORROW COALITION

Daily we see mounting social and environmental problems that threaten our communities and the survival of our global life-support systems. These problems underscore the need for an education that sheds light on the underlying causes of issues such as poverty, unemployment, and crime; and ecological concerns such as environmental pollution and natural resource depletion.

Miriam Weinstein's *Making A Difference College Guide* moves well beyond the traditional guides and highlights a wide range of innovative, programs and courses that provide practical, problem-solving approaches to some of the great issues of our time - issues that may ultimately imperil our future survival.

The book features colleges and universities that, through their development of programs and selection of faculty, demonstrate a concern for social responsibility, the quality of life, and the future of humankind. Most entries contain a description of the institution's philosophy and its approach to social and environmental concerns, and provide summaries of key programs designed to "make a difference."

The *Guide* highlights innovative programs at more traditional universities such as Tufts, Wisconsin, and Oregon; at well-known colleges such as Oberlin, St. Olaf, and Earlham, at less-known but valuable institutions such as Warren Wilson, Goshen and Prescott, and tiny but unique programs such as the Institute for Social Ecology, and the School for International Training.

A wide range of practical programs leading to good employment opportunities are covered in areas such as forestry, applied environmental technology, environmental engineering, natural resource management, community health, and social work.

The publication is obviously a labor of love; Miriam Weinstein is committed to promoting critical values needed for the twenty-first century such as environmental protection, conflict resolution, and social equity. *Making A Difference College Guide* reveals educational programs that will help students make the planet a better place for themselves and for future generations.

Walter Corson is a Senior Associate at Global Tomorrow Coalition, a not-for-profit alliance of nearly 100 U.S. organizations, institutions, corporations, and individuals committed to acting today to assure a more sustainable, equitable, and humane global future.

INTRODUCTION

Yes, you want to use make a difference, but you also want a good job after college. You also want to attend a college that actively supports social and/or environmental responsibility. So many colleges today claim to do so. This book, *Making A Difference College Guide*, profiles those unique institutions or departments for whom this is an abiding and genuine dedication. They are committed to public service, social change and environmental stewardship. And fortunately for you, the colleges and programs listed are also among the most innovative and engaging in the nation. Many of the colleges listed in this guide are perhaps unfamiliar not only to you, but to college counselors as well. Yet, when students and parents read about them, their eyes light up and the parent usually responds "Now, that's a school my child would like!" or "I wish I could have gone to a school like that!" I know you will be very happily surprised when you learn what American higher education at its best offers today.

As a parent who is a veteran of three college searches, including one for myself, I learned how ill equipped we were to make a good decision. My daughter and I conducted her college search from view books, college guides, help from a high school counselor, and my outdated recollections. Nowhere in this process did we ever look at a list of classes offered, much less descriptions of the courses she'd be taking. I wish we would've had a guide which not only shepherded us to these special colleges, but gave us the flavor what the classes would really be like. So, even if you don't have a clue as to what you want to study, look the class listings over - something is bound to spark your interest.

Colleges in this guide engage in the major issues of our day, especially environmental, women's, peace, and ethnic studies. You'll find programs as varied as marine biology, social work, outdoor education, teaching, public health, economics, natural resources, gerontology, forest engineering, and sustainable development. Interdisciplinary studies and opportunities for individually designed majors abound.

Do you need to attend a big-name school with an inch-thick catalog to get a good education? Not at all. Many of the most thoughtful socially committed and undergraduate-centered schools are small and often little-known. These institutions offer small classes taught by faculty who care more about teaching than research, and who are glad to see students outside of class. Consider the idea of being a top student in a little pond, rather than a middling student at a top school. Universities, on the other hand, can offer a mind-boggling array of majors, greater opportunities to participate in advanced research, and vast resources.

You'll notice the profiles in this guide are quite different than others you may have read. Schools were asked such questions as:

- How do you integrate your institution's mission with your educational approach?
- How do you foster ethics, critical thinking, social activism, responsibility to community, the Earth, and future generations?
- How do you foster sensitivity to minority and other world views?
- What kinds of community service are your students engaged in?
- What study abroad programs (particularly non-institutional) do you offer?
- Do you have recycling or energy conservation policies in force?

Each school has its own unique opportunities. Warren Wilson and Goddard students all work to operate and maintain their campuses. College of the Atlantic requires internships, Hampshire requires community service. During Goshen's "study-service term" program, students do service abroad, mostly in rural areas in third world countries. Students in Bethel's internship program have assisted migrant laborers and taught sustainable agriculture in Central America. If you would like your education outdoors, check out Prescott College, Audubon Expedition Institute and the School for Field Studies. Tufts University is pioneering environmental studies "across the curriculum," while Unity offers environmental majors exclusively. Most of the schools listed in the guide allow you to design your own major, and many offer opportunities for independent study. Naropa Institute attracts primarily older and re-entry students, while a few others serve adults through non-residential study. Oberlin, Berea and Bethel are among those having an historical ethic of concern for the disadvantaged, while Northland and Bemidji offer special programs for Native Americans. The Evergreen State College has gained nationwide recognition for its team teaching, core/multidisciplinary approach. Many of the schools have required courses in non-Western cultures, promoting understanding and tolerance in our increasingly diverse and multicultural society. All of these important and sometimes unique offerings will give you an educational experience that is both highly engaging and relevant. "Making A Difference" institutions offer many exceptional opportunities for growth. By participating in co-op education, community service and internships you'll gain not only a more integrated education, but also a genuine head start in finding employment after graduation. Whether you want to attend a research oriented university, a traditional liberal arts college with two or three thousand students, a small innovative farm based school, a Christian affiliated school, or a progressive school, you'll find them all here. Do note that the schools in this guide which characterize themselves as only moderately, minimally or even non-selective in their admissions process, all offer an excellent education both in and out of the classroom. Make sure you read Martin Nemko's "College Report Card - A Tool for Choosing from Among Your Top-Choice Colleges" on pages 12-18. Also read Tom Kelly's "Environmental Literacy" essay on pages 7-8 to help you decide where the environment fits into your educational and career plans.

If your interests lie in "environmental sciences" and "environmental studies" programs, get a catalog and examine the required and elective courses. A well balanced major will include courses from both the social sciences (sociology, economics, political science, anthropology etc.) and sciences (biology, geology, engineering etc) although not in the same proportion. Environmental science programs too often include no social sciences, and environmental studies programs are often weak in science. The social sciences educate you about the complex real world context of our problems, in which sciences needs to be understood. And science, like it or not, is a big part of the ball game.

You'll notice in reading the profiles that these schools have a particularly strong concern for active citizenship, and service to society. To quote President Clinton's speech on national service: "We'll ask young people to work, to help control pollution and recycle waste, to paint darkened buildings and cleanup neighborhoods. To work with senior citizens and combat homelessness and help children in trouble get out of it and build a better life.... We are a nation, with all of our problems, where people can come together across racial and religious lines and hold hands and work together, not just to endure our differences, but to celebrate them." Like President Clinton, we hope the ethic of service conveyed by these institutions guides you throughout your life. More and more graduates are choosing service oriented careers, or making volunteer work a significant part of their lives. Do read Nancy Rhodes' article "Community Service: Experience for a Lifetime" on pages 5-6.

Next comes the always burning question of "What work can I get when I graduate?" Many people fear that making a difference means a life of poverty. But there's good news in the section on career opportunities. These careers correspond to the myriad studies found in this guide. Some fields of work such as forestry, forestry engineering and paper sciences have tremendous demand for graduates. The need for people in environmental sciences and gerontology likewise is constantly increasing.

It is unfortunately true that nowadays, a college degree does not guarantee a job, much less a secure, interesting or high paying one. It is also true that if you are looking to make a better world, and if you are persistent in seeking it out, there is a meaningful career waiting for you. When your work is personally meaningful, you'll find both greater motivation to succeed, and greater job satisfaction. Perhaps you won't be able to measure the wealth you earn in dollars, but you will have the immeasurable gains that come from a life led in integrity, the joy of doing good work, of improving other peoples lives, and of caring for the earth

As for the expense of attending college, whether public or private, big or little, never be deterred from applying solely because of financial considerations. Every institution offers financial aid. If you need it, apply. Depending upon your financial circumstances, the cost to your family of sending you to an expensive school may not be any higher than attending a state college. It is always smart to apply early if you need financial aid.

Lastly, I have chosen to let the schools speak for themselves. I have neither the expertise nor the desire to rank or judge them. They are all special and worthwhile. Do take advantage of Martin Nemko's College Report Card to compare colleges you are considering.

The institution's profiles were written by the colleges especially for this guide and/or taken from materials provided by the college. In some cases, the study areas listed were chosen by the college, but more often than not, I have done the choosing. The list of class titles is given as a general indication of coursework - it is seldom a complete listing of courses available, and generally does not list introductory classes. As classes can change from year to year, the courses listed might not be offered during your enrollment. Also, note, I have included majors, minors and concentrations under "Making A Difference Studies." Some institutions have provided faculty biographies. I have included them because people with interesting lives are often more interesting teachers.

All the colleges were asked if they were actively seeking minority students. The good news for those of who who have minority status is that virtually every school said "Yes."

In the back of the book you'll find a number of helpful resources for your use. There is a state by state index of colleges, and a resources and bibliography section featuring an array of national groups and opportunities, as well as some practical reading. There are forms for you to use to contact colleges you want to know more about.

Healing is so urgently needed in our country and around the world. So, please, use this book to choose a college and perhaps a career for building a better world. My gratitude to you for joining with the many caring and courageous people all over the earth who are seeking to make a difference.

COMMUNITY SERVICE
EXPERIENCE FOR A LIFETIME
NANCY RHODES
CAMPUS COMPACT

Exciting changes are unfolding in community and public service at colleges and universities across the country, and if you want to serve the public good, I am happy to say you have arrived at just the right time to join in. Opportunities for you to engage in tremendously challenging, important, and rewarding community service while you are in school are becoming available like never before. Whatever issue motivates you, whatever level of commitment you bring, whatever your personal style and unique talents, there is a place for you to contribute, to truly make a difference, to have a real impact in peoples' lives -- and in your own.

Better still, you will find that at many colleges and universities community service is no longer limited to extracurricular activities that students undertake in their free time. Increasingly, service is being integrated with academic programs in ways that make the service more effective and the learning more profound. This powerful trend in education, called service learning, is breaking down the walls that separate campuses from communities, and is a major element in the national explosion of community service. Service learning represents a merger of the movement for education reform, which holds among other things that education can be improved through combining active learning, with the movement for responsible citizenship. These two movements agree that engaged citizenship in a democratic society is a learned behavior, a lifelong "habit of the heart," that can be acquired in part through service learning.

Perhaps the most exciting aspect of the student service movement is that it is largely led by students themselves. Today's students seek out quality service programs, and where programs do not exist, students are creating them. Look at students involved in service today, says a report on the service movement, and you will find "messy, fast-growing, and exhilarating action. These young people radiate confidence, energy, earnestness, and purpose. They are willing to work hard, they are willing to listen, they are willing to move ahead in confusion, and willing to make mistakes. Because of this, they have accomplished great things."[1]

Students are indeed doing great things, and the nation has taken notice and is following their lead. For instance, I work for a national coalition of university and college presidents which began several years ago when a group of presidents met and decided that they should take action to support students' community service efforts. Additionally, Congress has created the Commission on National and Community Service to channel funding to a wide range of service program And President Clinton has proposed a national service program that will provide stipends and educational benefits to young people engaged in community service. You are, as I said, in luck.

Now, to the business at hand. There are a few things to consider as you set about selecting a school that is right for you. First, I would encourage you to look closely at the service programs offered at schools you consider, as the nature and quality of programs vary a great deal. Many of the schools in this guide have exceptionally strong service programs. You will find that on some campuses service programs are described in admissions materials and are well known by admissions staff. But catalogs are only a starting point. Although it may not always be easy to find out what is going on, you should make inquiries. Use the telephone. Try especially to talk to participating students. Visit if you possibly can.

Second, find out who runs service programs. Programs are run by student organizations, by student life administrators, or by academic departments. Programs run by students will challenge your organizing and leadership abilities, but may take time away from direct service, while programs run largely by faculty or administrators will allow you to devote more time directly to service, but with perhaps less influence in the direction of the project. So it depends on what you are looking for and where your talents lie.

Likewise, consider issues. If you have a passion for a particular issue, such as HIV/AIDS, mentoring, natural resources, or migrant farmworkers, you might want to look for schools with service programs that address your issue.

Finally, I suggest you inquire specifically whether a school has a service learning program that integrates service with study. Combining your service with learning will help you understand deeply the subtleties and relationships between the subjects you study, the problems that we face together, and the institutions we have created to address them.

Service will change the way you look at the world, and will give you experiences available nowhere else. "Behind the studies, the rhetoric, and the ideological struggles lies one simple fact: service works. Not only are trees planted, old people cared for, the hungry fed, but young people learn a new version of their familiar selves; they meet in themselves strong, resilient, reliable, demanding, determined, likeable individuals who can change the world and change their own lives as well."[2] Good luck!

1. Judy Karasik, in a report for the John D. and Catherine T. Mac Arthur Foundation
2. ibid.

Nancy Rhodes is Acting Director of Campus Compact, The Project for Public and Community Service. Campus Compact is a project of the Education Commission of the States.

ENVIRONMENTAL LITERACY
A GUIDE TO CONSTRUCTING AN
UNDERGRADUATE EDUCATION
THOMAS H. KELLY, PH.D
TUFTS ENVIRONMENTAL LITERACY INSTITUTE

Because all human activities are dependent upon and have repercussions within the environment. you have an opportunity to make a difference no matter what your interests. Whether you major in marketing, biology, mathematics or music and you spend your professional life in industry, government or journalism, your actions will have an environmental impact. So, remember whatever your major is, in a certain sense, it is an environmental one.

Ask yourself then, what kind of impact do you want to make? Where do you want to make it? How do you want to make it? These questions have important implications for deciding on the kind of college education you want.If you are concerned about the environment and want your education to reflect that concern and strengthen your capacity to assess, evaluate and judge where you fit into the environment, think about these questions. Independent of your ultimate career choice, what knowledge, skills and experiences do you want from your undergraduate education? If you are concerned about the Earth, yet do not wish to choose an environmental career, consider the notion of "environmental literacy."

An environmentally literate person understands the nature of the interdependence between human activities and the non-human world. With a modern education, so often career-oriented, if we are to graduate environmentally literate citizens, environmental concerns must be incorporated across the curriculum and even beyond the classroom. The prominence of the environment and an ecological perspective emphasizing systems such as the biosphere within the liberal arts education is relatively new. Many educators now seek to connect a broad range of disciplines in an effort to grasp complex, large-scale ecological problems. This is a tall order because there is a fundamental tension between the broad inclusive character of environment, and the practical significance of specialization to the job market or graduate school.

Moreover, recognition of the need to understand the social aspects of ecological problems has introduced questions of racism, equity, human rights, national sovereignty and national security into the environmental debate. These aspects of ecological problems are now widely acknowledged to be part and parcel of these issues. Internationally, the scientific, educational and governmental communities agree that segregation of the so-called "natural sciences " from "social sciences" is a significant obstacle to environmental education. Accordingly, calls for interdisciplinary and multidisciplinary educational programs are being heard from many quarters. Prospective undergraduates should be aware that while intuitively appealing, interdisciplinary and multidisciplinary education are interpreted differently by different schools. It is one thing to take a collection of courses from different disciplines; it is another to integrate and internalize their contents so that you can apply them to your personal and professional life.

When you are evaluating schools and deciding what kind of education you want, one consideration is the degree of disciplinary integration. Does a given program simply offer varying menus of courses from different disciplines? Or, does it offer an integrating mechanism such as a core curriculum or a culminating course or project specifically designed to aid your incorporation of the material into thinking and action? Is there a sufficient range of sciences in the curriculum to provide a graduate with a basic understanding of the materials, energy and processes within which human activity occurs? But beware of a scientific bias in course requirements; make sure adequate study of cultural, political and economic aspects of the environment are included. How integrated are environmental perspectives with the curriculum of other majors such as international relations, chemical engineering or theater? In addition to these types of general questions, you should also frame questions specific to your interests. For example, does the university offer semester abroad programs in developing countries? To what degree does the curriculum employ field work or problem-based learning?

While a general awareness of environmental issues has been prominent since the late 1960's, colleges and universities often change slowly. Therefore you should get the most specific information you can about the school you are considering before making a choice. The institutions in this book are among the nations strongest in environmental curricula.

But of equal importance, you will be well served in your search for the best education for you, if you begin by asking questions of yourself.

Thomas H. Kelly, Ph.D. is the Director of the Tufts Environmental Literacy Institute, Center for Environmental Management at Tufts University

MAKING A DIFFERENCE IN THE WORLD
HOWARD BERRY
PARTNERSHIP FOR SERVICE LEARNING

You want to help people. You want to go abroad.

A service program can be a semester or a year in a poor country, serving the needs of the hungry, the homeless, the ill or handicapped, the very young or very old.It can be construction and repair work or teaching literacy; caring for the sick, supervising recreation for troubled teens; conducting research or doing office work for an economic development or environmental agency or a museum.

Whatever your individual talents and goals, there is a point to consider carefully: the program should be based on mutuality; giving and receiving. Obvious? Yes, but there are programs which are designed to give you a fine experience, but without reference to the host culture. And there are some which expect you to work hard but pay no attention to your own needs.

A service-learning experience is not easy, and shouldn't be. But if you approach it with flexibility, openness, and a willingness to learn - you too will encounter the host culture in a way not possible as a tourist or a traditional study abroad student, and you will be satisfied with your contribution to the people and society, and they with you.

Our agency, Partnership for Service Learning, is a not-for profit consortium of colleges, universities, service agencies and related organizations united to foster and develop programs linking community service and academic study. Over 1500 students from 180 colleges have participated for recognized academic credit in its programs.

Aaron Romano participated in a PSL project while a student at Bard College. A Jewish-American, he worked in a Christian-Jamaican church-based community center providing holistic (physical, mental and spiritual) services to people from low income neighborhoods. At first he felt uneasy, but he soon realized "our religious tenets shared the common principle that one who asks shall receive, and we were to assist in this process. Throughout the semester, I befriended doctors, nurses, teachers, priests, rabbis, and others leaders of the community who were involved in helping Jamaica keep it's head above water. I discovered the majority of Jamaicans are very concerned with the state of their country. Many are willing to devote their lifetimes to ameliorating the oppressive economic and social conditions. Never before have I encountered a place where people were willing to give so much and expect nothing in return. Here is where the essence of love is taught; and with love happiness soon follows."

Students often find that their ideas about what constitutes service are challenged by the values of their host culture. John Hathaway spent a semester in Ecuador and learned to face the differences between his notion of service and that community and the service agency. "The feelings and help of gringos come second in this organization. I realize now that that is how it should be."

Service learning addresses many of the complaints about higher education in this country. Concerns about its efficacy and value, doubts about the teachability of students coming into college who are alienated from the educational process, frustration about inability to find jobs upon graduation, and lack of education for increasing globalization beset education. Educators find it difficult to teach community in a world where the traditional ideas of community no longer work.

It is here that the concept of service-learning comes into the picture. Service learning involves far more than opportunities to work while pursuing studies. It is an integrating volunteer experience, in another culture, designed to improve sense of values, to provide new knowledge, and to assist in the relief of human suffering. Service-learning is based on some quite simple premises. Learning is easier when rooted in practical experience. Service learning programs enrich both learning and experience by providing them with meaning. By linking formal study, formal evaluation and formal expectation with service, it is not an interlude in formal education but a part of it. That the best way to learn the values of sharing and service is by deriving them from concrete situations, where the human need to cooperate is absolutely clear. Volunteer work requires a willingness to put others before self, a willingness to give up something material in order to receive something spiritual in return. That the right way to learn self-worth is by observing one's ability to better the self-worth of others. Living in another culture is the best way to prepare young people for the multicultural and globalized world of today and tomorrow. Programs take place in other cultures to broaden students' horizons to the maximum, to teach them what is relative about their cultures, and to teach them to view their sense of self and their acquisition of knowledge through the values of another culture. That students who have been through such experiences are better able to deal with the world of work, more employable, more mature. Lastly, when all of this has gone on, there is something left behind and that something is good. A student who participates leaves a measurable improvement in the lives of others and hence in society.

International service-learning puts new life and vigor into liberal education for the 21st century, fights valuelessness and materialism, and that helps students go on to live more useful lives in the new multicultural, fragile, yet infinitely absorbing world that is before us.

Howard Berry is the President of Partnership for Service Learning. This essay draws heavily on an essay entitled "Service, Values, and a Liberal Education" by Dr. Humphrey Tonkin, President of Hartford University, and Chair of the Partnership for Service Learning Board of Trustees.

THE WESLEYAN CHALLENGE

Expanding the reach of its historic commitment to community service, Wesleyan University has announced a summer service competition for high school students.

The Wesleyan Challenge offers three high school sophomores and juniors the chance to improve their communities by implementing a summer service project of their own design. These students receive $5,000: $2,000 for the project and $3,000 toward tuition at the college of their choice.

The program, funded by the generous of an alumnus, is philosophically consistent with the Clinton Administration's national service initiative. In 1994, Eli Segal, President Clinton's Director of National Service, served on the panel judging the student entries. During a speech kicking off the Wesleyan Challenge, he remarked,

> " It's in the identical spirit of the national service law,
> which I oversee. It rewards young people financially
> for their commitment to their communities and its a
> clarion call to our young people sitting here today, that
> even before their college years, even before they've
> become eligible to participate in national service, that
> the ethic of service can be alive and can be borne by
> challenging young people, by investing in them, not just
> as recipients of our benevolence, but as service
> entrepreneurs..."

"We see the Wesleyan Challenge as a powerful statement about the principles of the University," said President William M. Chace. We hope the challenge will inspire high school students to think creatively about solutions to the problems facing their communities and the nation."

Applicants are invited to submit written proposals to Wesleyan by March 1 detailing a public service project they would undertake in their communities. Each proposal must identify goals, cost estimates and local resources and organizations that might be involved. An adviser must also provide a recommendation.

In April, ten finalists are brought, all expenses paid, to the Wesleyan campus for interviews with the panel of judges. During the summer, the winners put their ideas into action, guided by their advisers and members of the Wesleyan Community. 1994 finalists came from as close as Connecticut, Pennsylvania and New York, and as far as South Carolina, California, Illinois, Florida, Texas and Puerto Rico.

Applications are available by writing: **The Wesleyan Challenge**
Wesleyan University, P.O. Box 7070, Middletown, CT 06459
or by calling 1-800-43-WES-GO.

THE COLLEGE REPORT CARD
A TOOL FOR CHOOSING FROM AMONG YOUR TOP-CHOICE COLLEGES
MARTIN NEMKO PH.D.

Directions

There are 47 items on the Report Card. They are the major factors that affect students' success and happiness at college. Put a checkmark next to the 5-15 factors you consider most likely to affect your success and happiness.

Make a copy of the Report Card for each college you're considering.

Over the coming months, you'll have the chance to learn how each college measures up on your 5-15 factors: by reading college guides and materials from the colleges, talking with your counselor and college students home for vacation, asking questions at college nights, phoning college personnel and students, and making a campus visit. (See "How to Test Drive a College" on page 16). A primary source of information for each item is listed alongside it. Write what you learn in the margins of each college's Report Card.

Important!!! You can get information on most of the items by phone. For example, to talk with students, call the college's switchboard (the phone numbers are available from directory assistance and have the call transferred to a residence hall front desk, the student newspaper office, or the student government office.

By spring of your senior year, you'll have a wonderful basis for choosing your college. After you've finished recording what you learned, compare the report cards, then choose your college based on your gut feeling as to which one will best promote your intellectual, social, emotional, and ethical development.

THE COLLEGE REPORT CARD
FOR_____ COLLEGE/UNIVERSITY

The Students

1. To what extent are you comfortable with the student body: intellectually, values, role of alcohol, work/play balance, etc.

In the Classroom

2. What percentage of the typical first years class time is spent in classes of 30 or fewer students? (*Ask students.*)

3. What percentage of class time is spent in lecture versus active learning? (*Ask students.*)

   Most educators agree that learning is often enhanced when students are active; for example, participating in discussions, case studies, field studies, hands-on activities. It's tough to achieve active learning in an auditorium. It's particularly important that first year classes be small because frosh are just getting used to college-level work. Students who might be tempted to space out or even play hooky in a large lecture class, should pay special attention to class size.

   Many colleges report a misleading statistic about class size: the faculty/student ratio. This statistic typically ranges from 1:10 to 1:25, even at mega state universities, evoking images of classes of 10-25 students. The faculty/student ratio is deceptive because it often includes faculty that do research but never teach, or at least never teach undergraduates. The faculty/student ratio also includes courses that you're unlikely to take. What good is it that Medieval Horticulture has three students if Intro to Anything has 300? Hence, the previous two questions are important.

4. How easy is it to register for the classes you want; e.g., do students register by telephone? Are enough sections of classes offered? (*Ask students*)

5. If you are attending a large school, are there special programs that enable you to get into smaller classes: e.g., honors programs, college-within-a-college, living-learning centers? How are students selected for these programs? (*Read college guides and admissions material.*)

6. What percentage of your instructors would you describe as inspirational? (*Ask students.*)

7. What letter grade would you give to the average instructor? (*Ask students.*)

8. Does the college make available to students a booklet summarizing student evaluations of faculty? (*Ask students.*)

   Such a booklet makes it much easier to find good instructors. Also, its presence suggests that the college is more concerned about student rights as a consumer than it is about covering up professors' failings.

9. In a typical introductory social science or humanities course, how many pages of writing are typically assigned? In an advanced class? (*Ask students.*)

10. Does feedback on written work typically include detailed suggestions for improvement or just a letter grade with a few words of feedback? (*Ask students.*)

11. Must all assignments be done individually, or are there sufficient opportunities to do team projects? (*Ask students.*)

12. Is the institution strong in your major area of interest?

13. If you might want a self-designed major, is this a strong point at the school or an infrequently made exception. (*See catalog, ask students*)

14. Are there mechanisms for integrating different disciplines: interdisciplinary seminars, team teaching, internships, capstone classes? (*See catalog, ask admissions*)

Intellectual life outside the classroom

15. Describe and evaluate the advising you've received. (*Ask students.*)

16. How easy is it to get to work on a faculty member's research project? (*Ask students and faculty in your prospective major.*)

   Working under a professor's wing is an excellent opportunity for active learning, also when students become part of the research effort, they feel more like an member of the campus community.

17. To what extent do the viewpoints expressed on campus represent a true diversity of perspectives rather than, for example, just the liberal view or just the conservative stance? (*Ask students and faculty.*)

18. How frequently do faculty invite students to share a meal? (*Ask students.*)

19. How much does the typical student study between Friday dinner and Sunday dinner? (*Read college guides, ask students*)

20. Do faculty live in student residence halls? Does it encourage good faculty-student interaction? (*Call a residence hall front desk.*)

The remaining questions in this section can probably best be answered via a phone call or a visit to the academic affairs office.

21. How does the institution assess a prospective faculty member's ability to teach?

   Ideally, undergraduate institutions should require prospective undergraduate faculty members to submit a teaching portfolio consisting of videotapes of undergraduate classes, student evaluations, syllabi, and conduct a demonstration class at the freshman level. Many colleges only require prospective faculty to do a demonstration of a graduate level seminar in their research area. That says little about their ability to teach undergraduates.

22. Recognizing that this will vary from department to department, how likely is it that a good teacher who publishes little will get tenure?

23. On your most recent student satisfaction survey, what was the average rating for academic life? For out-of-classroom life?

   This is the equivalent of asking hundreds of students how they like their college. If they say that the institution doesn't conduct student satisfaction surveys, you've learned that the institution doesn't care enough to assess student satisfaction.

24. How much money per student is spent annually on helping faculty to improve their teaching? (not to include money for research-related sabbaticals and conventions.)

   Colleges frequently espouse the importance of good teaching. The answer to this question lets you know if a college puts its money where its mouth is.

25. What is done to ensure that students receive high quality advising?

   For example, does faculty get special training in how to advise students? Does advising count in faculty promotion decisions? Can students and advisors, via computer, see what courses the student has taken and yet must take?

Co-Curricular Life

26. Does the new-student orientation program extend beyond the traditional 1-3 days? (*Ask students, consult admissions brochure, and/or catalog.*)

27. What percentage of freshmen, sophomores, juniors, and seniors can obtain on-campus housing? This affects campus community. (*Consult admissions material, ask admissions or housing office.*)

28. Describe residence hall life. How close is it to the living-learning environment described in admission brochures? (*Ask students.*)

29. How attractive is student housing? (*Ask students. Tour facilities.*)

30. How well did you like your freshman roommate? This item assesses the quality of the college's roommate-matching procedure. (*Ask students.*)

31. Is the school's location a plus or minus. Why? (*Read college guides, ask students.*)

32. How many crimes were committed on or near campus last year? How admissions reps for the "crime pamphlet." (*Each school is required to provide one.*)

33. What is the quality of life for special constituencies; e.g., gay, adult, minority, or handicapped students? (*Read admission materials, ask students, phone the office that serves that constituency.*)

34. How strong is the sense of community and school spirit among the students? (*Read college guides, ask students.*)

35. In the dining hall, do students primarily eat in homogeneous groups: for example international, racial groups, etc. (*Ask students, observe first-hand.*)

36. How extensive are the opportunities for community service? What percentage of students participate in it? (*Ask students, the career center, service office.*)

The "Real" World

37. How extensive are the internship opportunities?

    Internships embody active learning, allow students to bridge theory and practice, try out a career without penalty, and make job connections. (*Ask students, contact the career center.*)

38. How good are the career planning and placement services? (*Ask upperclass students*)

    Most colleges offer some career planning and placement, but the best ones offer critiques of videotaped mock interviews, the SIGI or Discover computer career guidance systems, video-interviewing with distant employees, extensive counseling, many job listings, on-campus employee interviews, and connections with alumni. (*Ask students and personnel at the career center.*)

39. In your field, what percentage of students get jobs or into graduate school? What percentage go into service-oriented careers? (*Ask students, faculty in your prospective major, ask at the career center.*)

Overall Indicators of the Institution's Quality

40. What percentage of incoming freshmen return for the sophomore year? (*Consult college guides, ask admissions rep or call the office of institutional research.*)

41. What percentage of students graduate within four years? Five years? (*Consult college guides, ask admissions rep, or call the office of institutional research.*)

    Graduation rate depends in part on student quality: the better the students, the higher the college's graduation rate. But take note if two institutions with similar S.A.T. averages have very different graduation rates. The one with a higher graduation rate will generally have more satisfied students.

42. What should I know about the college that wouldn't appear in print? (*Ask everyone.*)

43. What's the best and worst thing about this college? (*Ask everyone.*)

44. In what ways is this college different from_____College? Ask about a similar institution that you're considering. (*Ask admissions rep, students, perhaps faculty.*)

45. What sorts of students are the perfect fit for this school? A poor fit? (*Read college guides, ask everyone.*)

46. What is the total cost of attending this college, taking into account your likely financial aid package? (*Ask the financial aid office.*)

47. What other information about the school could affect your decision? e.g., beauty of campus, food, a graduation requirements you object to, percent of students of your religious or ethnic group. (*Consult catalog, college guides, ask admissions rep.*)

HOW TO TEST-DRIVE A COLLEGE
MARTIN NEMKO PH.D.

College A or College B? A visit is the best key to deciding. You wouldn't even buy a jalopy without popping the hood and test-driving it. With a college, you're spending thousands of dollars and four or even six years of your life, so better take it for a good spin.

Trouble is, many students make a worse decision after a visit than they would have made without one. A college can feel so overwhelming that many students come away with little more than, "The campus was beautiful and the tour guide was nice."

Here's how to put a college through its paces.

Preparing

1. Plan to visit when school is in session. Visiting a college when it isn't in session is like test-driving a car with the engine off.

2. Call ahead. Ask the admissions office if you can spend the night in a residence hall, perhaps with a student in your prospective major. If you think it might help, make an appointment for an interview. Get directions to campus, a campus map, and where to park. Also find out when and from where tours are given.

3. Reread the college guides. If you're just about to visit, that seemingly boring profile of Sonoma State may become fascinating. It can also raise questions, like, "The book describes Sonoma's Hutchins School of Liberal Studies as excellent. Is it?"

4. Review the questions on the College Report Card.

The Visit

Write what you learn on the College Report Card. Especially if you're visiting more than one college, the differences between them can blur.

Here are the stops on my campus tour. If you're with parents, split up, at least for part of the time. Not only can you see more, but it's easier to ask questions like, "What's the social life like?"

The Official Tour

Take the tour mainly to orient you to campus geography, not to help you pick your college. Tour guides are almost always enthusiastic, unless, of course, they're in a bad mood. The tour guide, however, is usually a knowledgeable student, so while walking to the next point of interest, you may want to ask some questions.

Grab Students

I know it's scary, but grab approachable students in the plaza or student union and ask a question. Most love to talk about their school. You might start with, "Hi, I'm considering coming to this school. Are you happy here? What would you change about the school? What should I know about it that might not appear in print?"

In addition to students at random, consider dropping by a residence hall and talking with the student at the front desk. Or pay a visit to the student government or student newspaper office. Folks there know a lot about life on campus. While you're at the newspaper office, pick up a few copies of the student newspaper. What sorts of stories make the front page? What's in the letters to the editor? Athletes should query players on the team, oboeists should quiz orchestra members.

The key is: never leave a campus without talking with at least five people that the admissions director did not put in front of you. Don't just speak with who's paid by the school, speak with who's paying the school. Like at high school, some people love the school and others hate it, but talk with ten people, and you'll get the picture.

A Dining Hall and/or the Student Union

Sample the food. Tasty nuggets or chicken tetrachloride? Are you a vegetarian? See if there's more than salad bar and cheese-drenched veggies.

While you're in the dining hall (or in the student union), eavesdrop on discussions. Can you see yourself happily involved in such conversations?

Most colleges claim to celebrate diversity. The dining hall is a great place to assess the reality because, there, integration is voluntary. Do people of different races break bread together?

Bulletin boards are windows to the soul of a college. Is the most frequent flyer, "Noted scholar speaks," "Political action rally" or "Semi-formal ball"?

Sit In On A Class

Best choices are a class in your prospective major, a required class, or in a special class you're planning to enroll in, for example, an honors class.

At the break, or at the end of the class, stop a group of students and ask them questions. If it's a class in your prospective major, ask students how they like the major and what you should know about the major that might not appear in the catalog.

How to Visit 10 Classes in Half an Hour

Rather than following the standard advice to "sit in on a class" which only lets you know about one class, ask a student for the name of a building with many undergraduate classes.

Walk down its halls and peek into open doors. What percentage of classes are alive and interactive? In what percentage is the professor droning on like a high schooler reciting the pledge of allegiance with the students looking as bored as career bureaucrats two days from retirement?

Some students say that they are too shy to peek into or sit in on classes, but it's worth conquering the shyness. Shouldn't you look at a sample of classes before committing to four years worth?

A Night in the Dorm

It's an uncomfortable thought. "I'm a dippy high school kid. I'll feel weird spending a whole night with college students." Luckily, it usually ends up being fun as well as informative. A bunch of students will probably cluster around you, dying to reveal the inside dirt.

You'll also learn what the students are like: Too studious? Too raunchy? Too radical? Too preppy? At 10:30 P.M. on a weeknight, is the atmosphere "Animal House", an academic sweatshop, or a good balance?

Are the accommodations plush or spartan? One prospective student found a dorm crawling with roaches. You won't get that information on the official tour.

Beware of Bias

We've already mentioned the peril of an overzealous tour guide. Here are other sources of bias in a college visit:

Timing

You visited a college on Thursday at noon. That's when many colleges are at their best. Students are buzzing around amid folks hawking hand-crafted jewelry or urging you to join their clubs or causes, all perhaps accompanied by a rock band. But if you were to arrive at 4:30, even the most dynamic college won't seem as exciting.

Weather

No matter how great the college, rain can't help but dampen enthusiasm for it.

The Campus

Chant this 10,000 times: "Better good teachers in wooden buildings than wooden teachers in good buildings." As mentioned earlier, it's so easy to be overwhelmed by ivy-covered buildings, lush lawns, and chiming bell towers. A beautiful campus is nice, but don't let it overwhelm other factors.

Colleges begin to melt together after a while, however, so you might want to take photos of each campus.

After the Visit

Finish recording what you've learned on the College Report Card immediately after leaving campus. Especially if you've visited a number of colleges, it's easy to confuse key features of one with another: "Was it North Carolina-Asheville or St. John's that had great vegetarian food?"

Probably, additional questions about each college will come to mind after you leave. Write them down and send them to your college interview as part of a thank you note which expresses your appreciation for the time spent and the advice you received.

The Decision

After you get home, ask yourself four questions:
- Would I be happy living and learning with these types of students for four years?
- Would I be happy being instructed by these professors for four years?
- Would I be happy living in this environment for four years?
- Will this college help me achieve my goals?

If it's yes to all four, you may have found your new home.

Congratulations.

Martin Nemko, Ph.D., is an Oakland, California-based consultant
to families and colleges on undergraduate education.

MAKING A DIFFERENCE CAREERS

African-American Studies See Ethnic Studies

Agricultural Engineers Design systems and strategies that preserve and protect our water and soil resources, regarding various engineering aspects of food and fiber production. Many work in developing countries helping with appropriate technology for increasing food production and quality while using human and natural resources responsibly.

Agroecology (The study of sustainable agriculture - more commonly known as 'organic farming') Graduates are in demand in farming, agribusiness, teaching, research and government.

American Studies Graduates find work as journalists, lawyers, government workers, teachers, business people, historical preservationists, and museum workers.

Anthropology Majors find work in federal, state, and local government, law, medicine, urban planning, business, and museums. They often go on to graduate work in anthropology as well, for a career in teaching.

Atmospheric Science See Meteorology

Child Development Careers as adoption counselors, child development specialists, educational consultants, working with handicapped children, hospital childlife specialists and go on to graduate work for Marriage & Family Counselor degrees. They work in crisis centers, hospitals, and both private and public agencies at both the local and national level.

Civil Engineers Conceive, plan, design, construct, operate and maintain dams, bridges, aqueducts, water treatment plants, sewage treatment plants, flood control works, and urban development programs. They are employed by governmental agencies at all levels and by engineering contractors, private consulting firms and in the areas of teaching, research, materials testing, city planning and administration fields.

Community Health Educators Work as school health educators, community health educators, family planning educators, environmental health specialists, occupational safety specialists, public health investigators, consumer safety investigators and OSHA inspectors.

Conservation Law Enforcement Graduates find work with state and federal governments as game wardens conservation officers, special agents for U.S. Fish & Wildlife, wildlife inspectors, border patrol agents, park rangers and state troopers

Economics Prepares students for careers both nationally and internationally in business labor, government, public service, or law.

Entomologists (Those who study insects) Work in the area of Integrated Pest Management which is essential part of organic farming. They work to understand the role of insects in the natural world and how they interact with man. They seek safe and effective solutions to insect problems in urban environments and agriculture.

Environmental Education Can lead to work in park and natural preserve administration, aquarium management, environmental advocacy organizations, nature writing, photography and documentation, teaching in elementary and secondary schools, and government work for environmental agencies.

Environmental Engineers Work in the areas of control of air & water pollution, industrial hygiene, noise & vibration control, and solid & hazardous waste management. Graduates find work in industry, consulting firms, and public agencies concerned with air and water pollution control, water treatment, and waste mgm't.

Environmental and Forest Biology Careers as animal ecologists, aquatic biologists, botanists, conservation biologists, consulting biologists, environmental assessment specialists, environmental conservation officers, fisheries biologists, natural resource specialists, ornithologists, park naturalists, plant and wetlands ecologists, public health specialists, sanctuary managers, soil conservationists, toxicologists, waterfowl biologists, wildlife biologists, game biologists, entomologists.

Environmental Health Specialists Work for state governments enforcing and administering laws governing water, food, and air contamination, noise, land use planning, occupational health hazards, and animal vectors of disease.

Environmental Studies Majors find a myriad of careers from cartographers, community resource development, cultural impact analysis, to environmental lobbyist, interpretive naturalist, park managers, recycled paper promoters, to wilderness survival instructors. Graduates also find work as pollution analysts, environmental journalists, air quality aides, transportation planners, pollution measurement technicians, environmental affairs directors, recycling co-ordinators, environmental educators, energy conservation specialists and legislative researchers.

Environmental Toxiology Those not going on to graduate study find work with government agencies, universities, industry and research and consulting firms in the areas of residue analysis, environmental monitoring, forensic toxicology, animal toxicology, environmental health and safety and pest control.

Ethnic Studies Graduates for work in community service organizations concerned with opportunities and problems of various ethnic and racial groups. They work as affirmative action officers, Equal Opportunity representatives, human relations specialists, peace officers, ombudsmen, urban specialists, diversity directors, educational specialists and lobbyists. Preparation for graduate work in the social sciences, law and humanities, and for work in municipal, state and federal government.

Fisheries Work in management, law enforcement and public information-education phases of fisheries work with national and international agencies as well as with regional, state and local government. Increasing opportunities are available with private industry interested in conservation, hydropower companies, and an expanding recreation business. Careers in research, administration, or teaching .

Forest Engineers Work in the areas of water resources (including water supply for urban areas and ground water aquifer protection) pollution abatement, and hazardous waste management. They design and plan collection systems to store and transport water, timber and energy structures, pollution abatement systems, and energy management. Careers as energy efficiency specialists, energy planning supervisors, environmental engineers, hydrologists, pollution control engineers, road engineers, survey party chief, water rights engineers, forest engineers, cartographers, ground water investigators, and natural resource engineers.

Forestry Graduates find work as foresters, arborists, environmental consultants, forest ecologists, timber buyers, urban foresters, land use specialists, forest economists, interpretive naturalists, consultants, environmental scientists, outdoor recreation, environmental conservation officers, naturalists, outdoor recreation, policy makers, forest protection work, including fire, insect and disease control. Managerial work planning timber crop rotations, and evaluating the economics of alternative forest management plans. Jobs far exceed the number of graduates each year.

Forest Ranger Graduates find work as county park rangers, environmental conservation officers, forest firefighters, forest rangers, forestry aides, survey party chiefs, engineer's aides, and forestry technicians. Jobs in forestry and surveying fields far exceed the number of graduates each year.

Fuel Science Graduates find work seeking to provide reliable energy sources without adverse environmental effects. They are employed by industry, government and utilities, as well as continuing on to graduate school.

Geology Geologists seek new resources, while insuring the most environmentally responsible means of doing do, ensure preservation of land and water quality, formulate plans for restoration of degraded lands. Career opportunities include industry, government and education. Many students continue on to graduate school in urban planning, engineering, environmental studies etc.

Geography Careers with environmental and resource management, location and resource decision-making, urban and regional planning and policy questions, and transportation in government, private, non-profit and international agencies.

Gerontologists Work in human service positions with the elderly or preparation for graduate school.

Human Services Work in advocacy, program development, management, direct service and case management in child-welfare agencies, drug and alcohol programs, crisis intervention settings, working in group homes for adolescents, community action programs, emergency housing programs, parole and probation. May provide case management, needs assessment, advocacy, crisis intervention and stabilization, and supportive task-oriented short term counseling.

Integrated Health Studies See Community Health

International Agriculture Development Careers in helping to solve hunger problems in Third World countries. This may involve working at the local level with government, private business, church or philanthropic organizations. Equally suitable for students with or without agricultural background.

Labor and Industrial Relations Graduates find employment in business, government, and labor organizations as labor relations specialists, personnel and human resource specialists, researchers, organizers, consultants and professionals in mediation and arbitration. The degree is also good preparation for graduate or law school.

Landscape Architects Work as city planners, coastal specialists, coastal zone resource specialists, community planners, environmental planners, land designers, land use planners, landscape architects and contractors, park landscape architects, regional, site, and transportation planners.

Landscape Horticulture See Urban Forestry

Land Use Planners Work with state or federal regulatory agencies, regional planning commissions, consulting firms and municipalities.

Marine Biologists Find careers in marine research, education and adminstration in marine industries and aquaculture, as well as further graduate study and research.

Medical Anthropologists (The study of the relationship between culture and health - a growing discipline for persons involved with the health needs of ethnically diverse populations.) Employment areas include local, state, federal and voluntary health agencies, and preparation for graduate programs.

Meteorologists (Persons who study the atmosphere) This field is important in environmental, energy, agricultural, oceanic and hydrological sciences. Graduates find careers with industry, private consulting firms, government, or continue on to graduate school.

Native American Studies Graduates teach social sciences, work in tribal governments and communities, and prepare for graduate work in anthropology, history, sociology, or professional training in law or business.

Natural Resources Planning & Interpretation Soil conservationist, environmental journalist, natural resources librarian, park ranger, rural county planner, environmental education leader, naturalist, hydrologist, information specialist.

Natural Resources Management Graduates work as public affairs specialists, soil technicians, wildlife biologist/ managers, plant curators, park ranger/managers, environmental planners, city planners, soil conservation planners, shellfish biologists, naturalists, and hazardous materials technicians. (See fisheries, forestry, wildlife...)

Natural Resource Sciences Careers in professional areas with a holistic perspective on resource management and research. Graduates are employed by all major public and private land management and wildlife organizations. They work as foresters, range conservationists, wildlife biologists, park managers, information specialists, game managers, consultants, researchers, and in developing countries.

Oceanography Graduates work as oceanographers, marine biologists, aquatic biologists, water pollution technicians, research assistants, earth scientists and environmental specialists.

Outdoor Education & Interpretation Careers in designing and administering recreation programs, guiding groups in wilderness adventures, counseling and working with diverse populations (troubled youth, handicapped people, senior citizens). Work with state, federal, private recreation departments, environmental education centers, camps, schools, groups such as Outward Bound.

Paper & Science Engineering Careers in recycling, paper making, and waste treatment, hazardous waste mgm't, oil spill prevention, environmental monitoring.

Peace & Conflict Studies Careers in arms control and public policy, third world development and human rights, the faith community, the Peace Corps, the United Nations, domestic social and economic justice, civil rights, mediation and conflict resolution. Preparation for law, journalism, education, government, and communications

Political Science (The study of predicting, explaining, and evaluating political behavior, beliefs etc.) Graduates find socially relevant careers in public service, political analysis and teaching. They attend graduate school in areas such as law, teaching, social work, journalism, public administration and public policy.

Public Administration Graduates work in administrative positions, as well as personnel, budgeting, planning, and public relations, and in substantive policy areas ranging from health and human services and environmental protection to defense, criminal justice, transportation and taxation. Work in city and town management, regional planning commissions, the state budget office and administrative positions in education, national and international agencies.

Public Health Careers as program analysts, mid-level administrators, technical staff persons, department heads in all areas of the health services delivery, and in the regulations field that require policy development, implementation, and evaluation.

Range Managment / Resource Science Careers are available as range conservationists, range managers, natural resource specialists, environmental specialists, soil scientists, park rangers, biological technicians, and agricultural inspectors.

Science, Technology and Values See Technology and Society

Sociologists Find work as consultants to business and government, as social change agents (such as community organizers,) politicians, educators and diplomats. They find careers as urban planners, youth counselors, employment counselors, public opinion analysts, social ecologists, industrial sociologists, correctional counselors, probation officers, health services consultants, and personnel management specialists..

Social Workers Work in areas of health care, services to the elderly, community practice, rehabilitation, youth work, mental health, services to children and families,, substance abuse, residential treatment, the developmentally disabled and employment services. They work in nursing homes, public schools, and probation offices.

Soil Science Graduates work in conservation planning, wetland identification and delineation, land reclamation, sediment & erosion control, land use planning, site evaluations, waste management, soil fertility mgm't, computer modeling of nutrient and pesticide movement, and with international institutions and organizations.

Technology and Society Employment is found with private industry, consulting companies, environmental foundations, and government in the areas of policy analysis and formulation, planning, risk analysis and environmental impact assessment.

Urban Forestry & Landscape Horticulture Leads to careers in landscape design and contracting, urban forestry, park supervision, garden center management, arborists, and city foresters.

Wildlife Studies Wildlife biologist, wildlife manager, fish & game warden, conservation officer, range conservationist, forestry technician, park ranger, soil scientists, naturalist, environmental planner, agricultural inspector, wildlife refuge manager, preserve manager, fisheries technician, and studying rare and endangered species. Work with state and federal environmental agencies and groups such as the Audubon Society and The Nature Conservancy.

Women's Studies Is an asset to careers in such fields as education, social service, government, business, law, the ministry, journalism, counseling, health and child care. More specialized work is found in battered women's shelters, rape counseling services, and in displaced homemaker centers. They work as women's health care specialists, political advocates, psychologists, and teachers.

MAKING
A
DIFFERENCE
COLLEGES

· Please note, Making A Difference Studies do include some minors.

ANTIOCH COLLEGE

650 Students   Yellow Springs, Ohio   Moderately Selective

Antioch College was founded in 1852 by educational reformer Horace Mann as a pioneering experiment in education which offered the first "separate but equal" curriculum to both men and women and stressed that there should be no bars for race, sex, or creed. Today, Antioch continues to dedicate itself to the ideas of equality, "whole-person" education, and community service.

Antioch students are expected to reach beyond conventional learning. They are encouraged to become courageous practitioners, intelligent experimenters, and creative thinkers. Both the faculty and the students strive towards the common goals of refinement and testing of ideas through experience, and of extensive student participation to mold both the campus and the community.

Antioch is committed to internationalization and to peace. The Headquarters of the International Peace Research Association, an association of peace researchers and educators from more than 70 countries, is located on campus. Antioch encourages its students to have a balanced respect for all of life—for one's self, for others, for society, and for the Earth. Empowered by their education, students are encouraged to empower others.

To accomplish its mission of enhancing classroom education with hands-on experience, Antioch has one of the most challenging cooperative education programs in the nation. Just a few examples of positions which Antiochians continue to hold include environmental science jobs in Parana State, Brazil; The National Abortion Federation in Washington, DC: and the Peace Child Foundation in Fairfax, Virginia. The College is scheduled on a calendar of four quarters; Fall, Winter, Spring, and Summer. During two quarters per academic year, students take jobs throughout the country and around the world which give them not only career experience, but also knowledge of different cultures, peoples and independent living. The variety of experience this provides is substantial. One environmental science student, for instance, worked as an environmental education assistant on a sloop on the Hudson River, at a resource center in Minnesota, researched rare plants in Appalachia, cared for injured birds in a raptor rehabilitation project in St. Louis, and then traveled around studying issues of importance in the Northwest. The Co-op Faculty maintains a network of 300 employers who hire students on a regular basis. Advisers assist students in choosing, financing, and evaluating their co-ops, as well as dealing with unexpected problems.

During the two quarters which are not spent on the job, students take part in an academic program which relies on utilizing the strengths of each individual, a willingness to both speak and listen critically, and an international, multi-cultural focus. Professors apply their lessons to "the real world" by bringing politics, world events, and students' co-op experiences into discussions. Classes are offered in the morning, afternoon, and evening, and are evaluated not by grades, but with written evaluations. The performance of each individual in class is assessed both by the professor and the student.

Antioch recognizes that an important part of today's education involves the ability to live and work in the multinational and multicultural society of the 21st Century. In order that students learn about the geography, customs, and traditions of other peoples, the school mandates an in-depth experience of 3-12 months in a cross-cultural environment (either inside or outside of the U.S.). Students can take advantage of the Antioch Education Abroad program, which has included Buddhist Studies programs in Bodh, India, a Comparative Women's Studies Term in Europe, and a British Studies program in London.

Another integral part of Antioch campus life is Community Government. Decision-making councils contain students, faculty, and administrators who strive to consider the many views of the community regarding administrative policy, academic programs, curriculum, budget allocations, tenure, new programs, quality of campus life and matters such as publication standards and social activities etc.

A wide variety of independent groups, such as Survivors of Sexual Offense, Third World Alliance, and Women's Center, exist on the Yellow Springs campus, and visitors often lecture or hold workshops on issues ranging from the Los Angeles Poverty Department, to ritual abuse, to Japanese theater. With the community as small as it is, everybody knows, works, and studies with everybody else. With only 650 students and 58 faculty, the College nurtures close-knit relationships between students, faculty, and administration. Because of this, a common sense of responsibility for the campus prevails. This responsibility manifests itself in an extensive recycling program, a student-authored sexual offense policy, an organic garden, and more.

The College's history of experimentation, its commitment to questioning traditional values and practices, and its willingness to act on its beliefs have had a profound impact of generations of Antioch students. Their achievements represent the living legacy of the Antioch educational experience. Antioch students approach their education, as well as their lives following graduation, with a serious resolve to tackle important issues, question the status quo, and work toward constructive change. Antioch's success carrying out its basic educational mission - empowering students to make a worthwhile difference - is its proudest and most enduring tradition.

Glen Helen, the College's 1000 acre nature preserve, a registered Natural Landmark complete with medicinal springs located right across from campus often serves as a laboratory for science-related courses. It also offers opportunities for hiking, horse-back riding, cross country skiing, canoeing, rock-climbing, rappelling and solitude.

With its Little Arts Theater, a health food store, a town library, the tiny village of Yellow Springs is a safe haven where students can find the essentials. The town offers an array of restaurants and off-beat shops, as well as seasonal street fairs. Antioch alumni, staff, and faculty account for a sizable percentage of the village's population of 4,000 people.

MAKING A DIFFERENCE STUDIES

Environmental Studies

Media and Social Change
Tropical Environments
Water and Water Pollution
Evolution of Landforms
Soils and Civilization

Natural Resources and Environment
Environmental Botany
Field Botany
Introduction to Solar Energy
Wildlife Ecology

- **Plants & People**   Plants of the world including economic, agricultural, medicinal, forest, and harmful plants, as they relate to and are used by people. Global and cultural issues will be addresses, i.e., how ethnic food preferences relate to available plants, economic and social basis for rain forest and other habitat destruction, and the herbal medicine tradition. Historical issues will be addressed, i.e., the development of agriculture and its effects on societies.

International Relations & Peace Studies

Our majors learn a modern conception of the world that transcends the idea that international relations happens only between national governments and that peace is simply the absence of war. The major develops academic skills and sets up international and cross-cultural experiences that empower students as world citizens and encourage them to think globally and act locally. Includes both negative and positive peace, which relates to direct and indirect or structural violence, and multi-disciplinary peace theories of interpersonal, inter-group, and international relations. Peace Net, a global computerized peace information network, is in the library for student use.

Introduction to Peace Studies
The World as a Total System
Gandhi: Truth and Nonviolence

Global Peace Movements in Information Age
Self Realization East and West
Issues in International Politics

- **Prospects for Peace in the 21st Century: Alternative Futures**   This course will consider probable and possible global peace developments in the 21st century. Issues covered will include 21st century war, environmental conflict, cultural and ethnic conflict, human rights, poverty, community conflict and micro-violence as well as possibilities for zones of peace, world government, and the further development of non-violent relationships.

- Faculty Bio **Paul L. Smoker** (Lloyd Professor of Peace Studies and World Law; M.Sc and Ph.D., Lancaster University, England) Paul has taught Peace Studies and International Relations for more than 25 years at universities in Europe, North America and Asia. He is Secretary General of the International Peace Research Ass'n, a world-wide academic association of peace researchers and peace educators. He has published a number of books and more than eighty academic articles in journals, recent publications including *Trident Town: Action-Research and the Peace Movement*. His current research includes an international project on reconceptualizing security to include political, social, economic, ecological, cultural and technological dimensions; and work on increasing the effectiveness of global peace movements.

Women's Studies

Women in Music
The Feminist Press
Feminist Theory
Women in Cross-Cultural Perspectives
Contemporary Latin American Thought on Women

Non-Traditional Literature by Women
Women and Minorities in Management
Human Sexuality
Poetry by Women

International/Cross-Cultural Studies/Anthropology

Our program equips students with the scholarly and critical skills they need for personal and intellectual growth and for their social contribution. The systematic placement of human belief and behavior in society and culture; ways to compare and contrast their own cultural assumptions; the historical, geopolitical and social contexts of environmental, local and global human problems. Cross-cultural studies is unique in the college curriculum: it frames inquiry and proposes strategies for problem-solving in the 21st Century.

Cultural History of Latin America
Japanese Poetry
Spanish Readings and Conversation
The Aztec and Mayan Civilizations
Cultural Aspects of Perception
History of Traditional Japan through Literature

Human Rights: Latin America
Tribalism, Ethnicity and the Nation State
Spanish Dramatics and Radio Workshop
Asian Theater Seminar
The Middle East: Its People and Culture

African and African American Studies

Black Women in White America
Intro to Drum & Dance of W. Africa
Race, Class & Nationalism: S. Africa
Society Health and Disease in Africa
From Africa to the New World: Peoples and Cultures of the African Diaspora

Race and U.S. Law
Literature by Black Women
Field Project in Cross-Cultural Studies
African-American Intellectual Thought

- Faculty Bio **Joseph R. Jordan** Assoc. Prof. of African/American Studies (B.A. Norfolk State Univ; M.A., M.S., Ohio State Univ, Ph.D., Howard Univ.) Joseph has, throughout his professional life, sought to combine his intellectual pursuits with political and community activism. He has served as co-chair of the Southern Africa Support Project, and as director of the Institute for African-American Writing. He has worked as a Senior Analyst in African Affairs at the Library of Congress and has also taught at Howard University. His research interests include current expressions of the African-American intellectual tradition and revisting the idea of the Black aesthetic. He also maintains an interest in southern African liberation struggles and solidarity organizations.

Social and Behavioral Sciences

Management of Non-Profit Organizations
Fascism
Urban Economics
Politics and Change in the Middle East
Minority Group Relations

The Economics of Developing Countries
Urban Sociology
Political Change: Non-Western Societies
Sex, Gender and Identity
Development, Sociology and Social Policy

- **Women and Minorities in Management** Theoretical as well as practical issues concerning the expanding role of women and minorities in organizations, particularly in mangement positions. Diverse range of economic and organizations. Theories examined with respect to division of labor, authority-power relations, and gender/race. Career management, stereotyping, communicators, networking.

Student Body: 20% state, 61% women, 39% men, 11% minority
Faculty: 59% male, 41% female, 18% minority
1994-5 Costs: $20,216   Apply by 2/1
• Field Studies   • Co-op Education   • Vegetarian Meals
• Study Abroad   • Individualized Majors

Use form in back to contact: Office of Admissions
Antioch College   Yellow Springs, Ohio 45387
1-800-543-9436

ARIZONA STATE UNIVERSITY

33,000 Undergraduates   Tempe, Arizona   Moderately Selective

MAKING A DIFFERENCE STUDIES

Environmental Resources in Agriculture

Enviro. Resources Sciences and Humans	Watershed Management
Range Ecosystem Management	Forest Ecosystem Management
Wildlife Habitat Relations	Soils Fertility
Natural Resource Conservation	Natural Resource Planning
Land Reclamation	Applied Systems Ecology

Urban Planning

Theory of Urban Design	Environmental Planning
Ethics & Professional Practice	Urban Planning
Environmental Impact Assessment	Urban Housing Analysis
Environmental Planning Economics	Preservation Planning

Landscape Architecture

Ecology & Conservation	Landscape Architecture
Theory of Urban Design	International Field Studies in Planning & LA
Planning & Development Control Law	The Living World
Landscape Plants	Introduction to Urban Planning
Landscape Construction	Landscape Planting Design

Elementary Education/ Indian Education Track   Fourth and fifth year classes.

Methods of Teaching Indian Students	Curriculum & Practices for Indian Education
Counseling the Indian Student	Problems of Teachers of Indian Students
Community Schools in Indian Education	Admin & Mgm't of Indian Education Programs

Family Literacy in Language Minority Communities
Role of Tribal, State & Federal Government in Indian Education
Development of Indian Cultural & Language Materials

- **Foundations of Indian Education** Historical Development of Indian Affairs and Indian education, including contemporary educational issues, traditional Indian concepts of education, and Indian cultures.

Social Work

Introduction to Social Work	Community Resources
Human Behavior in Social Environment	Social Policy and Services
Social Work Practice	Ethnic/Cultural Variables
History of the City	Planning & Development Control Law

Anthropology   Women's Studies

Student Body: 74% State, 48% women, 52% men, 10% minority
1994-95costs: Residents $5,638   Non-Residents $11,784
Rolling Applications
• Co-op Education   • Study Abroad   • Individualized Majors

Use form in back to contact: Undergraduate Admissions Office
Arizona State University   Tempe, AZ 85287
(602) 965-7788

ARMAND HAMMER UNITED WORLD COLLEGE

200 Students   Montezuma, New Mexico   Very Selective

Through international education, shared experience and community service, the United World College enables young people to become responsible citizens, politically and environmentally aware, committed to the ideals of peace, justice, understanding and cooperation, and to the implementation of these ideals throughout the world.

The UWC movement can be traced to Dr. Kurt Hahn, founder of the Outward Bound Trust. A refugee from Hitler's Germany, Dr. Hahn conceived of an education that could transform "the love of liberty and the love of country" into a common love of humankind. He determined that the student body would be drawn from young people of all nations and races. The age range, 16 to 19 years, targeted those who, he believed, were at an impressionable age, students with established cultural roots who understand the world situation yet are young enough to accept the discipline of living together in a residential community of hard academic and physical service work. The first UWC opened its doors in Wales in 1962. Since then, the system has grown to eight schools with HRH Prince Charles at the head of all United World Colleges.

In a rigorous two-year curriculum, students work for their International Baccalaureate degree. Administered from Switzerland, and recognized by colleges and universities throughout the world, the IB is a well-balanced, integrated curriculum that thoroughly prepares students for the challenges of higher education. UWC students may gain advanced standing as sophomores in universities in the United Sates.

Throughout its first decade, the fully-accredited Armand Hammer United World College has called on 30 years of UWC experience to develop strong programs. The Armand Hammer UWC sustains the conviction that its students can contribute significantly to international understanding and service, and thus to peace on the globe.

Students may also choose the Environmental Program which concentrates academic study, three terms of environmental or recycling services, an extended essay and a one week project. Students also design or lead new environmental activities.

Service is an integral part of the International Baccalaureate program. There are two broad divisions to the service program: Community Service and Wilderness Service. Students can choose to pursue either or combine the two. Students work in day care centers, local hospitals or the state mental hospital and serve as tutors to local school children or as companions to the elderly. On weekends, students work in homeless shelters, help renovate community buildings and reconstruct historic adobe churches. The aims of the Community Service program are to foster compassion and a service ethic on a personal and social level.

In Wilderness Service, students learn how to become self-sufficient in the wilderness, including map reading, navigation, rock-climbing, search and rescue techniques and environmental awareness. The college search and rescue team is called out frequently to help find missing hikers, skiers and hunters.

The college has also introduced a voluntary program in conflict resolution that addresses global issues. Students learn how to facilitate group meetings to find common ground and bring about consensus.

MAKING A DIFFERENCE STUDIES

New students are required to select six subjects for study for two years, one subject from each group listed below. At the end of the first semester, they choose which three they will take at a higher level, and which three at a subsidiary level.

1 Language A: The student's best language. Instruction is in English, French and Spanish. All students take a course in World Literature.
2 Language B: A second language, English, French, Spanish and German are offered.
3 Society and Culture: Economics, History and Social Anthropology
4 Natural Sciences: Biology, Chemistry, Physics and Environmental Systems
5 Mathematics
6 Art, Music or a second option from Groups 2, 3 or 4.

All courses are taught in English, other than additional language courses. However, students may write their International Baccalaureate exams in English, French or Spanish.

- **Social Anthropology** Survey of major anthropological concerns, emphasizing the comparative structural and functional analysis of institutions. Students acquire some familiarity with alternative anthropological approaches. Urbanization, the individual and culture, the anthropological study of change and planned change also surveyed.

- **Contemporary History** This survey course outlines 20th century world history, emphasizing the following themes: the causes, practices and effects of war; the rise and rule of single-party dictatorships; and East-West relations after 1945.

- **Economics** How can society allocate its scarce human and physical resources? Who decides, in theory and in practice, what the economy will produce? How are problems such as inflation and unemployment to be understood? Develops skills in economic analysis with an emphasis on applying theory to existing world economic problems.

- **Biology** Comprehensive study of a broad range of topics, including ecology, genetics and physiology of plants and animals. Development of cellular and molecular biology.

- **Theory of Knowledge** Compulsory course encourages students to reflect critically on disciplines they are studying and the knowledge they are acquiring. It is taught partly in regular class and in special sessions covering several days. Sources and varieties of knowledge; types of proposition; valid and invalid reasoning; scientific method and the problem of induction; the social sciences, the problem of free will, historical knowledge and causation; moral and aesthetic judgments; and, What is Truth?

- **Faculty** The international faculty at The Armand Hammer United World College are chosen for their teaching experience and their commitment to the ideals of the United World Colleges. Current faculty members come from India, Canada, Germany, Colombia, Barbados, South Africa, Great Britain and the United States.

Student Body: 75% International, 25% United States
1994-95 costs: $16,500   Financial Aid Available   Apply By 2/1
• Recycling program in place

Use form in back to contact: Admissions Office
Armand Hammer United World College
P.O. Box 248   Montezuma, New Mexico 87731
(505) 454-4220

AUDUBON EXPEDITION INSTITUTE
NATIONAL AUDUBON SOCIETY
100 Students   Based in Belfast, Maine   Very Selective

The Audubon Expedition Institute offers an extraordinary educational journey. AEI's philosophy comes directly from years of creating and living in our unique educational environment - North America. The journey, which began as an educational experiment twenty five years ago, has successfully become a viable educational model.

Nature has always been and continues to be our best teacher. The places we have visited, and the people who inhabit them, have guided our thoughts. AEI has changed and grown as environmental and student needs have changed. The lessons have been transforming, and through our experiences we have created an academic program that speaks to the environmental and educational needs of today.

AEI offers an opportunity to actively experience nature and people as parts of a whole. The Institute's program fosters a thorough understanding of the world of plant, animal, air, earth, and spirit - the world where community, relationships, and life are of primary importance.

AEI offers small community living as a challenging avenue to experience and examine life. By using the school community as a microcosm of larger systems, students learn to apply fresh insights and skills from their lives both to the political and social structure of society, and to the workings of natural systems.

AEI believes in open and honest communication as a route to personal growth. We foster the development of clear and honest written and verbal communication, as well as a healing and open relationship with ourselves and others, in order to promote interpersonal understanding.

Audubon's program promotes educational excellence through structured, self-directed field studies, hands-on experience, and traditional academics. AEI integrates challenging outlooks with progressive ways of learning in nature to encourage the evolution of independent thinking, self-discovery, and scholastic competency.

At AEI, each student is encouraged to cultivate individual, spiritual growth. Developing a spiritual relationship with the environment is of primary importance in understanding the inherent connections between people, nature and culture.

AEI encourages a lifestyle that leads to the integration of humanity and nature. By providing ethical, philosophical, and practical skill development in ecological studies, we prepare the individual for a life of service as a global citizen. AEI invites students to consider that their physical, emotional, intellectual and spiritual well-being can lead to global health. The Institute encourage students to approach their relationship to the Earth with the care and reciprocity that allows all persons to seek their fullest potential.

Participation in AEI's Bachelor's degree program is an exciting opportunity for a student to broaden his or her experience in preparing for careers in education, public policy, conservation, small and non-profit business, industry or other science, or environmental work. The environment becomes your educator as you immerse yourself in the study of culture and nature. Students develop skills in such diverse subjects as ecology, geology, English, psychology, history and anthropology melding the sciences with the humanities to bring a holistic overview to each student's journey in education. The faculty members guide students in expanding their communication skills and broadening their environmental outlook. Each student's vision is cultivated through direct contact with diverse cultural groups, studies in nature, idea exchanges among students and faculty, and analysis of expedition experiences.

Undergraduate students may participate in the field program for one semester, a full year, (two semesters), three semesters, or two years (four semesters). AEI's Quest Program described below is an individually designed Independent Study/Internship that takes place during a student's third year with AEI. Students may wish to participate with Audubon Expedition Institute immediately following high school as a post-graduate year instead of taking a year off before college. Credits taken with AEI can generally be applied towards a student's undergraduate degree. Many students come as sophomores or juniors in order to enhance their classroom experiences. Most colleges accept credit either directly from AEI or from Lesley College in Cambridge, Massachusetts with which our program is affiliated.

Students can receive a Bachelor of Science degree in Environmental Education from AEI and Lesley College. The undergraduate program sequence of 64 AEI credits (equivalent of four traveling semesters), plus 64 additional liberal arts credits can be arranged in several ways. Up to 3 semesters taken with AEI may be applied to the following degrees granted by Lesley College: B.S. in Education, B.S. in Human Services, B.A. in Liberal Studies, B.S. in Self-Designed majors, or an A.A. in Liberal Arts.

Quest is a student-designed, junior or senior year personal "expedition" to seek educational and career settings that complement the Audubon/Lesley B.S. degree. Quest may take the form of an internship, an apprenticeship, an independent study project or a combination of these during the third year.

A limited number of Advanced Placement high school students may also enroll in the AEI program. Students are given the opportunity to challenge themselves academically in a supportive, experiential setting while earning both their final high school credits as well as Lesley College credits. Students take the combination of high school and college courses while traveling and participating fully as Expedition members. They are involved in every aspect of the educational process, from selecting and planning activities to carrying them out and evaluating them. The Advanced Placement program is only offered during students final semester of high school.

Audubon Expedition Institute also has a 2 year fully accredited graduate program offering a Master of Science in Environmental Education.

MAKING A DIFFERENCE STUDIES

Following is a sample of AEI programs and regions visited. While no one bus visits all of these places in the course of a year, nor does each bus necessarily have all the experiences listed, this list gives a brief glimpse of the scope of the program.

- **Pacific Northwest Semester** Southwestern British Columbia, Washington, Oregon, Northern California. Explore strikingly different ecosystems including the Sierra Mountains, the Hoh Rain Forest, and Mount Saint Helens. Listen to a Makah Indian story teller recite legends in her traditional tongue, investigate highly controversial logging practices, study sea lions on the Oregon coast, and hike on trails through old-growth redwoods.
- **Southwest Semester** Arizona, New Mexico, Southern Utah, Southern Colorado. Backpack, explore, and ski cross-country among the canyons, buttes, mesas, and desert ecosystems of the Four Corners area. Discover and explore ancient Anasazi cliff dwellings, then experience the ceremonies of their descendants, the Hopi Indians. Water scarcity, grazing, and mining are major environmental struggles in the Southwest.
- **Southeast Semester** Florida, Georgia, Louisiana, South and North Carolina, Tennessee. From wading through the Everglades in search of unusual birds, to West Virginia hiking in the Smoky Mountains during the spring wildflower extravaganza, the Southeast provides a rich tapestry of folklore and natural history. Talk with old-time musicians, wrestle with development issues, visit a citrus plantation and work to protect endangered wildlife.
- **Mountain/Plains Semester** Wyoming,Colorado, Montana, South Dakota. Rocky Mountain geology, grassland ecology, national park mgm't, water issues, and endangered species are the academic backdrop for this semester. Discover the difference between the Lakota-Sioux Indian and European/American influence upon this bioregion and explore some of North America's best known parks.
- **Canadian Maritime/New England Semester** Newfoundland, New Brunswick, Nova Scotia, Maine, New Hampshire, Vermont, Massachusetts. Glacial geology, coastal and tundra ecology, and forest biology accent this semester. Spend a day with an old-time fisherman, canoe in the northern Maine woods, and be immersed in a tidepool during a day of estuarine ecology. Issues surrounding forest management, acid rain, and hydro-electric projects are highlighted.

These experiences translate into course work in the following manner:

First Year Courses

Ecology of Place	English as a Means of Self-Expression
People, Land and Traditions	Physical Education: Camp & Outdoor Ed.
Learning Communities	Physical Education: Health and Wellness

- **Ecology of Place**--Survey the biomes, ecosystems, microsystems and geological features which comprise the bioregion. The ability to visualize and conceptualize geologic processes and principles which have shaped the earth and its life are emphasized. An understanding of the interrelationships of all life as well as humanity's position in the natural world is stressed. This course will examine natural systems with a deep ecological perspective in addition to a more traditional scientific approach.

Second Year Courses:

Applied Ecology

Practicum in Environmental Education

Human Diversity

Methods of Independent Learning & Self-Directed Study

Eco-Philosophy

Special Topic in Ecology

- **Eco-Philosophy**--Our post-industrial society is in the midst of a transition, with the outcome still unknown. This course offers students an opportunity to personally explore a newly-emerging ecological world view which pursues wisdom and is spiritually alive, life-oriented, socially-concerned and environmentally-sensible. At the core of this philosophical journey is the art of asking questions that open hearts and minds to a healthy dialogue. In this time of deep personal and social change, such questions encourage us to expand our ecological consciousness and increase our reverence for natural wisdom.

Third Year "Quest" Courses:

Voice of Nature

Survey of Personal Growth

Environment As Educator

Internship

- **Life Systems Communication** Examines the functioning of earth's ecosystems on a global scale. Based on the Gaian hypothesis that the planet Earth is alive and that all life has a common interest in self-preservation, this course identifies the basic communication processes between critical ecological and geological systems. Earth communication is compared to the various means by which people communicate.

- Faculty Bio **Susan Klimczak** (M.S. Environmental Ed., Lesley College) Susan worked for nine years as an engineer specializing in communications. Her work includes community organizing around feminist issues, renovating shelters for the inner city homeless, volunteering in a prison and living on a permaculture demonstration farm. A published writer, she is enthusiastic about Environmental Justice, sustainable agriculture, multi-cultural education as well as Quaker and Eastern philosophy.

- Faculty Bio **Hank Colletto** (M.S. Environmental Ed., Lesley College) Hank has been part of a consensus-run community land trust where he built a solar, earth-bermed home, and was active in grassroots environmental organizations. As an energy conservation consultant, Hank presented workshops on photovoltaics, superinsulation, solar construction techniques and solar heating. His work as an environmental education trip leader adds to the foundation of his teaching career. Hank's humor and storytelling are an integral part of the bus experience and he finds particular joy in guiding students on a transformative journey in search of their dormant inner wildness.

Student Body: 50% men, 50% women   • Actively seeking students of color

1994-95 costs: $13,388 (one semester $7,852)

Add'l per credit fee if arranged through Lesley College.

• Team teaching   • Individualized majors   • Exclusive seminar format

Use form in back to contact: National Audubon Society Expedition Institute

P.O.Box 365   Belfast, Maine 04915

(207) 338-5859

BASTYR COLLEGE

328 Students   Seattle, Washington   Moderately Selective

"The ordinary doctor is interested mostly in the study of disease. The nature curist is interested more in the study of health. His real interest begins where that of the ordinary doctor ends."

Gandhi

Founded in 1978 as the John Bastyr College of Naturopathic Medicine, Bastyr College is the first accredited school of natural healing in the United States. The College trains naturopathic physicians, and offers baccalaureate degrees in nutrition, Oriental medicine and applied behavioral sciences, graduate degrees in nutrition, Acupuncture, and certificates in Midwifery and traditional Chinese herbal medicine.

The College's philosophical orientation honors and reflects the unique and worldwide traditions of natural medicine: the treatment of the whole person, prevention of disease, teaching patients how to take responsibility for their own health, working with each individual's inherent healing ability and using natural, non-toxic therapies. Its curriculum recognizes and utilizes the enormous amount of information that scientific research brings to the understanding of health and disease. The Natural Health Sciences Programs at Bastyr provide unique two-year upper division programs that lead to the Bachelor of Science degree.

There is a growing recognition of the importance of traditional and natural health care practices throughout the world. Midwifery, acupuncture, and botanical medicines are a few of the practices that are recognized and supported by the World Health Organization. We believe that effective solutions to the "health care crisis" being experienced in many of the developed countries must include the principles and practices of natural medicine. Bastyr College is a leader in the effort to create an international, intercultural understanding of - and commitment to education in - natural health care. In addition, Bastyr has been recognized by the United Nations Educational, Scientific and Cultural Organization (UNESCO).

Bastyr College is playing a pioneering role in the development of science-based natural medicine in the United States. The College's mission includes the pursuit of scientific research on the use of natural therapies in the management and treatment of health care problems and in the prevention of chronic disease. Students are engaged in primary clinical research at the college's outpatient teaching clinic. Faculty members from Bastyr College are participating in a number national agencies, such as the Office of Alternative Medicine at the National Institutes of Health, the Office of Technology Assistance and the Task Force on Health Care Reform.

The Leadership Institute of Seattle, LIOS has been preparing students to become successful consultants, managers and leaders in the nation's organizations for twenty years. LIOS expands the Bastyr College focus on wellness to an organizational level. The LIOS campus is located in Bellevue.

The baccalaureate program in Oriental Medicine is the first half of a three year program that leads to the Master of Science in Acupuncture. The LIOS/Bastyr College M.A. and B.S. program offers unique instructional settings which effectively combine experiential learning and skills development with a strong theoretical base. These degree programs are directed towards practitioners in business, professions and human services who want to further develop themselves as leaders. If you care about natural, "holistic" approaches to life and health, and if you want an education that will give you science-based training in natural health care, Bastyr College can help you put your values into practice.

MAKING A DIFFERENCE STUDIES

Prior to enrolling, students must have completed 90 quarter credits.

Oriental Medicine—Two Year Program

Meridians & Points
Traditional Chinese Medicine Diagnosis
Traditional Chinese Medicine Pathology
Fund'l Principles: Chinese Medicine
Counseling
Psychology & Treatment of Addiction
Acupuncture Therapeutics
Microbiology
Organic Chemistry

Anatomy & Physiology
Tui Na
Acupuncture Techniques
Clinical Observation
Traditional Chinese Medicine Herbology
TCM Prepared Medicines
Disease Processes
Biochemistry
Medical Terminology

Traditional Chinese Herbal Medicine Certificate Program

Intro Traditional Chinese Herb Medicine
TCM Nutrition
Practice Management/Ethics
Pharmacology of Botanical Medicine
Advanced TCM Materia Medica and Formulations

TCM Prepared Formulas
Pharmacy of Botanical Medicine
Oriental Medicine Electives
Herbal Clinic & Preceptorship in China

Nutrition

Community Nutrition
Counseling Principles
Food Science
Field Observation
Core Nutrition
Nutrition and Mental Health

Nutrition in Natural Medicine
Disease Processes
Chemistry of Foods
Epidemiology
Recipe Adaptation
Maternal and Infant Nutrition

Bastyr College is now offering certain of the undergraduate through Distance Learning. For more information on these offerings, call 206-523-9585

Student body: 30% state, 75% women, 25% men, 15% int'l
For priority consideration, Apply by: 4/1
1993 costs: Nutrition: $5625   Acupuncture & Oriental Medicine: $8570
• Low Cost Health Care at the Natural Health Clinic   • No Housing   • Vegetarian Cafeteria

Use form in back to contact: Director of Admissions
Bastyr College
144 Northeast 54th Street   Seattle, WA 98105
(206) 523-9585
For LIOS Program contact: Director of Admissions
LIOS   1450 - 114th Ave. SE   Bellevue, WA 98004-6934
(206) 635-1187

BELOIT COLLEGE

1,100 Students   Beloit, Wisconsin   Very Selective

Beloit College prepares leaders for the 21st Century by emphasizing problem solving and critical thinking skills. The pace of the social and technological changes
already taking place globally isn't going to slow down. It will be the citizens who
know how to keep up with that pace, the ones who can deal with change effectively,
and the ones who are unafraid to ask questions who will excel in the future. Life is
the test Beloit College wants you to pass. The liberal arts structure provides a learning
environment that will lead you on a path to a life of productive and active citizenship.

The concept of active citizenship is so important at Beloit that is has now made
community service a requirement for all of first-year students. This is done through
the "First-Year Initiatives Program," a program that links you from the day you arrive
on campus to an experienced professor and a group of your peers. The professor will
teach one of your first semester courses, and serve as your academic advisor and mentor. Rebuilding nature trails and serving breakfast to schoolchildren are just two of
the many types of community service projects FYI students have done. FYI is just the
beginning of volunteerism for many of our students. Student volunteers have traveled
to, among other places, Guatemala, the Netherlands, Alaska, and even Beloit,
Alabama, doing such things as building schools, teaching schoolchildren, conducting
inventories of bird populations, and researching acid rain.

Pluralism, the idea of a society with numerous distinct, ethnic, religious, and cultural groups peacefully co-existing, is another concept we stress. At Beloit, you share
your learning experiences with peers from 47 states and 40 countries. It's just as likely
your roommate will be from Mississippi or Nevada, as it is that they're from Finland
or Zaire. What they share is a kind of practical idealism, a deep respect for individuality and diversity, and a commitment to making diversity work. It's no wonder that in
several recent years Beloit has had the highest proportion of graduates volunteering
for the Peace Corps of any school in America.

There are more than 100 clubs and organizations that can help you find your cultural and social niche at Beloit, and you can always start your own club if one of those
isn't what you're looking for. One of the most active clubs is the Outdoor
Environmental Club which spearheads the campus' recycling program.

Finding your own direction is far too personal an adventure to be standardized.
At Beloit you can invent yourself; there is no lengthy list of requirements, no rigid
formula for choosing a major, no mold in which you are expected to fit. Students are
often encouraged to build a larger program of study through our interdisciplinary studies program. For example, if none of the regular minors meets your needs, you can
explore a social interest through an interdisciplinary minor.

There are literally hundreds of directions to go at Beloit. You'll have plenty of
help, if you want it. But ultimately you will make the decisions about your future.
Beloit's commitment is to provide you with the resources that will allow you to make
critical and productive connections between thought and action in all aspects of your
life.

MAKING A DIFFERENCE STUDIES

Environmental Geology
This dep't is a member of the distinguished Keck Geology Consortium, providing majors outstanding opportunities to participate in summer research activities in US and overseas.

Enviro Geology and Geologic Hazards
Sedimentology
Natural History
Foundations of Economic Analysis
Geologic Field Methods

Mineralogy and Crystallography
Hydrology
Challenge of Global Change
Marine Biology
Field Excursion Seminar

Biology Tracks in Environmental, Behavioral, Mathematical, Medical, Molecular Biology
Botany
Behavioral Ecology
Comparative Physiology
Microbiology
Biological Issues

Environmental Biology
Population Biology
Zoology
Molecular Biology and Biotechnology
Developmental Biology

Philosophy and Religion
Biomedical Ethics
Personal Freedom and Responsibility
Violence and Non-Violence
Hebrew Scriptures
Islam

Business Ethics
Philosophy of Science
Logic
Oriental Philosophy
20th Century Theology

Government and International Relations
Women and Politics
Civil Liberties
Communist & Post-Communist Systems
Parties and Groups in American Politics
American Presidency

Principles of Government and Politics
The Politics of Developing Countries
Politics of Advanced Industrial Democracies
Theories of International Relations
American State Gov't and Politics

- **International Organization and Law** Political foundations of int'l institutions and law. Focus on transformation of the UN, the growth of specialized agencies and contemporary legal framework. Problems of int'l peace and security, arms control, economic development, social welfare and human rights in international organizations.

Interdisciplinary Studies
Individually developed majors have included women, environment and change; choreography of the universe; set-design for educational TV, African studies; environmental design.

Energy Alternatives
Liberal Education and Entrepreneurship
Sense of Place: Regionalism in America
Circumstances of Agriculture in US

Town and City in the Third World
Mass Communication in a Modern Society
Women, Feminism, and Science
Cultural Resource Management

Photographic Images as Recorders of History and Social Change

Sociology   Women's Studies   Health Care Studies

Student Body: 23% state, 58% women, 42% men, 8 % minority, 11% int'l, 14% transfer
Faculty: 70% male, 30% female
1994-5 costs: $20,090   Rolling Applications   Apply by 3/1 for financial aid priority
• Exclusive Seminar Format   • Team Teaching   • Individualized Majors   • Vegetarian Meals

Use form in back to contact: Admissions Office
Beloit College   700 College Street   Beloit, WI 53511
(608)363-2500   (800)356-0751

BEMIDJI STATE UNIVERSITY

4.750 Undergraduates   Bemidji, Minnesota   Moderately Selective

"The Americans were rich in cultural diversity long before the arrival of the first Europeans. American cultures were reflected, by then, in more than two hundred language families, evolved through centuries of migration, intermingling, and the building and changing of traditions. In the relatively short time since the first Europeans have arrived, explorers, immigrants, and slaves have brought new cultures from virtually all corners of the world, each facing the inevitable challenges of preserving the old traditions, values, and identities while adapting to the new.... We are and will remain intolerant of intolerance!"

Minnesota Manifesto

MAKING A DIFFERENCE STUDIES

Geography Tracks in Regional & Land Use Planning; Park & Recreation Planning; Recreation-Park & Archaeology; Economic Planning & Development; Social Planning

Introduction to Human Geography	Aerial Photography and Remote Sensing
Weather and Climate	Site Analysis and Planning
Geography of Population & Settlement	Urban Geography
Land Use Analysis & Planning	Regional Planning Methods
Environmental Conservation	Introduction to Community Recreation
Environmental Perception	Field Botany

Environmental Education & Interpretation / Elementary Teaching Credential

Program designed for pre-service and in-service educators from educational institutions, organizations, and gov't agencies, community leaders, interested individuals, and students.

Group Processes	General Ecology
Archery	Introduction to Crafts
Environmental Conservation	Intro to Enviro Education and Interpretation
Taxonomy of Seed Plants	American Nature Writers

Field Experiences: Environmental Education and Interpretation
Organization and Administration of Environmental Education and Interpretation

International Studies / Global Perspectives Track

Cultural Anthropology	World Regional Geography
Religions of Preliterate Societies	Comparative Economic Systems
Women in Literature	Global Peace and Justice Issues
The Global Economy	United Nations
Intercultural Communication	Sociology of Religion
International Conflict	Geography of Population and Settlement
Human Services and Social Planning	Regional Planning Methods

Minority Group Studies / Elementary Teaching Credential

Cultural Anthropology	Ethnic & Minority Group Relations
Intercultural Communication	Parent-Child Relations: Contemporary Family
U.S. Ethnic and Minority History	World Regional Geography
Women and History	Sociology of Religion
Intro to Human Geography	Women's Issues

Applied Psychology   Tracks in Human Services / Family and Community Health

Interpersonal Skills
Child and Adolescent Psychology
Family systems
Criminology
Neuromuscular Relaxation
Psychosocial Adjustment to Handicapping Conditions

Basic Counseling Techniques
Psychology of Adulthood and Aging
Family Violence
Human Responses to Death
Parent-Child Relations in Contemp. Family

Social Work / Chemical Dependency

Intro to Social Welfare
Social Welfare Policy
Abnormal Psychology
Psychology of Adjustment
Chemical Dependency: Prevention and Intervention

Social Work Practice
Bureaucracy & Society
Chemical Use, Abuse, & Dependency
Human Relations

Health

Health is defined as a dynamic, ever-changing condition of well-being within the interactive relationships of intellectual, social, emotional, physical, and spiritual functioning.

Human Anatomy
A Lifestyle for Wellness
Physiology of Exercise
Courtship & Marriage
Women's Issues
Community Health
Health & Drug Education
Program Planning, Promotion & Administration

Chemistry of Drugs
Technology of Neuromuscular Relaxation
Learning & Cognition
Family Violence
Nutrition
Consumer Health
Theoretical Foundations of Health

Indian Studies   Tracks in Public Administration & Social Services

Designed to provide Ojibwe and other Indian students with a viable academic area of study that is relevant to their heritage and diversity.

Ojibwe Culture
North American Prehistory
American Indian Literature
American Indians in the 20th Century
Contemporary Indian Issues
Survey of American Indian Art
Tribal Government

Elementary Ojibwe
Archaeology & Ethnology of Minnesota
Indians of Canada
American Indian Lands
Federal Indian Law
Advanced Ojibwe Crafts
Ethnic & Minority History

Indian Studies / Elementary Teaching Credential

Native North Americans
Indians of the United States
American Indian Literature
History of the Ojibwe
Elementary Ojibwe
American Indian Social Welfare Perspectives

Education of Amer. Indian Children & Youth
Curriculum Development: Indian Education
Minnesota History to 1900
Ojibwe Culture
Introduction to Ojibwe Crafts

Student Body: 98% state, 49% women, 51% men, 6% students of color
1994-95 costs: Residents $5984   Non-Residents $8609   Apply By 8/15

Use form in back to contact: Office of Admissions
Bemidji State University   Bemidji, MN 56601-2699
(218) 755-2000

BEREA COLLEGE

1500 students   Berea, Kentucky   Very Selective

Berea College, located in the foothills of the Cumberland Mountains, aims to fulfill it's mission as a Christian school "primarily by contributing to the spiritual and
material welfare of the mountain region of the South, according to young people of
character and promise a thorough Christian education, with opportunities for manual
labor as an assistance in self-support."

The seal of the College bears the inscription "God has made of one blood all peoples of the earth" which epitomizes Berea's belief in human-kind which should unite
all people as children of God. It is hoped that men and women going out from Berea
will further interracial understanding and that they will be courageous in opposing
injustice and wrong.

Berea's distribution requirements for cultural area studies insures that each student will be able to demonstrate an understanding of some aspects of culture other
than his or her own; a recognition of, and sensitivity to, similarities and differences in
cultures; and an expanded perspective on a world of plurality of cultures. For
Freshman Seminar all students select a series of courses designed to involve them in a
critical study of the topic "Freedom and Justice" as it relates to the commitments of
Berea College, to Appalachia, the Christian faith, the kinship of all people, or the
dignity of labor. Similarly, students in the teacher education programs at Berea are
asked to think deeply about the nature of teaching, learning, and schooling within
the contest of the college's commitments: to able students who are economically disadvantaged; to the Christian ethic and to service; to the dignity of labor; to the promotion of the ideals of community democracy, interracial education, and gender
equality; to simple living and concern for the welfare of others; and to service of the
Appalachian region.

As an integral part of the educational program, each student is expected to perform some of the labor required in maintaining the institution, thus to gain an appreciation of the worth and dignity of all the labor needed in a common enterprise and
to acquire some useful skill. The aim is to make available a sound education to students who are unable to meet usual college expenses, but who have the ability and
character to use a liberal education for responsible, intelligent service to society.

Through the fellowship of meaningful work experiences, an atmosphere of democratic social living prevents social and economic distinctions and instills an awareness
of social responsibility. Student industries include broomcraft, weaving, woodcraft
and wrought iron work, the products of which are sold to the public from the student
run giftshop and hotel. Students also participate in running the college farm and
poultry farm.

Berea's campus comprises 140 acres. Farm lands, including the experimental farms,
piggery, and poultry farm cover 1400 acres. The college also owns a 7,000 acre forest.

Admission to Berea is limited to students whose families would have a difficult
time financing a college education without assistance. Financial need is a requirement
for admission.

MAKING A DIFFERENCE STUDIES

General Studies- Core Courses

Community Building
Freedom and Justice: The Third World
Housing: American Dream or Nightmare
Politics of Food
Immigrants and Minorities
Sacred Earth, Sacred Relationships

Health Decisions: Justice and Autonomy
Women, Society and Mental Health
Technology, Culture, Belief
Community and Spirituality
Values in Conflict
Labor, Learning and Leisure

- **One Blood, All Nations: Cultural Diversity & Environmentalism.** Major issues concerning tensions between advocacy for cultural diversity and environmentalism, especially the environmental concept of a global commons. Achieve a deeper understanding of the issues contained within the concepts of kinship of all people and a way of life characterized by plain living; deeper understanding of the relatedness of these concepts; and understand how these concepts generate questions of freedom and justice.

Black Culture

Introduction to Afro-American Studies
Slavery & Afro-American Culture
Afro-American Music: An Overview
Black Emancipation & Reform in the U.S.
Critical Issues of Black Americans in the Twentieth Century

Afro-American Literature
Contemporary Afro-American Experience
Race in America
Sub-Saharan Black African Art

Appalachian Culture

Appalachian Literature
Appalachian Problems and Institutions
Appalachian Music

Appalachian Culture
Health in Appalachia
Appalachian Crafts

- **Community Analysis: The Appalachian Case** Study of history, demography, social structure and forces promoting social change in Appalachian rural communities. Sociological approach to understanding concept of community, its various systems, institutions and groups. Community problem-analysis orientation. American, European, and Third World communities examined looking at content and method.

Child and Family Studies

Principles of Food Science
Human Environments
Family Relations
The Exceptional Child
Contemporary Family Issues

Child Development
Advanced Child Development
Guidance of the Young Child
Cross Cultural Perspectives on Family
Family Resource Management

Nursing	Agriculture	Sociology

Student Body: 80% from Southern Appalachia, 15% national, 9% minority, 5% int'l.
1994-95 costs: All tuition costs are met by the college through the work program. Students and their families are responsible for room and board, $3023 for which financial aid is available.
Rolling Applications
• Field Studies   • Co-op Work Study   • Study Abroad
• Core or multidisciplinary programs   • Individualized majors

Use form in back to contact: Office of Admissions
Berea College   CPO 2344   Berea, Kentucky 40404
(606) 986-9341

BETHEL COLLEGE

576 Students   North Newton, Kansas   Moderately Selective

Bethel is a liberal arts and sciences undergraduate college affiliated with the General Conference Mennonite Church. Its 450-year-old Anabaptist heritage is the wellspring for a vibrant academic Christian community of faculty and students with a tradition of combining academic excellence with a commitment to social justice, service to others, peacemaking and conflict resolution.

The College offers 26 majors and four professional and preprofessional programs leading to the Bachelor of Arts, Bachelor of Science, or Bachelor of Science in Nursing. The College has a deserved reputation for excellence in preparation for the professions and graduate study.

The following excerpts from the College's goals study summarize its educational mission:

- A Christian, Church - Related College. By word and example, Bethel attempts to help persons discover what it means to be committed to Christ in today's world. Believing that authentic faith comes from free conviction and not from indoctrination or conformity, Bethel promotes freedom, openness, and voluntarism.

- Liberal Arts is the heart of the undergraduate educational experience. Such a program requires the development of basic and integrative skills and exposure to major subject areas and methodologies. Committed to a search for values that transcend the physical world, Bethel is concerned with ideas that matter, with questions relating knowledge to values, and with the implications and types of life that result from such inquiries.

- Peace Education. Bethel's distinctiveness, by heritage and conviction, includes a deeply-rooted commitment to peacemaking, service, and conflict-resolution. The urgency of this focus is self-evident in a nuclear world. Both Christian and secular education have a special responsibility to seek ways to cope creatively and nonviolently with the human and environmental needs of our global community. Therefore the College seeks to study and practice ways of peacemaking and reconciliation in society both in its core curriculum and in specialized programs.

- A Systems Approach in an Interdependent World. In a world of specialization and fragmentation the great need of our time is for coherences, to understand that we live in a world of linkages. Therefore Bethel seeks to provide an environment that assists in the integration of the worlds of faith, learning and work. In our world of linkages and finite resources, Bethel supports a conserving desire to accent the beauty of simplicity and to live more with less. Such a goal is also a more convincing witness to the developing nations of our world and to our understanding of Christian stewardship.

As evidence of these commitments, all Bethel students must meet a Global Awareness requirement to help prepare them to live in a shrinking world of increasing complexity. In order to meet this requirement, the student must pass a global issues seminar or spend at least thirty days in an approved situation where the student is exposed to a culture which is significantly different from her home environment.

Each student also must satisfy a Convocation Requirement. Convocation is an all-school assembly which generally meets twice weekly during the term. Guest lectures, performing groups, and audio/visual presentations provide students with a wide-ranging exposure to issues in politics, society, religion, the arts and sciences. The convocation experience is designed to help build community, broaden horizons, and allow exploration of basic value issues. Sample convocations from last year included the film "Man, Oh Man: Growing Up Male in America"; a lecture on "Human Rights in the 1990's" by Curt Goering, Senior Deputy Executive Director of Amnesty International, USA (and a Bethel College alumnus); a lecture on "Housing for the Poor" by Millard Fuller, President of Habitat for Humanity International. Finally, the special awareness is reflected in the fact that fifty percent of the Bethel faculty have been engaged in overseas (non-military) service and study.

As a community we expect our members to be responsible to each other in seeking the health, growth, and development of self and others; to guard the dignity and worth, and to promote the equality and empowerment of self and others, to value volunteerism, and participate in service to others; to work through conflicts without force, intimidation or retreat; to promote relationships that are free from sexual discrimination, sexual coercion, exploitation and abuse; to keep the environment safe and clean; and to nurture the spiritual awareness and development of self and others.

Bethel encourages students in the education program to consider teaching in schools of another culture or in a multicultural setting. Those students interested in pursuing such a course are encouraged to do their student teaching in these environments. The Director of Teacher Education arranges for student teaching in accredited inner-city schools inside or out side of Kansas, American Indian schools, or even overseas schools as the demand arises.

Bethel seeks to arrange and supervise international placements for students interested international internships or directed study abroad, or in the USA. Some of the recent placements have been in a rural development and environmental health program emphasizing water resources with the Mennonite Central Committee in Burkina Faso, West Africa; a directed study of the gender factor in communications in Nicaragua; working with a Migrant Farm Workers Project in Missouri, and an International Development internship with Granja Loma Linda, a training and demonstration center for methods of sustainable agriculture for hillside farms; and working with a Mexican organization on the forefront of environmental eduction and action at the community level throughout Mexico. Bethel has recently added a new program that provides students the opportunity to spend an entire semester in Mexico. This program involves intensive Spanish language study and an internship placement in the student's major field of concentration. While in Mexico, students live with a Mexican family and immerse themselves in Mexican culture. There are no added costs (above regular Bethel College tuition) for participating.

The Service Learning Program recognizes the learning experience gained through voluntary service and affirms the Mennonite heritage of concern for one's neighbor. Students entering an approved voluntary service program or having at least seven months left in a service program may receive up to 14 hours of college credit.

MAKING A DIFFERENCE STUDIES

Global Studies

Integrates study of our environment, development (what we do in attempting to improve our lot within that abode), peace and justice (how we react to unequal sharing of our planet's resources). The topics are inherently interwoven and international, hence multidisciplinary and cross-cultural.

Global Studies—Environmental Studies

Emphasize the holistic understanding of environmental systems and an appreciation of the relationship of the environment to human life quality.

Introduction to Environmental Science	Environmental Biology
Environmental Monitoring & Management	Ecology
Social & Physical Geography	Development Economics

- **Environmental Decision-Making** Sudy the various systems of evaluation in environmental decision making: decisions under uncertainty; risk analysis; long-term and short-term values. Methods of environmental decision making, environmental impact analysis process, environmental regulations, and environmental law. Team taught.

- Faculty Bio: **Dwight R. Platt,** Ph.D. (Univ of Kansas) has been Director of Sand Prairie National History Reservation since 1966, and was Chairman for eight years of the Scientific Advisory Panel to Save the Tallgrass Prairie. He was a visiting professor at Sambalpur University in Orissa, India, as well as an Education Technician with the American Friends Service Committee there.

Global Studies—Peace Studies

The nature and causes of human conflict, the factors which contribute to peace with justice, and the processes by which conflict can be managed creatively to bring about fundamental social change. The program includes study of global relationships, conflict between groups and institutions within nations, and conflicts within small groups and among persons.

Conflict Resolution Theory & Practice	Majority/ Minority Relations
Peacemaking & International Conflict	Theories & Strategies of Social Change
Summer Peace Institute for Teachers	Just War in American History
Christian Social Ethics	Public Policy for Global Issues

- **Nonviolence Theory and Practice** The philosophical and religious foundation, theory, history, and practice of nonviolence as a method of social change. Special attention to Mahatma Gandhi and Dr. Martin Luther King, Jr.

- Faculty Bio: **Duane K. Friesen,** (Th. D. Harvard) was Symposium Director of "Peacemaking in the Middle East: The Role of Judaism, Christianity & Islam" and a Research Fellow at the Ecumenical Institute for Advanced Theological Research in Jerusalem. He was also a member of the Executive Committee, Consortium on Peace Research, Education and Development.

Economics & Business

Development Economics	Comparative Economic Systems
Public Policy & Finance	Public Policy for Global Issues

- **Business Ethics & Social Responsibility** Business as a social institution and moral theory as it applies to business. Course centers on both theoretical and practical aspects of social responsibility of the modern industrial corporation as well as the institutional values and goals. Case studies in what role, if any, ethical and social responsibility play in corporate activity an decision making.

Global Studies—International Development

This program emphasizes rural and urban development among the poor. It seeks to meet the need for better prepared workers in International Development emphasizing cross-cultural understanding, an appreciation for the dignity of the poor and the complexity of their struggles, and a broadly - based study of development theory. The major gives a better understanding of how foreign policy, international aid, and foreign debt influence development.

Public Policy for Global Issues

Transcultural Seminar

Principles of Sustainable Agriculture

Development Economics

Relief, Development & Social Justice

Energy Issues & Appropriate Technology

International Health

Theories & Strategies of Social Change

Global Issues in Environment, Human Conflict and Development

- **Rural Development in Central America/Mexico** A hands-on experience, travel course to one or two of the following countries: Mexico, Guatemala, El Salvador, Honduras, Costa Rica, Nicaragua. Seminars and field experiences to learn about the problems and possibilities for rural development, social change, and conflict resolution. The problems of food production, population growth, rural to urban migration, and degradation of the environment will be studied. Emphasis upon trying to hear and understand those who suffer the consequences o f underdevelopment.

- Faculty Bio: **Paul McKay, M.S.** (Cal Polytechnic State U. 1973) was Area Representative for Central America for 11 years with World Neighbors, Inc. He was Director for two years of the Chimaltenango Development Program in Guatemala, and Extension Agent, Guatemalan Extension Service for the American Friends Service Committee in Guatemala.

Special Education Concentration

Strategies for Behavior Management

Consultation Skills for Special Educators

Characteristics of Adolescents with Handicap

Early Intervention for Handicapped Children

Education and Psychology of the Exceptional Individual

Practicum with Preschool-Aged Children with Handicaps

Methods for Facilitating Development in Infants with Special Needs

Methods for Teaching Children and Youth with Mental Retardation at Educable Level

Off Campus Study

Biology/Anthro Field Trip to Belize & Guatemala Study of tropical marine, fresh water terrestrial biology and archaeological history and contemporary life in two Central American countries.

Social Work   Nursing

Student Body: 67% state, 57% women, 43% men, 14% students of color, 9% transfer
• 28 male faculty, 24 female faculty
1994-95 costs: $12,320   Apply By: 8/15
• Life Experience Credit   • Team Teaching   • Non-resident Degree Program
• Nursing Outreach Program   • Co-op Work Study   • Evening Classes   • Vegetarian Meals
• Recycling policies in force

Use form in back to contact: Admissions Office
Bethel College
300 East 27th Street   North Newton, KS 67117-9989
1 (800) 522-1887

BROWN UNIVERSITY

5,500 Undergraduates   Providence, Rhode Island   Most Selective

Very few centers of higher education can honestly claim tooffer their students the best of both worlds: the breadth and depth of auniversity's resources, and the intimate experience of an undergraduate liberal arts college. Brown offers this rare balance. Recently implemented "University Courses" emphasize synthesis rather than survey, and focus on the methods, concepts, and values employed in understanding a particular topic or issue. Using a single discipline or interdisciplinary approach, they introduce students to distinctive ways of thinking, constructing, communicating , and discovering knowledge. This emphasis has spawned unusual interdepartmental concentrations and programs. For example, biomedical researchers have worked with the departments of Philosophy and Religion to create a concentration in Biomedical Ethics. The Health and Society concentration pulls together the fields of human biology, community health, economics, and the social and behavioral sciences to examine health care systems and address policy issues at the local, national, and international levels.

Collaborations between faculty and undergraduates in research, course development and teaching have resulted in research on the impact of TV advertising on election campaigns, developing mathematical models of predator-prey interactions in marine ecosystems; and cataloguing materials for the study of race relations in Brazil.

Brown students have designed and implemented a wink-controlled wheelchair for parapalegics, converted an unused carriage house into the University's Urban Environmental Laboratory, collaborated with engineering professors to build a "clean air" automobile, and worked at a missionary hospital in Kenya.

Brown President Vartan Gregorian noted "more than ever, we need to recover a sense of the wholeness of human life and to understand the human condition.... We need to admit questions of values to the arena of discussion and debate. The moral argument of a poem, the social implications of a political system, the ethical consequences of a scientific technique, and the human significance of our responsibilities should have a place in classrooms and dormitories. To deny that place is to relinquish any claims or any attempt to link thought and action, knowing and doing."

Brown's emphasis on civic and social responsibility, and on bridging the gap between academia and the world beyond, provides opportunities to integrate community work with their academic and career goals. The Center for Public Service coordinates its activities with various academic programs, including Public Policy, Health and Society, Urban Studies, and Environmental Studies. Students volunteer with educational, social service, health, government and cultural organizations. Faculty and staff serve too: the Taubman Center for Public Policy is working with the city of Providence to develop a comprehensive antipoverty program, and the Allan Shawn Feinstein World Hunger Program tackles the issue of starvation amid plenty.

With Brown's extraordinary array of religions, ethnicities, and nationalities, students tend to find common ground through academic, extracurricular, and social interests, as well as through cultural ties. Experiencing that diversity first-hand is, for many, one of the most rewarding aspects of the Brown experience.

MAKING A DIFFERENCE STUDIES

Public Policy and American Institutions
Ethics and Public Policy
Woman and Public Policy
Public Policy and Higher Education
Social Welfare Policy
Political Research Methods

Environmental Regulation
Education and Public Policy
Law and Public Policy
Housing & Community Development Policy
The Price System and Resource Allocation

Development Studies
African History and Society
Slave Community
Culture and Health
Nuclear Weapons: Technology and Policy
Women & Health Care
Burden of Disease in Developing Countries

Population Growth and the Environment
Issues in Minority Health
Gender in 20th Century American Sport
Shaping of World Views
Anthropological Issues in World Population
Possibilities for Social Reconstruction

Biology & Medicine Track in Community Health
Culture and Health
Research in Health Care
Economic Development
International Environmental Issues
Red, White & Black in the Americas
The Culture of Postcolonialism

Health Care in the U.S.
Ideology of Development
Comparative Sex Roles
Social Change in Modern India
Third World Political & Economic Issues
Comparative Policy and Politics: East Asia

Biomedical Ethics
Ethical Issues in Field of Mental Health
Ethical Issues in Pediatric Medicine
Moral Problems
Religious Ethics and Moral Issues

Ethical Issues in Preventive Medicine
The Aims of Medicine
Moral Theories
Sociology of Medicine

Ethical Issues in Research and Use of Biomedical Technology

Sociology
Economic Development & Social Change
The Family
Social Inequality
War and the Military
Environmental Sociology

American Heritage: Racism & Democracy
Population Growth and the Environment
Race, Class and Ethnicity: Modern World
Women in Socialist & Developing Countries
Social Structures & Personal Development

- **Industrialization, Democracy and Dictatorship** Examines the interrelations between economic development and political change. Does economic development encourage democratization in today's underdeveloped countries as it did in W. Europe? Does rapid economic change foster revolutionary movements? Does sustained economic growth require authoritarian rule? What is the impact of multinational corporations on political conditions in developing countries?

Women's Studies   Environmental Studies   Aquatic Biology   Urban Studies

Afro-American Studies   Education   International Relations   Public Policy

Student Body: 3% state, 51% women, 49% men, 26% students of color, 9% int'l
1994-95 costs: $27,850   Apply By 1/1

Use form in back to contact: Director of Admission
Brown University   Providence, RI 02912
(401) 863-2378

BRYN MAWR

1105 Students   Bryn Mawr, Pennsylvania   Most Selective

Bryn Mawr is a liberal arts college in both the modern and traditional senses. Its curriculum is modern in offering a full range of subjects in the arts, sciences, and social sciences, but the College is also traditional in its commitment to the original sense of "liberal arts" — the studies of a free person.

Bryn Mawr believes in a broad education which prepares students to be free to question or advocate any idea without fear. This kind of education results in graduates who are determined to change society. Among Bryn Mawr graduates are the domestic policy adviser to Vice President Albert Gore; the deputy director of the U.S. Office of Management and Budget; the medical director of the only women's health clinic in Nairobi; federal judges, children's legal advocates, teachers at every level, and a much higher than usual percentage of women who are in positions to improve society — in this country and around the world.

Individual responsibility with a concern for the community are prime traits of Bryn Mawr students. The college believes that the pleasure of knowledge is insufficient if that knowledge does not lead to social action. Too many people act without knowing and too many highly educated people won't act on behalf of others. Bryn Mawr seeks students who wish to use their education, not merely for personal enrichment but to be fully contributing, responsible citizens of the world. Mary Sefranek, Class of '94, is a good example of our philosophy in action. She was one of twenty USA Today All Academic Team winners in 1994 for, among her many accomplishments, the work she has done with the Roberto Clemente Middle School in Philadelphia. Mary created a special program for this low-income, primarily Hispanic public school, including teams of Bryn Mawr student tutors and field trips. She is one of many Bryn Mawr students active in volunteer projects.

Bryn Mawr's students are from 48 states, Puerto Rico, D.C., and 51 other countries. American minorities make up 25% of the students. Several students from South Africa not only voted in the first free and open election in 300 years, they worked at the Philadelphia Absentee Ballot Center to help their compatriots vote. The unusually high percentage of foreign students means everyone learns first-hand about real world problems. Bryn Mawr is among a handful of private colleges which give financial aid to foreign students. A recent CBS Sunday Morning News show featured four Bryn Mawr students in a segment called "Women of the Revolution." Students from Kuwait, the People's Republic of China, Rumania, and South Africa talked about their hopes that their BM educations would be put to use for their people at home.

The Minority Coalition, an organization representing all of the minority student organizations, enables minority students to work together to increase the number of minority students and faculty, and to develop curricular and extra-curricular programs dealing with United States minority groups and non-Western peoples and cultures.

Bryn Mawr is one of the very few colleges and universities with an honor code. The honor code characterizes a philosophy of mutual respect between students, faculty and administration.

MAKING A DIFFERENCE MAJORS

Geology

Mineralogy and Mineral Paragensis	Stratigraphy/Sedimentation
Crystallography and Optical Mineralogy	Low Temperature Geochemistry
Principles of Economic Geology	Introduction to Geophysics
Tectonics	Structural Geology

- **Environmental Geology** Issues affecting land use and management of the environment including natural geologic hazards, forces shaping the earth's surface, energy
  sources, waste disposal, and urban planning. Labs focus on local environmental issues.

Peace Studies

War and Cultural Difference	Nationalism in Europe
Social Inequality	Intransigent Conflict
Schools in American Cities	The Culture of the Cold War
Ethnic Group Politics	Great Powers and the Near East
Germany Since 1914	Slavery and Emancipation: British & U.S.

Conflict and Conflict Management: A Cross-cultural Approach

Growth and Structure of Cities

This interdisciplinary major challenges the student to understand the relationship of spatial
organization and the built environment to politics, economics, culture and society. Students
pursue their interests through classes in planning, art and architecture, archaeology, and in
social and natural sciences including anthropology, economics, geology, sociology, and history.

Urban Culture and Society	The Form of the City
Ancient Greek Cities and Sanctuaries	Comparative Urbanism
Latin American Urban Development	Topics in Urban Culture and Society
Modernization	Survey of Western Architecture
Topics in History of Modern Planning	Ethnic Group Politics

Chinese Notions of Time and Space: Garden, House, and City

Anthropology

Sex, Culture and Society	Medical Anthropology
African Ethology: Urban Problems	Language in Social Context
Linguistic Anthropology	Cultural Ecology
Psychological Anthropology	Gender Differentiation
History of Cultural Theory	Traditional and Pre-Industrial Technology
Origins of Civilization and the State	Ethnography of South Asia

Feminist and Gender Studies

Feminism and Philosophy	The Family in Social Context
Patterns in Feminist Spirituality	Topics in European Women's/Gender History
Studies in Prejudice	Women in Early Christianity
Women in Science	Gender, Class and Culture

Women in Contemporary Society: Third World Women

Student Body: 14% state, 100% women, 25% minority   Apply By: 1/1
Faculty: 50% male, 50% female, 12% minority   1994-95 tuition, room and board $26,165
• Team Teaching • Individualized Majors • Core/Multidisciplinary Classes • Vegetarian Meals

Use form in back to contact: Office of Admissions
Bryn Mawr College   Bryn Mawr, PA
(610) 526-5152

CALIF. STATE POLYTECHNIC UNIVERSITY

8,000 Undergraduates   Pomona, California   Very Selective

MAKING A DIFFERENCE STUDIES

Biology
Environmental Conservation
Bio Perspectives on Contemporary Life
Field Studies in the Southwest
Water Pollution Biology
Fresh Water Biology

Marine Ecology
Principles of Ecology
Population Ecology
Chaparral Biology
Tropical Biology

Mechanical Engineering: Energy Systems Option
Energy Management
Heat Power

Solar Thermal Engineering
Building Energy Calculations

• **Alternative Energy Systems** Fossil fuel systems; viable alternative energy sources, solar, geothermal, wind, biomass, hydro and ocean; resources, conversion, storage and distribution. Environmental impact and economics of alternative systems.

International Agriculture Development
Emphasizes development of ecologically sound food production and marketing techniques.
Agricultural Ecology
Rural Development Project Analysis
Environmental Technology and Culture
Ethical Issues in Agriculture
Agricultural Co-ops

Animal Agricultural Science
Farm Management/ Low Income Agriculture
Planning in Developing Nations
Global Resources for Food
Tropical Agriculture

Environmental Engineering
Soil Mechanics
Aquatic Ecology
Construction and Engineering Law
Computer Programming & Numerical Methods

Water Supply Engineering
Environmental Resource Systems
Elementary Surveying

Architecture
Energy Conservation
Latin American Architecture
Consciousness and Community
Cities, Citizens and Urban Planning
Environmental Conservation

Solar Design Applications in Architecture
Behavioral Factors in Architecture
Living with the Land
Promise and Crisis
The Architect and the Development Process

Agricultural Engineering Dep't is at the forefront in application of drip or trickle irrigation methods as adapted to agriculture/landscape irrigation systems design and conservation of water.
Environmental Engineering   **Landscape Architecture**
Environmental Health Specialist   **Outdoor Recreation Administration**
Black; Hispanic; North American Indian Studies   Women's Studies

Student Body: 82% state, 41% women, 59% men, 43% students of color   Apply By: 11/30
1994-95 estimated tuition: Residents $1443 Non-residents $246 additional per unit
Housing: Priority given to first year students. Architecture applications accepted in November only

Use form in back to contact: Admissions Office
Cal State Polytechnic U   Pomona, Pomona, CA 91768
(909) 869-2000

CALIFORNIA STATE UNIVERSITY - SACRAMENTO

20,000 Undergraduate Students   Sacramento, CA   Moderately Selective

MAKING A DIFFERENCE STUDIES

Environmental Studies
Environmental Ethics
Environment & the Law
General Ecology
The Ecology of Shelter
Land Economics

International Environmental Problems
Quantitative Methods for Environments
Energy Economics
Environmental Politics & Policy
Climate

Social Work / Community Organizing, Planning and Administration
COPA has a long tradition from efforts of social reformers of the New Deal, rank and file orga-
nizers of the 30's to the war against poverty in the 60's. Emphasis on advocacy and social action.
Planning and Administration
Law and Social Work
Advocacy, Theory and Practice
COPA Policy and Services
Theories, Community Organizing, Planning and Administration

Field Instruction
Immigrant and Refugee Service
Human Behavior and Social Environments
Social Work Practice in Community Organizing

Social Work
Welfare in America
Issues and Services in Aging
Child Welfare Services
Black Women in America
Politics of the Underrepresented

Crimes Without Victims
Poverty and Homelessness in America
La Mujer Chicana
Asian-Americans: Status and Identity
Women and the Economy

Health and Safety Studies / Community Health Option
Healthy Lifestyles
Disease Prevention
Human Ecology and Health
Public Health Administration
Community Health Planning

Community Health
Mental Health
Epidemiology
Alcohol and Drugs
Consumer Health and Self Care

Communications
Critical Analysis of Messages
Children and Television
Communication & American Culture
Media Issues and Ethics
American Women in Media and Arts

Interpersonal Communication Skills
Violence and Communication
Intercultural Communication
Conflict Resolution Thru Communication
Film as Communication: Third World Emphasis

Child Development
Families Under Stress
Issues in Parenting
Language and Learning
Human Development
Biology: A Human Perspective

Cross Cultural Child Development
Self-Concept and Role theory
The Family and Social Issues
Adolescent Development
Family Life Education

| Economics | Philosophy | Biological Conservation |
| Aquatic Biology | Asian Studies | Women's Studies |

Use form in back to contact: Director of Admissions
CSU Sacramento   Sacramento, CA 95819
(916) 278-3901

55

CSU, SAN FRANCISCO

19,102 Undergraduates   San Francisco, California   Moderately Selective

MAKING A DIFFERENCE STUDIES

NEXA Program (Science and Humanities: A Program For Convergence)

Science and Culture
Time in Human Consciousness
The Nuclear Revolution
Split Brain/Split Culture?
Exploration
Science as Social Process

Mythic and Scientific Thought
Words, Culture and Change
The Feminist Revolution
Animal Rights: A Multidisciplinary

The City in Civilization

- **Words, Culture and Change** How culture (including technology, social organization, religion, etc,) shapes and is shaped by language across the ages. Preliterate cultures.

Labor Studies

Intro to Study of Labor
Union Structure and Administration
Women and Work
History of Labor in the U.S.

Researching Labor Issues
Labor and Government
Industrial Sociology
Labor Economics

Holistic Health

Holistic Health: Western Perspectives
Holistic Health and Human Nature
Psychosomatics and Stress Management
Orthomolecular Dietary Therapy
Regulation
Environmental Health
Ethics of Medicine

Holistic Health: Eastern Perspectives
Chinese Perspectives in Holistic Health
Chinese Body-Mind Energetics
Foundations of Biofeedback & Self-

Healing Practices of the World
Traditional Sciences of Indian America

- **Psychobiology of Healing** Foundation, ramifications and practices of therapeutic touch and healee-healer interaction. Topical presentations of the healing process.

Intercultural Skills Program

Cultural Awareness
Intercultural Communication
Culture and Personality
Ethnic Relations: Int'l Comparisons
Intracultural Communication

International Negotiation
Sociolinguistics
Kinship and Social Structure
Language and Culture
Anthropology and Folklore

La Raza Studies

Oral History and Traditions
Philosophy of La Raza
La Raza Women
La Raza Journalism
Acculturation Problems of La Raza
Central Americans in the U.S.

Socioeconomics of La Raza
La Raza Community Organizing
Psychodynamics of La Raza Family
Latino Health Care Perspectives
Indigenismo
Community Mental Health

Student Body: 98% state, 58% women, 42% men, 55% minority
1993-94 fees: Residents $3232   Nonresidents $246 add'l per unit   Apply By 8/1

Use form in back to contact: Director of Admissions
San Francisco State University   San Francisco, CA 94132
(415) 338-1111

CALIFORNIA UNIVERSITY OF PENNSYLVANIA

5,983 Undergraduates   California, Pennsylvania   Moderately Selective

MAKING A DIFFERENCE STUDIES

Teaching Credential / Environmental Studies
Man and His Environment
Ecosystems Ecology
Wildlife Techniques
Game and Habitat Management
Physical Geography

Environmental Biology
Man and His Physical World
Outdoor Activities
Recreation and Park Administration
Human Ecology

Environmental Resources /Environmental Pollution
Contemporary Issues in Biology
Air Quality Monitoring
Environmental Regulations
Introduction to Oceanography
Solid Waste Management
Ecosystems Ecology

Earth Resources
Economic Geography
Climatology
Coastal Geomorphology & Marine Resources
Water and Wastewater Analysis
Environmental Research Problems

Environmental Conservation
Principles of Biology
Wildlife Techniques
Plant Ecology
Water Pollution Biology
Biometry

Biotic Communities
Soil Science
Environmental Research Problems
Conservation of Biological Resources
Ornithology

Wildlife Biology
General Zoology
Principles of Wildlife Management
Land Use Planning
Urban Planning
Principles of Biology

General Botany
Plant Taxonomy
Mammalogy
Ichthyology
Environmental Physiology

Urban Studies
Survey of Urban Affairs
Political Economy
Urban Transportation
Housing and Housing Policy
History of Urban America
Urban Sociology

Municipal Government
Urban Geography
Recreation for Phys./Emotionally Handicapped
Practicum in Urban Affairs
Organizational & Administrative Behavior
Community Action & Neighborhood Gov't

Social Work   Gerontology   Meteorology   Early Childhood Ed.
Special Education: Community Services/Community Living Arrangements A.A.

Student Body: 90% state, 50% women, 50% men, 6% minority
Faculty 56% male, 44% female, 8% minority
1993-94 costs: Residents $6564   Nonresidents $9957   Apply By 8/1
• Single Parent Programs   • Team Teaching   • Evening Classes   • Vegetarian Meals

Use form in back to contact: Director of Admissions
California University of PA.   250 University Ave.   California, PA 15419
(412) 938-4404

CARLETON COLLEGE

1700 Students   Northfield, Minnesota   Very Selective

Carleton is one of the nation's most respected small liberal arts colleges, unusual for its location in the Midwest. Its vital intellectual community draws students from all fifty states and 15 other countries. Co-educational since its founding, Carleton has a long history of encouraging original thought and a sense of intellectual adventure through rigorous study of traditional academic disciplines, complemented by a wide offering of electives and interdisciplinary programs.

One such program, which appeals to students interested in environmental studies, is the Technology and Policy Studies concentration which explores the implementation of emerging technology into public policy. Faculty in the program are drawn from several departments including economics, geology, and sociology. Other students interested in environmental studies, however, major in the natural sciences, taking advantage of one of the strongest undergraduate programs in the country.

Carleton's setting is distinct, with a 400-acre arboretum bordering the campus. The "Arb," as it is called by students, consists of a variety of habitats, including floodplain forest, wetlands, prairie, and a pine plantation. Used for both research and recreation, the arboretum is governed by students, who both decide what preservation projects are undertaken, and do the actual work themselves.

Students at Carleton have a long history of activism, involving themselves in over one hundred organizations on campus. Acting in the Community Together, or ACT, is one of the most popular. Through this umbrella volunteer organization, students administer over forty separate community-based programs, and were commended for the last two years by the Governor of Minnesota. Selected as the Minnesota hub campus for the national organization, COOL (Campus Outreach Opportunity League), ACT now serves as a consultant for other campus service programs.

Carleton encourages students to engage in honest discussions on issues of difference, whether based on gender, race, ethnicity, socio-economics, or political viewpoint. Through both informal discussion and coursework, the College aims to expose members of the community to perspectives that have developed outside of, in opposition to, or in ways only dimly visible to the dominant culture in which most of us have grown up and been educated. Before first-year students arrive at Carleton, they are invited to participate in a "Common Reading" of a book such as *July's People* by Nadine Gordimer or *Donald Duk* by Frank Chin. When they arrive on campus, the students meet with faculty and staff in their homes to discuss the book. In order to fulfill the "Recognition and Affirmation of Difference" requirement, students must take a course centrally concerned with another culture; with a country, art, or tradition from outside Europe and the US, or with issues of gender, class, race or ethnicity

With over 60% of its students participating in off-campus studies, Carleton operates of of the largest study abroad programs on any college campus. In an average year, Carleton students are on over 85 different programs. Whether it be in Nepal, Costa Rica, or Kenya, Carleton students gain not only an unusual academic experience, but also an invaluable personal one.

MAKING A DIFFERENCE STUDIES

Biology
Biology for the Humanist
Spring Flora
Marine Biology
Tropical Rainforest Ecology
Field Investigation in Tropical Rainforest Ecology (in Costa Rica)
Biology Field Studies and Research (in Australia/New Zealand)

Biology of Conservation
Introductory Botany
Ecology
Biology of Non-Vascular Plants

Technology and Policy Studies
Information, Society and Democracy
Environmental Policy and Politics
Public Policy and the Human Fetus
Intro to Environmental Geology
Congress, Campaign Money & A National Energy Strategy

Technologies and Their Societies
Water and Western Economic Development
Environmental Chemistry
Technology Policy Project

Sociology/Anthropology
Population and Food in Global System
Biography and Ethnography
Nationalism and Ethnicity
Islam and the Middle East
Explorations of Diaspora Populations
Conquest and Encounter: Europeans and Indigenous Peoples in the "New World"

Class, Power and Inequality in America
Economic Anthropology
Schooling and Opportunity in Amer. Society
Comparative Study of Developing Societies
Ethnology of Central America & Caribbean

Political Science
Science, Technology and Politics
Parties, Interest Groups and Elections
Urban Politics
Political Theory of M. L. King
International Conflict and War
Social Movements and Protest Politics

Liberal Democracy and Social Democracy
Feminist Political Theory
Urban Political Economy
Gender Discrimination&Constitutional Law
American Security and Arms Control
Urban Racial and Ethnic Politics

- **Poverty and Public Policy** Focus on the relationship between race, class, gender and poverty in the U.S. Students will analyze various explanations for the growth of the underclass and homelessness as well as public policy strategies for reducing poverty.

Economics
Comparative Economic Systems
African Economic Development
Political Economy of Capitalism
Economics of the Public Sector
Environmental Health Economics
Economics of Poverty, Discrimination and the Distribution of Income

The Economics of Apartheid
Political Economy of the Third World
Economics of Human Resources
Economics of Natural Resources &
Economics of Poverty

Educational Studies Concentration
Women's Studies

Natural History Concentration
African/African-American Studies

Student Body: 24% state, 49% men, 51% women, 16% minority, 2% int'l
Faculty: 68% male, 32% female, 9% minority
• Team teaching • Individual majors • Exclusive Seminar Format • Vegetarian Meals
1994-95 Comprehensive Costs: $23,375   Apply By: 2/1

Use form in back to contact: Dean of Admissions
Carleton College   Northfield, MN
(507) 663-4190

CLARK UNIVERSITY

2,100 Undergraduates   Worcester, Mass.   Very Selective

For the spirited, independent, inspired learner, Clark University can offer the best of many worlds; combining the advantages of the intimate, liberal arts college and the distinctive, research university; prompting students to venture beyond classroom and laboratory into the community, across cultures, and even across the globe. Clark is dedicated to being a dynamic community of learners able to thrive in today's increasing interrelated societies. More than 70 percent of classes have fewer than 20 students.

The special strength of Clark's programs stems from a fruitful integration of teaching and research. Clark has attracted a faculty that is committed to excellence in teaching and original scholarship. Clark's academic community has long been distinguished by the pursuit of scientific inquiry and humanistic studies, enlivened by a concern for significant social issues. Clark especially contributes to understanding human development, assessing relationships between people and the environment, and managing risk in a technological society. In Clark's classrooms and laboratories, professors try out new ideas and recount their firsthand experiences with, for example, measuring Chernobyl's radioactive fallout in Europe, or helping villagers use resources more effectively to produce food in Kenya, Somalia, and Zimbabwe.

Clark's programs focusing on environmental change are among the very best in the country. Many Clark students are interested in helping alleviate the world's ills, among them: acid rain, depletion of the ozone layer, drought, overdevelopment, and nuclear risk.

Clark was one of the first universities in the country to offer an undergraduate major in the interdisciplinary field of Environment, Technology, and Society. The E.T.S. Program is designed for students who hope to contribute to the solution of complex societal problems such as environmental protection, energy policy, technological hazards, and risk analysis. Degree requirements emphasize a firm grounding in natural science coupled with considerable exposure to social science and public policy perspectives. The E.T.S. Program offers some thirty problem-oriented and methodological courses and a variety of special projects and internship experiences.

The International Development and Social Change program focuses on questions of equity, growth, and development at a time when developing countries are increasing their influence on the world's economic, political, and social systems. Clark recognizes that most problems transcend national boundaries, and the program emphasizes ways in which individuals can identify effective local action in the context of global change. The program serves students from developing nations as well as industrialized countries. Topics of particular interest include participation in local institutions, roles of women and community organizations, rural development, and geographic information systems.

Each year, 250 Clark students from every major take advantage of off-campus experiences earning one to four course credits, either paid or unpaid. One student recently interned at the UN, working in the office of the press secretary to the Secretary General. Others have interned at the US Dept of Health and Human Services, Planned Parenthood, the Audubon Society, and National Clean Air Coalition.

MAKING A DIFFERENCE STUDIES

Cultural Identity and Global Processes

Dramatic growth in transnational and global phenomena has led to the existence of a global community that has significantly contributed to the demise of the nation-state. Yet, at the same time there is a resurgence of cultural identities in both regional and local contexts.
Cultural Identities and Global Processes   Race, Migration, Gender and Ethnicity
The Creation of Nationalisms, Nationalist Cultures, and Symbols

- **Culture, Consumption, & Class in Local & Global Contexts** Focuses on consumption as it is culturally and ethnically determined, gendered, classes, and impacted upon politically by both individual consumers and capitalist producers. The ways in which consumption is linked to the identity values are explored. A central theme is the interplay between the forces of the world market and cultural identities, between local and global processes, and between consumption and cultural strategies.

Cultural / Humanistic Geography

American Land, American Mind
Culture Landscape
Agriculture in Third World Economics
Cultural and Political Ecology
Cultural Ecology in Humid Tropics

World Population
Cultural Ecology in Arid Lands
The End of America: Los Angeles
Driving Forces of Global Change
Race, Migration, Gender and Ethnicity

Before and After Columbus: Ancient Middle America and Impact of the Conquest

Regional / International Development / Political Economy

Geography of the Third World
Political Economy of Underdevelopment
Development Problems
Politics, People, and Pollution

Economic Development and Policy Analysis
International Division of Labor
Dev. Theories and Philosophies of Change
Land & Development in Latin America

Overcoming World Hunger - Agricultural Research and International Development
Money, Banking and Finance in Developing Countries

- **Gender, Space & Environment** How gender is reflected in the landscape, in our settlement and land use patterns, in environmental history, and in our present ecological science and practice from the global to the local level. Feminist and other alternative explanations of the gendered nature of knowledge, access, use, and control of space and resources in a variety of environments, past, present, and possible.

Environment, Technology and Society

To enable individuals to deal with technical issues is a social and political context and to do so with an acute awareness of the short and long range limitations of the natural environment to respond to human interventions. Students are encouraged to obtain academic year internships or paid summer jobs. Placements have included the International Atomic Energy Agency in Vienna, the Mass. Energy Office, and the Mass. Office of Coastal Zone Mgm't. The program also offers an integrated B.A./M.A. option with a minimum of 5 years study.

Introductory Case Studies
Economy and Environment
Energy Systems, Economics & Policies
Environmental Hazards
Risk Perception
Medical Ethics
Conflict Resolution

Introduction to the Global Environment
Technology and Social Change
Environment and Society
Limits of the Earth
Decision Analysis for Environmental Mgm't.
Environmental Health
Groundwater Resources

Environmental / Resource Management

The Global Environment

People, Ecology and Global Village

Gender, Resources and Development

Social Forestry and Development

Societal Responses to Global Change

Forest Hydrology Field Methods

Technology and Social Change

Locating Hazardous Facilities

Nature and Culture in the Ancient World

Management of Arid Lands

Environment and Society

Int'l & Comparative Resource Policies

Physical Geography of Human Systems

Biogeography

Tropical Ecology

Earth Science and Development

Urban Ecology: Cities as Ecosystems

Environment and Disasters

Watershed Ecology

Land Degradation

Physical Environment of Arid Lands

Oceanic Islands: Geology and Ecology

Agriculture and Grazing

Peace Studies

Peace Net international computer network access is available for student use

Introduction to Peace Studies

Arms Control

Development Problems

Global Capitalism

Social Movements

Politics of War and Peace

United States and the New Europe

Conflict Resolution

Local Action, Global Change

Race and American Society

Philosophy

Personal Values

Social and Political Ethics

Legal Ethics

Politics and Human Nature

AIDS: Ethics and Public Policy

Medical Ethics

Business Ethics

Women and Philosophy

Feminist Theory

Idealism

Women's Studies

Gender and Film

Women in Hispanic Literature

Women in Society

American Jewish Life

Gender, Resources and Development

History of American Women

Women and Social Change

History of African-American Women

Policies, Projects and Strategies for Change: A Focus on Gender

Women and Militarization in a Comparative Politics Perspective

American Politics and Public Policy Urban/Social and Economic/Planning
Sociology   Psychology   Screen Studies

Student Body: 23% state, 55% women, 45% men, 9% minority, 15% int'l, 18% transfer
1994-95 cost approximately: $23,000   Apply By 2/15, Early Decision 12/1
Housing: Special interest houses include "global environment house"

• Service Learning Programs   • Internships   • Core/Multidisciplinary Classes
• Individualized Majors   •Team Teaching • Vegetarian and Kosher Meals

Use form in back to contact: Dean of Admissions
Clark University, Admissions House
950 Main St.,Worcester, MA 01610
(508) 793-7431

COLLEGE OF THE ATLANTIC

225 Students   Bar Harbor, Maine   Very Selective

"A student is a light to be lighted, not a glass to be filled."
William H. Durry, Jr.

College of the Atlantic was created at a time when, for many students, it was becoming evident that conventional education was inadequate to prepare them for effective citizenship in an increasingly complex and technical society. The founders envisioned a pioneering institution dedicated to the interdisciplinary study of human ecology. Their goal was a college in which students could overcome the narrow points of view and integrate knowledge across traditional academic lines. COA's curriculum especially focuses on developing conceptual frameworks for the solution of human and ecological problems. As we approach the twenty-first century these problems include equitably addressing the use and distribution of global resources, preventing nuclear war, and developing a mechanism to insure lasting peace.

COA is a college for the environmentally and socially committed individual. Being willing to take a stand on an issue, to show compassion for others, to recognize and promote the interconnectedness of all species and systems - all are characteristics of many students who choose COA. The mission at COA is to equip students with the knowledge, understanding, enthusiasm, and sensitivity to solve complex environmental and social problems from a humanistic perspective. Truly interdisciplinary thinking requires new methods for synthesizing and utilizing knowledge. In an interdisciplinary academic culture the boundaries among disciplines are minimized. Scientific analysis joins with humanistic and aesthetic understanding. Insights from specialized knowledge are combined and contribute a fuller understanding of complicated issues.

Responsible citizenship also requires collaborative attitudes and skills. This is a central concept at COA and the main rationale for a commitment to participatory governance and consensus building. It is exemplified by creative ways to run meetings, resolve disputes, utilize computer technologies, or work partnerships with outside communities.

At COA, students work on real issues from the beginning of their studies rather than after they are "educated". Individual courses of study are created by students as they work together with faculty to expand their academic horizons and develop their sense of responsibility. The outcome is an education that builds competence and confidence for life-long learning and prepares effective citizens and leaders for the decades to come.

In order to remain interdisciplinary and help students see the connections between all academic disciplines, COA does not break down into academic departments. Courses at COA are distinguished by three resource area: Arts and Design, Environmental Sciences, and Human Studies. One facet of the Human Studies resource area is the innovative teacher certification program about which the Maine

State board of Education noted "As a Board and as policy makers we have often talked about excellence... at College of the Atlantic we experienced excellence in education."

At College of the Atlantic each student is responsible, with the help of an advising team, for designing his/her own academic program. Upon entering the College, students are assigned an advising team with whom they meet to plan and evaluate their studies. At the end of the first academic year, students choose a permanent advising team, comprised of one faculty member, one student, and an optional third member of the COA community. Combining courses in Arts and Design, Environmental Sciences, and Human Studies, independent study courses, group tutorials, an internship, and a Senior Projects, each student tailors their education to their specific academic interest.

Internships are a required facet of the program at COA. Recent internships by students include work at Acadia National Park, Bimini Biological Field Station, Canadian Wildlife Foundation, Consumer Energy Council, Friends of the Earth, New Alchemy Institute, World Peace Camp and the Solar Energy Research Institute.

Another requirement of the COA degree is contribution of time and energy to the building of the college community. This obligation can be fulfilled by serving on an established or ad hoc committee, or with a community action group such as the Environmental Action Resource Network. Students can help with the production of a college publication, serving as an advisor, or helping to manage an essential system such as scheduling students or organizing a COA forum.

To introduce students both to outdoor recreational activities and to one another, the College coordinates optional outdoor orientation trips for entering students. Staff members and older students lead these trips which sharpen outdoor skills and encourage the development of friendships. Recent trips have included canoeing the Allagash, canoeing a series of Maine Lakes, hiking along the Appalachian Trail to Katahdin and bicycling through the Maritimes and coastal Maine.

The College itself is located in the town of Bar Harbor on Mount Desert Island, Maine, where Acadia National Park is also located. The large, scenic island is connected to the mainland by a causeway. Living on MDI introduces one to a preservation ethic—an ethic that encourages people to develop a sense of history and to value the buildings, gardens, parks, and open space in their community. COA's curriculum and the political-social climate of the island encourage students to join with residents in developing land-use policies to insure the islands uniqueness will be preserved.

The College's location enables students to participate in many outdoor activities. Nearby Acadia National Park has over 50 miles of carriage paths and 100 miles of open trails. Students regularly jog and bike, hike and rock climb, windsurf, canoe, and sail on the island lakes and in Frenchman Bay, and in the winter cross-country ski, snowshoe and skate. Students frequently participate in organized weekend camping trips to northern and western Maine and nearby New Hampshire.

MAKING A DIFFERENCE STUDIES

Environmental Sciences

Brings together the biological and physical sciences in exploration of the earth's systems by using the scientific method of identification and investigation, tracing ecological and evolutionary patterns, studying natural communities, and understanding the interactions of people and natural systems.

Animal Behavior   Biology I and II;
Biology of Fishes   Bio-Organic Chemistry
Ecological Physiology   Conservation of Endangered Species
Gender and Science   Geology
Marine Ecology   The Gulf of Maine
Ornithology   Plants and Humanity
Plant Taxonomy   Women in Science.

- **Marine Mammals** This course is primarily an introduction to the biology of whales, porpoises and seals, concentrating particularly on species that frequent New England waters, but also including other species or habitats as directed by current events and student interest. Practical work includes study of skeletal anatomy, study of prey species, visits to harbor seal ledges, visit to observe gray seals, evaluation of anew whale museum, and a whale watching trip to observe humpback whales feeding.

Human Studies

By synthesizing the humanities with the social sciences, the human studies resource area provides students with a wide and diversified perspective on human nature. Through these courses students focus on aspects of the contemporary human condition and are challenged to blend ecological concerns with classical human studies.

Humans in Nature   Technology and Culture
Critical Theory to Feminist Theory   Environmental Journalism
Environmental Law   History of American Reform Movements
International Environmental Law   Women and Men in Transition
International Peace In Theory and Practice Issues in Regional Resource Management
Literature and Ecology   Literature of Third World Women
Medicine and Culture   Outdoor Education and Leadership
Philosophy of Nature   Science and Society
Use and Abuse of Our Public Lands   Women's History and Literature
White Water and White Paper: Canoeing / Conservation

- **Environmental Education and Communication Lab: Using Media Arts in the Schools** This lab provides a theoretical and practical introduction to an environmental education methodology, which employs audiovisual media as documentary and artistic means of expression. The approach combines active, self-determined, and experiential learning with future oriented questioning aimed at identifying collective problems in the life-world of the learners and proposing solutions. The lab is carried out at a local school. Thematic issues may include local planning, place and community, and teenage issues on Mt. Desert island.

Arts and Design

The curriculum not only fosters artistic development but also gives students the opportunity to immerse themselves in design problems and to find solutions to them by combining aesthetic theory with an understanding of ecological, economic, and energy constraints.

Architectural Survey

Art, Media, and Environmental Studio

Introduction to Video Production

Photography I and II

Projects in Theater Workshop

Design and Activism

Environmental Design

Presentation Skills

Primitive Art

Women in the Visual Arts.

- **Land Use Planning Studio** What are the key physical aspects that make Mount Desert Island so appealing to residents and visitors? What aspects are essential to retain the integrity of that landscape into the future? As the island towns and the national park develop their comprehensive plans, the answers to these questions should guide future growth and preservation/ conservation. Students analyze the physical makeup in terms of types of development and the scenic, cultural and natural resources of a specific area on the island. The purpose of this analysis is to determine what defines the "quality of life" for residents as well as tourists.

Teacher Certification K-12

Approximately 20 percent of COA graduates are engaged in graduate studies or employed in the field as naturalists, environmental educators, and classroom teachers.

Environmental Design: Learning Spaces

Perspectives on School and Society

Intro to Philosophy of Education

Qualitative Research in Schools

Mainstreaming the Exceptional Child

Curriculum and Instruction in the Secondary Schools

Practice Informed by Theory in the Integrated Curriculum

Environmental Education and Communication: Using Media Arts in the Schools

Art, Media, and the Practice of Learning

Mainstreaming the Exceptional Child

Learning Theory

Intellectual History of Schools

- Faculty Bio **Etta Mooser** (Ed.D. Columbia University) heads COA's innovative teacher certification program. Her specialty areas include curricular innovation, ethics in education, and learning and environment. She has recently been appointed to the Maine State Advisory Committee to the Office of Truancy, Dropout, and Alternative Education.

Student Body: 15% state, 60% women, 40% men, 10% minority, 20% transfer
Faculty: 56% male, 44% female
1994-95 Costs: $19,101   Apply By 3/1, 2/15 for financial aid
Dining arrangements are cooperative with students sharing housekeeping & food preparation duties.
Many students choose to find their own housing in Bar Harbor or elsewhere on the island.

• Individualized Majors   • Core/Multidisciplinary Classes
• Exclusive Seminar Format • Team Teaching   • Vegetarian Meals

Use form in back to contact: Admissions Office
College of the Atlantic   Bar Harbor, ME 04609
(207) 288-5015
(800) 528-0025

COLORADO COLLEGE

1900 students   Colorado Springs, Colorado   Very Selective

Students come to Colorado College knowing they will have the opportunity to explore their values and discover their place in society. Students find a community that listens and challenges, provides and delivers. Professors dedicated to teaching respond to student initiative and independence. Students interested in the people, cultures, and land of the American Southwest come to Colorado College for its distinguished Southwest Studies program. CC's location and programs are ideal for those whose wonder and concern for the natural world is integral to their education. The College encourages students to pursue their goals for serious independent research. CC provides resources -- students, faculty, programs, and location -- for those who wish to discover themselves, to learn how to answer difficult questions, and to understand how they can best serve their community.

In 1970, Colorado College students and faculty decided they wanted to enhance the school's liberal arts curriculum by implementing a new schedule that allowed for in-depth study, extended field trips, and ample opportunity for independent study. This move resulted in the Block Plan which divides the academic year into eight three-and-a-half week segments called blocks. Students take one course during each block and faculty teach only one. Unrestricted by time and place, teachers can schedule class sessions to best suit the material. As a result, students learn through participation and "hands-on" exploration. Classes can spend entire days in the library or a museum gathering data for research projects; classes in geology, economics, and sociology can take prolonged field trips, studying their subject in the appropriate environment.

Because of its location and the interests of students and faculty, Colorado College has become a leader in the study of the American Southwest. Southwest Studies is interdisciplinary, asking students to understand the "big picture," to weave together various cultural and historical perspectives with the literature and language of the indigenous people and an understanding of the area's natural environment.

With one of the highest percentages of Native American and Hispanic students at a liberal arts school, the campus is alive with a Southwest flavor. The College's Hulbert Center for Southwest Studies, sponsors visiting scholars and events, and such topics as "Unmasking the Past to Face the Future: American Indian Women" and "How to Read the Writing on the Wall: Graffiti in Urban Settings." Some professors take their class to live on a Navajo reservation for a month, visit Hispanic communities in Colorado, or to examine the southwest terrain in the Four Corners region. The "Baca" campus, at the base of the Sangre de Cristo Mountains is ideal for studying the flora and wildlife of the Southwest and is accessible to multi-cultural communities with which Colorado College holds close ties.

While CC does not have an actual environmental studies department, learning about the natural world and protecting the environment permeate the academic and extra-curricular life. Students design their own major in environmental advocacy or environmental sciences, constructing their curriculum by choosing from a vast plate of environmental and other relevant courses. Every major takes a block or two for independent work. For instance, one spent a month in Belize, Central America studying the impact of economic development on an island near the barrier reef; seeing relationships between economics, biology, sociology, and political science.

Students' environmental interests aren't limited to the academic forum but merge into a way of life. Almost every year, students band together to form an environmental theme house. This past year, students lived together in a house dedicated to bringing an awareness and respect of nature to Colorado Springs children. Another group, EnAct (Environmental Action) offers opportunities for activism, education, and outreach, while coordinating a campus-wide recycling program. In addition, the Outdoor Recreation Committee is CC's most popular organization on campus, leading trips up mountains, down rivers, and through valleys for students of all abilities and experience; focusing on student leadership and environmental reverence.

Over half the student body contributes to Colorado College's community service program, which has expanded its resources tremendously because of student initiative in the past five years. The Center for Community Service helps coordinate volunteers and provides students with the resources and connections to contribute to the community. Community service thrives primarily on the efforts of students who generate the enthusiasm and the ideas. One student was recently honored with a national community service award for her leadership in the implementation of a soup kitchen.

For those who want to get involved, 15 volunteer groups address many sections of society, from the economically disadvantaged to the elderly to under-privileged children. Students takes advantage of the Block Plan's four-and-a-half day "mini-vacations" that fall between classes by traveling to places such as Denver, San Luis Valley, Chicago, or New Mexico to assist communities facing economic instability, or serve the local community with mentoring programs for middle school students, or with Habitat for Humanity, providing decent, affordable housing for low-income families.

The College supports independence and creativity with opportunities for research and independent study. For instance, since 1971 nearly 100 students have bred, monitored, and studied falcons with Professor Jim Enderson, the leader of the Western Peregrine Falcon Recovery Team for the U.S. Fish and Wildlife Service. Through their efforts, they have downlisted the Peregrine falcon from "endangered" to "threatened" in many parts of the West.

CC is one of the top schools in Watson fellowships for projects that demonstrate commitment, significance, and imagination. 1993's winners will live with single parent families in France to see how state initiatives affect economic and social conditions; researched alternative cancer treatments in Europe; and studied Catholic missionary groups (one traditional theology, one liberation theology) in Central America.

Colorado College's strengths work together to create a unique environment. Programs like Southwest and Environmental Studies have risen due to the school's unmatched location, and flourished because of the extended field trips afforded by the Block Plan. Colorado College graduates consistently find themselves relying on their well-rounded education, their problem-solving abilities and communication skills.

MAKING A DIFFERENCE STUDIES

Environmental Studies
Ecology
Environmental Economics
Public Policy Making
Atmospheric Physics
Nature and Civilizations

Intro to Environmental Chemistry
Mineral Resources, Problems and Policies
Energy Systems in a Technological Society
Environmental Ethics
Global Industrial Relations

Biology
The Flowering Plant
Field Botany
Ecology
Animal Cell Physiology
Plant Environmental Physiology

Winter Ecology
Field Zoology
Field Studies in Coral Reef Biology
Entomology
Parasitic Protozoa

War and Peace in the Nuclear Age
The Dawn of the Nuclear Age
War, Violence and the Humanities
Foundations of Nonviolence
Int'l Human Rights: Theory and Practice

The Non-Violent Tradition in Literature
Morality in War
Freedom and Authority
War & Peace in Nuclear Age

* **The Anthropology of War and Peace**   Social and cultural factors that predispose human societies to engage in or avoid armed conflict; explanations for warfare in anthropological literature; the art of warfare in non-Western industrialized societies.

Philosophy
History of Environmental Ethics
Science, Technology, and Values
Ethics
Business Ethics
Philosophy of Science

Philosophy of Feminism
Intro to Social and Political Philosophy
Philosophy of Education
Philosophy of Mind
Asian Philosophies of Feminism

* **History of Environmental Ethics**   Views of the natural environment expressed in philosophy, science, mythology, religion, literature, and art from the beginnings of Western civilization to the present. Origins and development of environmental ethics. Relations between professed ideas about nature and actual practices of exploitation, stewardship, conservation, and preservation   Some comparisons with non-Western cultures.

Southwest Studies
Geology and Ecology of the Southwest
Southwest American Indian Music
Ethnohistory of the Southwest
Arts and Cultures of the Southwest
History of the Southwest Since the Mexican War

Chicano Politics
Literature of the Southwest
Southwestern Ecosystems
American SW: The Heritage and the Variety

Economics and Business
History of Economic Thought
Economics of Poverty
Business Ethics
Economics of Labor
Economic Development
Natural Resource Economics

Households and Markets
Social Impact of Business
Legal Environment of Business
Political Economy of Defense in War & Peace
Economics of Discrimination
Economics of International Finance

History

Origins of Modern Science
War and Society Since the Renaissance
History of 20th Century Europe
Black People in the U.S. Since Civil War
Modern France & Italy: Fascism, War and Resistance
Witchcraft and the Witch Craze in Early Modern Europe

Education in the West
The Jews in Modern Europe
Women in America Before the Civil War
Women and Children in the Western Past

- **Greek History and Philosophy: Origins of Western Culture** Aegean and Greek texts with emphasis on those ideas formative in shaping Western culture. Development and transformations of these ideas in early Christian era, the Enlightenment or Modern Age. Rise of individualism and its conflicts with community, ritual relationships to nature vs. separation and exploitation, the relation of theology to the ordering of experience, and how psyche both forms and is formed by its relationships to community, nature, and god(s).

Asian-Pacific Studies

Global Perspectives in Education
Asian American Literature
Buddhism
Asian-Americans in U.S. History
Ritual in Asia and the Pacific
Asian-Pacific Economic Challenge for North America

Chinese Aesthetics and Ethics
U.S. Foreign Policy in Asia
Hinduism
Indonesian Music
Contemporary China

Women's Studies

Gender and Science
Native American Women of the West
Feminist/Womanist Ethics
American Women in Industrial Society
Psychology of Women

Black Women, Fiction & Literary Tradition
Women, Literature and the Family
The Family Before Industrialization
Myth and Meaning
Women and the Media

- **Ecofeminism** The interconnections between feminism and ecology. Ecofeminism explores the links between systems of domination such as sexism, racism, economic exploitation and the ecological crisis. Assess criticisms of ecofeminism and evaluate the potential of this philosophy for political practice.

Sociology

Social Issues in American Sport
Social Psychology
Patterns of Human Intimacy
Racial Inequality
Chicanos in American Society
Human Consciousness

Inequality
Sociology of Education
Nature of Sexual Inequality
Blacks in American Society
Indians and American Society
Women in Development

Religion   Political Economy   Ethnomusicology

Student Body: 29% state, 51% women, 49% men, 13% minority, 12% transfer
Faculty: 67% male, 33% female
1994-95 Costs: $21,332   Apply By 1/15
• Individualized Majors   • Core/Multidisciplinary Classes   • Study Abroad
• Exclusive Seminar Format   • Team Teaching   • Vegetarian Meals

Use form in back to contact: Director of Admissions
Colorado College   14 E. Cache la Poudre
Colorado Springs, CO 80903
(800) 542-7214

COLORADO STATE UNIVERSITY

20,000 Undergraduates   Fort Collins, Colorado   Moderately Selective

MAKING A DIFFERENCE STUDIES

Range Ecology / Land Rehabilitation Option

Prepares students to manage the vegetation and soil resources on rangelands for land management or related industries. Meets U.S. Civil Service requirements for a range conservationist and soil conservationists.

Animal Sciences
Natural Resource Ecology s
Agriculture/Natural Resource Economics
Principles of Range Management
Grass Systematics
Range Ecosystem Planning
Agriculture Experimental Design

Rangeland Improvements
Surface Mining Rehabilitation
Range Ecogeography
Soil Fertility Management
Range Animal-Habitat Interactions
Range Plant Production and Decomposition
Land Use and Water Quality

Landscape Architecture

History of the Landscape
Landscape Architecture Site Design
Landscape Resources Analysis & Design
Land Use Planning
Landscape Plants

Landscape Architecture Urban Design
Social Aspects of Natural Resource Mgmt
Ecology of Landscapes
Introduction to Soil Science

Forestry Tracks in Forest Biology, Forest Management, Forest Fire Science

Fundamentals of Forestry
Forestry Field Operations
Forest Mapping
Integrated Resource Management
Plant Physiology
Decision Making in Forest Resources
Forest Fire Management
Forest Management Science

Forest Mapping
Wildland Fire Measurements
Forest Ecology
Forest and Shade Tree Pathology
Introduction to Natural Resource Analysis
Timber Harvesting and the Environment
Natural Resource Policy and Administration
Timber Management

Natural Resources Journalism

Agric/Natural Resource Economics
Attributes of Living Systems
Principles of Wildlife Management
Public Speaking and Discussion
Photojournalism
Economics of Energy Resources
Remote Sensing of Natural Resources

You and Media
Environmental conservation
Environmental Ethics
Sociology of Rural Life
Media and Society
Economics of Urban and Regional Land Use
Geographic Information Systems

Conservation Biology

Population Ecology
Maintenance of Biotic Diversity
Disturbed Lands
Environmental Toxicology
Wildlife Ecology
Range Ecogeography

Environmental Conservation
Population: Natural Resource & Environment
Ecology of Landscapes
Forest Ecology
Methods of Landscape Analysis
Politics and Natural Resources

71

Entomology

Beekeeping

Aquatic Insects

Population Ecology

Insects, Science & Society

Range and Livestock Insects

International Crop Protection

Insect Pest Management

Agricultural Pesticides

Teacher Endorsement/ Biology - Natural Resources

Introduction to Soil Science

Principles of Plant Biology

Environmental Conservation

Bioclimatology

Plant Identification

Geography of Natural Resources

Environmental Economics

Principles of Forest Management

Gerontology

Perspectives in Gerontology

Social Work with Social Gerontology

Nutrition and Aging

Death, Dying and Grief

Handicapped Individual in Society

Adult Development and Aging

Biology of Aging

Housing and Design: Special Populations

Philosophy of Aging

Family Financial Resources and Public Policy

Nonprofit Agency Administration

Intro to Nonprofit Agency Administration

Nonprofit Agency Fund Raising & Mgm't

Accounting

Human Development & Family Studies

Human Diversity Issues

Marketing/Public Relations

Volunteer Management & Service Leaning

Management Fundamentals

Sociology

Psychology

Social Work

Community Dynamics and Development

Sociology

Social Problems in Contemporary. Society

Population: Natural Resources & Enviro

Public Opinion in Mass Society

Comparative Urban Studies

Sociology of Religion and Medicine

Contemporary Race-Ethnic Relations

Social Stratification

Collective Behavior and Social Movements

Technology, Culture and Society

Social Change

- **Comparative Majority-Minority Relations** Discrimination, ideology, power, policy issues in the U.S. and selected societies; application of basic concepts in student's self appraisal.

Economics

Issues in Environmental Economics

Economics of Natural Resources

Labor Economics

Poverty and Income Distribution

Economics of Outdoor Recreation

Economics of Urban and Regional Land Use

- **Economics of Energy Resources** Supply, consumption, trends and projected demand for alternative energy resources in domestic and world perspective; the economics of public energy policies.

Student Body: 75% state, 50% women, 50% men,10% minority, 3% int'l

1994-95 costs: Residents $6,700   Non-Residents $12,988   Rolling Admissions

Use form in back to contact: Director of Admissions

Colorado State University,   Fort Collins, CO 80523

(303) 491-6909

CORNELL UNIVERSITY

12,750 Undergraduates   Ithaca, New York   Most Selective

MAKING A DIFFERENCE STUDIES

Natural Resources
Food, Population & the Environment
Resource Mgm't & Environmental Law
Environmental Conservation
Res. Mgm't in Yellowstone
Science & Politics at Toxic Waste Sites

Teaching in Natural Resources
Principles of Conservation
Nat. Res. Policy, Planning & Politics
Religion, Ethics & the Environment

Agricultural and Biological Engineering
Engineering practice in biological/ physical systems represented in agriculture and its supporting industries and agencies, environmental or resource protection agencies, and int'l engineering. Environmental quality, safety and preservation of soil, water, and energy resources.
Soil & Water Management
Principles of Aquaculture
Enviro Systems Analysis
Biomass Conversion Processes for Energy & Chemicals

Treatment & Disposal of Agric. Wastes
Intro to Energy Technology
Bioenvironmental Engineering

Soil, Crop, and Atmospheric Sciences
Sustainable Agriculture
Soil & Water Management
Environmental Biophysics
Atmospheric Air Pollution

Weed Science
Hydrology & the Enviro
Soil, Water & Aquatic Plants

- **Biogeochemical Cycles, Agriculture, & the Environment** The impact of agriculture on aspects of the global biogeochemical cycles is discussed and illustrated with current agric. and environmental issues. Topics include sustainable agriculture, effects of nitrogen fixation, acid rain, global warming, and land disposal of wastes.

City and Regional Planning
Environment & Society: A Delicate Balance
Urban Economics
Environmental Politics
Urban Housing: Sheltered vs. Unsheltered Society
The Global City: People, Production, & Planning in the Third World

Intro to African Development
Gender Issues in Planning & Architecture
American Indians, Planners, & Public Policy

- **The Progressive City** A review of attempts to incorporate the interest of working-class and poor constituencies through majority control of local governments. The role of the city in class formation; historical perspectives on urban political administration; contemporary populist, socialist, and progressive urban governments.

Rural Sociology Tracks in Development Sociology; Population, Environment & Society; Social Data and Policy Analysis
Human Fertility In Developing Nations
American Indian Tribal Governments
International Development
Technology and Society
Land Reform Old and New

Intro to Rural Sociology
Environment and Society
Gender and Society
Population Dynamics
Gender Relations, Ideologies, & Social Change

- **Global Patterns of International Migration** How migration flows are changing in an increasingly interdependent world. Permanent, refugee, labor, illegal, brain drain migration from perspective of receiving and sending countries. Economic policies.

Biology and Society

Religion, Ethics and the Environment

Living on the Land

Writing as a Naturalist

Ecosystems and Ego Systems

Land Resources Protection Law

Ethics and Health Care

Women and Nature

Ecology and Social Change

In the Company of Animals

The Politics of Technical Decisions

- **Global Climate and Global Justice** Attmepts to organizae int'l cooperation to prevent fundamental changes in global climate have produced disputes between rich states and poor states. What is fair when rich and poor cooperate to deal with a common threat? Liberal, communitarian, feminist, and Third-World views.

Economics

Economic Development

Economic Problems of Latin America

International Trade Theory and Policy

Public Finance: Resource Allocation & Fiscal Policy

Practical Aspects of Business Mgm't of Worker Enterprises

Economics of Participation & Workers' Mgm't.

Practice & Implementation of Self-Mgm't.

Economics of Defense Spending

- **Technological & Product Base of Worker Enterprises: Ecology & Solar Energy Applications** Designed to deepen students knowledge of worker's self-management and cooperation through learning about and construction of simple energy-related technologies. to be produced in workers enterprises.

American Indian Program

Ethnohistory of the Iroquois

American Indian History

Content & Form of Iroquois Democracy

Indians of Eastern N. America

American Indian Philosophies: Power and World Views; Native Voices

Resistance & Adaptation: Native American Responses to the Conquest

Ethnohistory of the Haudenosaunee: The Six Nations Iroquois Confederacy

Near Eastern Studies

Islamic History

Jews of Arab Lands

Islam in South Asia

Intro to Islamic Law

The Islamic Resurgence

International Relations of the Middle East

Problems of Ethnicity, Religion & Interest: Russia, Central Asia & the Mid East

Africana Studies

Racism in American Society

Black Resistance: S Africa & N. America

African Civilizations & Culture

African Socialism & Nation Building

Oppression & the Psychology of the Black Social Movement

Social & Psychological Effects of Colonialization & Racism

Politics & Social Change in the Caribbean

Women's Studies   Outdoor Education   Asian American Studies

International Agriculture   Science and Technology   Policy Analysis

Hispanic American Studies   Ecology & Evolutionary Biology   Human Services

Civil & Enviro Engineering   Field & International Study   Marine Science

Student Body: 44% state, 43% women, 57% men, 23% minority, 4% int'l

1994-95 costs: Residents $13,840 Nonresidents $21,000 to $25,000 Apply by 1/1

• Field Studies   • Third World Study Abroad   • Individualized majors

Use form in back to contact: Undergraduate Admissions Office

Cornell University, Ithaca, NY 14850-2488

(607) 255-5241

EARLHAM COLLEGE

1,100 Students   Richmond, Indiana   Very Selective

"Earlham is a Quaker college, affiliated with the Religious Society of Friends. 'Friends', the name Quakers prefer to use, is also a key to academic and community life at Earlham. Academic life at Earlham is shaped by the Friends commitment to openness to new truth, and by the belief that each of us can grasp the truth.

Earlham strives to be a special kind of learning community, one in which people are honest with each other and themselves, a community in which people are encouraged to be friends, not rivals. We aspire to an academic integrity rooted in trust. We believe that learning takes place most effectively in a cooperative environment. As a Friends college we support cooperative learning, and try to create a community of trust that makes such cooperation possible, for we are convinced that we can all learn from each other. Cooperation requires trust rather than the mutual suspicion that pervades much of our society. We encourage people to study together, and to share tasks. Faculty do not usually proctor exams because people are expected to be honest.

Earlham's distinctive learning community rests also on another value important to Friends and indeed, to the search for truth - respect for other persons. None of us has a monopoly on the truth. Freedom to inquire, to pursue truth where one is led, happens best in a supportive community. In a true learning community people are challenged to do their best. There is open and honest argument about rival theories, but that argument does not degenerate into personal attacks. At Earlham we strive to keep the classroom - and the residence hall discussion - safe places for persons, but dangerous places for ideas, for it is by challenging ideas that we grow.

Because diversity enriches the education of us all, Earlham seeks a multiformity of students and faculty. Diversity requires a heightened sensitivity of each of us in the way we listen and in how we speak to each other. The College protects or promotes no group over another. We are all colleagues embarked on a shared journey to discover truth. Because we may find different paths, Earlham values individual freedom, but not at the expense of respect for those who are different or whose ideas we find disagreeable. Respect means we avoid thoughtless expressions that are genuinely hurtful to others. It also requires that we not demean those with whom we disagree. Insulting language is unacceptable at Earlham.

Earlham values social justice and peaceful resolution of conflicts. Students and faculty have many opportunities to work for justice and to give of themselves in service. Following the example of early Friends, we seek not only to avoid violence, but to remove the causes of violence. Much of Earlham's Community Code concerns ways to mediate disputes, rather than simply to punish offenders.

Earlham values simplicity in living, understanding simplicity as avoiding that which is unnecessary, to free us to focus on the essential. We seek a community life that is balanced and whole, with the proper focus on learning, but also room for social life, athletics, and recreation.

Community life at Earlham is based on the assumption that we are a community of adult learners, who can take responsibility for their lives and be supportive of others. Students, staff, and faculty share in governing the College through a system of joint committees. As much as possible, Earlham tries to reach decisions by consensus, by arriving at what Friends call a "sense of the meeting" that is shared by all involved.

We combine the highest academic standards with a very supportive and cooperative environment. We try to structure community life at Earlham to draw out the best that is in each member of the community, in social as well as academic life. Earlham has high ideals; finding ways to live up to them is part of that adventure."

Richard Wood, President

Earlham has always recognized the need for providing students with basic knowledge about American and world cultures. "An Earlham education stresses the idea of global connectedness. A commitment to programs such as women's studies, African/African-American studies, and Asian studies is a commitment to helping students see things from someone else's point of view. The other things - compassion understanding, humanity- follow naturally ." (Anthony Bing, Professor of English) Students often design their own majors, including Outdoor Education, Social Thought, and Latin-American Studies.

Many students collaborate with professors on research and creative projects. Recent projects include experiments in molecular biology focusing on the search for a cure for leukemia, a study of the responses of the American peace movement to conflict in the Middle East, and a research seminar on women, social movements, and temperance reform. Students frequently participate in field study research, whether in Puerto Rico, Kenya, the Galapagos Islands or nearby areas in Indiana to study bird migration, or Quaker libraries to study Quaker women. One in five students participate on research teams, gaining experience that applies directly to graduate school and careers. Additionally, sixty percent of students participate in internships.

Earlham offers 25 off-campus study opportunities to 17 different countries including Mexico, Colombia, Kenya, China, Japan, and the Czech Republic. Students live with families in their homes and often work in social service agencies or along-side their hosts. Most students participate on at least one international study program.

Most Earlham students also participate in community service, logging over 18,000 hours last year. Students tutor in high schools, participate in Big Brother/Big Sister programs, work with senior citizens, mentor young children, and volunteer at the local YMCA.

Earlham's 600 acre back campus of ponds, woods, and meadows serves as a biological field station as well as the site for the College's observatory and farm.

MAKING A DIFFERENCE STUDIES

Conservation Biology

Understanding and preserving the diversity of life forms on earth. Those working in the field apply the principles of ecology, animal behavior, evolutionary biology, and genetics as well as insights from related disciplines such as geology, economics, and management. Students have designed and conducted projects in Puerto Rico on how spider populations have responded to environmental changes wrought by hurricanes; while others carry on long-term studies of turtle and iguana populations in the U.S., Mexico and the Bahamas.

Ecological Biology

Ornithology

Population and Community Ecology

Biological Diversity

Field Botany

Tropical Biology Interterm

Field Biology Training Program at Manomet Bird Observatory, Massachusetts

Environmental Chemistry

Students have conducted studies of acid rain heavy metals, and pesticide residues. Currently students are doing research on trace mercury in the environment using a new ultrasensitive technique available at only a few places in the nation. The Earlham Analytical Chemistry Lab, the only facility of its kind within an undergraduate institution provides water and wastewater analysis for local industries and other customers.

Techniques of Water Analysis

Chemical Dynamics

Instrumental Analysis

Organic Chemistry

Environmental Chemistry

Biochemistry

Quantum Chemistry

Chemistry in Societal Context

Peace and Global Studies

War, the roots of violence, non-violent alternatives, conflict resolution, and social justice.

Culture and Conflict

Politics of Global Problems

Conflict Resolution

International Law

Moral Education

Introduction to Philosophy: Food Ethics

Methods of Peacemaking

Theories of International Relations

Religious Responses to War and Violence

Technology and Arms Control

- **Christian Ethics & Modern Moral Problems** Development of Christian ethics in relation to other ethical alternatives and contemporary moral problems. Consideration is given to such topics as love, justice, sexuality, violence, pacifism, and issues in medical ethics. Particular attention is paid to the nature of the moral self so as to illumine personal decisions.

Human Development and Social Relations

Draws on the resources from the departments of psychology, sociology / anthropology, philosophy, education, and biology. The program aims to teach how to work on a one-to-one basis with individuals in a large scale institutional or bureaucratic setting.

Theories of Human Development

Persons and Systems

Social Science and Human Values

Field Study

Social Relations

Human Biology

Comparative Cultures

Institutions and Inequality

Frontiers of Psychological Inquiry

Counseling & Psychotherapy

Women's Studies

Introduction to Women's Studies

Women and Literature

Psychology of Women

Feminism, Ecology and Peace

Feminist Theory

Women and Men in American Society

Women, Political and Social Change

Self-Defense for Women

Management

Because business and social concerns increasingly cross borders and engage diverse ethnic and social groups, Earlham's longstanding emphasis on cross-cultural education offers a particular advantage for future managers. Managers often make moral and ethical choices about how to interact with workers, and how to use the Earth's resources. Management students explore such issues in an environment that encourages personal responsibility and social concern.

Nonprofit Organization and Leadership
Work and Culture
Programming and Problem-Solving
Public Administration
Japanese Economic Development
Conflict Resolution
Health, Medicine and Society
Business Policy
Industrial Organization and Public Policy
Political & Econ. Development of Pacific Rim

International Studies

Development of the Pacific Rim
Japanese Arts
Theories of International Relations
Culture and Language
Politics of Latin America
Culture of Mesoamerica
Military Authority and Democracy
Theories of Comparative Economics
American Foreign Policy
Political Economy of Int'l Trade & Payments

Japanese Studies

Solid grounding in the language and culture of Japan. Combines study of Japanese language and civilization with extensive work in various disciplines, including history, political science, psychology, religion, economics, education, sociology /anthropology, and fine arts.

Introduction to the Study of Japan
Japanese Arts
Religion of East Asia
Education and the Family in Japan
Super Japanese
Readings in Japan Culture
Politics of Japan
Senior Seminar

African/African-American Studies

African-American Literature
Southern African History
History of Africa Before 1880
Institutions and Inequality
African-American History
Intro to African/African-American Studies
History of Africa After 1880
African-American Religious History

Sociology/Anthropology

Comparative Cultures
Social Action Lab
Health, Medicine and Society
Poverty and Culture
Sociology of Religion
Institutions and Inequality
Social Service Lab
Drug Use in Society
Urban Studies
Socio-Historical Perspective: Black Experience
Applied Anthropology
Culture and Conflict

Environmental Geology   Education   Wilderness

Student Body: 17% State, 54% women, 46% men, 12% minority
Faculty: 63 men, 45 women, 18 multicultural
Average Class size in a first year classroom: 18-20
1994-95 Comprehensive Costs $20,343   Apply By: 2/15

• Team Teaching   • Individualized Majors   • Service-Learning Programs   • Study Abroad
• Core/Multidisciplinary Classes   • Vegetarian Meals   • Energy conservation policies in effect

Use form in back to contact: Director of Admissions
Earlham College   Richmond, IN 47374
(317) 983-1600

EASTERN MENNONITE COLLEGE

960 Students   Harrisonburg, Virginia   Moderately Selective

Eastern Mennonite College places outstanding academics into the context of global awareness and active Christian involvement. The college's unique Global Village Curriculum builds on the belief that we are all interdependent in ways which can affect the survival or destruction of civilization. Eastern Mennonite educates students to use their talents to improve the welfare of humanity by working for peace, by promoting just social structures, and by aiding access to basic human resources for life and dignity.

This educational perspective is rooted in the 450 year old Anabaptist-Mennonite tradition. EM's particular theological principles include the Bible as the authoritative guide for faith and life, the church as a community of work and worship, and discipleship as the mark of an authentic life. Discipleship implies an active faith characterized by simplicity of life, peacemaking (the active pursuit of justice and reconciliation, including refusal of all participation in the military), evangelism and Christian service.

The cornerstone of this approach to learning is Eastern Mennonite's Cross Cultural Program, one of the strongest programs in international and cross cultural education in the country. EM students study in a wide range of international and domestic location such as Central America, the Middle East, Europe, China, Japan, Russia, Africa, Mexico, Los Angeles, New Orleans and American Indian reservations.

On these cross-cultural study tours, led by EM's faculty, students receive an education that reaches far beyond the classroom. The larger world serves as a laboratory for testing and refining knowledge, no matter what a student's major. Eastern Mennonite students have life-changing experiences which broaden their world view and give them expanded possibilities after graduation. On campus, Eastern Mennonite is a vibrant community bringing together students from a rich variety of cultural and religious backgrounds. With about 1,000 students, EM is a good size - large enough for a full range of quality programs and activities, but small enough so students are not lost in the crowd. Personal relationships with professors are part of every student's experience.

Faculty practice what they teach, demonstrating the creative possibilities of devout faith combined with serious reflection. The moral and intellectual persuasiveness of faculty comes from significant engagement in congregational life, Christian service, and public demonstrations of love for learning and the life of the mind. Creative teaching and learning affect the mind and character of the student. At its best education engenders in students a sense of idealism and responsibility, a sense of reverence and an awareness of the ambiguities of life.

In addition to the college's strong theater, athletic, and music programs, students participate in a wide array of extracurricular clubs and events. Students quickly discover that at Eastern Mennonite success is measured not only by what they achieve after graduation, but how they have developed along the way.

MAKING A DIFFERENCE STUDIES

Biology

Environmental Science

Plant Pest Management

Ecology

Soil Science

- **Agroecology** Explores agricultural ecosystems, especially in food deficit countries. Physical, biological, social, and economic bases of agroecology are examined using a variety of sources and case studies. Attempt is made to appreciate traditional agricultural rationality, and to investigate the effects of modification of existing agroecosystems.

International Agriculture

Designed as a background for work in countries with food scarcities.

Anthropology and Social Change

Farm Business or Management

Sociology of Development

Food and Cultures

Development & International Economics

(Integrated) Plant Pest Management

Community Nutrition

Emphasis on nutritional needs in developing countries and low income areas of the U.S.

Food and Population

Community Nutrition

Food and Cultures

Anthropology and Social Change

Sociology of Development

Nutrition Fundamentals

Biochemical Investigations

Microbiology

Peace and Justice

Conflict Resolution and Peacemaking

Peace and Justice in the American Context

Anthropology and Christian Mission

Development and International Economics

Mediation and Conflict Transformation

International Conflict and Peacemaking

Human Behavior & Social Environment

Sociology of Development

- **Peace and Justice in the Global Context** We analyze the interwoven nature of religion, theology, economic perspectives, int'l organization, models for social change (development, revolution etc.) and missionary activity in the creation, maintenance and change of social systems. Civil religion, Third World Theology, int'l economic organization, and development as they relate to peace and justice.

Socio-Economic Development

Social Systems and Social Problems

Conflict Resolution and Peacemaking

Sociology of Development

Peace and Justice in Global Context

Anthropology and Social Change

Social Policy Analysis

Food & Population

Development and International Economics

Camping, Recreation and Youth Ministries

Wilderness Experience Seminar

Outdoor Living Skills

Backpacking

Technical Rock Climbing

Camp Leadership

Outdoor Education

Environmental Science

Camping, Recreation, Youth Ministries

Human Services Skills

Conflict and Peacemaking

Student Body: 35% state, 58% women, 42% men, 7% minority, 3% international
1994-95 Costs: $13,450   Apply By: 8/1
• Team Teaching   •Third World Study Abroad   •Core/Multidisciplinary Classes

Use form in back to contact: Ellen Miller, Director of Admissions
Eastern Mennonite College   Harrisonburg, Virginia 22801
1-800-368-2665

EASTERN MICHIGAN UNIVERSITY

26,000 Students   Ypsilanti, Michigan   Moderately Selective

MAKING A DIFFERENCE STUDIES

Labor Studies
Labor Economics
Communication in Negotiation
Collective Bargaining
Economics of Women
Human Resource Management
Unionism in the Public Sector

U.S. Labor History
Minority Workers in Labor Market
Employment Law
Industrial Psychology
American Labor Unions
Labor and Government

Public Safety Administration
Intercultural Communications
Public Policy Analysis
Managing Public Safety Agencies
Arson Investigation
Emergency Preparedness Planning
Racial and Cultural Minorities

Public Administration
Public Relations and Public Safety
Police in Modern Society
Hazardous Materials
Drug Use and Abuse
Methods in Sociological Research

Occupational Therapy
General Psychology
Life Span Human Growth & Development
Tools and Materials
Developmental Activities
A View of Occupational Therapy

Human Physiology
Health Care Issues
Programming for Adulthood and Aging
Programming for Early Childhood
Field Work/Practicum in O. T.

Historic Preservation
Historic Preservation
Location and Site Analysis
Land Economics
Cultural Geography
Indians of the United States
Principles of City & Regional Planning

Settlement Geography
Environmental Psychology
History of American Architecture
Construction Systems
Introductory Archaeology
The Urban Community

Social Work   Tracks in Family and Children's Services; Health Care Services
Family Centered Practice
Substance Abuse
Social Work, Sex, and the Family
Separation, Loss, and Grief
Practice Issues With Women
Social Work Practice/Health Care Settings

Practice Issues With People of Color
Group Work With Children & Families
Social Wk. w/ Physically/Mentally Handicapped
Psych. Perspectives: Prejudice & Discrimination
Health & Illness Problems Through Life Span
The Interdisciplinary Health Care Teams

Therapeutic Recreation   Sports Medicine   Conservation & Resource Use
Urban & Regional Planning   Gerontology   Geography

Student Body: 92% state, % men, % women, % minority
1993-4 Costs: MI or OH residents $6651   Non-residents $10,611   • Migrant Worker Residency Factor

Use form in back to contact: Office of Admissions
Eastern Michigan University   Ypsilanti, MI48197
(313) 487-3060

EUGENE LANG COLLEGE
NEW SCHOOL FOR SOCIAL RESEARCH

350 Undergraduates   New York, New York   Moderately Selective

Eugene Lang College offers a distinctive liberal arts education with an interdisciplinary focus designed for engaged and independent-minded students. The College is a vital intellectual community which aims to foster in its students a critical self-consciousness about the process and purpose of knowing. Students at Lang College are encouraged to participate in the creation and direction of their education.

Lang students are firmly grounded in the liberal arts. They work in depth in an area of their choosing, often doing original projects with an active faculty as a rich resource. The challenge of the experience produces graduates for whom critical thinking has become a way of life.

The liberal arts curriculum of Eugene Lang College is special. It is open and flexible; students design their own programs of study with their academic advisors. It is innovative and creative: many Lang courses explore topics that cross traditional academic boundaries and approach classic texts and traditional subjects from new perspectives. It is diverse and inclusive: Lang courses include works, voices, perspectives and ways of knowing of different peoples and different cultures. The curriculum is challenging and demanding; the small classes (15 students maximum) the emphasis on reading primary texts, the use of writing and revision as a way of learning - these hallmarks of the Lang educational program mean that students work hard and feel responsible for active participation in their classes. Most classes are conducted in seminar format. Seminars permit the most direct engagement of students with the material and the opportunity for close relationships with faculty.

Eugene Lang College offers students five broad areas of concentration, within which a student maps out an individual path. A student's particular course of study within the concentration consists of 8 to 10 courses leading to relatively advanced and specialized knowledge of an area of study. The concentrations are highly interdisciplinary, allowing students to make connections between varied modes of thought and different approaches to topics and ideas. These come under the broader headings of Cultural Studies; Mind, Nature and Values; Social Inquiry; Urban Studies; and Writing, Literature and the Arts.

Eugene Lang College believes that internships are central to undergraduate liberal education. Students earn college credit while contributing to the wider community and gaining a variety of skills available through hands-on work experience. Examples of internships include work with Madre, a women's aid organization raising money for health, prenatal and education programs in Central America and the Middle East; National Organization for Women; The Institute for the Development of Earth Awareness; the Interfaith Center on Corporate Responsibility; Homes for the Homeless; People Against Sexual Abuse; The Rainforest Alliance; The War Resisters League; and The Wetlands Preserve "New York City's only environmental nightclub".

Following is a general introduction to the areas of study offered at Eugene Lang:

- Social Inquiry This concentration brings together a wide range of courses from such disciplines as history, political science, economics, anthropology, and sociology. Students interested in this area of study benefit from the New School's renowned Graduate Faculty of Political and Social Science. Students may take courses in the Graduate Faculty once they are advanced enough.

- Mind, Nature and Values This concentration is the principal location for study in philosophy, religion, science and psychology, especially as the issues and questions from these disciplines exist in relation to each other and in specific social and historical contexts. Mind, Nature and Values takes as its starting point the central question: How do human beings know and live in the natural, spiritual and moral worlds they inhabit? Each of the fields of study constituting the area makes distinctive claims about how to address and answer this question.

- Cultural Studies Whatever courses a Lang student chooses, no matter what the concentration, they will involve issues and perspectives of different peoples and different cultures, including those historically underrepresented in academic study. Cultural studies permits students to develop paths which focus directly on issues of the creation and representation of identity in social and historical contexts. In this concentration, the students take interdisciplinary approaches to theories of identity and difference and how they relate to political practice and to the practical, everyday experiences of individuals.

- Urban Studies This concentration brings a multi-disciplinary focus to bear on the history, development, politics and problems of contemporary urban life. It is also directed to students who seek a more direct pathway to additional training and careers in the area of public policy. The concentration makes the city an object of study and uses New York City as an educational laboratory and resource. It unites theoretical inquiry with field experience, academic internships, and urban research.

- Writing, Literature and the Arts This concentration enables students to pursue literary studies, the writing of prose and poetry, and the discipline of theater. At the same time it seeks to establish connections among these and other art forms that are usually studied in isolation. Students examine works and traditions in a broad cultural context, framing political and aesthetic questions about issues such as the silencing and empowering of voice, or changing interpretations of artistic traditions.

Students may avail themselves of the University Tutorial Program, enabling advanced undergraduates to work with scholars located in other divisions of the University. Individually, or in groups of two or three, students construct a directed reading course in the area of the tutor's particular expertise and interest.

Eugene Lang has school wide efforts (including hiring practices) to promote sensitivity and understanding about racial, religious and gender differences

MAKING A DIFFERENCE STUDIES

First Year Studies

Feminist Focus on Men	Approaches to Historical Inquiry
The Economic Way of Thinking	Physical Models of Reality
Writing as Re-Vision	Conflict, Identity and the Written Voice

Sugar and Spice: Coming of Age and the Social Construction of Gender
Order Out of Chaos Gender and Culture in the Modern Western World
Political and Social Change in America; The 1960's
World Science and Social Change: Then and Now
Holistic Science: An Analysis of Science in Contemporary Society

- **Inventing Reality: What to Believe in What the Media Tells Us** We will examine the role the media plays in creating/inventing the reality about which it wants to or claims to be reporting. We'll talk about how business and government manipulate journalists and editors in order to advance political/economic agendas and ideologies and the extent to which journalists and editors willingly participate in that manipulation. We'll talk about the meaning of press freedom in a country where, as conservative critic James J. Kilpatrick has approvingly noted: "Freedom of the press belongs to anyone who owns one."

- **The Living City** . This course provides a cursory introduction to the ways of understanding the complexities of the city, but also offers an alternative to exploring the city in written form alone. This course attempts to integrate the ideas of urban theorists with a perspective of "the street." Students are sent throughout the semester into 'the field' - specified neighborhoods in Lower Manhattan to work up projects on such topics as architecture and built environment, immigrants, deindustrialization and gentrification.

- Faculty Bio **Sara Ruddick Ph.D.** (Harvard) Sara Ruddick has taught at New School for Social Research, New York University and Haverford College. She is a consultant for Union Graduate School, on the editorial board of Peace and Justice, and a member of Network for Women in Development. Professor Ruddick received a Ford Foundation Grant for Faculty and Curricular Development in Women's Studies, and organized a conference on Simone de Beauvoir. She is a prolific writer and has been extensively published.

Upper Level Studies

Gay and Lesbian Latino Voices	Feminist Inquiry
Fem. Critiques of Reason and Sexuality	Feminist Psychology
Love, War and Work	Women in the City
Virtue and Politics	Ecology and Politics

Little to X to Shabazz: A Hero for Daily Living
National Identity and Ethnicity in Latino/a Literature and Films
The Politics of Sexuality in African-American Literature
Social Experience of Men in Post-War America
Ecology in Perspective: Science, Technology and Power
Drugs, Ethnicity and Urban Communities

- **Global Boundaries: International Relations Beyond the State**   The recent emergence of a "global culture" coincides with the increasing globalization of vital issues such as poverty, health, identity, and the environment. We will focus on issues such as: the global status of women, the representation of dominated peoples in the West, the power of global cities, the international circulation of knowledge, and the claims of the post-colonial societies and the individuals within them. Students will explore the ways identities, knowledge, images, people, and state power and capital circulate across national borders.

- **Holistic Science: An Analysis of Science in Contemporary Society**   How and why is contemporary science becoming more interdisciplinary? What new discoveries have helped this process? What is chaos theory? Quantum physics? episodic evolution? dynamic biological systems? What are the philosophical, political, cultural, and economic consequences of these trends? We will explore these questions to become more informed about the political and cultural nature of scientific and technological thought and practice within world capitalism.

- Faculty Bio   **Ann Snitow**   A cultural critic, literary scholar, and feminist theorist and activist, Ann Snitow teaches a wide variety of courses in literature, gender, and cultural studies. Well known nationally and internationally, Ann Snitow is a leading example of the "public intellectual," whose work regularly appears in such places as The Village Voice and Dissent. She has most recently established The Network of East-West Women which has brought scholars and activists in the women's movements in Eastern Europe and the USA together for the first time.

Joint BA/BFA Parsons School of Design Program - Architecture Program

Students in the architecture program have been developing mixed income housing projects for 3 sites in New York's depressed Lower East Side. The program was launched with a grant from Housing Opportunities for the Promotion of Equality, an organization that lends money to women and minority-owned companies. Community Access, a not-for-profit organization that develops housing, and the NY State Division of Housing and Community Renewal were involved in the project. The state initiated the project with the idea of creating useful, practical, architecturally interesting affordable housing.

Student Body: 30% state, 60% women, 40% men, 18% students of color, 5% int'l
1994-95 costs: Tuition $14,710,   Apply by 2/1, 7/1 for transfers
Room & board only for students coming from beyond NYC $5,230
Average students in a first year classroom: 15
Eugene Lang has recycling and energy conservation policies in effect.

• Core/ Multidisciplinary programs   • Individualized Majors
• Exclusive Seminar Format   • Kosher/ Vegetarian Meal Option   • Internships

Use form in back to contact: Jennifer Fondiller, Director of Admissions
Eugene Lang College
65 West 11th Street   NY, NY 10011
(212) 229-5365

THE EVERGREEN STATE COLLEGE

3,136 Undergraduates   Olympia, Washington   Moderately Selective

Evergreen is a challenging, free-spirited and continually evolving community founded on the values of cooperative learning, open inquiry and diversity. It provides high quality undergraduate education through its unique curriculum of liberal arts and sciences characterized by inter-disciplinary studies. Evergreen is nationally famous for its quality of personal instruction that bridges the gaps between disciplines, teaching students to engage ideals, concepts and problems in a unified, interdisciplinary manner. Close faculty-student contact is evidenced at all levels of the curriculum, and collaborative teaching and learning activities are common to all programs. Evergreen's fundamental mission is to assist students in learning how to learn and continue developing their skills in a world of increasing diversity, interdependence and moral complexity.

Evergreen approaches its mission with the tools of a traditional college: the disciplines of the humanities, arts, natural sciences and social sciences. However, those disciplines are transformed at Evergreen into teaching and learning experiences characterized by:

- interdisciplinary learning communities that immerse students in complex and diverse perspectives, fostering development of cooperation, communication and integration skills
- internships and applied projects to bridge theory and practice;
- small classes and narrative grading, requiring active involvement of students even at the beginning level
- independent study options and self-evaluations in which students take responsibility for their own learning
- a campus environment that actively celebrates diversity as a resource for learning.

Evergreen strives to produce graduates who are distinguished by their ability to communicate, their self-reliance as learners and researchers, their ability to conceptualize and to solve problems, their comfort with diversity and complexity, and their commitment to personal integrity and the public good.

Students enroll in a single comprehensive program (block) rather than several separate courses. These comprehensive programs bring groups of students and faculty teams, each sharing a different area of expertise, into extended contact - a quarter or the entire year - allowing them to work intensively in ways that encourage intellectual growth and comradery.

Students design their own areas of concentration (majors) in consultation with faculty. First-year students ordinarily enroll in a Core Program. The themes of these programs vary from year to year. Each Core program stresses interdisciplinary learning, writing, seminar skills and research skills. Each of the Core Programs is an integrated study that combines several activities: seminars, individual conferences with faculty members, lectures, field trips, laboratory work -- whatever is appropriate. Evergreen also offers a variety of programs in eight interdisciplinary specialty areas: Environmental Studies, Expressive Arts, Knowledge and the Human Condition,

Language and Culture Center, Management and the Public Interest, Native American Studies, Political Economy and Social Change, and Science, Technology and Health. Students may design concentrations in American studies, anthropology, biology, communications, community service, ecology, economics, energy studies, environmental studies, ethnic studies, European studies, human development, humanities, marine biology, philosophy, physical sciences, political science, pre-law, pre-medicine, psychology, public administration, small scale agriculture, social sciences, sociology, urban studies, visual arts, and zoology, among others.

Faculty are hired and evaluated primarily on the quality of their teaching, not on the basis of their research or publishing success. On the average, Evergreen faculty spend nearly one-third more hours in direct teaching contact with students than is the norm at most public institutions of higher education.

Evergreen offers a variety of ways to study different cultures both in Olympia and abroad. The curriculum offers a variety of year-long programs with an international theme. Students may also pursue options to study abroad through individual learning contracts, group contracts or programs offered by other universities. Recent off-campus study included a trip to the rainforests in Costa Rica, a trip to the Caribbean to study "Voices of Revolution and Tradition" and a study trip to Russia.

More than half of Evergreen's students complete one or more internships by the time they graduate. This compares with a nationwide figure of less than two percent. Although most internships are conducted in southwest Washington, they are available throughout the state, nation, and in other countries in both the private and public sectors. One student worked as a river ranger with the U.S. Forest Service in the Grand Canyon, guiding researchers working on an environmental impact statement, another as a marine mammal researcher, tracking and documenting the habits of gray whales off the California coast; as an English tutor at a refugee center; and another as an affirmative action/minority and women owned business compliance specialist.

Evergreen's Organic Farm has received national recognition. Thirteen acres of bustling agricultural and academic activity are located on the west edge of campus. A wide array of crops are grown to demonstrate which vegetables, fruits, berries and nuts do well in the region without use of pesticides or commercial fertilizers.

Students participate in the governance of the college in a variety of ways. Student representation is encouraged in all task forces investigating particular issues or preparing drafts for college-wide policies. Students fund a variety of organizations that provide cultural, informational, social, recreational, spiritual and educational services and activities. Current organizations include Asian/Pacific Isle Coalition, Bike Shop, Childcare Center, Environmental Resource Center, KAOS-FM, Bisexual, Gay, Lesbian Resource Center, Jewish Cultural Center, Jurassic Substance Abuse Education Group, YWCA, Peace and Conflict Resolution Center, Recreational Sports, Umoja/African American Student Organization, Women of Color Coalition, Union of Students with Disabilities, Women's Center, and the Wilderness Center.

Evergreen graduates tend to carry their sense of involvement and social responsibility with them in their careers as educators, entertainers, social workers, environmental engineers, lawyers, journalists, administrators, care providers, counselors, artists, entrepreneurs, and business people.

MAKING A DIFFERENCE STUDIES

Core Studies for First Year Students (48 credits each and team taught)
Politics of Identity: Cultural Crossings   Water
Humans and Nature in the Pacific NW   Looking Towards the 21st Century
Problems Without Solution???

- **Hard Choices: Public and Private Decision Making in the Contemporary World**
  Although it can be difficult, making choices is an inevitable part of private and public
  life. This program explores facets of decision making by individuals, small groups, and
  large organizations such as corporations, voluntary nonprofit groups, scientific communities and governments. Focus on tension between efforts to make decisions more
  "rational" and the circumstances that limit or preclude such rationality. Examination
  of the ethical, political, and social dimensions of making choices. Issues of lying, secrecy and fabrication, as well as those raised by political and social conflict when dealing
  with the environment, gender relations, the economy and rights of diverse groups.

Environmental Studies
The faculty are experienced in, and committed to, providing students with practical experi-
ence through field work and projects that serve the people and organizations of southwest
Washington and the Pacific Northwest. Environmental Studies is closely related with
Political Economy & Social Change, and Science, Technology and Health.
Hydrology (16 cr.)   Nat. Hist. & Conservation: Latin Amer. (32 cr.)
Salmon (16 cr.)   The Marine Environment (32 cr.)
Practice of Sustainable Agriculture (24-32 cr.)
Community Development: Local and Global Perspectives (48 cr.)
Geography and Environment: Systems in Conflict (32 cr.)
Conservation Biology and Restoration Ecology (16 cr.)

Knowledge and the Human Condition
Construction of Community (16 cr.)   The Search for Community (32 cr.)
Afro-asiatic Roots of Greek Myth (16 cr.)   Knowledge, Truth and Reality (32 cr.)

- **The Tyranny of Reason** (16 cr.) The socio-political structures of the West, since at
  least the 17th century, have enshrined a certain agenda and quite specific methods of
  thinking about that agenda as the very meaning of intelligence, reasonableness, modernity, seriousness and even humanity. Some consequences have been laudable and world-
  transforming. Other consequences, in addition to environmental ones, have been psy-
  chologically, socially and politically disastrous. Central goal is to evolve an understanding of human beings which is respectful of the power of human reason, while situating it
  less tyranically among our diverse capacities: and an approach to agenda-setting which is
  more democratic and appreciative of our diverse agendas and ways of being in the world.
  Feminist and post-modern critiques. Philosophical and psychological interfaces.

Science Technology & Health Tracks in Energy Studies; Health and Human Biology
Sense of Place: The Languages of the Individual, the Community and Nature
Psychological Counseling: A Multicultural Focus

- **Energy Systems** Starts with skill-building and background study, and finishes with
  major community-oriented projects related to energy. Concentrate on households
  and other small-scale applications where architecture, climate, economic pressures
  and personal values interact in challenging ways. Solar, conservation, and other "soft
  path" approaches will get close attention. (48 cr.).

Expressive Arts

Moving Image Theater

Politics, Power and Media

Different Drummers

Introduction to Music and Dance

Telling the Story

Student Originated Studies

- **Earthworks: Introduction to the Performing Arts** Skill development work, as well as theories of performance in ritual theater, non-Western performance, and activist theatre (political, feminist and ecological). Work with guest artists, journal-keeping, research reflections and partner writing. Develop performances for "Earthworks: performance Collaboration in Nature." Students may develop their creative work from political, social, ecological and/or historical points of view that emphasize the connection between human and other species, and between the human and the earth.

- Faculty Bio: **Gail Tremblay** (B.A., Univ. of New Hampshire, M.F.A.,U. of Oregon) An artist, writer and teacher, Tremblay's work has been exhibited nationally. She also serves on the national board of the Women's Caucus in the Arts.

Native American Studies

The major goal is to provide an open alternative education opportunity through experiencing a Native American philosophy of education which promotes self-determination, individual research, goal setting, internal motivation and self-reliance. This program is designed to serve Native American students who are interested in enriching their unique cultural heritage and developing strategies for self-determination in a pluralistic society, and students interested in learning about their own traditional cultures and values including the dynamics of change in a pluralistic society.

Home: The Hospitality of the Land

The Indigenous Voice

c(ART)ographies

Tribal: Reservation Based, Community Determined

Sense of Place: The Languages of the Individual, the Community, and Nature

Political Economy and Social Change

Integrates anthropology, economics, history, law, political science, philosophy and sociology as a way of understanding the modern world, and as a set of tools for analyzing contemporary public problems, locally, nationally and globally.

Political Economy & Social Change (32 cr.)   Cold War: Origins and Consequences (16 cr.)

A Usable Past: Our Historical, Political and Economic Legacy

Management and the Public Interest (48 credits)

This program focuses on the private business sector, but also gives attention to public and not-for-profit sectors. Values, ethics and the public interest are addressed throughout the year. Special emphasis is placed on development of analytical and people skills.

Science and Human Values

Student Body: 75% State, 55% Female, 45% Male, 12% students of color, 20% transfer
Faculty: 63% male, 37% female, 22% "people of color"   Apply By: 3/1
1994-95 Tuition: Residents $2,256, Non-residents $7,973 Room & Board $4,266
 • Team Teaching • Prior Learning Credit   • Co-op Education   • Study Abroad
  • Vegetarian Meals • Part-time Degree Program • Exclusive Seminar Format

Use form in back to contact: Admissions Office
The Evergreen State College   Olympia, WA 98505
(206) 866-6000

GEOCOMMONS COLLEGE YEAR
GAIA EDUCATION OUTREACH INSTITUTE
8 to 20 Students   Temple, New Hampshire   Very Selective

Geocommons College Year is a new project committed to education for the love of life. Each semester students and faculty build a unique learning community around the question: What fundamental knowledge, skills, arts, and relationships do we need to lead lives that are sustainable, creative, compassionate, and fulfilling? Participants survey what they know about environment and world, self and society, body and soul. Each one traces his/her story back through histories of family, place, community, culture, species, life forms, and Earth forms to one's origins in the stars and first great flash of the universe. What are the hopes and fears, desires and needs of person and planet? Can we create maps for meeting these needs? Where are the boundaries of my being if ocean and star were once my home? In pursuit of these questions Geocommons College offers an extraordinary journey into conscious community, sense of place, ecological literacy, the universe story, cross-cultural perspectives, sustainable studies, mindful awareness, and life celebration.

Students may choose the fall Foundation Semester in New England and/or the winter International Communities Semester in Europe and India. Eight to twenty students and faculty, ages 18 to 75, are based at a farm and wilderness site in southern New Hampshire. College credit for courses in sustainability, food and society, and other subjects are available from the University of New Hampshire.

During the year participants will:
- Immerse themselves in the comprehensive story of the universe, integrating science, humanities, arts, and world spiritual traditions. Deepen their relationships with self, others, Earth, & spirit.
- Serve local communities and schools in helping to identify resource flows of energy-water-food-materials-wastes, quality-of-life needs, and strategies for developing a sustainable bioregion.
- Participate in exemplary, innovative communities here and abroad; share in their successes and struggles to put ideals into action; discover the richness of diverse cultures and environments.
- Practice living mindfully with awareness and compassion in a daily balance of studies, physical work, artistic expression, meditation, recreation, community life, reflection, and celebration.

Geocommons College Year is a program of Gaia Education Outreach Institute, a non-profit organization that promotes life-centered education through community, ecology, and spirit. GCY students participate in the design and construction of Monadnock Geocommons Village, a small eco-community being developed at the college site. The "Geocommons" is a place, its natural systems, and the people who consciously inhabit this place for the good of the whole Earth community. A central goal of GCY is learning how to build the Geocommons wherever one lives.

MAKING A DIFFERENCE STUDIES

Credit granted by UNH can usually be transferred to other schools. The approach is interdisciplinary and wholistic. Learning methods include lectures and dialogue, reading, composition, theory and practice, and demonstration and evaluation. Participants keep journals and portfolios of their work and to share special interests in presentations. Core courses include:

- Studies for a Sustainable Society: combines ecological audits with study of the elements of sustainability and their application in real life situations.
- The Universe Story: traces the unfolding of cosmos, Earth, and humans from scientific, historical, and poetic-spiritual perspectives.
- Food and Society: examines the cultural and personal significance of food in its historical, psychological, social, political, and economic aspects; immersion in cross-cultural diets.

Foundation Semester (September to mid-December)

Studies, community living, and physical work at the farm campus alternate with local community service, a wilderness experience, three weeks in intentional communities, and field trips. Students and faculty share cooking, gardening, maintenance, games, singing, and many other activities plus the ups and downs of community life. The mood is one of awakening and intense exploration while encouraging simple healthy living and time for quiet self-reflection.

International Communities Semester (January to mid-May)

This term ideally follows fall term preparations offering immersion in cross-cultural and environmental issues. After a short orientation, students journey for three months to exemplary, innovative communities in Scotland, France, and India. They work side by side with community members in schools, reforestation projects, farms, and kitchens. They encounter high ideals, authenticity, successes, failures, remarkable personal stories, and daily committed action. These are powerful, inspiring, learning laboratories that provide some of the "good news" of our planet. Communities visited have included Findhorn, Plum Village, Auroville, and Mitraniketan. In April students return to NH for five weeks of synthesis, portfolio completion, service project presentations, evaluation, and closing celebration.

Sustainable Community Service

Geocommons College participants are starting to work with local schools, businesses, officials, and organizations to help build a sustainable bioregion. They are planning to:

- Conduct environmental audits, including quality-of-life needs.
- Initiate a Sustainability Resource Bank to include skills, tools, assets, and interests that people are ready to share for the well-being of their bioregion.
- Develop plans and take actions for a sustainable future.
- **Faculty,** adjuncts, and friends bring many years of teaching experience in traditional and alternative schools and colleges. They range from UNH and Harvard professors to biodynamic farmers; from writers, artists, and activists to alternative technology specialists. Director Bruce Kantner has been a teacher, organic farmer, international service volunteer, and participant-designer in innovative schools and communities.

1994-95 fees for tuition, room, board, academic credit, and travel: fall semester $3,800
winter semester $7,800; both semesters $11,000. Some small scholarships are available.
Apply by July 15 for fall and by September 30 for winter.

Use form in back to contact: Gaia Education Outreach Institute
Derbyshire Farm, Temple, NH 03084
(603) 654-6705

GODDARD

Goddard College invites students interested in finding out something about experimental and progressive education, and to consider what it might mean to them. Progressive education is a transforming process. Goddard's mission is to help people change themselves and to help them work to change the world, with lifelong learning as the basic tool. Within and outside the college, Goddard students are asked to join in struggle against the ignorance and prejudice that engender overpopulation, nationalism and war, alienating work, racism and sexism, homophobia, and poverty.

Newspapers, radio and television daily report increasing threats to the world's environments: the clear-cutting of rain forests wherever they flourish; the poisoning of rivers, streams, ponds, and lakes by acid rain in Vermont and elsewhere, the accumulation of toxic wastes; the weakening of the atmosphere's protective ozone layer by the emissions of fluorocarbons; global warming and the climatic changes it threatens.

Never has there been a greater need for transformative education: learning that leads individuals to see the world in a new way - as a precious jewel, unique in the universe, facing socio-ecological dilemmas created by the human species. Education must lead these persons to search together for effective solutions, "thinking globally and acting locally," recovering the true humanity of humankind.

Goddard's smallness has contributed to the success of its graduates: students know each other and their faculty closely; they learn how a community works. Like their Vermont neighbors, they learn to cope: to plan, to economize, to recycle, to make do, to take initiative, to create their own recreation. They learn that study and work, education and vocation - the work in the world that calls one to become part of it - are inseparable.

North-central Vermont contributes to the learning. This is an environment always beautiful, sometimes harsh, rewarding to become part of, fascinating to study. One cannot hide from the weather. Goddard people are continually aware of nature: the changing color on the mountains, the deer and occasional moose to watch out for on country roads, the wildflowers in spring, summer, fall, the birds who come for the summers. One learns that one is truly part of - that one cannot live apart from - this web of life.

College people talk about improving skills, developing a broad understanding of society, teaching disciplined thinking (and a discipline.) But what about the heart, the spirit? Of what use is a mind packed with theory and method unless it is wedded to a knowledge of self, and a passionate involvement with life and the welfare of the planet? It is the whole person - intellect, passion, heart, spirit - whose needs are the starting point for a plan to learn, and whose purposes commit her or him to carrying out the plan.

Goddard education may be described in images or analogies: a circle, a bridge, a door or window or gate, a dance. The Goddard learning process is circular: as the conclusion of one learning experience evokes the need for the next, the learning cycle begins again. In a more physical sense, Goddard group studies and other meetings are circles, students and faculty sitting around a room, all learning from what everyone has to contribute.

Because the faculty emphasize collaborative learning and community involvement, the college can be a bridge from self-centered individualism to contributing individuality. Many students discover Goddard to be a bridge from the passive learning of lectures and exams to active, participatory learning. Then there is the exciting bridge between ideas and actions, from the creative urge to the created product. These bridges lead to the most important bridge; that which a Goddard student builds between a changing self and a changing world. Goddard opens a door to one's inner self as the source of energy for learning. It opens many windows on the world, and helps students correlate what they see from varied perspectives.

Progressive education has its own language. The emphasis is on learning as change. Individuals are important, but their individuality is understood in the context of interdependence. The words "whole " and "holistic" recur, emphasizing that persons and experiences cannot be fragmented. Undergraduate campus study is centered around Group Studies, so named to emphasize the importance of collaboration in learning. Some group studies are called "Foundation" studies because their aim is to introduce a student to a particular way of looking at and acting in the world - ecology or anthropology or literature and writing for instance. There are "Advanced " studies to help students explore problems, issues, and skills beyond the base knowledge into applications of living and learning. The Goddard curriculum is different each semester, because students needs and the society change. Examples of possible study at Goddard typically, although not always fall under the following areas: Business, Leadership, and Community Organization; The Natural and Ecological Sciences; Psychology and Counseling; Feminist Studies; Multicultural Studies; Teacher Education; History and Social Inquiry; Writing and Literature; Performing Arts; Visual Arts; Media Studies and Communication.

Goddard College also has an off-campus study program. Students use campus facilities only during the week-long residencies that begin the Off-Campus semesters. They plan large scale independent study during the residencies, and carry out their study plans at home, and keep in touch with their faculty mentors through correspondence. An additional 325 students pursue graduate and undergraduate studies in the off-campus mode.

The Work Program is a required part of the curriculum. Through it, students help maintain and operate the college, at the same time reducing their tuition expenses. Two hours a week is on a meal team in the college dining room and kitchen; six hours a week is in one of many jobs: shelving or signing out books in the library, assisting in one of the offices, operating the student bank, working in the college woods, gardening and many other tasks. Work, in particular, and practical activity, in general, have special value in progressive education. Values are involved, ethical judgments may need to be made, the social and moral worth of a product or process evaluated. Additionally, the college work program reduces college costs.

MAKING A DIFFERENCE STUDIES

Goddard "resource areas" are not "departments," and the studies listed for each often draw on resources from other areas. The Goddard curriculum is different each semester, because student needs and the society change. The "recent group studies" listed here under each area description are some of those offered during the past three years.

Natural and Ecological Sciences

Holistic Health & Healing
Mind-Body Interaction
Global Issues & Ecology
Environmental Ed. in Elementary School
Computer Programming

Nutrition
Design &Construction: Solar Greenhouse
Gaia: the Earth as an Organism
The Biology of the Cell
Aquatic Ecology

- Faculty Bio: **Charles Woodward** (M.A. Goddard) Teaches environmental science. Mr. Woodward's interests include biological and environmental sciences, environmental management and restoration, and sustainable agriculture; environmental education.

Business, Leadership, and Community Organization

How can people make a living and also make a life in socially responsible ways? Communities are places where both can happen, if there is acting on thinking: a socially responsible job, and a constructive and creative life.

Organizational Problem Solving
Grant Proposal Writing
Biographical Studies of Leaders for Social Change
How to Market Your Creativity Without Selling Out
The Community Service Project: Internships in Central Vermont

Money & Power: Problematic Relationship
Group Dynamics for Middle Management

Feminist Studies

Women, a majority rather than a minority, are challenged to invent a future qualitatively different from the historic (though not, perhaps, the prehistoric) past. The feminist perspective suggests the possibility of a world characterized by resistance to violence as a way of settling interpersonal and international disputes: by the rejection of exploitation of individuals, groups, cultures, and other life forms; and by a hope for a society based in life-giving wholeness, not life destroying fragmentation and competition. Feminist concerns are dealt with in every curriculum area.

Defining Feminism: Who We Are
Goddess Religion
Lesbian Ethics
The Gender of Language
Refugee Voices: Women, Violence & Human Rights
From Victim to Hero: Women's Fiction, Women's Lives

History of Feminism
Women's Ways of Knowing
Women's Relationships
Women's Lives: Studies in Culture & Class

History and Social Inquiry

Cultural, political, and social history are rich resources for understanding current world news. Especially relevant is "Modern" history - what has happened since the late 17th century. The current history of post-colonial cultures, including Native American history, is essential to an understanding of contemporary world tensions. Recent group studies include:

The Nature of Truth & Proof
Something About the Sixties
Who's Calling the Shots: Secret Government in America
History of Nature & Humanity's Relation To It

Mexico: It's History & Culture
Global Political Economy

Multicultural Studies and Cultural Anthropology
Development Problems in Third World   Myths as Mirrors of Culture
Mayan Art   Intro to Navajo Culture (in Arizona)
T'ai Chi & Kung Fu: Philosophy & Practice   Cross-Cultural Approach to Health & Healing
Religion & Spirituality in a Cross-Cultural Perspective
Rich Folks/Poor Folks: an Examination of Daily Life

- **Mayan Studies** A series of group studies related to the Mayan culture of Meso-America, culminating in a three- week study of the tour of the Maya lands in southern Mexico - including sites in Chiapas and Yucatan. We will meet with farmers, community leaders, government officials and development workers.

- Faculty Bio **Hong Yue Go M.A.** (Goddard, M.A. Beijing Teachers College) "A good education should not only help students with their academic progress, but also help them to discover themselves and the real meaning of their lives, help them to learn how to challenge themselves in their life journey. I feel life is a struggle, not a struggle with the world around us, but a struggle with our inner world, with weakness in our will. We must overcome this inner weakness in spirit before we can truly give to others."

Education and Teaching
To earn a teaching license, you study human development, educational philosophy, social issues affecting education, and new as well as traditional teaching methods. Goddard's program for the education of teachers was recently reviewed and highly praised by the Vermont State Dep't of Education.

- **A Sense of Place; A Study of a Bio-Region** Students will learn to find a connection to a sense of place. We will look at many perspectives of what it means to live here and study this region's geography, history, and ecology. How did those factors shape both the people who first settled here and the people who live here today. Will provide a framework for those interested in integrating learning and teaching.

Performing Arts
African & African American Music   Indonesian Gamelan: International Orchestra
The Life and Times of the Guitar   Improvisation/Dance Theatre Performance

Student Body : 15% state, 58% women, 42% men, 10% minority, 52% transfer,
1994-95 costs: $19,040   Rolling Admissions

• Non-Resident Degree Program   • Exclusive Seminar Format
• Individualized Majors   • Life Experience Credit   • Study Abroad
• Day care   • Housing for Single Parents   • Vegetarian/Vegan Meals

Use form in back to contact: Admissions Office
Goddard College   Plainfield, VT 05667
(802) 454-8311   (800) 468-4888

GOSHEN COLLEGE

1,000 students   Goshen, Indiana   Moderately Selective

With a Mission Statement that lists developing "informed, articulate, sensitive, responsible Christians" seeking to become "servant leaders for the church and the world" as its focus and a general education program that was the first in the nation to require international education, making a difference permeates everything about Goshen College. Owned and operated by the Mennonite Church, one of three historic "peace churches," the college has attracted attention as being a place where values are "lived as well as taught."

Central to that living out of values has been Goshen's international education requirement. Since 1968, about 85 percent of GC students have fulfilled the requirement by taking part in the internationally recognized Study-Service Term (SST) program. In the program, students spend a term in a culture significantly different from the United States, usually at the same cost as a term on campus. Students typically spend the first seven weeks of the term living and learning in a major city, studying the language and culture of the country. The second half of the term is spent in a service-learning assignment, usually in a rural setting and often related to the student's major. Education majors have taught in schools and nurses and pre-medicine students often work in clinics and other health-related settings. Goshen was instrumental in opening up the People's Republic of China to undergraduate students, developing the first exchange program between a U.S. college and the country. Currently, the school offers programs in Costa Rica, the Dominican Republic, the Ivory Coast and Germany. Goshen students will travel to Indonesia for the first time in 1994. Other SST sites have included Haiti, Honduras, Belize, Guadeloupe, Nicaragua, and Korea. Other students fulfill the international education requirement by taking part in other approved study-abroad programs or by taking on-campus courses focusing on intercultural studies.

But international education at Goshen isn't limited to a 13-week term in another country. Each year, around 70 students from more than 30 countries are part of the student body of 1,000. Most GC faculty leaders have lived and worked outside of the country and many bring their international experiences to the classroom. International education at Goshen also plays a significant role in the programming of the school's Multicultural Affairs Program.

Students minoring in environmental or related studies such as biology or environmental education can study at the college's nearby Merry Lea Environmental Learning Center, a 1,150-acre plot of bogs and meadow. Outdoor enthusiasts also find the center within easy riding distance by bicycle. Visitors can also spend the day hiking the trails of the facility, enjoying the hundreds of species of plant and animal life. Adjoining campus is Witmer Woods, another source of environmental study.

The college also offers a minor in peace studies. Activities around peace include the annual peace oratorical contest, the peace play, the C. Henry Smith lectureship, Students for Shalom, public lectures and conferences. Some courses are taught in "real-world" settings, including Guatemala, Ireland, Chicago and Washington, DC.

MAKING A DIFFERENCE STUDIES

Environmental Studies

General Ecology

Environmental Ethics

General Ecology

Geology

Water Resources

Field Botany

Agriculture in the Tropics

Marine Biology

Field Experience in Environmental Education

Land Resources

Ornithology

- **Conservation**   A study of the need for and the best methods of conservation of our national resources from an ecological approach. Emphasis on ecological principles related to populations, soil, water, forest, wild life pesticides, waste, pollution and energy. Includes first-hand study of natural areas, erosion, conservation practices, impact of humans and all-day field trips.

Peace Studies

Prosocial Behavior

Issues in Peace Studies

Violence and Nonviolence

Peace Workshop

War and Peace Systems

Peace Studies Practicum

Third World Theologies

War, Peace and Nonresistance

Introduction to Economic Development

Contemporary Women's Issues

Seminar in Personal Violence

- **Doing Theology in a Latin American Setting**   The complex issues which face the Christian church in Guatemala. Anabaptist, Protestant and Roman Catholic approaches to missions and service activities in Guatemala examined. Mayan and Ladino cultures will be studied. Lectures, field trips, journaling, group Bible study and small group discussions provide an opportunity to investigate religious issues in Guatemala.

Women's Studies

Marriage and Family

Liberation Theologies

Spiritual Writings of Women

Women's Growth and Development

Womanhood and the Cultures of the U.S.

The Bible and Sexuality

Social Problems

Contemporary Women's Issues

Women in Text and Image

Intercultural Studies

Communication Across Cultures

Comparative Economic Systems

African Societies and Cultures

International Politics

Introduction to Linguistics

World Geography

Asian Religions

Race and Ethnic Relations

First/Third World History

International Literature

Community Development

The Far East

Student Body: 44% state, 57 % women, 43 % men, 9% minority, 7% int'l.
Average students in a first year class: 16 students   61% male faculty, 39% female faculty
1994-95 Costs: $11,150   Rolling Admissions
• Life Experience Credit   • Team Teaching   • Individualized Majors
• Vegetarian Meals   • Recycling and energy conservation policies in effect
• Approximately 85% of students study abroad

Use form in back to contact: Admissions Office
Goshen College,   Goshen, IN 46526.
(800)348-7422   (219)535-7535

GRINNELL COLLEGE

1,322 Students   Grinnell, Iowa   Very Selective

Ask students, faculty, and staff what it is about Grinnell that distinguishes it from other liberal-arts colleges, you will hear their agreement that Grinnell fosters a strong sense of community where individuals are respected for who they are and what they believe -- where differences can be expressed and appreciated. Grinnell is a place where great ideas and global issues are considered and debated. The debate over these significant issues is encouraged in the classroom, continued throughout the campus, carried into the community, and extended beyond Grinnell. Students leave Grinnell with the belief that they can and should make a difference in their careers and communities. The tone of the place is self-confident.

Grinnell is an institution informed by a pioneering spirit: a willingness to experiment and a commitment to community. Grinnell seeks and produces good students who are also concerned citizens, people who take an active part in the campus community and later in the world. The college has traditionally been a community with a conscience. Grinnell's pioneering past began in 1846, when New Englanders with strong Congregational, social-reformer backgrounds established the college. The college was named after abolitionist minister Josiah Bushnell Grinnell. Influenced by Grinnell's educational and social idealism, the college blended academic accomplishments with a sense of service to the world beyond the campus.

In 1959, Grinnell College established the Travel Service Scholarship Program, a precursor of the Peace Corps, which provided funds to send graduating Grinnell seniors to developing countries for a year to assist with language instruction, village work projects, or other special needs.

In 1989, Grinnell became the second college in the country to establish a Peace Corps Preparatory Program, a program of courses and experiential learning designed to prepare students for international volunteer service in the Peace Corps or other volunteer organizations.

"Grinnell stresses three qualities above all—individualism, social commitment, and intellectual self-reliance. Our interest is not to produce undergraduate specialists devoted to narrow pursuits. We want to develop thinking individuals who continue the process of learning, caring, valuing, and questioning" stated President Emeritus Glenn Leggett.

Grinnell's pioneering present again links educational goals with society's realities. The college believes, as do leaders in business, government, and industry, that today any liberally-educated person must be able to analyze problems quantitatively and must be aware of the nature of technology and its impact on society. Corporations have taken note of a long-term AT&T study in which the best records for managerial progress and performance went to employees with humanities and social sciences degrees. Grinnell graduates not only join businesses—they can be found in large numbers in the public sector—the Peace Corps, political campaigns, public official staffs, environmental coalitions, public and private education. For many, the social consciousness developed at Grinnell becomes a life-long commitment.

The interdepartmental General Science program allows students freedom to explore other areas of the curriculum as well and provides the broad background preferred in elementary-school teaching, interdisciplinary science fields such as psychobiology, and environmental science. A 365-acre environmental research area is also near campus.

Students who major in Chinese customarily spend the first two years on campus, the third year in the People's Republic of China, Taiwan, or Hong Kong, and return to Grinnell for the senior year. Grinnell is actively involved in Russian-American exchanges. The college annually hosts a visiting professor from Russia and offers four students from St. Petersburg the opportunity to study at Grinnell. The college sponsors its own interim study tour that allows 25 students and their instructors to visit Russia during winter break.

To introduce students to differing voices and ideas, Grinnell brings to campus many prominent thinkers. Lecturers have included the founder of United Farm Workers Cesar Chavez, Watergate prosecutor Archibald Cox, the Consul General of Japan, and Chilean author/ activist Ariel Dorfman. Recent symposia and conferences have focused on such topics as "Poverty and Homelessness" "The Small Town in America" "Nuclear Disarmament," and "Rethinking the Family from Multicultural Perspectives."

Grinnell students also join in campus and community life. As high-school students, three-quarters did volunteer work. At Grinnell, they take part in student activities and organizations, including the Environmental 100 Action Group; Javanese Gamelan Ensemble; Andean music group; The Young, Gifted, and Black Gospel Choir; Amnesty International; Model UN; and Animal Rights Coalition. Also active on campus are the Juggling Club; Ultimate Frisbee; Stonewall Coalition; the Concerned Black Students; the Multi-ethnic Coalition;, Native American Interest Group; the Politically Active Feminist Alliance; Poverty Action Now; Women in International Development;, and Student Organization for Latinas/Latinos.

Many students keep one foot in the world beyond the campus by taking a part in the town of Grinnell and surrounding cities and towns - including work with Head Start, Habitat for Humanity, the Native American Tutoring Project, local school systems, and church groups. A monthly newsletter published by the Community Service Center informs the campus community of volunteer activities and opportunities. The CSC welcomes student-initiated projects and encourages students to link service activities with academic interests and career exploration.

Outdoor activities are organized by the Grinnell Outdoor Recreation Program. Students decide on the group's activities: cross-country skiing, backpacking, sailing, caving, whitewater canoeing, and others. GORP provides training workshops and has equipment students can use at no charge. Campus members of the Environmental 100 Action Group promote environmental awareness and engage in nature-oriented activities.

MAKING A DIFFERENCE STUDIES

Environmental Studies

Students may participate in off-campus study programs in Tropical Field Research in Costa Rica or at the ACM Wilderness Field Station.

Ecology

Human Ecology and Adaptation

Evolution and Ecology

Resource and Environmental Economics

- **International Politics of Land and Sea Resources** Analysis of the international politics of the conflict between the developed nations of the north and the developing nations of the south for control of the world's resources and over a new economic order. The impact of national decision-making processes, international organizations, cartels, and multinational corporations. Case studies on fuel, mineral, and food crises, and law-of-the-sea negotiations.

First Year Tutorials

Latinas and Their Worlds

The Health Care Crisis

Russia and the West

Children and the Legal System

Biotechnology: Bountiful Harvest or Bitter Harvest?

Autobiography of Social & Political Struggle

Varieties of Nationalism in Europe

Practice &Theory of Public&Commercial TV

Culture in the Americas: Conflicts & Visions

Technology Studies

Philosophy of Technology

Bridges, Towers, and Skyscrapers

Decision Making

Organizations and Their Members

Evolution of of Technology

Electronic Music

Solar Energy Technologies

Technology Assessment

Latin American Studies

Latin American Cultures

State and Society in Latin America

International Economics

Political Economy of Developing Countries

Minority Relations

Economic Development

- **Dilemmas of Third World Development** Historic and current debated about Third World social development and constraints on policy choices, in selected Latin American, Africa, and Asian societies. Population, urbanization, quality of life, education, value transformation, political consensus building, minority relations, relations with industrialized countries.

Sociology

Dilemmas of Third World Development

Self and Society

The Black Community

Men and Women in Family and Society

Asian Americans: Immigration and Assimilation

Social Movements in the 20th Century

Social Inequality

Minority Relations

Industrialized Societies: U.S. and Japan

Afro-American Studies   Gender and Women's Studies   Anthropology

Student Body: 15% State, 53% women, 47% men, 10% minority, 10% int'l.
Faculty: 63% male, 37% female, 7% minority
1994-95 Costs: $20,680   Apply By 2/1
• Individualized Majors   • Field Studies   • Study Abroad   • Vegetarian Meals

Use form in back to contact: Office of Admission
Grinnell College   P.O. Box 805   Grinnell, Iowa 50112
(515)269-3600

GUILFORD COLLEGE

1,200 students   Greensboro, North Carolina   Moderately Selective

"It takes a whole community to educate one person."

The African proverb has unique relevance for the kind of experience you would have as a student at Guilford College. Here, learning is a cooperative effort shared by all members of the college community. Located in Greensboro, North Carolina and founded in 1837 by the Society of Friends (Quakers), Guilford College is the third oldest coeducational college in the nation and the oldest in the South. It offers a distinctive four year liberal arts and sciences education in the Quaker tradition. This heritage stresses spiritual receptivity, candor, integrity, compassion, tolerance, equality and strong concern for social justice and world peace. Growing out of this heritage, the college emphasizes educational values which are embodied in a strong and lasting tradition of coeducation, a curriculum with intercultural and international dimensions, close individual relationships between students and faculty in the pursuit of knowledge, governance by consensus and a commitment to lifelong learning.

While embracing many traditional educational goals and methods, the college also promotes innovative approaches to teaching and learning. Both students and faculty are encouraged to pursue high levels of scholarly research and creativity in academic disciplines. Guilford particularly likes to explore interdisciplinary and intercultural perspectives and to develop a capacity to reason effectively, to look beneath the surface of issues, to understand the presuppositions and implications of ideas, and to draw conclusions incisively, critically and with fairness to other points of view. The college desires to have a "community of seekers" individuals dedicated to shared and corporate search as an important part of their lives. Such a community can come about only when there is diversity throughout the institution a diversity of racial and cultural backgrounds, a diversity of older and younger perspectives, a diversity of beliefs and value orientations. As a community, Guilford strives to address questions of moral responsibility, to explore issues which are deeply felt but difficult to articulate, to support modes of personal fulfillment and to cultivate respect for all individuals.

Guilford students tend to be aware politically and concerned about issues. Many of them are involved in volunteer services, serivces on and off campus and believe that those opportunities are an important part of their educational experience. Guilford students have many opportunities to be involved on campus in ways that will contribute to personal growth. On every major college committee there is at least one student member. Students are part of decisions which impact the college significantly: setting tuition, deciding budgets, assisting faculty and administrators with strategic planning, articulating the perspective. The student viewpoint is respected here.

Students may grow through active participation in any number of groups that share affinity housing meaning that you would actually live with a group of students who have a common interest or concern. During the year, housemates discuss shared interests and collaborate on activities and projects that increase awareness of issues in the community. During the 1994-95 academic year, affinity houses at Guilford focused

101

on the following areas: Awareness of Handicapped Children Gender Awareness/ Equality, Habitat for Humanity, Self Esteem of Young Children, Men Against Sexual Assault, Greensboro Beautiful (Ecology), Guilford Geology Workshops for Children, Substance Abuse Awareness, Issues of Sexual Identity, Recycling and Environmental Concerns.

Students also become involved in social outreach. Through Project Community, student committee, students volunteer time with Delancey Street, a nationally recognized two year drug and alcohol rehabilitation home that serves as an alternative to the prison system; Turning Point, the rape crisis and child abuse agency of Greensboro; Gateway Center, a facility that cares for the physically challenged; or through serving as a tutor in adult literacy programs offered in conjunction with local elementary schools.

A group of student volunteers traditionally spends the spring break holiday helping local residents of Johns Island, South Carolina with construction and renovation work on housing and area facilities. Guilford students also have participated in similar work camps on the Cherokee Indian Reservation in North Carolina and have, in this past year, traveled to southern Florida to assist residents in their efforts to recover from the damage wrought by Hurricane Andrew, and to inner city Philadelphia to assist in clean up efforts aimed at restoring a Quaker cemetery.

One of the most important advantages of a Guilford education is that students have the opportunity to work directly with faculty. Often faculty who are involved with research projects will include their students in the project. To his courses in criminal justice, Barton Parks brings his own extensive experience in aiding those caught up in the throes of the judicial system. He helped start a successful dispute settlement center which mediates everything from neighborhood disagreements to criminal charges. Student interns and justice and policy studies majors are active participants in the operation of the center.

Psychology professor Richard Zweigenhaft, who coauthored *Jews in the Protestant Establishment* and *Blacks in the White Establishment?*, is also an avid basketball player and has developed a course on the psychology of sports. Zweigenhaft frequently encourages his students to undertake independent research projects. A recent collaboration between Zweigenhaft and student Michael Cody on *The Self-Monitoring of Black Students on a Predominantly White Campus* was published in the *Journal of Social Psychology*.

A collaborative program entitled *Teaching in the Multicultural Classroom* was developed by Guilford student Darlene Whitley and sociology/anthropology professor Vernie Davis. The program, presented to teachers and principals in the Guilford County, North Carolina public schools, presented anthropological concepts and examined cultural situations faced by teachers and administrators. The program encouraged teachers to use the multicultural makeup of a student body as a constructive resource.

MAKING A DIFFERENCE STUDIES

Geology

Physical Geography
Environmental Geology
Energy and Natural Resources
Crust of the Earth

Historical Geology
Marine Geology
Hydrology
Exploration Geophysics

- **Seminar West**   Summer course, including four weeks of camping and hiking, to study the American West. Geologic process of mountain building and erosion and their impact on man - history, prehistory, environment, literature and art.

Justice and Policy Studies

Offers students study and participation in community service, focusing on the criminal justice system and related public service institutions, including community based organizations.

Intro to Criminal Justice
Trust and Violence
Conflict Resolution Strategies
Criminal Justice Policy and Practice
Public Administration

Youth in Trouble
Building Community
Ethics in Justice and Policy Studies
Media and Community Relations
Punishment and Corrections

- **Family Violence**   Wife abuse, child sexual abuse and rape/sexual assault. Causal factors, psychology of victim and offender, societal impact, treatment & intervention strategies.

Religious Studies

Myth, Dream, Metaphor
Religion and Social Issues
Islam
Feminist Theology
Primitive Myth

History of Religion in America
Quakerism
Hebrew Bible
East Asian Religions
History of Christianity

Peace and Conflict Studies

Peace, War and Justice
Community and Commitment
Conflict and Cooperation
Revolutionary Central America
International Politics

Nonviolence: Theories and practice
Personal and Social Change
Women/Body/Voice
Personal and Social Change
International Economics

Philosophy

Business Ethics
Journalistic Ethics
Hegel and Marx
Theory of Knowledge
Topics in Contemporary Philosophy

Ethics
Social and Political Philosophy
Mind and Nature
Modern Western Philosophy
Philosophy of Religion

Sports Medicine	**Women's Studies**	**Environmental Studies**
3/2 Pre-forestry with Duke	**Economics**	**Education Studies**

Student body: 30% state, 48% male, 52% female, 10% minority, 5% int'l, 15% transfer
Faculty: 61% male, 39% female, 3% minority   Average number of students in first year class: 18
1994-95 Comprehensive Costs: $18,774   Apply By: 2/1
• Individualized Majors • Core/Multidisciplinary Classes • Vegetarian Meals • Recycling Policies

Use form in back to contact: Director of Admissions
Guilford College   5800 W. Friendly Ave.   Greensboro, NC
(800) 992-7759   (910) 316-2000

HAMPSHIRE COLLEGE

1200 Students   Amherst, Massachusetts   Very Selective

In 1970, 200 students came to Amherst, Massachusetts to take part in an extraordinary new experiment in liberal arts education. Hampshire College has since grown to 1,200 students, and its position in higher education is secure. But true to Hampshire's original philosophy, an atmosphere of challenging accepted ideas, of intellectual and social ferment, still permeates the college.

Hampshire's innovations include the breaking down of barriers between academic disciplines, and fostering an integrated, dynamic view of knowledge; actively involving students in their own education; and connecting academic work to "real-world" issues and problems. All faculty and courses are organized into four Schools: Humanities and Arts, Social Science, Natural Science, and Communications and Cognitive Science. An anthropology professor daily rubs elbows with historians, psychologists, and political scientists. Faculty trained in different disciplines often "team up" and offer courses together. For instance "Women's Bodies, Women's Lives," was taught by a physiologist, a writer, and a sociologist.

Hampshire's founders were convinced that students would be better prepared for a rapidly changing society if they were also expected to carry out research and independent projects, and pursue internships and field studies. The student headed to law school works for a Congressional representative in Washington; a student concerned about the problems of refugees goes to SE Asia to work for the Red Cross.

Virtually all Hampshire students incorporate internships or other off-campus experiences into their academic programs. The Program in Public Service and Social Change assists students in finding placements in human service agencies or social action organizations. The college maintains close ties with all study and service programs in Third World Countries. Students are also required to perform community service, and to incorporate a non-Western or multicultural perspective into their work.

Students collaborate with faculty mentors to design an individualized program of study. Concentrations typically embrace several subjects; a student concentrating in environmental studies might take courses in biology, politics, Third World studies, even literature. She might work at a local conservation area, or conduct research on the effect of habitat destruction on local wildlife populations. In the absence of course requirements, students design programs that reflect their most passionate interests and concerns. The typical question, "What's your major?" might elicit "Well, I'm interested in health care in Third World countries, so I'm taking pre-med courses and studying African history and reading about the philosophy of medicine. Next term I'll be working in a rural clinic in Nigeria."

Some 85% of Hampshire students go on to graduate or professional school. Almost 20% run their own businesses, everything from restaurants to yogurt companies, to design-and-construction firms. Still others are working as physicians, writers, lawyers, college professors, scientists, school teachers and social workers. Having learned at Hampshire to take charge of their own lives, and to change the society around them, the college's alumni are engaged in doing just that.

MAKING A DIFFERENCE STUDIES

School of Natural Science   Programs in Agricultural Studies, Coastal & Marine Studies, and Women and Science.

A strong effort is made to view the scientific concepts in broader historical, social, and philosophical contexts. The agricultural program centers around facilities on our 800 acre campus which include the Farm Center and the bioshelter, a laboratory for the study of hydroponics, solar aquaculture, nitrogen fixation, plant and fish physiology, and passive solar energy. Extensive field opportunities include the Northeast Marine Environmental Institute, a field station on Cape Cod, and in Belize. Women and Science is an informal program studying scientific theories about women and the impact of these theories on women's lives, biology, health nutrition, and how women's participation in science might impact science.

Marine Ecology Seminar
Environmental Science and Politics
Agroecology
Biology of Poverty
Women's Bodies, Women's Lives
Land Degradation and Society
Pollution and Our Environment
Sustainable Agriculture
The Science of Disarmament
Health in America Before Columbus
War, Revolution, and Peace
Energy Resources and Technology
Agricultural Research &Technology in Developing Countries
Energy and Society: History, Geography and Politics
Bugs and Drugs: Naturally Occurring Medicines and Pesticides

- **The World Food Crisis** Hunger in the midst of plenty has been called an absurdity and obscenity. How can we understand it? What can we do about it? What are the political, economic, and ecological sources of famine? Are they natural disasters or human folly? Is overpopulation really a problem or just a political smokescreen? How is food actually produced and at what cost to the environment? Are pesticides and other chemical inputs really necessary?

School of Social Science

The faculty have worked to create a curriculum in a variety of problem areas which reflect their interest in social institutions and social change.

Political Justice
Poverty and Wealth
Third World Development
Land Degradation and Society
World Food Crisis
Power and Authority
Making Social Change
Culture, Gender, and Self
Politics of the Abortion Rights Movement
Pueblo Indians: Change and Adaptation
Democracy in Third World
Poverty, Patriarchy, and Population
Inter-American Environmental Economics
Gendered Cities

- **Psychology of Oppression** Focus on the psychology of racism, sexism, anti-Semitism, heterosexism, ageism, and the oppression of members of the poor and working classes. Exploration of the commonalties of these various forms of oppression and to examine the costs and benefits to members of the dominant and subordinate groups. Collusion, benign neglect, internalized oppression, denial, and development of allies.

School of Humanities and Arts

Art and Revolution
Technoculture
Caribbean Crossing
Chicano Narratives
Latin America History Through Fiction
Women's Lives, Women's Stories
The Harlem Renaissance
Feminist Challenges to Art History
Ethnic Expression in America
Gender, Race, and Class: U.S. History

- **Literatures of Colonialism** How the experience of colonialism is framed by writers differently positioned in the contrasting histories of colonial exploitation. Three different experiences of colonialism: the British and French in Africa, the U.S. in Central America.

School of Communications & Cognitive Science

Culture Industries
Topics in Media Criticism
Political Culture
Moral Issues and the World of Work

Moral Theory
Culture and Human Development
Developmental Language & Learning Disorders
Eurocentrism in Philosophy

- **Producing Cable and Community Television** Learn to produce live television shows by learning to work in the TV studio, doing research, and working together on TV crews. Examples of community and cable TV shows will be viewed and discussed critically to contextualize the work produced in class within the larger cable TV community.

Population and Development

A multidisciplinary framework within which to comprehend population dynamics and reproductive rights issues internally. How fertility, mortality, and migration issues are shaped by colonialism, gender inequality, the organization of economic production and international division of labor.

- Faculty Bio **Benjamin Wisner** Henry Luce Professor of Food, Resources, and International Policy (B.A., UC Davis, M.A., Univ. of Chicago, Ph.D. Clark Univ) He has worked for 21 years, mostly in Africa, but also in south Asia, Brazil, and the Caribbean, in solidarity with popular struggles to satisfy basic needs for food, water and sanitation, health care, shelter, and eduction. more recently he has been working on the growing problem of hunger and homelessness in the US. His recent research has concerned socially appropriate technology for co-production of food and biomass energy, land reform, refugee settlements, and Africa's economic reconstruction.

Education Studies

The first emphasis is on child development, cognition, and the classroom, and includes language acquisition, environmental education, multicultural education, gender roles. The second emphasis is on schools as key social and cultural institutions; i.e. the changing character of school's missions and purposes, public policy, the economics of education, social mobility (particularly for racial minorities) and family studies.

Third World Studies
Feminist Studies Program
Civil Liberties & Public Policy

Food, Resources, & International Policy
Peace and World Security Studies

Student Body: 50% men, 50% women, 9% students of color
Faculty: 50% women, 50% men, 14% people of color
1994-95 costs: $26,820   Apply by 2/1
Hampshire College has 5000 sq. ft. of solar collectors for energy conservation.
• Required Community Service   • Team Teaching •Individualized Majors   • Vegetarian Meals

Use form in back to contact: Director of Admissions
Hampshire College   Amherst, MA 01002
(413) 549-4600

HOBART AND WILLIAM SMITH COLLEGES

Hobart 1,100 men   William Smith 850 women
Geneva, New York   Very Selective

Hobart College for men and William Smith College for women provide a distinguished liberal arts program within a co-ordinate system that establishes equality as the model for women and men, and offers a curriculum that promotes this model. Recognizing that psychological needs and socialization of women and men may differ in our culture, the methods employed to unite the social with the academic experiences will differ somewhat for women and men.

The history of H&WS is a record of bringing together the traditional and the innovative. The Colleges have been leaders in the development of general curricula, interdisciplinary teaching, and the interrelation between the rigorous pursuit of intellectual goals and reflection on their social consequences. Themes of gender awareness and global awareness span the curriculum, and inform the lives of students. All first-year students are required to attend acquaintance rape prevention workshops in single-sex settings. The men's workshops organized and facilitated by upper-class men are nationally recognized as a ground-breaking program.

The academic program of the Colleges stress the interconnections of knowledge and the dependence of one field upon another. Hobart and William Smith have sought professors whose interests span many fields. It is not unusual for professors to teach courses in two or more departments on a regular basis.

Most students of Hobart and William Smith Colleges will have had some kind of off-campus/international learning experience by the time they graduate. Whether the experience is teaching literacy skills to Native Americans in South Dakota, studying haiku in Tokyo, or living with a Russian family in Siberia, students at the colleges understand the value of "breaking away" to discover something about themselves and others. Students are also encouraged to look into the programs of Partnership for Service Learning, which offers terms in Jamaica, Ecuador and England. By enabling students to encounter the cultural differences between our own society and other parts of the country and the world, they become sensitized to major world issues and are encouraged to reflect on their own cultural identity

The outdoor recreation program provides both structured and unstructured recreational opportunities for outdoor enthusiasts. The program sponsors a combination of courses, clinics, and outings throughout the school year. Hiking and backpacking, orienteering, kayaking, winter camping, Nordic skiing, alpine skiing, horseback riding, canoeing, sailing, cycling and ice skating are available.

The Colleges maintains a 108 acre biological field station and preserve for ecological studies, with 40 ponds, a hardwood forest, swamps, marshes, and a large variety of wildlife. The HWS Explorer, is a 65 foot vessel for student and faculty research activities.

H&WS's Environmental Studies Summer Youth Institute is a 2 week interdisciplinary program for high school students. The program is an introduction to a variety of environmental issues and perspectives on nature. Students do in research on the Explorer and learn about a range of topics in environmental policy, economics and ethics.

MAKING A DIFFERENCE STUDIES

Environmental Studies

The Natural Science Perspective
Natural Resource and Energy Economics
Sociology of Environmental Issues
Population Crisis in the Third World
Natural & Agric. Ecosystems of Mexico

The Social Science Perspective
Senior Integrative Experience
Technology and Society
Environmental Geology
Philosophy of Natural Science

- **The Humanistic Perspective** Examines ways in which theories of culture and the significance of cultural artifacts have been use to examine America attitudes toward the natural world. Designed to introduce the student of American culture to methods of cultural analysis. Provides a chronological overview of the evolution of American views of the natural world, touching on attitudes towards Native Americans, natural resources, gender and nature, human uses of animals and development of agribusiness.

First Year Seminars

War and Society in America
Adolescence in Cross Cultural Perspective
Resisting the Melting Pot: -Construction of Identities in the U.S.
Food Systems: Deciphering Food Systems at the Global, National, and Individual Levels

Educational Opportunities: 40 Year Assessment
Prejudice, Discrimination and Responsibility

Second Year

Students are required to take bidisciplinary courses such as the following:

The Third World Experience
Men and Masculinity

Contexts for Children in a Changing Society
Alcohol Use & Abuse: Cause & Consequences

American Studies

American Indian Texts and Testimonies
Sex and Power
African-American History

The Education of Minorities
Women in American History
Slavery in the Americas

Patterns: The Shaping of Natural and Human Realities in American Cultures

- **Discovery/Invasion: The Native American Experience of the European Colonization of N. America** History of the Americas usually is examined from the perspective of the Europeans who invaded and conquered Native Americans, rather than from that of the indigenous people who were subjugated. Impact of European trade, disease, settlement, and warfare on the native populations of N. America, and policies of land acquisition and "Indian" removal developed by the U S government, and of the wars against the native peoples of the Great Plains. Special attention will be given to the ecological effects of these processes.

Anthropology and Sociology

Feminist Social Theory
Sociology of Minorities
Action Anthropology

Environment and Culture: Cultural Ecology
Sex Roles: A Cross-Cultural Perspective
Third World Women & Political Mobilization

Pattern and Process in Ancient Mesoamerican Urbanism

- **Sociology of Environmental Issues** Technological fix and social value definitions of environmental issues, how occupational and residence patterns are involved with the perception of and response to environmental issues, urban policies as aspects of environmental issues, stress involved with current life styles and occupations, the personal, group, and social responses to resolve environmental problems.

Philosophy

Justice and Equality
Economic Justice
Facts and Values
Morality and Self-Interest
Philosophy of Medicine

Philosophy and Feminism
Environmental Ethics
Liberty and Community
Experience and Knowing
Critical Thinking & Argumentative Writing

Economics

Environmental Economics
Women and International Development
Political Economy of Co-op Production
Environmental Policy

Women in the Economy
Natural Resource & Energy Economics
Political Economy of Race
The Political Economy of the Right

Religious Studies

Religion and Class Struggle
Toward Inclusive Theology
New Heavens, New Earths

Therapy, Myth and Religion
History of East European Jewry 1648-1945
God, Gender, and the Unconscious

The Question of God/Goddess: Metaphoric and Philosophical Origins

- **Sacred Space** Comparative approach to explore the meaning, function, and structure of space for religious persons. "Wanderings" of the Australian aborigines, habitation modes of American Indians, the Peyote pilgrimage of the Huichol Indians of Mexico, the Hindu Temple, the Buddhist Stupa and the individual as cosmos in yoga.

Off-Campus Study

Geneva, Switzerland The term focuses on issues that confront international organizations headquartered in Geneva, including UN agencies, and non-governmental agencies such as religious, human rights, women's, and youth groups.
The Struggle for Justice and Human Rights in a Global Perspective

- **Conflict, Conflict Resolution, and the Struggle for World Peace** The emphasis here is on public international law, on its reciprocal relationship to the U.N. structure, and on the problem of conflict regulation within the U.N. structure and outside of it. We look at the origins and current structure of public international law, at the U.N. structure, and at conflict-management techniques at the international level.

Dominican Republic Semester length program is designed to offer students interested in the Spanish-speaking Caribbean and Latin America the opportunity to study on site an Hispanic culture and a society of the Caribbean region from an interdisciplinary perspective.
The Dominican Economy
Africana-Latino Studies: Social Problems of the Dominican Republic

- **An Education in the Dominican Republic** This seminar is conducted in Spanish, and is accompanied by a community workplace assignment to be chosen from teaching English as a second language; rural community development; teaching/recreation for street children; or work in a community health clinic.

Education   Geoscience   History

Student Body: 40% state, 12% minority, 3% int'l.
1994-95 costs: $25,280   Apply by 2/15
• UN Semester • Individualized Majors • Study Abroad

Use form in back to contact: Director of Admissions
Hobart College and William Smith Colleges
Geneva, NY 14456
Hobart (800) 852-2256   William Smith (800) 245-0100

HUMBOLDT STATE UNIVERSITY

6,250 Undergraduates   Arcata, California   Moderately Selective

Set between redwood groves and the Pacific Ocean 270 miles north of San Francisco, Humboldt State University is a campus of choice, not convenience. The northernmost institution in the California State University system, the campus tends to attract from afar students who are more adventurous and self-reliant.

The intimate, natural setting and small class sizes foster friendliness and close faculty/student relationships. Thus undergraduates enjoy uncommon privileges: broad access to computers, equipment, and laboratories including the university forest, greenhouse, marine laboratory, and electron microscope.The University is traditionally known for its sciences and natural resources programs such as forestry and wildlife

The intimacy of the campus mirrors the sense of community along California's North Coast. In the small-town atmosphere, students learn they can make a direct, positive difference in the lives of others. And they do, through programs for senior citizens, recycling, science outreach, legal counseling, health education, and other concerns. Many students acquire a long-lasting sense of social commitment, as evidenced by Humboldt's historically high proportion of graduates who enter the Peace Corps.

The University welcomes the challenges and opportunities of a diverse and rapidly changing society. To this end, it is a community striving to value diversity, to be inclusive, and to respect alternative paradigms of behavior and value systems. The missions of Humboldt State includes the development of a fundamental understanding of the interdependent web of life; and the cultivation of the capacity of individuals for self-initiative, self-fulfillment, and autonomous and responsible action.

Humboldt State has a remarkable array of resources. Students from fisheries, oceanography, geology, biology, and other majors get a chance to test experiments and work on research projects at the university's Marine Laboratory in the coastal town of Trinidad, not far from the main campus. The nearby bay and Pacific Ocean provide rocky and sandy intertidal and subtidal habitats for further study. The university also has an 88-foot seagoing vessel available for the primary purpose of providing instructional experiences on the ocean. Students also find many instructional and research opportunities at a 300-acre Dunes Preserve, managed by HSU in behalf of the Nature Conservancy. The dunes, bounded by the Pacific Ocean and the and River Slough, contain rare natural habitats of the California coast, where research can be conducted in a protected ecosystem. At the edge of Humboldt Bay are 150 acres of city-and-state-owned sanctuary which benefit students in botany, fisheries, environmental resources, engineering, biology, wildlife, and natural resources interpretation. Among the projects are a unique, national model natural wastewater treatment process designed by a HSU professor: a co-generation system using methane digesters; and an aquaculture program devoted to rearing salmon, trout, and oysters in treated wastewater. Students interested in appropriate technology have a unique opportunity at the Campus Center for Appropriate Technology. Students combine theory and practice at the center, a live-in, working demonstration home, including photovoltaic and wind electric systems, a solar hot water system, a greenhouse passive heating system, a composting privy, a graywater system, and organic gardens.

MAKING A DIFFERENCE STUDIES

Environmental Resources Engineering
Principles of Ecology
Environmental Health Engineering
Environmental Impact Assessment
Solid Waste Management
Water and Wastewater Treatment Engineering

Introduction to Design
Renewable Energy Power Systems
Solar Thermal Engineering
Soil Mechanics

Forestry: Forest Resource Conservation (pending approval)
Wilderness Area Management
Forest Resources Protection
Natural Resource Management in Parks
Forest Ecosystems and People
Forest Remote Sensing & Geographic Information Systems

Natural Resource Economics
Advanced Forest Ecology
Forest Administration
The Forest Environment

Oceanography
General Oceanography
Sampling Techniques and Field Studies
Estuarine Ecology
Beach & Nearshore Processes
Solid Earth Geophysics

Biological Oceanography
Physical Oceanography
Marine Primary Production
Zooplankton Ecology
Field Cruise

Environmental Ethics
Environmental Ethics
Ethics and Action
Forest Ecosystems & People
Case Studies in Environmental Ethics
Conflict Resolution in Natural Resources

Water Pollution Biology
Natural Resource Law
Sociology of Wilderness
The Conservation Ethic

Appropriate Technology
This minor is especially useful for students wishing to volunteer for the Peace Corps or other overseas development work.
Whole Earth Engineering
Technology and the Environment
Politics of Appropriate Technology in the Third World

Appropriate Technology
Human Ecology

> **Politics of Appropriate Technology** Political dimensions of theory and practice of appropriate technology in industrialized and nonindustrialized societies. Emphasis on political concepts such as participation, decentralization, equality and peace.

Natural Resources Interpretation
Contemporary Topics in Economics
Oral Interpretation
Natural Resources Public Relations
Intro. to Natural Resources Interpretation
Human Resource Management in Park and Recreation Area

Nature Writing
Intertidal Ecology
Interpretive Graphics
Natural Resources and Recreation

Natural Resources Planning
Economic Geography
Wildlife Ecology and Management
Natural Resources Regulatory Processes
Watershed Management
Ecosystem Analysis

Natural Resource Economics
Origin and Classification of Soils
Range Management Principles
Applied Geology for Resource Planning
Resource Planning in Rural Communities

Water Resource Policy

Intro to Native American Water Rights
Forest and Range Hydrology
River Morphology
Water Resource Policy

Western Water Politics
Water Resource Development
Intro to Water Quality
Water Law

- **Watershed Management** Basic hydrology. Influence of vegetation on environment and water. Techniques of managing wildlands for increased usable water yields. Field observations and planning for protection and rehabilitation of watershed values.

Rangeland Resource Science

Plant Ecology
Range Policy
Grazing Influences
Range Economics
Range Wildlife Nutrition
Principles of Wildlife Management

Posionous Plants
Agronomy
Range Development and Improvements
Range Analysis
Soil Fertility
Range Management Principles

Peace and Conflict Studies

Foreign Relations of the U.S.
International Mass Communication
Myths of War and Peace
International Relations
Psychology of Prejudice

Comparative Economic Systems
Paths to the Center
Intercultural Communications Workshop
World Religions
Military Sociology

Indian Natural Resource, Science, and Engineering

A support program for American Indian and Alaskan native students.
Introduction to Indian Law
Native American Water Rights

Tribal Government
Natural Resources & Science Field Experience
Natural Resources and Sciences Management / Research Career Work Experience
Native American Perspectives on Natural Resources Management

Social Work

Community resources and provision of service intervention in small town and rural areas
Social Work & Social Work Institutions
Volunteer Experience
Social Policy
Intro to Psychology

Cultural Anthropology
Social Work Methods
Human Behavior and the Social Environment
Social Work Research

Indian Teacher & Educational Personnel Program provides Native students the opportunity to complete requirements for credentialing as teachers, counselors, administrators for Indian communities and public schools. Emphasis on American Indian teaching methods and materials.

Environmental Toxicology   Fisheries   Wildlife
Native American Studies   Ethnic (Black & Chicano) Studies

Student Body: 98% state, 53% men, 47% women, 11% minority   Apply by: 11/30
1993-94 fees: Residents $1,752 Room & Board $4,000   Non-resident tuition $246 add'l per credit
• Credit for Prior Learning   • Individualized majors   • Study Abroad

Use form in back to contact: Admissions and School Relations
Humboldt State University   Arcata, CA 95521
(707) 826-4402

INSTITUTE FOR SOCIAL ECOLOGY

Plainfield, Vermont

"What is nature? What is humanity's place in nature? And what is the relationship of society to the natural world? In an era of ecological breakdown, these have become searing questions of momentous importance for our everyday lives and for the future that we and other life-forms face. They are not abstract philosophical questions that should be relegated to a remote, airy world of metaphysical speculation. Nor can we answer them in an offhanded way, with poetic metaphors or with visceral, unthinking reactions. The definitions and ethical standards with which we respond to these questions may ultimately decide whether human society will creatively foster natural evolution or whether we will render the planet uninhabitable for all complex life-forms, including our own."

Murray Bookchin, Co-Founder, Director Emeritus, and faculty member of the ISE from *The Philosophy of Social Ecology*

The Institute for Social Ecology was established in 1974 at Goddard College and incorporated in 1981 as an independent institution of higher education for the purpose of research, education and outreach in the field of social ecology. The Institute incorporates principles drawn from nature: mutualism, unity through diversity, cooperative action, and non-hierarchical organizational forms into the structure, content and intent of it's educational programs. We use local communities as a framework for examining problems which have global implications. Our educational approach integrates study, critique, and creative action into a holistic process which fosters self-understanding, cultural knowledge, and a deeper sense of people's relationship to nature.

The mission of the Institute for Social Ecology is the creation of educational programs that enhance people's understanding of their relationship to the natural world and to each other. That understanding, by necessity, involves the Institute in programs that deepen a student's awareness of self and others, helps her or him to think critically and to expand her or his perception of creative potentialities for human action.

Our focus on people's relationship to the natural world integrates studies in the Social Sciences, Arts, Humanities, and the Natural Sciences. The purpose of our programs is the preparation of well-rounded students who can work effectively as constructive participants in the process of ecological reconstruction. We are committed to making out programs financially accessible to a diverse student body.

The Institute's programs reflect it's commitment to the idea that creative human enterprise can foster a more ecological future. Toward that end, the Institute offers both community education and academic programs, sponsors research projects and community activities, and produces educational materials and publications. A unique aspect of the Institute for Social Ecology is this integrated approach.

The learning goals of the Institute for Social Ecology are:
- The development of a student's understanding of how the principles of social ecology - mutualism, cooperation, unity through diversity, feminism and egalitarianism - incorporate into the student's life.
- The development of a student's analytical abilities - the skills of critical thinking.
- The development of a student's ability to act creatively to affect positive change in both the cultural and natural environments.
- The development of the student's ability to communicate effectively - the ability to articulate ideas clearly in spoken and written form.
- The development of a student's understanding of self and the world through the exploration of the holistic perspective of social ecology and specialized knowledge in at least one of it's component fields.

The Institute for Social Ecology offers the following programs:

Ecology and Community is a four week, intensive educational experience which includes courses, seminars, workshops, colloquia and lectures. This program also contains an optional fifth week called "From Theory to Practice". Participants will examine ways in which they can take what they have learned from the Ecology and Community program into their home communities. Nine college credits are available. The Ecology and Community Program is also the starting point for those who wish to embark upon the non-residential Master of Arts in Social Ecology program.

Design for Sustainable Communities is a two-week long intensive studio and practicum dealing with ecologically oriented community design and planning. Students can receive up to six credits for this program.

The Institute for Social Ecology draws an international group of students annually whose ages range from 17 - 70, with the average age being 24. Many participants in these programs are activists who do not attend for academic purposes, however, quite a few people transfer credit to other institutions. Credit transfer can also be arranged through Goddard College for an additional fee.

The Institute for Social Ecology's programs are held at Goddard College, which comprises 250 acres of woodlands and meadows. Goddard's facilities include a library, an organic vegetable garden, a solar greenhouse and a community radio station.

The ISE's programs are best suited to mature, self-directed students who are capable of independently pacing themselves. The programs are often extremely intensive and offer a total immersion in the field of social ecology. ISE attempts to build a community of learners and social ecologists during our time together. ISE often receives comments to the effect of "This month (the Ecology and Community program) has been the single most intense and exciting educational experience I've ever had. I only wish that it were not limited to one month each summer" and "I have made more intellectual gains in these four weeks than I have over my past three years at U. of..."

The ISE is involved in several projects, such as publication of a bi-annual newsletter and "Society and Nature: the International Journal of Political Ecology" an annual conference on social ecology, and the Social Ecology Network.

MAKING A DIFFERENCE STUDIES

Ecology and Community

Ecology and Society	Community and Development
Soil, Food and Community	Community Health
Agriculture and Food Systems Issues	Ecofeminist Direct Action
Reconstructive Anthropology	Advanced Concepts in Feminism & Ecology
Advanced Concepts in Social Ecology	Native Amer. Perspectives on Social Ecology
Feminism and Ecology	Ecological Economics & Community Develop't

Fifth Week Course: From Theory to Practice -- Community Organizing & Direct Action

- **Ecological Technology: Architecture and Society** Examines technological issues in community development, planning, and design in the context of the following questions: How can we create a regionally adapted architecture that supports and enriches our damaged ecosystems? How can we integrate the principles of preventive and holistic health into the disciplines of architecture and urban design? How can architecture best express and serve decentralized and democratic communities?

- Faculty Bio: **Louis Mannie Lionni** (B.S. Arch, MIT) Mr. Lionni has taught architecture at Pratt Institute and City University of NY. He currently serves on the planning board and practices in Burlington, Vermont with a focus on housing and community facilities in low and moderate income areas.

Design for Sustainable Communities is a two week, six credit studio and practicum which acts as an introduction to the range of issues involved in planning sustainable communities: ecological land use planning, sustainable agriculture, legal constraints on development, energy use, waste recycling, community economics, the nature of community, and the nature of design as a process of giving physical form to goals and ideas.

- Faculty Bio: **Nina Veregge** (S.M. Arch.S.) Ms. Veregge is a registered architect with an extensive background in residential and commercial design. She has taught at Kansas State University, Boston Architectural Center and the national Engineering University in Managua, Nicaragua. Fee for this course is $900

Colloquia, Lectures and Workshops

Environmental Racism	Activist Art and Community
Reconstructing the Inner City	Ecology and Spiritual Renewal
Native American Perspectives,	Radical Environmental Politics

Neolithic Mythologies & the Emergence of Hierarchy
Iroquoia: The Next 500 Years: Politics of the Imagination

- **Towards an Ecological Economics** The contradiction between the present capitalist process of supranational concentration of power and the requirements of an ecological society are becoming more apparent every day. How we might constitute a new economics with the perspective of social ecology? We will address ecological sustainability, direct democracy, and decentralization based on local economic self-reliance. We will outline not only the utopian ideal, but how to begin making the transition today.

1994 Comprehensive fees: $1850, Fifth Week $125   Rolling Admissions

Use form in back to contact: Institute for Social Ecology
P.O. Box 89   Plainfield, VT 05667
(802) 454-8493

INTERNATIONAL HONORS PROGRAM

30 Students   Based in Boston, Mass.

"As I reflect on my year with the International Honors Program, I realize that I was able to reach people and places I never could have on my own. IHP brought me the fireflies dancing in the trees of a coconut grove village in Thailand and the splendor of the sun setting as the full moon rose over the high ridges of the Himalayas. All the myth, power, tradition and spirituality that modern society has neglected is still alive and fundamental to people worldwide. These ideas, which raise questions of survival and the role of humans in the preservation and destruction of our fragile ecosystems, are seldom discussed in classrooms, but are the basis of IHP." (Roopali Phadke, IHP '93, Wellesley College '94)

Founded in 1958, the International Honors Program offered in cooperation with Bard College offers a small group of 30 students per year the opportunity to study and travel around the world, working with an international faculty and living with families in most locations. The itinerary for the 1994-95 program is: Boston, England, Spain, India, Thailand, New Zealand, Mexico, Belize, Washington DC. This year's program will combine academic study in the areas of ecology, biology, anthropology and sociology with on-site examination of governmental policies and independent projects concerned with ecological balance, the environment and indigenous cultures.

IHP's Global Ecology Program offers students a curriculum of courses entitled *Nature, Society and Sustainablility* that examine ways of understanding the Earth and its inhabitants as a single complex system, and considers patterns of action within the context of global ecology. This program is the fifth year focusing on Global Ecology under the leadership of Edward Goldsmith, publisher of The Ecologist magazine, and an experienced faculty team. The approach to the topic is through a combination of academic study and visits to centers around the world where global issues are being addressed through programs of action and research. IHP faculty leadership will be provided by at least one professor in each country in addition to meetings with local academics, environmental experts and activists.

IHP's Global Ecology programs have helped launch many graduates on careers in the environmental field, with government, NGO's and as advocates on the grassroots level.

Each year's program is composed of approximately 75 percent undergraduates, and 25 percent recent graduates, mid-career professionals, and occasionally teachers on sabbatical. Although course work is at the undergraduate level, several students have obtained partial graduate credit for their work with IHP. Students come from a mix of academic backgrounds. While many are majoring in ecology-related fields, recent IHP students have also brought to the Program an interest and expertise in art, philosophy, architecture, engineering, politics, music and history.

IHP encourages and supports an active network of alumni, and in 1994 established a formal mentoring program to connect recent graduates with students from the past 35 years of IHP.

MAKING A DIFFERENCE STUDIES

Nature, Society and Sustainablility

- **Ecological Balance and the Environmental Crisis** This course will provide an understanding of global ecology in terms of physical, chemical and biological mechanisms. these mechanisms are dynamically interlinked to generate a mutually dependent set of processes that maintain the stability of the oceans, the soil and the atmosphere. From this perspective a study will be made of environmental and climatic factors that most affect our ability to feed ourselves and our welfare in general.

- **Organisms and Their Evolution** This course will focus on the properties of cells of cells and organisms as revealed in their life cycles. The roles of genes and the environment will be examined in relation to patterns of stability and change in life strategies.

- **Economic Development and Sustainability** Economic development has been a major goal for the last fifty years, and though it may have provided benefits, it has also caused environmental degradation and social disruption. We consider the concept of development itself as well as the development experience in the different countries visited. Role, past record and current policies of multinational corporations, World Bank, Int'l Monetary Fund, and Food & Agricultural Organization of the UN will be examined.

- **Society, Culture and Ecology** This course focuses on relationships between individuals and larger socioeconomic conditions which converge in the utilization of "natural resources," examining inequalities and conflict as well as cooperation and possibilities for change at this convergence.

Itinerary

Boston (1 week) Meet other students, first homestays, first assignments. Orientation and introduction to faculty and the diverse parts of the global ecology equation. Perspectives on local and global environmental concerns. Half-day Outward Bound program.

England (5 weeks) Study at the Wadebridge Ecological Centre and at Shumacher College. Meet with James Lovelock, originator of the Gaia thesis, scientist and author, and others from England's highly effective environmental movements.

Spain (3 weeks) Experience tradition and development in rural Andalucia, one of the least industrialized parts of western Europe, but now seeing massive change as Spain seeks closer integration within the European Community. Visit Coto Donana and Grazalema National Parks.

India (7 weeks) Confront first-hand the problems of population, health issues, energy and development with physicist and feminist Vandana Shiva. Lengthy field studies in Himalayas offer a unique opportunity to work with Chipko activists. Sustainable energy use.

Thailand (4 weeks) Compare urban issues of air and water pollution in Bangkok with rural villages. Visit Community Forest Project and salt fields. Analyze effects of lignite mining and forest encroachment on village life. Visit Karen "hill tribes" and explore forest ecosystems.

New Zealand (6 weeks) Explore unique vegetations in the rain forest and Mt. Ruapehu regions, the active thermal regions, and the geology of Hokianga. Study coastal ecology, wading bird habitats, sewage and waste management. Indigenous populations and Maori culture.

1994-95 tuition $18,250 plus airfare. Apply by March 15

Use form in back to contact: International Honors Program
19 Braddock Park   Boston, MA 02116
(617) 267-0026

IONA COLLEGE

5,352 Students   New Rochelle, NY   Moderately Selective

Iona College takes its name from the isle of Iona located in the Inner Hebrides just off the west coast of Scotland. It was to this tiny island that the Irish monk Columba came in A.D. 563 to establish an abbey from which missionaries went forth to teach and evangelize. The island of Iona became a center of faith and culture that contributed significantly to the civilization of Western Europe. In 1940, the Congregation of Christian Brothers founded Iona College in New Rochelle, New York. The name Iona signifies the college's fundamental purpose; a synthesis of culture and faith and faith of life. Enriched by the cultural multiplicity within our society, the college further expresses this tradition in terms of action on behalf of justice and of participation in the transformation of the world.

There is a vision for Iona that its constituents be engaged in the task of building a concerned community. Iona believes that through this experience its members will be better prepared to work toward such a community within their families, places of employment, and neighborhoods, as well as in the nation and the world.

Iona has as its purpose the education of its students through intellectual discipline and a developing awareness of self, structured upon increasing understanding of their cultural, religious, and social heritage. Iona endeavors to develop informed, critical, and responsive individuals who are equipped to participate actively in culture and society.

Iona's Center for Campus Ministries offers vast opportunities for students in the areas of Peace and Justice Education and volunteer service activities. Iona has dedicated student groups such as Amnesty International, Project Earth, and Pax Christi that put a focus on helping to change the world today. As part of a unique commitment to creating positive change, there are on-campus activities such as environmental awareness, multicultural education and a Holocaust remembrance. Iona's committment to assume a leadership role as an institution dedicated to Peace and Justice is evident every November as the college celebrates the "Week of the Peacemaker" recognizing the great works of peacemakers throughout history. The weeklong celebration includes lectures, seminars, and performing arts events. Past visitors on this week include Mother Theresa, Coretta Scott King, the Dalai Lama, and geologian Thomas Berry.

Another natural way for students to express their faith is through service activities. Iona students serve communities locally at soup kitchens, Project S.W.A.P. (Stop Wasting Abandoned Property), an inner-city rebuilding project; the Midnight Run, in which students bring food, clothing, and companionship to NYC's homeless; and the Lord's Pantry, which involves students delivering meals to homebound patients with AIDS. Students serve regionally as well, travelling during winter and spring breaks to Appalachia to assist in building homes in poor communities while learning about the history and culture of the Appalchian region. There is also a semester long program in Bonita Springs, Florida, where students work with migrant workers. Iona students even serve internationally and have travelled to El Salvador to live in community with the people of El Salvador while helping to build cinder block homes. There are service learning credit options for many of these programs.

MAKING A DIFFERENCE STUDIES

Biology Track in Ecology
The Department has a collaborative internship for students to do research with the Osborn Laboratories of Marine Sciences of the NY Zoological Society at the NY Aquarium.

Ecology	Microbiology
Oceanography	Microbial Ecology
Invertebrate Zoology	Science, Technology and Society
The Life of Green Plants	Parasitology
Genetics	Assessing the Environmental Future

Peace and Justice
All faculty have made a commitment to directly address issues of peace and justice in a global and/or ecological perspective. Three week summer intensive courses in Ireland and with Native Americans of the Lakota tribe in South Dakota.

War and Peace in American Society	Conflict Solving for Children
Sacred Cosmology	Race to Save the Planet
Ethics and Business	Health Care Ethics
Contemporary Peacemakers	Latin American Politics
The Homeless of New York	Environmental Health
Service Learning: Appalachia	Service Learning: Urban Immersion

- **Iona Peace Institute in Ireland** The opportunity to experience Ireland's social and political realities, its spirituality and cultural achievements in an integrated and lively way. Analysis of the roots of injustice, notably Ireland's "Great Famine" and "troubles", and exploration of possible routes to resolution of injustice and reconciliation.

Economics

Health Economics	Economics of the Arts: Performing & Visual
Economics of Labor	Economics of Poverty and Discrimination
Urban Economics	Women in the Labor Market
Public Finance	Assessing the Energy Future
Economics of Global Resources	Environmental Econ. & Sustainable Develop't
Changing Role of Women in the Economic Development of the U.S.	

Political Science

American Political Thought	International Relations
Politics and Criminal Justice	Peace and Justice in the Contemporary World
Politics and the Mass Media	Campaign Politics
Third World: Politics of Development	Latin American Politics
Soviet and E. European Systems	Public Administration

Social Work	**Gerontology**	**Urban Studies**
Women's Studies	**International Business**	**Philosophy**

Student Body: 93% state, 44% men, 56% women, 33% minority, 5% transfer
Faculty: 66% male, 34% female, 5% minority   Average number of students in first year class: 22
1994-95 Costs: $17,480   Rolling Admissions
• Weekend/Evening Classes • Service-Learning Classes • Life Experience Credit
• Team Teaching • Vegetarian Meals

Use form in back to contact: Office of Undergraduate Admissions
Iona College   715 North Ave. New Rochelle, NY
(800) 231-IONA

JUNIATA COLLEGE

1,150 Students   Huntingdon, Pennsylvania   Moderately Selective

At Juniata, students engage in learning experiences that focus on the students ability to meet changing world conditions with confidence and flexibility. Juniata helps make students more comfortable with the technological world as it is, yet helps students become more socially and environmentally conscious to shape the world as they want it to be. Juniata offers students the hands-on experience that brings learning to life. Its Peace and Conflict studies program is sanctioned by the United Nations and serves as the model for programs at institutions nationwide.

MAKING A DIFFERENCE STUDIES

Peace and Conflict Studies
Introduction to Conflict Resolution
Intro to Peace and Conflict Studies
Anthropology of War and Peace
Social Violence in Latin America
Peace and International Internship

Rebellion, Religion and Pacifism
Nuclear Weapons: Threat and Response
Latin American Revolutions
The Holocaust
Third Party Roles in the Mgm't of Conflict

Sociology/Anthropology
Minorities
North American Indian Ethnography
Inequality and Opportunity in the U.S.
Death and Dying
Social Problems and Social Welfare
Sociology of medicine

The American Family
Aging and Society
Anthropology of War and Peace
Child and Family Services
Social Welfare Policy and Services
Cultures of the World

History
The Fascist Era: 1918 to 1945
Religious Sects in America
The Holocaust
Witchcraft in Western Civilization
History of Science

20th Century American Wars
Oriental Religious Heritage
1492: Contact, Conquest and Consequences
Appalachia & America: Images & "Realities"
Latin American Civilization

Political Science
Public Policy Analysis
American Political Thought
Law and Society
South Asia Since Independence
Politics of the Soviet Union

Comparative Communism
Public Administration
Politics of Developing Nations
Politics of the Middle East
Legal & Public Affairs Internship

Environmental Studies   Geology
Pre-Forestry / Pre-Environmental Mgm't 3/2 Program with Duke

Student Body: 77% state, 54% women, 46% men, 3% minority
1994-95 Costs : $19,310   Apply By 3/1
• Adult and Continuing Education   • Vegetarian Meals

Use form in back to contact: Director of Admissions
Juniata College   Huntingdon, PA 16652
(814) 643-4310   (800) 526-1970

KALAMAZOO COLLEGE

1,270 Students   Kalamazoo, Michigan   Very Selective

The mission of Kalamazoo College is to prepare its graduates to better understand, live successfully within, and provide enlightened leadership to a richly diverse and increasingly complex world. Founded in 1833, this nationally recognized college of liberal arts and sciences has developed a distinctive tradition of excellence in the fulfillment of this mission. In the 1960's Kalamazoo's visionary educational leaders developed and implemented a four-part curriculum plan. The "K" Plan interweaves the traditional and the innovative to create a comprehensive undergraduate program that provides a foundation in the liberal arts along with global, experiential, and independent learning opportunities.

The cornerstone of the program is the liberal arts course work. The small campus environment fosters a positive learning community in which professors and students interact closely. The main focus of the faculty is on teaching, and contributions from the student and professors are equally valued.

Over the past 30 years, nearly 90% of Kalamazoo graduates have studied overseas. The Foreign Study option is key to developing a global outlook. All students may choose to study overseas, regardless of major, and it is financially feasible due to a special grant that subsidizes travel costs. Students pay no more than they would for on-campus study. There are many locations available through Kalamazoo and Great Lakes College Association programs, including some sites geared toward specific interests. Whenever possible, students live with native families to provide maximum cultural interaction and exposure to foreign language.

Through the Career Development option students are able to gain experience in a given field. The Career Development Center on campus provides counseling and resource materials to help students locate internship positions or design research or creative projects to test out their classroom knowledge in a "real-life" situations. The possibilities are limitless, as students' choices show: from doing research with manatees at Mote Marine Laboratories in Florida, to joining Common Cause for Grassroots/Advocacy lobbying in Washington, DC, digging at an archeological site in Scotland, to founding the Women's Resource Center on campus.

The Senior Independent Project is the required element of the "K" Plan. Students design their own project with help from a faculty advisor. As one student said, "It makes you take on a more active role in your education." Students present papers on topics ranging from AIDS research, to the feminist movement in Spain, to Native American painting. Many complete internships at the same time, in both domestic and international settings.

The effects of these learning experiences are evident in the students and on the campus. Students have a perspective on situations all over the world, which enriches the college community. They learn to adapt to many situations and be sensitive to differences in others -- skills that cannot be learned in the classroom. One graduate concluded "I can think of no other place that prepares you for the way the world really is today. My experiences at "K" have been the best preparation for the future."

MAKING A DIFFERENCE STUDIES

Foreign Study Program / Kalamazoo Foreign Study Centers

With 85-90% student participation, and subsidized costs, students attend programs of varied lengths at the following special interest locations (other non "K" locations also available)

Africa:
Dakar, Senegal
Freetown, Sierra Leone
Nairobi, Kenya

South and Central America:
Oaxaca, Mexico
Quito, Ecuador

Europe:
France: Strausbourg, Clermont-Ferrand, Caen
Germany: Munster, Erlangen
Spain: Caceres, Madrid

Asia:
Beijing, China

Public Policy and Urban Affairs

All students will engage in either a sustained volunteer experience, a National Issue Forum, or an off-campus internship in a policy-related position.

Public Finance and Fiscal Policy
Environmental and Resource Economics
Women and the Western State
Schools, Prisons and Public Policy
Managing the Earth: Culture, Politics and the Environment

Political Economy
Politics, Parties and Public Opinion
Urban Sociology
Ethics and the Common Good

African and African American Studies

Ecology of Africa
Class, Race & Ethnicity
Music of World Cultures
Race Relations in America
Urban Politics

Ethnology of Africa
Economics of Less-Developed Countries
Contemporary Africa: Historical Perspectives
Liberation Theology
Traditional Religions of Africa & America

Sociology and Anthropology

Medicine and Society
Methods in Social Research
Women in Cross-Cultural Perspective
Class, Race and Ethnicity
Cultural Integration and Ethnic Pluralism in the U.S.

Social Problems
Applying Social Research
Peoples and Cultures of Latin America
Growing Old in America

Religion

Religious Rites,Rituals and Ceremonies
Ethics and the Common Good
Class, Culture and Religion
Religious Founders and Reformers
Theology and Modern Culture
Liberation Theology

Islam
Buddhism
Native American Religion
Modern Jewish Thought
Modern Catholic Theology
Theological Ethics

African, East Asian, Latin American, Russian, and Western European Studies

Women's Studies   Human Development   Japanese, Chinese, Russian, African Language

Student Body: 70% state, 45% men, 55% women, 11% minority
Faculty: 67% male, 23% female, 6% minority • Avg. number of students in first year classroom: 16
1994-95 Tuition $21,273 Aapply by: 2/15 • Actively seeking minority students
• Land-Sea Orientation • Service Learning • Core/Multidisciplinary Classes • Vegetarian Meals

Use form in back to contact: Admissions Office
Kalamazoo College   1200 Academy St.   Kalamazoo, MI 49006
(800) 253-3602

LONG ISLAND UNIVERSITY
FRIENDS WORLD PROGRAM

145 in FWP   Southampton, New York   Moderately Selective

"While all life is being threatened by increasing military might and ecological ruin, a rising tide of quiet voices from all parts of the world reminds us that only knowledge inspired by justice and compassion has the power to save us and save the life sustaining power of the earth. We must listen to and learn from such farsighted scholars, professionals and others and search for those emerging concepts - globally applicable and globally acceptable - which can provide a basis for a saner future"
Morris Mitchell, First President, Friends World College

Very few colleges offer a program like Friends World; an experiential education by total immersion into other cultures. The program stands alone in two important aspects. The first is the faith in students. Friends World believes that intelligent young men and women have the ability, and the right to be deeply involved in determining their own educational plans. FW trusts them to be capable of gathering, absorbing, and synthesizing knowledge through their own experiences.

The second is Friends Worlds belief that all nations of the world need citizens who are educated to see beyond their own borders, and to recognize that individuals share in the responsibility for the future of the planet.

With eight program centers and campuses around the world and a student body and faculty drawn from twenty-two countries, Friends World Program is uniquely international. The Program is designed for students who want to assume greater responsibility for their own lives and learning. The Program's worldwide facilities offer students the opportunity to live, study, and work in two or more foreign cultures while earning an accredited B.A. degree; to design individual programs of study based on their personal interests and goals; and to combine academic study with field experience and internships. While acquiring a balanced liberal arts education, including fluency in one or more foreign languages and an appreciation of the culture and values of several world regions, students have an opportunity to carry out in-depth study and gain practical experience in their chosen field. In addition, they develop a deeper understanding of and a broader perspective on current world issues.

In addition to the North American Center, located in Southampton, NY, there are centers in London, China, Japan, Kenya, Costa Rica, Israel, and India. The goal of Friends World is to encourage students to treat the entire world as a university, to take the most urgent human problems as one basis of their curriculum and, to seek designs together for a more human future.

While students do not have a major, in the traditional sense, they develop individual study plans in such areas as Afro American studies, agriculture, animal behavior/wildlife studies, anthropology, archaeology, area studies (African, Asian, European, Latin American, and Middle Eastern), communications (film, journalism, photography, and video), community health, community organization and development, criminal justice and comparative legal systems, dance, economics, education, environmental studies/ecology, fine arts and crafts, holistic and natural healing, human services, Native American studies, nutrition, peace studies and conflict resolution, philosophy, psychology/counseling, rainforest ecology, religion, sociology, Third World development, United Nations studies, and women's studies.

The learning process is a carefully planned combination of academic study and field experience. The Program involves classroom study, immersion language training (often including homestays), and independent fieldwork in at least two foreign countries. Under the guidance of an international faculty, students develop skills and competence in a major academic field by combining book research, hands-on experience, and analytical writing. Friends World students typically spend at least two years abroad working with center faculty to design and carry out field studies (such as internships, apprenticeships, and investigative research) in several cultural settings. For example, they have studied Gandhian nonviolence in India, desert agriculture in Israel, animal behavior in Kenya, and holistic healing and acupuncture in Japan. Students have worked with a feminist publishing cooperative in Paris, interned with a Congressman in Washington, researched agrarian economic development in Costa Rica, apprenticed with a modern dance company in Munich, worked with the United Nations in New York, and interned with a legal center in London. Many other projects range from anthropology to zoology.

Founded in 1965, sponsored by the New York Yearly Meeting of Friends (Quaker), Friends World is non-sectarian. About 180 students are in the program, comprising about 14 percent of the total student population of Southampton College. Students come from all over the U.S., and other countries as well; most are 18-22 years old, with about 30 freshmen and 25-30 transfers in each Fall class. Visiting students from other colleges may also join Friends World for 1 or 2 terms -- a popular option.

As a record of their learning growth, students maintain journals or portfolios of their work. The journal replaces the usual requirements of assignments and examinations in serving as a means of evaluating and awarding credits. Students do not receive grades, nor do they take traditional classes. Usually 15-16 credits are earned by successfully completing each semester's work.

On campus dining facilities include a wide variety of choices for vegetarians. Outdoorsy types are drawn to the rural, seaside location on Long Islands East End. Recreation options include sailing, swimming, biking, camping, surfing, and enjoying some of the most beautiful beaches on the East Coast.

Environmental awareness is high on the Friends World Southampton Campus. The Long Island area places a high priority on land preservation, and many understand and protect the fragile beach ecology. Through the marine biology department, Southampton is a "resident expert" monitoring local shellfish populations, water quality, and erosion studies.

MAKING A DIFFERENCE STUDIES

Experiential projects, field studies, seminars and workshops.

In **North America,** students have done 15 credit projects in such areas as:
- Peace Studies with the American Friends Service Committee
- Native American rights with Big Mountain Offense/Defense League in Arizona
- Arms race issues with SANE/FREEZE • Homeless issues in NYC
- World hunger issues with the Institute for Food & Development Policy in CA.
- Mediation & creative resolution at a school in CA.
- Wilderness camping with troubled youth in Florida
- Alternative magazine production with Co-op America
- Media accuracy with Fairness & Accuracy in Reporting, NYC
- Working in international business with the Council on Economic Priorities
- Also, internships with UN NGO: World Council on Religion & Peace; assisting ethnic concerts and workshops in NYC; researching dolphins and seals in CA; sustainable agriculture and farm design in Arizona; and community open space development in Boston.

- Through the **South Asian Center, Bangalore, India.** students have worked in rural development and health education, done botanical research in Malaysia, conservation research with the World Wildlife Fund and taught Tibetan children in Nepal.

- At the **Latin American Center, San Jose, Costa Rica,** students have interned at a zoo, done rainforest botanical studies, participated in community health & nutrition programs in Nicaragua, and done biological field research in Guatemala.

- At the **East African Center in Kenya,** students studied village development, worked promoting appropriate technology, studied the historical role of women in Somalia, and learned about community health and traditional medicine in Nairobi.

- Students interning at the **Middle East/Israel Center in Jerusalem, Israel** have been archaeological field assistants, done an anthropological study of Bedouin women in Sinai, and studied arid-zone agriculture in the Negev.

- At the **China Center in Hong Kong/Hangzhou, China/Taiwan,** studies have included "Calligraphy and Politics", the Origins of Chinese Buddhism, The Chinese Writer as Social Activist, and Korean Nationality in Jilin Province.

- Through the **European Center in London,** projects have included film and video internships,an apprenticeship to an environmental publisher in Ireland, a study of the role of women in Portugal and the history of French feminism from 1860 to 1940.

- At the **East Asia Center in Kyoto, Japan** projects include the study of integration of Western and Eastern medical practice,US foreign policy in regard to Korea and Indonesia, and business mgm't and quality control in Japan, Taiwan and Singapore.

Field Advisors: Friends World students have their education enriched by working with many leading professionals and specialists. They have included Dr. Helen Caldicott, founder of Physicians for Social Responsibility; Jenny Watson of Amnesty International; and Bernadette Valley, Friends of the Earth, London.

Student Body: 50% state, 75% female, 15% male, 10% minority   Faculty: 50% female, 50% male
1994-95 Tuition $11,800   Room, board, travel and personal expenses average about $6,000
Rolling Admissions   Avg. students in first year classroom: 15
• Vegetarian Meals   Life experience Credit   • Exclusive Seminar Format   • On-Campus Recycling

Use form in back to contact: Friends World Program, Office of Admissions
Southampton Campus, LIU   Southampton, NY 11968
(516) 283-4000

LONG ISLAND UNIVERSITY
SOUTHAMPTON COLLEGE
1,300 Students   Southampton, New York   Moderately Competitive

Southampton's commitment to the environment began when the college opened in 1963. The seacoast location was chosen in order to have access to a wide variety of marine environments to study. Located on the eastern tip of Long Island, the college is in one of the most ecologically beautiful and fragile areas of the country. Bordering on the Atlantic Ocean with miles of barrier beach, dunes, salt marshes, bays, pine barrens, endangered wildlife, and a fragile groundwater aquifer, the area is a kind of living environmental laboratory. The delicate relationship between water, wind and land has made environmental protection a priority here since early times. Local groups like the Peconic Land Trust and national groups like the nature Conservancy have long been active in this area. In the midst of such natural beauty and activist spirit, Southampton is ideally suited to preparing young environmentalists to undertake the research, plan the programs and create the policies that will make a difference in our world.

Campus four different environmental study programs are offered: Environmental science, Environmental Education, Environmental Studies and Marine Science. All are designed to prepare students for graduate study of a professional career in environmental work. The programs are interdisciplinary, combining courses from several academic areas. The college is one of two in the country with a marine research station on campus.

The Environmental Science Program is designed to give students the experience and training to compete successfully for positions in the environmental field, one of the fastest growing employment areas in the country. The program offers a unique multidisciplinary curriculum developed by faculty in consultation with employers in the environmental field. Southampton prepares young scientists to deal with some of the world's most critical environmental issues. In Environmental Biology, problems may include the effects of harmful substances on ecosystems, the deforestation of tropical forests, the loss of biodiversity and protection of wildlife resources. In Environmental Chemistry, scientists study chemical species in water, soil and air, solid and hazardous waste management, acid rain, ozone depletion and global cycling of toxic substances. Environmental geologists explore such topics as pollution of surface and ground water, coastal processes, sedimentation and erosion.

Southampton is one of the few institutions in America that offers an undergraduate degree in Marine Science. In the past 17 years, the Marine Science Program has graduated 14 Fulbright Scholars, an extraordinary record for a small school. A fully equipped Marine Station on Shinnecock Bay houses aquaculture and water quality labs, teaching labs and classrooms, and research equipment. The 44-foot Paumanok is used for coastal research while the Shinnecock, a 35-foot platform craft, is used for bay and estuary work. Every winter a group of marine science students and professors travels to the South Pacific for a four-credit course in Tropical Marine Biology to study in some of the most pristine and exotic areas of the world including Australia's Great Barrier Reef and the Fiji Islands.

The Environmental Studies major is designed for students who wish to prepare for careers in environmental planing and policy. The course work and field experiences are aimed at helping students develop essential tools and skills in economic analysis and decision making, natural resource management and computing. Students are offered a variety of opportunities for "hands-on" work with Suffolk County environmental planning offices. Suffolk County has some of the most progressive planning and health requirements in the nation, and continues to be a region with vast public commitment to environmental protection. Students who choose to focus on alternative agriculture and energy sources may take internships on agricultural projects coordinated by the Friends World program centers in Kenya, Costa Rica, India and Israel, or they may participate in an experimental garden project on campus.

Environmental Education is a new concentration in the Biology major that emphasized nautral history and is designed for students who love the out-of-doors. The program's main emphasis is interpretive naturalism -- how we explain the natural world to others and how we use the natural environment to teach scientific principles and aspects of environmental concern. A significant aspect of the program is an outdoor experiential component. All students participate in experiences that provide outdoor leadership skills and expose them to work in environmental education or to study in unusual and challenging environments.

"SEAmester," a unique program at Southampton, allows students not only to study the ocean environment, but to live it. For nine weeks they travel on board the *Spirit of Massachusetts,* a 125-foot schooner modeled after a turn of the century fishing schooner. Students earn up to 16 academic credits while undertaking responsibility of crewing the gaff-rigged schooner. SEAmester students sail almost 3,000 miles, stopping at ports of call to examine unique ecosystems, or "heave to" for oceanographic stations at sea while studying coastal ecology, navigation, and marine science. Field work includes studies of the finest reefs in the Caribbean to the mudflats of North Carolina. A coral reef becomes an intense experience when you dive from the ship to do a field laboratory on the reef front. Fish anatomy becomes unforgettable as you perform a megadisssection on a fresh 12 foot tiger shark.

Southampton has the largest concentration of undergraduate marine and environmental science faculty on the East Coast. They bring a diversity of backgrounds and interests to the Environmental Programs -- from environmental planning and management, to marine natural products, from energy conservation to beach processes, environmental law to marine mammals.

Experience counts, and at Southampton Campus students get it through cooperative education and internship placements with land use planners and leading scientists in prestigious institutions throughout the country. Southampton emphasizes field work, giving students valuable experience and helping them make contacts before they graduate. Students may earn up to 16 credits in off-campus work. Typical placements include The U.S. Environmental Protection Agency, New York City Aquarium, Woods Hole Oceanographic Institute, Outward Bound and the National Wildlife Federation.

MAKING A DIFFERENCE STUDIES

Marine Science Tracks in Marine Biology; Chemistry; Geology

Introduction to Cell Biology	Plant Biology
Quantitative Chemical Analysis	Marine Ecology
Geochemistry	Biology of Plankton
Marine Operations and Research	Evolution
Physical Oceanography	Mineralogy
Coastal Processes and Marine Geology	Geophysics and Global Tectonics

Environmental Science Tracks in Biology, Chemistry, Geology

Ecology	Microcomputer Analysis and Report Writing
Environmental Inventory	Biochemistry
Physical Geology	Hydrology
Environmental Law	Environmental Impact Assessment
Technical/Scientific Writing	Chemical Oceanography

- **Environmental Chemistry** A multidisciplinary study of the sources, reactions, transport, effects and fates of chemical species in water, soil, and the atmosphere and the influence of human activity on these chemicals. Biogeochemical cycles, water pollution and treatment processes, microbial transformations of pesticides in soils, trace metals, sources and reactions of atmospheric pollutants and their effects.

Environmental Studies

Society and the Environment	Public Policy
Environmental Sociology	World Population Problems
Regional Planning & Enviro Protection	Environmental Psychology
Alternate Agriculture and Society	Ethics
Field Biology	Coastal Zone Resources

- **Global Environment** Study of international relations from an environmental perspective and an analysis of efforts by the UN in improving the human environment.

Sociology

Society Through film	The Community
Social Problems	Contemporary Issues in Drug Abuse
Community Field Service	The Sociology of Aging
Social Minorities	Cross-Cultural Child Development

- **Science, Technology and Society** Historical, ethical, ecological and social perspectives are used to define the broader context in which the practice of science and the adaptation of technology occur. value free science is discussed with reference to the Nazi doctors and development of the atomic bomb. Technological displacement of workers, social responses to "killer" diseases, high risk and nuclear technologies.

Environmental Education　　　　**Biology**　　　　**Psychobiology**

Student Body: 65% state, 42% male, 58% female, 18% minority, 25% transfer
Faculty: 85% male, 15% female, 3% minority
1994-95 Costs: $11,800　　　Rolling Admissions
• Field Studies　• Life experience Credit　• Vegetarian Meals

Use form in back to contact: Carol Gilbert, Office of Admissions
LIU, Southampton　　Southampton, NY 11968
(516) 283-4000

MANCHESTER COLLEGE

1,000 Students   Manchester, Indiana   Moderately Selective

Manchester College has a long tradition of combining learning and values. It's goal, as presented in the mission statement, is "to graduate people who possess ability and conviction." Manchester recognizes that change cannot come from conviction alone, that those who ardently desire to build a better world need real world skills to accomplish those goals. At Manchester College, skills and abilities are developed through rigorous preparation in a student's academic major(s) and broad coursework in the liberal arts. Graduates leave well trained for graduate school or their first job.

Manchester's mission statement also speaks best to it's core values: "Within a long tradition of concern for peace and justice, Manchester College intends to develop an international consciousness, a respect for ethnic and cultural pluralism, and an appreciation for the infinite worth of every person. A central goal of the College community is to create an environment which nurtures a sense of self-identity, a strong personal faith, a dedication to the service of others, and an acceptance of the demands of responsible citizenship." Manchester College is an independent, co-educational college in the liberal arts tradition, and is committed to continue in the tradition of social concern which is a mark of the Church of the Brethren, its supporting denomination.

The Peace Studies Institute plans college-wide conferences featuring speakers, debates on issues of public policy, and workshops. Manchester also offers an unusually large number of scholarships to students majoring in Peace Studies.

Students at Manchester College experience excellence, develop and strengthen commitments, find community, are committed to serving others, shape a global perspective, and find success. The curriculum allows varied combinations of majors and minors, both in allied fields (history and political science) and across disciplines (physics and peace studies, music and gender studies). Students take advantage of travel opportunities through Brethren Colleges Abroad (a semester or year at campuses in China, France, Ecuador, England, Germany, Greece, Japan, Spain and Mexico) and during the three and a half week January Term. In 1994, Jan Term classes went to Cuba, Costa Rica, Nicaragua, Jamaica, Hawaii, Florida, and Russia, and students were involved in NASA research, health, fitness and wellness internships, field experiences in peace studies and psychology, and many other off campus opportunities.

Manchester's emphasis on developing abilities and convictions shapes the academic and extra curricular experiences of students in every major. Action-oriented student groups are open to all students. They include Amnesty International, the Environmental Group, Habitat for Humanity, prison visitation teams, Death Penalty Awareness, Women's Advocacy Group, and many others. Students also participate in the Peace Choir, retreats, coffee houses, concerts, lectures and discussion forums, and local and national conferences.

Other special resources include the 100 acre Koinonia Environmental Center, including a 5 acre natural lake and woods, just 11 miles from campus. The retreat building provides class and seminar rooms and environmental laboratories. Koinonia has become a retreat and learning center for church and college groups.

MAKING A DIFFERENCE STUDIES

Environmental Studies Tracks is Interpretation-Education and Technical Studies
Over 20 years old, this program was founded before "environmentalism" became popular.

Environmental Philosophy

Plant Taxonomy

Science and the Environment

Field Biology

Fundamentals of Chemistry

Environmental Studies Practicum

Ecology

State and Local Politics

Environmental Science

Historical Geology

Peace Studies Tracks in Interpersonal and Intergroup Conflict, International and Global Studies, Religious and Philosophical Bases
The Peace Studies program founded in 1951, was the first in the nation. Nearly all majors participate in a Peace Studies practicum, an internship, or a year of study abroad.

Current Issues in Peace and Justice

Religions and War

Philosophy of Civilization

International Politics

Confucian and Buddhist Worlds

Microeconomics

Literature of Nonviolence

Analysis of War and Peace

Environmental Philosophy

Conflict Resolution

The Brethren Heritage

Peace and Justice

Social Work
The Social Work program has an excellent reputation among professionals in the region. resulting in strong placement rate for interns and graduates.

Introduction to Human Services

Social Service Policy

Social Welfare as an Institution

Juvenile Delinquency

Human Behavior and the Social Environment

Race and Minority Group Relations

Gerontology

Social Work Practice

Psychology
Students interested in psychology and conflict resolution find an exceptional opportunity in Manchester's mediation program--the Reconciliation Service, one of only a few in the country where students are active participants in mediating disputes for students and outside groups.

Cross-Cultural Psychology

Psychology of Mediation and Conciliation

Psychology of Learning

Psychology of the Young Adult

Counseling Theory and Practice

Psychology of Childhood

Gender Studies
Based on the theory that gender is a cultural construct, not a naturally given aspect of personality, Gender Studies calls on us to reflect on the role gender plays in our lives and in society.

Introduction to Gender Studies

Feminist and Womanist Theology

Self and Society

Women in European History

Women in Literature

Women in the Arts

Women in American History

Feminist Theory

Student Body: 86% state, 50% male, 50% female, 6% minority, 3% int'l, 14% transfer
Faculty: 60% male, 40% female • Actively seeking minority students
1994-95 Costs: $14,290   Rolling Admissions
• Service-Learning Programs • Individualized Majors • Core/Multidisciplinary Classes

Use form in back to contact: Jolane Ogden, Office of Admissions
Manchester College   609 College Ave N. Manchester, IN 46962
(219) 982-5055

MARLBORO COLLEGE

275 Students   Marlboro, Vermont   Moderately Selective

If we are to survive, it will take a combination of an objective mind and a humane spirit. Marlboro strives to develop both qualities and hence we leave prepared to front these issues in a meaningful way.

Founded in 1947, Marlboro's inception was fueled by a vision of individualized learning and educational merit. Marlboro's goal is to teach students to think clearly and learn independently, to develop a command of concise and correct written language, and to aspire to academic excellence, all while acting responsibly in a self-governing community. Such insistence on independent thought, clearly expressed vision, and responsibility toward others has produced compassionate and involved world citizens dedicated to making a difference in their own lives and in those of all around them. Liberal by nature, Marlboro students begin college with boundless idealism. Marlboro celebrates this idealism by helping each student strengthen his or her skills and background to become more effective members of the global community.

Essential to such an experience is the Plan of Concentration, which allows students to self-design a curriculum tailored to their interests. The Plan, a two-year course of study in which juniors and seniors design and implement an academic program leading to a bachelor's degree, varies enormously in both content and style. Students conduct their studies under the close guidance of one or two faculty members who suggest a coherent sequence of coursework in small classes, (on average eight students per class), seminars, and individual Oxford-style tutorials. However diverse, Plans share a common outcome. Every Marlboro graduate knows that he or she has gained the ability to define a problem, set clear limits on an area of inquiry, analyze the object of study within those parameters, evaluate the results of research or artistic production, and report articulately on the outcome of a worthy project. These are very important and powerful skills in the arena of progressive change.

While there is no question that many barriers have been broken down, the world is becoming a more volatile place, threatened by overflowing population, a dying ecosystem, and a resurgence of ethnic hatred that presents us once more with the glaring reality of humankind's inhumanity to its own. Marlboro's World Studies Program, run in association with The School for International Training in Brattleboro, VT, embraces the premise that we must develop an understanding, acceptance, and celebration of the World's diversity through intercultural education.

The program is designed to help motivated students acquire the cultural framework, practical skills and intellectual tools necessary to analyze global developments against the backdrop of history, in the light of differing values and traditions. Students study broadly within the liberal arts, focusing increasingly on a particular area of inquiry within the context of Western and non-Western cultures; they acquire foreign language proficiency and cross-cultural skills; then, in the junior year, they experience living, working and studying in a different culture. Interns have traveled to over thirty different countries world-wide, from Ireland to Bali, and return holding not only a much broader global perspective, but also increased insight and maturity.

They reach the culmination of their studies by producing a finished Plan - a work that fuses their academic and intercultural experience and results in a truly world view, one which is often continued in their later work.

Outside the World Studies Program, students individually arrange study-abroad semesters or internships both in other countries and at other colleges and universities in the United States. The College also sponsors several field trips each year, such as scientific expeditions to tropical, desert, or mountain environments; outdoor adventures in mountain climbing or white-water rafting; and a theater trip to England each winter.

To the faculty at Marlboro, the term "Environmental Science" is synonymous with the term "Human Ecology," that is, a study of the way that humans interact with their environment. Such a broad definition suggests that an interdisciplinary or cross-disciplinary approach is warranted, and indeed, students should study the environmental sciences from the special perspective and knowledge of the arts, humanities, social sciences, and natural sciences. The integration of various disciplines into a coordinated approach to environmental questions is the challenge of this field. Each student majoring in environmental science must develop an in-depth familiarity with one or more approaches to solving problems. One cannot, for example, reasonably address the problems associated with acid rain without knowing something about biology and ecology, resource economics, public policy and political institutions, international relations, environmental chemistry, and meteorology.

The interdisciplinary nature of Marlboro also allows great flexibility for students who wish to study gender issues. Students focus on women's studies throughout the curriculum, and similar to work in environmental sciences, a broad perspective in all areas of the liberal arts coupled with a specific focus within a discipline or cross-discipline provide each student with multi-faceted and thus, more informed work.

Along with the academic challenge, Marlboro has a tradition of community service. To some degree this can be attributed to a highly distinctive aspect of Marlboro: the Town Meeting structure by which the College is governed. Town Meeting serves as a training ground for its members to participate in the democratic process and assume a considerable measure of personal responsibility for the health of the community, both at Marlboro and beyond our bounds.

Marlboro also offers a very active outdoors program. The main activities are rock climbing, backpacking, caving, canoeing, cross-country skiing and winter camping. The surrounding environment is ideal for both instruction and recreation in these areas. The Outdoors Program offers trips each weekend on a first-come basis. The program owns most of the equipment needed and loans this to students at no charge. While some students try an activity only once for its "thrill" potential, others continue and advance to a high level of proficiency.

MAKING A DIFFERENCE STUDIES

Environmental Sciences

Students must study broadly throughout the curriculum, developing an aesthetic sense in the arts, an appreciation of the foundations of civilization in the humanities, a view of the inner workings of past and present human societies in the social sciences, and a firm grounding in basic physical and biological principles in the natural sciences. On the advanced level, students draw from a broad academic base and focus their studies to a specialized goal. Students on Plan must have one of the program faculty as the major sponsor.

World Energy Issues	Pollutants: Conservation Biology & Policy
Global Environmental Issues	God, Man, and Nature
The Philosophy of Nature	Solar Energy & Building Design
Climactic Change	Perception of the Environment
Ecosystems	Alternative Institutions
Public Policy & Endangered Species	Recovery Strategies
Energy Policy Issues	Wetland Policy and Protection in Vermont

Interaction Between The Role of Wildlife in Community Development
Tropical Deforestation Forest Practices and Management in the U.S
Relation Between Range Management and Public Policy on Grazing of Public Land
Environmental Law and Natural Science w/ Emphasis on Coastal Zone Mgm't Act

- **Ethnobiology** This course includes three distinct but interrelated segments: 1) an examination of how people in different cultures classify plants and animals; 2) a study of contemporary and historical events in the Americas in which resource consumption, environmental destruction, and native land rights are linked; and 3) a brief survey of medical anthropology, the study of medical belief systems within particular cultural contexts.

World Studies Program

World Studies Program students are expected to gain a general education through the liberal arts and to develop skills as international citizens. These general goals include: an introductory knowledge of world history and cultures; an understanding of contemporary global issues; competence in cross-cultural communication, recognition of difference in cultural values, and experience working and learning in another culture; proficiency in a second language; and a basic knowledge of one world region (geography; economic and environmental systems; culture and history).

Central America Politics	Topics in Human Understanding
Southern African Politics	Professional Development
Economic Development	Mesoamerican Studies
Foreign Languages	Language in Culture
Third World Development	Russian and Soviet Studies,
Seminar in Policy Studies	Inuit Healing Techniques
Gender and Healing in Tunisia	Tibetan Subcultures in Exile
Tourism and Tradition in Balinese Dance	History, Language,&Ethnic Identity in Ireland
Changing Roles of Women in East Africa	Cultural Responses to Develop't in Uganda

- **Introductory Seminar for World Studies** The course is designed to help students situate themselves in time and place, and begin to think historically, culturally, and geographically. We discuss concepts and issues relevant to the contemporary world and to historical experience, in global comparative contexts.

Biology

General Biology

Plant Ecology

Plants of Vermont

Conservation Biology

Plant Diversity

Animal Behavior

Biogeography

Community Ecology

Pollination Ecology

Alpine Plant Ecology

Field Course in Tropical Biology (Mexico, Guatemala and Belize)

- **This Biology of Deserts** An examination of the physiological and ecological adaptations possessed by organisms living in the world's deserts. Some emphasis on the taxonomy of the US desert biota. Course will culminate in an extended field trip to the Chihuahuan (Texas,) Sonoran (Arizona,) and Mojave (California) Deserts.

Gender Studies

Gender Studies are incorporated throughout the curriculum through various disciplines, such as american studies, philosophy, world studies, theater, art history, literature, sociology, psychology and the sciences. In almost all cases, gender studies are interdisciplinary.

Research in U.S. Women's History

A Feminist Critique of Philosophy of Science

African American Women Writers

Prostitution in America Plans

Women, Science and Objectivity

Feminism and Drama

Two French Feminists

Working Women in the Progressive Era

Artistic Development of Modersohn-Becker, O'Keefe, and Virginia Woolf

Contemporary African-American Women & The Search for Identity

The Relationship between Women and Nature in Victorian Post- colonial Fiction

Economics

Political Economy

Environmental Policy

U. S. Capitalism

Organizations, Environments & Public Policy

Economic Anthropology

Politics of Deforestation

The Soviet Economy

Solid Waste Mgm't in Rural New England

Decision Making: Individual, Interactive and Collective

- **Economic Justice** Considers the existing distribution of income and wealth, theories which attempt to explain this distribution, and programs which seek to change it.

- Faculty Bio: **James Tober** (B.A., UC Berkeley, M. Phil., Yale, Ph.D. Yale) Jim's doctoral dissertation was on Natural Resources for the Future. He was a Visiting Fellow and Research Scholar at Yale with the Program on Non-Profit Organizations, Institution for Social and Policy Studies, and was Co-director for two years of the World Studies Program. Jim's long-term research on wildlife policy has led to two books: *Who Owns Wildlife* and *Wildlife and the Public Interest*.

Student Body: 20% state, 50%-male, 50% female, 5% minority, 5% int'l

Faulty: 65% male, 35% female, 1% minority

1994-95 costs: $24,450   Rolling Applications

- Team Teaching   • Individualized Majors   • Exclusive Seminar Format
- Study Abroad   • Core/Multidisciplinary classes   • Vegetarian Meals
- Campus Wide Recycling Program   • Many buildings on campus are passive solar.

Use form in back to contact: Director of Admissions

Marlboro College   Marlboro, VT 05344-0300

(802) 257-4333

MIDDLEBURY COLLEGE

2,000 Students   Middlebury, Vermont   Very Selective

Middlebury is well-known as one of New England's outstanding small, residential, liberal arts colleges of long tradition. It was founded in 1800 and in 1883 became one of the earliest co-educational institutions. Middlebury is distinguished for its long international and multicultural tradition. Middlebury seeks those who wish not only to learn about themselves and their own traditions, but those who wish to expand their vision, to see beyond the bounds of class, culture, region or nation. Indeed, it could be said that the central purpose of a Middlebury education is precisely this transcendence of oneself and one's own concerns.

Since World War 1, the College has operated internationally known language programs. Middlebury views languages both as a means of communication, and as ways to learn more about a culture or a discipline. Four out of ten Middlebury students spend at least one semester abroad, experiencing another culture first-hand and bringing their new perspectives back to campus.

At Middlebury, the New England tradition of the town meeting takes on an international dimension at many of our symposia. His Holiness, the Dalai Lama, the exiled spiritual and political leader of Tibet, spent a week on campus as part of a conference called "The Spirit and Nature Symposium." A symposium on South Africa had international speakers - and a large audience: 140 stations of the American Public Radio.

First Year Students at Middlebury are required to elect one of a number of seminars that are designed from a perspective which makes connections among a number of traditional academic disciplines. Recent topics have included Environmental Issues for the Nineties: Crises and Resolution; Thinking About War; and Cries of Injustice: Black Protest and the Civil Rights Movement.

Middlebury college has a very active volunteer service program. Over 600 students volunteer each year. One of the oldest programs is Community Friends, in which students choose individuals in need from the following groups: children between the ages of 6-12, the elderly, people with mental retardation and mental illness. Students also work reading to the blind, and in affordable housing renovation. Students take ungraded internships for credit in various areas, from a clinic for parasitology in Thailand to the office of a local attorney.

The College has a partnership with De Witt Clinton High School (Bronx, N.Y.) whose student population is 99% minority. De Witt Clinton teachers have participated in workshops with Middlebury faculty, and students have conducted teaching internships at the high school during winter term. Middlebury also has three regional "diversity task forces" designed to help recruit and retain students of color. In addition, a rural outreach program focuses on first-generation, college-bound students of modest financial means.

MAKING A DIFFERENCE STUDIES

First Year Seminars
Theory and Practice of Nonviolence
Stories About Women
Voices Across Social Groups: How Do We Talk To Each Other?
Women and World Politics: Questions About Gender
Social Class & Ethnic Relations in America
Moral and Ethical Decisions in Public Life

Environmental Studies **Tracks in Conservation Biology; Enviro Geology; Enviro Economics; Geography; U.S. Enviro Policy; Environmental Perspectives in Literature and Writing; Philosophical & Comparative Perspectives;& Human Ecology.**
Visions of Nature
Ethics and the Environment
Social Movement and Collective Action
Environmental Economics
Methods in Ecology
Environmental Economics
Science and Society
Environmental and Natural Resource Policy
Native Peoples of North America
Environmental Geology
Religion, Ethic and the Environment
Perspectives on the Environmental Movement
Natural Science and the Environment
Philosophy of Nature

Geography
The Geography of Development
Population Geography
Surface Water Resource and Development
Energy Fuels and Mineral Development
Economic Geography
Geographic Perspectives on Middle East
Social Aspects of Environmental Issues
Women in the City

Northern Studies
*Polar Biota: Flora
Artic and Alpine Environments
*Northern Archaeology
Public Policy in Circumpolar North
*Indigenous Cultures of the Circumpolar North
*Community Development in Circumpolar North
*These classes are offered at the Center for Northern Studies in Wolcott, Vt
*Political Economy Of Resource Mgm't.
Northern Legal Issues
*Artic Policy Studies
Northern Resource Conflicts

Sociology/Anthropology **Concentrations in Social Inequality, Social Policy Issues, Health and Society**
Women, Culture and Society
Indian Society
Sociology of Women
Social Movements and Collective Action
Medical Anthropology
Medical Sociology
Native Peoples of North America
American Community Studies
Women in Social Thought
Chinese Society and Culture
Sociology of Education
Race and Ethnicity

Women's Studies   **Third World Studies**

Student Body: 5% state, 50% men, 50% women, 5% minority
1994-95 Costs: $25,750   Apply By: 1/ 15
• Field Studies   • Internships   • Individualized Majors
• Third World Study Abroad   • Mystic Seaport Program

Use form in back to contact: Admissions Office
Middlebury College   Middlebury, VT 05753-6002
(802) 388-3711

NAROPA INSTITUTE

200 Undergraduates   Boulder, Colorado   Moderately Selective

The approach to learning taken at The Naropa Institute, an accredited institution, is called "contemplative education." Through the practices of meditation and contemplative disciplines, learning is infused with the experience of awareness, insight, and friendliness to oneself and others. All members of The Naropa Institute community participate in creating an atmosphere that is gentle, dignified, and committed to intellectual, artistic, and spiritual development. Inspired in part by the tradition of Buddhist teaching, contemplative education at the Institute encourages the evolution of confidence, wisdom, and the desire to work for the benefit of others.

The educational programs presented at the college are rigorous; they are designed for students who are resourceful, willing to let go of habitual patterns of thought and feeling, and motivated to realize their potential. The Naropa Institute's missions is:

- To offer educational programs that cultivate awareness of the present moment through intellectual, artistic, and meditative disciplines
- To strive for excellence in all disciplines
- To exemplify the principles of The Institute's Buddhist educational heritage
- To encourage the integration of world wisdom traditions with modern culture
- To be nonsectarian and open to all

The goals of contemplative education are to deepen students' knowledge of themselves and their place in the contemporary world, to develop and strengthen personal discipline within a specific field of study, and to nurture the desire to contribute to the world with understanding and compassion. By working with these goals, students are preparing for the constant challenges and the rapid change of modern society with moral, intellectual, and spiritual responsiveness.

Cultivating awareness of the present moment is the heart of contemplative education. At The Naropa Institute, awareness is cultivated through meditation and other traditional and modern contemplative practices, as well as through intellectual and artistic disciplines. Faculty at the college have also been inspired to develop contemporary forms of awareness practice within their specific fields of study.

All fields of study are understood to represent the creativity of many people working in different ages, places, and cultural contexts. Naropa seeks to offer academic programs based on the inherent standards within the traditions being taught. From this point of view, students are asked to step beyond personal and cultural bias and to connect to a pluralistic understanding of the world.

Buddhist educational training is based on the three primary principles of meditation, discipline, and knowledge which lead to the discovery of egolessness. In Buddhist philosophy, egolessness means that what one experiences and understands as the "self" is not unchanging but rather continuously in process. Meditation refers to the cultivation of mindfulness and awareness. It is a foundation for self-knowledge as well as for compassion and service. Knowledge is realized through three levels of learning: listening to what is taught, examining whether it rings true and, finally, taking the subject to heart. In this way, knowledge is based on experience and can be expressed clearly in words and in actions.

The wisdom traditions of the world, which include the great religions, Native American traditions, hermetic teachings, and shamanistic cultures, offer insight into and guidance for contemporary society. By bringing these traditions of wisdom into the curriculum of modern education, a student's self-importance and limited perspective begin to dissolve.

Cultivation of mindfulness and awareness is a discipline that has been taught in many different traditions throughout history. Meditation and contemplative practices have value not as religious experiences per se, but as tools to stimulate curiosity and self-discovery. Appreciation of mindfulness and awareness, the benefits of synchronizing body and mind, and a need to go beyond a narrow sense of self are becoming increasingly widespread. There is a greater understanding of the role of mind/body interactions in healing processes, the value of awareness training in many professions, the role of intuition in science and commerce, the transcendence of self-interest in ecology and environmental ethics, and the change of management styles toward more cooperative and inclusive decision-making. Many students attend the Institute seeking an education that will train them to contribute to the world in this way.

The Institute's founder, Chogyam Trungpa Rinpoche, was a recognized "lineage holder" of Buddhist traditions. In 1963, he received a sponsorship to study comparative religion, philosophy, and the fine arts at Oxford University. He became widely recognized as one of the foremost teachers of Buddhism in the West. With the founding of The Naropa Institute in 1974, he realized his dream of creating a college that would combine contemplative studies with traditional Western scholastic and artistic disciplines.

Programs beginning in '94 include The Traditional Eastern Arts BA and Visual Arts, BA. The Traditional Arts program emphasizes traditional practices, handed down from generation to generation, in some cases since ancient times. Students learn to bring the essence of core body/mind disciplines; t'ai chi ch'uan, aikido, or yoga into alignment with livelihood, health, and creative expression as well as into their larger community. Creativity in the Visual Arts program is grounded in spontaneous appreciation and critical eye through the cultivation of awareness and specific skills in technique and theory in Eastern and Western traditions.

Programs beginning in '95 include: Engaged Buddhism, MA and Environmental Leadership, MA. Based on Buddhist philosophy and meditation, Engaged Buddhism prepares students for work as a Chaplain in social action in a variety of settings. The Environmental Leadership program trains students with a scientific understanding of ecosystems and human cultures to work in administrative positions, government and other environmental agencies.

The Institute's faculty members are distinguished by their involvement in the professional or artistic extension of their disciplines beyond the academic community. The faculty's involvement in the professional world contributes a high degree of immediacy and relevancy to the classroom. Naropa's faculty are an exceptionally committed group of educators.

MAKING A DIFFERENCE STUDIES

Environmental Studies Tracks in Anthropology, Ecology, Horticulture, and Native
American Studies
"When human beings lose their connection to nature, to heaven and earth, then they do not
know how to nurture their environment. Healing our society goes hand in hand with healing
our personal, elemental connection with the phenomenal world." Chogyam Trungpa, Rinpoche
Environmental Studies is taught from the perspective of "deep ecology," which trains both
the intellect, and intuition, an awareness of our dynamic interconnectedness with all being.

Small Farm Management	Ecology Practicum
Deep Ecology	Eco-Literature
Edible Plants and Survival Skills	Restoration Ecology and Changing Landscapes
Field Ecology	Field Botany
Vegetable Garden	Permaculture
Sustainable communities	Ethnomedicine Seminar

- **Contemplative Natural History & Gaia** Explores local natural history and our relationship to its climate, geology, plants, and animals as they coexist in ecosystems.
  Exploration will be grounded in the contemplative practice of the participants, and
  in short meditative practice in each class. Grounded in the Gaia hypothesis that the
  earth, and the life on/in the earth, has created its own ecology to maintain itself.

Contemplative Psychology Tracks in Buddhist & Western Psychology; Jungian
Psych, the Psychology of Health and Healing; and Transpersonal & Humanistic Psych.
Designed to deepen the student's self-understanding as well as to cultivate clarity, compassion,
and skill in interpersonal relationships. Work with one's personal process in order to develop
the courage and wisdom to genuinely help others.

Psychology of Healing	Psychology of Meditation
Healing and Music	Death as a Spiritual Teacher
Body Cosmology and Natural Healing	Dynamics of the Intimate Relationship
The Geshtalt Approach	Healing in Cross-Cultural Perspective
Archetypes and Collective Unconscious	Teaching Children in Contemplative Tradition
Tibetan Medicine	Buddhist Psychology: Maitri & Compassion
Psychology of Shamanism	Esoteric Christ: Jesus from a Jungian Perspective

- **Cognitive Studies 1** Explore ways in which one can cultivate an intellectual rigor of
  mind without abandoning one's perceptual ground. Refining one's sense of thought
  and integrating one's speech and inner gesture systems aid in bringing idea to form.
  Commitment, confusion, wonder, and chaos as possible agents for cognitive change.

Early Childhood Education
Applies traditional Asian contemplative ideas and practices to holistic teacher training.
Training in awareness, direct knowledge of learning styles, global perspectives on child-rearing,
children's studies, and educational and developmental psychology. Students intern at the
Institute's preschool, with 15 years of experience in developing a contemplative approach to
teaching young children.

Buddhist Educational Psychology	Body Mind Centering
Cultural Anthropology & Social Change	Nourishing the Teacher
Teaching & Learning Styles	Child Development and Creativity
Contemplative Parenting	Educational Admin. of a Child Care Center

- **Holistic & Contemplative Traditions of Teaching** An overview and comparison of
  contemplative and related holistic approaches to teaching children, focusing on the
  Shambala tradition, and including those of Steiner, Montessori, and Krishnamurti.

Dance/Movement Studies Tracks in Dance or Dance Therapy

Whether primarily interested in dance as an art form, or as a tool for working empathetically with others, this program provides ample ground for personal exploration. Our approach to dance synthesizes the spirit of sitting meditation, developing allegiance to the experience of the present moment, with an appreciation for experimental dance.

Body Mind Centering
The Dance of Haiti
Dance Therapy

The Dance of West Africa
Contact Improvisation
Contemplative Arts Practice

- **Dance Therapy 11** Focus on developing movement relationships through empathic movement and verbal exchange in dyads. This discipline supports increasing intimacy, which is the ground of the healing relationship, and, eventually, active participation in and support of another's process. Using the groundwork of increased authenticity of presence and movement, we will extend our clarified awareness of self and other into the movement process of group.

Religious Studies

Contemplative Christianity
Meditation Practicum
Contemplative Islam/Sufism
Buddhist Civilization
Women, Sufism, & Islam: Womanist Perspectives

Contemplative Religions of China and Japan
Tibetan
Contemplative Judaism: The Knowing Heart
Contemplative Hinduism

Traditional Eastern Arts

This program prepares students to be and act in the world.

T'ai Chi Chu'an
T'ai Chi Ch'uan: Sword Form
Shambala Meditation Practicum
Ikebana: Japanese Flower Arranging
Bugaku: Japanese Court Dance

Aikido
Yoga
Kyudo: The Way of the Bow
Japanese Tea Ceremony

Study Abroad: Nepal and Bali

Program provides a thorough introduction to the living traditions of meditation, philosophy, music, painting and dance presently flowering in both Nepal and Bali. Both programs infuse the cross-cultural educational experience with awareness of the personal journey.

Meditation Practicum
Balinese Gamelan Orchestra
Arts and Culture
Kathmandu Valley:Traditional Culture, Developing Nation

Buddhist Traditions
Balinese Dance
Independent Study and Travel

Theater Studies

Music

Student Body: 30% state, 55% women, 45% men, 5% minority
90% transfers   75% over 25 years of age
1994-5 costs: $17,300   Rolling Admissions

- Field Studies   • Individualized Majors   • Weekend/Evening Classes
- Life Experience Credit   • Core/Multidisciplinary Credit   • Vegetarian Meals

Use form in back to contact: Director of Admissions
The Naropa Institute   2130 Arapahoe Ave.   Boulder, CO 80302
(303) 444-0202

NEW COLLEGE OF CALIFORNIA

450 Undergraduates   San Francisco, California   Non-Competitive

Twenty years ago, New College began as a handful of students meeting in Father Jack Leary's living room. The College was founded as part of the nationwide movement for alternative education. While New College has both refined and broadened its original mission, it has held true to that mission. The critical and interdisciplinary study of the humanities, in an environment that respects students' individual needs and gifts and encourages them to take responsibility for their own learning and for the society they live in - this remains the core of New College. Our aim is to empower students by validating intuition and imagination as well as intellect, and by helping them develop tools with which to understand and affect the forces that have shaped both their fields of study and their own lives.

New College works to empower students in may way: through the advising or mentor relationship, which encourages students to reflect critically on their learning within an open dialogue; through small, discussion-oriented classes; through a core curriculum that stresses the ways that knowledge is socially created, transformed, and used; and through requiring students to work for a community organization

Finally, is the effort of New College to link the goal of personal development to that of social responsibility and committed social action. The empowerment and mutual respect that are so highly valued are qualities of human interaction that should shape every aspect of our society. It is hoped that the educational experience students have at New College will give them the confidence and knowledge they need to help bring this kind of society into being.

Education at New College is intended to be critical, activist, student-empowering, and multicultural.

- Critical   This means that all knowledge must be situated in its social, historical and cultural contexts. Moreover, New College looks at how knowledge develops in the context of relations of power.

- Interdisciplinary   New College challenges the division into specialized disciplines that characterizes the modern academy. While students are grounded in the languages, methods, and perspectives of a given discipline, this grounding is the basis for overcoming them. Students are urged to see the links between apparently disparate bodies of knowledge.

- Activist   Knowledge is not meant to be a key to privilege and power in a corrupt and unjust society, but a means of addressing the myriad social problems facing us locally and globally. This activist approach is directly facilitated through internships and practica.

- Empowering   At New College, this over-used word has real, concrete meaning. The Humanities Program empowers students by providing courses that foster critical and creative thought and by helping students develop the skills to use knowledge strategically in changing the world.

- Multicultural   To truly affirm the possibilities inherent in the "shrinking" of the world by modern communications is both to foster dialogue and to cultivate diversity. New College is committed to an ethnically diverse, gender balanced faculty; to a student community reflecting the diversity of the Bay Area; and to a curriculum that seriously engages the European tradition while also examining the history and cultures of Asian, African, Latin American, and tribal peoples.

The School of Humanities offers one of the few undergraduate arts programs that incorporates technical training with the study of the role of the arts in shaping society. Students first acquire the skills to bring the imagination to life through Performance, Video, and Visual Arts. They then learn to apply these skills in education, community organizing, therapy, and political activism.

Queer Consciousness and Cultures is a new program which explores the experiences and articulates the creativity of diverse cultures of lesbians, gay men, bisexuals and all those connected to challenging dominant relations around gender and power.

The Integrated Health Studies emphasis provides an interdisciplinary examination of the relationships between medicine, health, and society. It explores alternative approaches to medicine and health while encouraging an activist orientation that seeks progressive social change.

The average age of New College students is 28, with many in their thirties and forties, with 60% transfer students and many re-entry students. In the Weekend College, an intensive one year completion program for working adults, students tend to be in their thirties, forties and fifties. All students participate in a series of full weekend seminars held once a month, and design their own thesis.

MAKING A DIFFERENCE STUDIES

Majors at New College are self-designed from work in the following areas.

Ecological Studies
Designed to prepare students for careers in environmental activism. Students work in the classroom and in the community, learning through critical dialogue, creative problem-solving, and real-world activity. A multicultural, interdisciplinary, and activist philosophy infuses the emphasis with a breadth of understanding and analysis that is unique. Students completing the emphasis may sit for the California Environmental Health Specialist examination.

Nature as a Concept	Eco-Logics / Eco-Nomics
Eco-Literacy: Introduction to Ecology	Issues in Environmental Activism
Understanding Ecological Systems	

- **Science, Self and Society**   This class examines the "objectivity" of science, and explores experiences and analysis of how science is central to our everyday economic lives as well as the ways in which we interpret the world.

Arts and Social Change

Arts and Learning	Arts and Social Change
Performance/Urban Ritual	Community Theater making
Joy of Movement	Video Arts
Drama Therapy	Screenwriting and Propaganda

Integrated Health Studies

Interdisciplinary studies of medicine, health, and society; exploring the full spectrum of behavioral and social change to promote both individual and community health, health activism, preventive medicine, AIDS, women's health issues, environmental and occupational health, national health care plans. Students may combine studies with health-related work in an AIDS education project, a public health program, a women's health clinic etc.

Medical Anthropology
Health Promotion and Awareness
Living Anatomy Through Movement
Social and Psychological dimensions of Health and Medicine

Political Economy of Health Care
Feminist Theory and Women's Health
Health Studies: Strategies for Change

- Faculty Bio **Michael McAvoy** (M.A. in Medical Anthropology from Case Western Reserve University Ph.D. candidate at the Western Institute for Social Research.) is the Director of the Center for Community Action, Research, and Education at NC. Michael has long been active in community health, as the director of the People's Health Resource Center and the People's Medical School in the Haight Ashbury of the early '70s, and as founder of a free clinic in a Cleveland inner-city high school.

Indian Justice Systems

The only program in the country designed to turn out highly trained Native American personnel to participate effectively in the tribal court systems in their communities. This program is the first to offer a solid foundation for careers in the courts of Indian country as judges, advocates, court administrators, social service personnel, court clerks and related roles.

Politics and Society

The political, economic, cultural dimensions of social change, the social roots of power and conflict; alternative views and strategies for addressing environmental destruction, health care, crime, poverty, racism, sexism; visions & strategies for a more just & equitable society.

Fundamentalism
Political History of San Francisco
Global Political Economy
Social Problems/Social Visions
Feminist Perspectives on Class, Race & Ethnicity in the U.S.

Political Economy
Critical Moments in 20th Century US History
Schooling, Inequality, & Social Change
Working: For (or Against) a Living?

Queer Consciousness & Cultures

Creativity, Sexuality, and the Sacred
Cultural Notions of Self and Sexuality
Perspectives on Lesbian/Gay Experience

Queer Cultures, Queer Spaces
AIDS and Society
Fundamentalism & the Religious Right

Sports and Society

Students pursue their degree through seminars, independent study, and practica during the evenings and on Saturdays. Geared for careers in coaching, teaching physical education, youth guidance and career counseling, park and recreation directorship.

Growing Up Black
Organization and Team Dynamics

Interpersonal Communication
Youth Guidance Advising

Student Body: 54% women, 46% men, 7% Native American, 34% other minorities
1994-95 tuition: $7,400 or $315 per unit P/T   No housing   Rolling Admissions
• Weekend & Evening Classes   • Required Practicum
• Individualized Majors   • Life Experience Credit   • Exclusive Seminar Format

Use form in back to contact: Office of Admissions
New College of California   766 Valencia St.   San Francisco, CA 94110
(415) 626-0884

NEW COLLEGE OF CALIFORNIA
WORLD COLLEGE INSTITUTE
25 Students   San Francisco, California   Moderately Selective

The World College Institute Global Studies program is focused on the humane resolution of global issues -- social, economic and intercultural, including the environment and social justice. Community is highly valued and students, staff and faculty engage in decision making that affect all aspects of the program. An in-depth World Study abroad is also a central part of the program and a requirement for all students. Current World Study sites are Mexico and Nepal. Students may design their own course of study with their advisor; most choose among current concentrations:

Art & Society focuses on intercultural arts emphasizing world literature, ethnic studies, women's studies, popular art forms, and international artists concerned with social justice. Students are often interested in art as a bridge between cultures and traditional academic disciplines, as a creative tool in teaching, psychology, and self-discovery, and as a catalyst for social change.

Meaning, Culture & Change focuses on basic questions that confront human beings, using literature, art, psychology, philosophy, and religious studies. Students ask "What makes life meaningful for people?" "How do different cultures answer the same basic questions?" "How can people work more effectively to create change?" The emphasis prepares students for graduate study, or for work in areas ranging from journalism and teaching to social service and peace work.

International Environmental Studies focuses on global and environmental issues dealing with the relationship between humans and their natural environment. In the 21st century competition for scarce resources will increase; acid rain, ozone depletion and global warming are likely to worsen. This emphasis prepares students to address environmental problems world wide, and to integrate scientific principles with human values.

International Service & Development is designed for students interested in fields concerned with social, political and economic development of "Third World" nations in Latin America, Asia, Africa and marginalized communities within the US. The program provides flexible options to allow students to prepare for graduate study or for immediate work with private voluntary organizations or government agencies like the Peace Corps. The emphasis is grounded in experience and focused on grass-roots development.

Required internships of 270 hours give students an opportunity to apply their knowledge in the "real world" and to develop projects that complement and further their educational goals. many students choose to do one of these internships in their World Study country. Nora Kropp, with an emphasis in Int'l Service and Development interned in Nepal integrating her interests in women's reproductive health. She worked in a maternity ward as a caregiver, assisting with prenatal examinations and deliveries. With the health staff of Save the Children U.S. A., she worked in a rural mobile clinic that serviced children and pregnant women. Nora brought medicine into remote areas, planned immunization camps, and worked to improve government collection of data regarding rural health issues. A second student concentrated on deaf culture, studying Nepali sign language and working with The Forum for the Protection of Human Rights.

MAKING A DIFFERENCE STUDIES

Meaning, Culture and Change
Internships include work with Planet Drum Foundation, and the Native American Indian Community Services Center for Senior Citizens.

Worldviews and Consensual Reality	The Anatomy of Change
Pre-Patriarchal Roots of Civilization	Quest for Meaning in Myths and Fairy Tales
Mediation	"Third World" Women's Literature

International Service and Development
Internships included Casa El Salvador, Worldviews Int'l, Nepal, and Institute for Food and Development Policy.

Peasants and Social Change	Theories of Development
Visual Anthropology	Decolonization
Non-Government Organizations	Service and Idealism
Research Methods	Development and Environmental Economics

International Environmental Studies
Internships have included Rainforest Action Network, Institute for Sustainable Agriculture.

Environment, Culture and Development	Environment, Law and Planning
Environmental Ethics	Intro to Environmental Sciences
Environmental Engineering	Environmental Economics

- Faculty Bio **Mutombo Mpanya** (B.Sc. Institut Superieur de Commerce, Belgium, B.A. Bethel College, M.A. U of Notre Dame, Ph.D. U of Michigan) A native of Zaire, Mutombo has worked in international organizations concerned with environmental issues and food production. He served as a director of the Mennonite Central Committee, Zaire, and as a consultant to the United Nations and World Bank.

Art and Society

The Artist and Human Rights	Creative Process
Self in community	Contemporary World Literature

Mexico World Study Program
The Mexico program is based in the state of Michoacan. In the urban phase, students live with families and come together for classes, participation in cultural events, and excursions to sites of historic, artistic, religious, developmental and environmental significance. During the rural phase, students live with host families and participate in village activities. Examples of independent projects from previous programs include: Folk doctors and traditional medicine; volunteer work in an orphanage; working to save the great sea turtles with local villagers.

Nepal World Study Program
This program gives students a holistic and diverse experience of Nepali culture. The urban phase is centered in Kathmandu; in the rural phase students live with families in villages. Students complete a Field Study of Community Life entailing research including social, economic, ecological and religious aspects of the village, and a self-designed independent study. Examples of independent projects from previous program include: Beliefs in and uses of medicinal plants; Culture and religion in a Gurung village; and a women's weaving cooperative.

1993-4 Tuition $6,900 No Housing
Mexico and Nepal World Study Tuition $3,450 per semester plus room, board and travel expenses
Use form in back to contact: World College Institute
50 Fell St., San Francisco, CA 94102
(415) 455-9300

Ohio Wesleyan University student Vassi Johri '95 walks President
Clinton through a display describing Ohio Wesleyan's Summer of
Service program at the S.O.S. summit meeting in Washington DC.

Audubon Expedition Institute's unique field studies program takes
students on extended bus tours to different regions of the country.

Warren Wilson students often take time out on their campus in the Smoky Mountains to reflect upon their world and the new ways they are beginning to understand it.

Grinell's commitment to social responsibility has been a large part of its history. Students are encouraged to link community service to their academic interests. Students volunteers are pictured.

Education students at Rudolf Steiner Institute get hands-on experience in learning how to put on festivals at Waldorf Schools nationwide.

Environmental Management Program students at Rochester Institute of Technology gain an understanding of well construction. Here they install groundwater monitoring wells to sample for chemical pollution.

Penn State's environmental studies and public education programs are most visible at the University's Shaver's Creek Environmental Center, which has federal and state licenses to use birds of prey for public education.

Across the country students enjoy volunteering with Habitat for Humanity, helping to build affordable housing for low-income families.

NEW COLLEGE

OF THE UNIVERSITY OF SOUTH FLORIDA

536 Students   Sarasota, Florida   Very Selective

When New College opened in 1964, the college embraced four educational principles:
- Each student is responsible in the last analysis for his or her education.
- The best education demands a joint search for learning by exciting instructors and able students.
- Students' progress should be based on demonstrated competence and real mastery rather than on the accumulation of credits and grades.
- Students should have, from the outset, opportunities to explore in depth areas of interest to them.

The past thirty years have demonstrated the wisdom of these principles. During this period, the nation has largely succumbed to pressures for vocational training and depended heavily on passive and impersonal styles of learning. By contrast, New College has deepened its commitment to the liberal arts while seeking fresh ways to implement its conviction that active learning prepares a student for a lifetime of learning. Moreover, by serving undergraduates only, New College has been able to guarantee that instruction is by full-time faculty skilled as classroom instructors and as guides to students who pursue original research.

New College has renovated traditional academic structures, creating an academic program that provides opportunities for student/faculty collaboration unparalleled at the undergraduate level. Instead of grades and formulaic requirements New College features seminars and tutorials, independent study, and the undertaking of a senior thesis.

The contract system is New College's alternative to a "credit hours" approach to a college education. Credit hours measure learning by the accumulation of time in classes; the contract draws the student, along with her or his faculty advisors, into reflection on the appropriate educational goals for a given semester and on how a certain selection of courses, tutorials, service learning, and other activities might achieve those goals. This approach reinforces individual accountability while providing for flexibility and individualization.

Replacing grades with narrative evaluations places the focus on individual learning, not on scoring or competing with peers. The Independent Study Project (ISP), which takes place in January when no classes are scheduled, encourages concentration on a single topic, taking the form of library or laboratory research, an internship or field research, small group projects, or dramatic or musical productions. The senior thesis provides the opportunity to pursue one topic of interest in uncommon depth, in close collaboration with a faculty mentor.

New College, then, has developed around the premise that authentic learning is characterized by engagement, intellectual initiative, and a restlessness that keeps the learner in motion, much like a reader who cannot put down a book because it is so absorbing.

Flexible structure combines, in a community of talented people, to yield rich outcomes. Students founded and run a Center for Service-Learning that supports the linking of community service with academics. New College encourages students to consider the larger community and be mindful of the rest of the world. It asks that students live responsibly and consider the social ramifications of their area of interest. It asks that students test indoor classroom knowledge against real problems, that they explore and document some public decision-making process related to the environment, or complete a significant community service project related to their area of interest. It asks students to pose questions, then ask what difference the answers will make, and what difference those differences will make. New College asks students to find something they care about, passionately.

The unique Environmental Studies Program (ESP) attacks environmental questions from a multi-disciplinary, problem-solving perspective. In fact, it is a goal of new College that all graduates be environmentally literate. So, in additon to supporting students pursuing an ESP concentration, the Program now provides opportunities for all students to increase their level of environmental awareness and understanding.

A 1994 visiting evaluation team from the Southern Association of Colleges and Schools observed of the faculty: "At a non-traditional, tutorial-based honors college such as New College, the faculty are the lifeblood of success... Their dedication to teaching excellence, their scholarly productivity, and their significant loads of service-related duties are truly exemplary." In one of biology Professor Sandra Gilchrist's courses which stressed active learning, she worked with a group of students to construct a Biosphere Reserve simulation game. The game evolved during a student-initiated, semester-long group tutorial, and was eventually presented at an annual meeting of the American Zoological Society.

The Sarasota area excels in science as well as the arts. Many New College natural sciences and environmental studies students intern at the Mote Marine Laboratory in Sarasota, while students of archaeology and anthropology undertake museology internships at the nearby South Florida Museum.

New College seeks students with outstanding academic aptitude and a serious interest in disciplined inquiry, students for whom intense study with faculty in seminars and tutorials will have rich personal meaning. Sixteen percent of the fall 1993 entering freshmen were National Merit Scholars, and over 65 percent of the in-state members of the current student body are Florida Academic Scholars.

Law, medicine, ecology, scientific research, city planning, creative writing and journalism are among the fields that attract graduates. In business, they tend toward consulting and entrepreneurship. New College's 2,500 alumnae/i include a Rhodes Scholar; numerous veterans of the Peace Corps; a U.S. Congressman (Rep., Florida); recent Fulbright fellows in New Zealand and Germany; founder and director of an internationally recognized tropical zoological park; four women attorneys who have successfully argued cases before the U.S. Supreme Court; a senior biomedical scientist at the Scripps Research Institute; president of a 125-year-old women's college; winner of the Fields Medal in Mathematics (often referred to as the "Nobel in math"); a White House correspondent; founder of a ewe's milk creamery; a pioneer in atomic-force microscopy; and author/producer of a multi-part Discovery Channel on the sea.

MAKING A DIFFERENCE STUDIES

Environmental Studies

Senior thesis research grant proposals are a distinctive feature of the program. Students must prepare a proposal to define goals, timetables, and support needed for their research. The program provides logistical support, laboratory and study space, and assistance in locating information, funding, and regional resources. Past theses have examined barrier islands, wetlands, hazard perception, water management, environmental aesthetics, ethics, education and history.

Environment and Behavior
Biogeography
Field Botany
Environmental Botany

Ecophilosophy, Environment & Public Policy
Urban Sociology
Environmental Law
Environmental Plant Ecology

- **Green Campus Seminar** Examines the green campus or campus ecology movement. What can we learn from the campus itself? How can we best integrate built systems with the fragmented campus environment? Features practicing land managers as guest lecturers to address wildlife habitat, stormwater, transportation and other issues.

Biology

Students tend to have an eye towards research in the bio-medical sciences, psychology-neuro sciences, ecology, bio-systems, environmental sciences, and careers in medicine and dentistry.

Environmental Biology
Animal Adaptations
Field Botany Laboratory
Vertebrate Neuroanatomy

Coral Reef Ecology
Human Genetics
Invertebrate Zoology
Neurobiology

Anthropology

Students and faculty cooperate in projects ranging from archaeological digs in Central America to planning for the homeless in Sarasota, to studies of the creolization process in black English.

Ethnography: Theory and Practice
History of Anthropological Theory
Cultural Anthropology

Language, Culture and Society
Universal Experience of Aging
Myth & Ritual: Anthro Approaches to Religion

- **Museology Internships** Provides an opportunity to work with museum collections, which include archaeological artifacts, historical artifacts and documents, fossils and zoological specimens. Combine curatorial work with research and analysis of collections.

- Faculty Bio: **Anthony Andrews** (B.A. Anthropology, Harvard, MA, Ph.D. U of Arizona) is a widely published Maya archaeologist and ethnohistorian who has done extensive field work in Mexico and Central America. He supervises studies in archaeology, cultural ecology and Latin American ethnography, ethnohistory and urban anthropology.

Public Policy   Russian Language and Literature   International Relations

Student Body: 6% state, 52% women, 48% men, 12% minority, 30% transfers
Faculty: 62% male, 38% female, 3% minority   • Actively seeking minority students
1994-95 Costs: Residents $5697   Non-residents $11,580   Apply by 5/1

• Individualized Majors   • Service-Learning Programs   • Predominantly Seminar Format
• Field Studies   • Tutorials • Vegetarian Meals

Use form in back to contact: Admissions
New College of USF
5700 N. Tamiami Trail   Sarasota, FL 34243-2197
(813) 359-4269

NORTHLAND COLLEGE

775 Students   Ashland, Wisconsin   Moderately Selective

The abundant natural beauty of the northern lakes and forest of Lake Superior country provide the perfect setting for a school like Northland. Twenty years ago the faculty and staff of this century-old college committed themselves to a new vision; a liberal arts/environmental college. Since then, the idea that our natural and social worlds and that the knowledge they support are inextricably connected, has flourished and matured at Northland. A premise of the Northland educational mission is that we must strive to free ourselves from the alienating and self-destructive assumption that human beings live in isolation from the natural environment. The essence of human existence is that we live in two worlds: the world we have created and the world that created us. We dwell simultaneously in the human realm of institutions, cultures, and ideas as well as in the life-giving realm of nature. As long as we separate these two realms, we can never feel completely at home, at peace with ourselves and our environment. In our quest for wholeness, we affirm our deepest humanistic values.

Northland is unique in that it does not restrict its study of the relationship between humanity and nature to a few courses in ecology or environmental studies. Almost a third of Northland's courses may be said to have some clear relevance to environmental issues. If the human and the natural are indeed as intimately interwoven as we believe, that relationship can be, and should be, analyzed and appreciated from all perspectives: scientific, political, anthropological, philosophical, literary artistic, and recreation. In short, a concern for the natural world around us is a theme that runs throughout Northland's curriculum and its co-curricular activities. Northland College and the Sigurd Olson Environmental Institute recently gained national recognition by receiving the Certificate of Environmental Achievement from Renew America in association with the National Environmental Awards Council.

As a liberal arts college, Northland strives to bring about the maximum intellectual, social, personal, and physical development of its students. In the long run, a liberal arts education is the most practical form of training. The world is quickly changing and tomorrow's problems cannot be anticipated. Success in the future will depend, therefore, on the ability to cope with the unknown, to acquire new skills as the needs arise, and to gather knowledge about factual situations that could hardly have been imagined a decade earlier. In short, there is a demand for people who not only know what is needed now, but who are prepared and eager to learn what will be required in the future. A technical, overly specialized training prepares for today; a liberal arts education prepares for tomorrow.

A small college, Northland fosters an atmosphere in which there is a distinctive concern for both the individual human being and the natural world. We offer a value-sensitive education focusing on the liberal arts as a vehicle for understanding the disciplines, techniques and knowledge needed to function effectively in the modern world. Northland focuses on the study of our interactions with the environment, ranging from aesthetic and spiritual values derived from the great Northwoods and Lake Superior, to complex social and scientific issues. There is also emphasis on the study of human behaviors and interaction through traditional majors and interdisciplinary programs in such areas as environmental studies, outdoor education, cross-cultural and global understanding, education and business.

Emphasis is placed on individual relationships with faculty, field experience, practicums, internships, independent study, exposure to other cultures and travel abroad as well as cooperative and experiential experiences. The faculty is commited on part of faculty members to including environmental subject matter or methodologies in their classes whenever appropriate. Several classes are team taught in a multidisciplinary approach. Northland's 4-4-1 calendar year offers many opportunities for travel to other countries.

Several environmental and social issue conscious groups are active on campus. The Sigurd Olson Environmental Institute is the environmental education outreach arm of the college. The Timber Wolf Alliance, and Loon Watch are among the sponsored programs. The Institute provides educational programs to increase public understanding of the Lake Superior Bio-region and environmental issues as well as in-service training in environmental education for teachers. A school wide recycling program and a pesticide policy was initiated at Northland four years ago. An environmental policy is in place, and an environmental energy audit is done once a year. The Environmental Council, a college-wide task force, is designed to serve as the vanguard of environmental consciousness on campus. Students are encouraged to be involved in public policy issues both on the campus and in the larger community.

Northland's commitment to environmental education is evidenced by the Natural Resources Technician program to recruit minorities for the U.S. Forest Service, the Wisconsin Dep't of Natural Resources and the Great Lakes Indian Fish & Wildlife Service; the training of regional school teachers for expanded emphasis on the environment in Wisconsin classrooms, and the Apostle Island School, a cooperative educational venture with elementary and middle schools.

Lake Superior, the Apostle Islands, Chequamegon National Forest and dozens of freshwater lakes offer a natural setting for field studies. Outdoor Education majors may spend a full semester at the Audubon Center of the North Woods. Academic adventures abroad provide in-depth exposure to international culture and environments. Examples include the study of rainforest ecology in Costa Rica, tropical lowland ecology of Mexico, the mammals of Kenya, and natural history and evolution in the Galapagos.

Work experience is highly valued at Northland. Students have worked as interns with the Fish and Wildlife Service, Department of Natural Resources, nature centers, U. S. Forest Service, National Park Service, Sigurd Olson Environmental Institute, businesses, as well as other organizations. Students have started a volunteer service organization on campus to work with groups in the Ashland area as well as a service-learning program.

At Northland, students participate in many outdoor activities and excursions, from sea kayaking and biking to backpacking and cross country skiing. Our outdoor orientation program for freshmen gives new students an opportunity to canoe,kayak, study native woodland skills, study wildlife on Stockton Island, or participate in small group outdoor experiences.

Northland College is unique in its curriculum, small classes and natural setting.

MAKING A DIFFERENCE STUDIES

Secondary Education Certification in Environmental Education (6- 12)

We also offer a Social Studies Teaching Major in Sociology/Native American studies.

Concepts of Biology
Environmental Public Policy
Sociology of the Environment
Ecology

Environmental Education Curriculum Review
Concepts of Earth Science
Environmental Law
Teaching Practicum

- **Environmental Citizenship** Holistic investigation of what it might mean to live at peace with the earth, including philosophies, alternative lifestyles, and management skills necessary for participating in a democracy.

Environmental Studies/Sociopolitical

Soils
Environmental Ethics
Public Administration
Applied Problem Solving
Native Peoples and Rainforests

Environmental History
Expository Writing
Internship
Economics of Citizenship
Global Resource Issues

Environmental Studies/Biophysical

Environmental Modeling
Land and Water Use Planning
Land Forms
Dendrology

Concepts of Biology
Populations
Remote Sensing
Pollution Biology

Outdoor Education/Native American Major; Native American Studies Minor

Program includes student support and community education which provides credit and non-credit courses, workshops, and technical assistance to residents of reservation communities.

Introduction to Ojibway Language
Native American History to 1890
North American Indian Cultures
Native American Song and Dance
Native American World Views

Native American Cultures of Wisconsin
Native American History 1890 to Present
American Indian Literature
Native American Arts and Crafts
American Indian Law

- **Ethnobiology** A study of native American beliefs and values in regard to the natural environment. Use of plants and animals to meet basic needs, i.e. food, shelter, clothing, medicines, etc. The course is oriented toward field work and projects incorporating the traditional lifestyle of Native American people.

Government/Environmental Policy

Environmental Public Policy
Land and Water Use Planning
Sociology of the Environment
Environmental Ethics

Seminar in Environmental Law
Environmental Citizenship
Microeconomics
Policy Analysis Techniques

- **Global Resource Issues** Analysis of growing human pressures on scarce resources and fragile ecosystems as a result of population increase and national and corporate policies with special view to the potential for human conflict generated by same: e.g. oil crisis, desertification, competition for minerals.

Natural Resources Technician Program Certificate (64 credits)

Training in resource mgm't. for members of historically underrepresented populations.

Native American Storytelling
Forest Harvesting and Products
Wildlife Biology

Silviculture
Fisheries and Limnology
Mgm't of Outdoor Recreation Resources

Outdoor Education: Tracks in Natural History; Special Populations; Outdoor Ed/Native American; Outdoor Writing; Adventure Education

Teaching Assistantships, Field Activities, Outdoor Education Practicums

Whitewater Canoeing
Orienteering
Group Process and Communication
Camp Counseling and Administration
Therapeutic Recreation Design
Basic Wilderness Skills

Rock Climbing
Introduction to Outdoor Education
Winter Exploration and Interpretation
Search and Rescue
Environmental Education Curriculum
Urban Ecology

Ecological Ecosystem Interpretation of Natural Science
Philosophy and Theory of Experiential Education

Conflict and Peacemaking

Major has four components: Peace Strategies, Values & Ethics, Skills, and Directed Studies

War, Peace and Global Issues
Environmental Citizenship
Theory and Practice of Nonviolence
Human Relations Workshop
Global Resource Issues
Social Change and Social Movements

Nuclear Age
Exploring Alternative Futures
Conflict Resolution
Sociology of the Third World
Group Process and Communication
Conflict and Peacemaking

Government/Social Welfare Policy

Economics of Labor
Social Problems
Nature of Inequality
Social Change & Movements
Microeconomics
Global Resource Issues

Conflict Resolution
Crime, Deviance and Criminal Justice
Sociology of the Community
Population
Issues in Political Thought
Introduction to Public Administration

Sociology

Cultural Ecology
Sociology of Community
Sociology of the Third World
Group Process & Communication
The Nature of Social Inequality

Human Conflict
Sociology of the Environment
Exploring Alternative Futures
Modern Japanese Social Thought
Social Change and Social Movements

Forestry A Dual Degree BS/BS 3/2 Program with Michigan Tech U.

Natural Resources Mgm't BS/MS 3/2 program with U. of Michigan

Education   **Government**

Student Body: 35% state, 51% women, 49% men, 8% Native American, 5% other minority,
Faculty: 15% Minority
1994-95 costs: $13,970   Apply By: May 1
• Study Abroad   • Weekend or Evening Classes   • Co-op Work Study
• Service-Learning programs   • Day Care   • Team Teaching   • Vegetarian Meals

Use form in back to contact: Director of Admissions
Northland College   Box 115   Ashland, WI 54806
(715) 682-1224

OBERLIN

2,669 Students   Oberlin, Ohio   Highly Selective

As long as there has been an Oberlin, Oberlinians have been changing the world. As an institution and as a community, Oberlin is characterized by a heady spirit of idealism. Do Oberlinians arrive with the conviction that a single person's efforts can have far-reaching effects, or does Oberlin instill this idealism in them? Most likely it is a combination of the two, one reinforcing the other. Whatever its source, the results of this idealism are dramatic. It impels Oberlinians to be open to new perspectives, to rethink their positions when necessary, to speak their minds, to strive to make the world a better place. This spirit of idealism, this sense of conviction, unites the many different individuals in the Oberlin community. Students, faculty members, and alumni believe they can change the world.

What unifies this diverse and often opinionated group of students into a community of scholars? First, they are all extraordinarily committed to academic achievement. Second, their vision and progressive thinking - that Oberlin spirit of idealism - allows them to seize every opportunity as a learning experience. They educate one another on important issues, and they work to solve problems on campus, in the community, and in the world. Their ongoing debate is evidence of their willingness to confront issues that society often chooses to ignore. Oberlin students put their idealism to work on a variety of issues. Reflecting Oberlin's traditional concern for the betterment of humanity, about 30% of Oberlin graduates work in the field of education. Alumni also stay close to important social causes.

Oberlin was the first coeducational college in the country. Three women graduated in 1841, becoming the first women in America to receive bachelor's degrees. The admission of women caused Oberlin to be the center of controversy over coeducation for years.

Oberlin's decision to admit blacks in 1835 was in exchange for financial backing by two wealthy abolitionists. As a result of this decision, by 1900 nearly half of all the black college graduates in the country - 128 to be exact - had graduated from Oberlin. To put it in even greater historical perspective, in 1835, the state of Ohio was debating whether to allow blacks to attend elementary and secondary schools, and Southern states were drafting even stricter slave codes.

Once set on this progressive course, Oberlin became a center for abolitionism. The progressive impulse that inspired Oberlin's commitment to minorities and social justice in the 19th century and in the 20th century spurred innovations in academic and campus life. Programs focusing on cultural diversity have been part of Oberlin's new-student orientations since the early 1980's, and training sessions on similar topics are offered periodically to employees. While Oberlin has never been a utopia, neither has it been willing to give up its quest for perfection. Oberlin moves ahead in our changing world by continually reclaiming its proud legacy of dedication to social justice and inspiring all Oberlinians to change the world for the better. In 1991 Oberlin began requiring students to take at least nine credit hours in courses that deal with cultural diversity in order to graduate. Faculty members also are incorporating materi-al on the environment, the experience of minorities and women, and other new areas into current courses, as well as developing new courses in these areas.

Freshman and sophomore colloquia are interdisciplinary, seminar style courses in which enrollment is limited to 10 first-year and five second-year students. This small size allows students to become familiar with the give-and-take nature of class discus-sions at the college level. Recent colloquia include "The Religious Thought of Mahatama Gandhi" "The Personal is Political: Representations of Activist Women in American History" "The Palestinian-Israeli Conflict" and "Explaining Social Power."

Students frequently work as research assistants for their professors. Biology stu-dents have assisted in research on the use of rock dust to remineralize soil and increase its fertility. Six students worked on a sociology survey investigating problems encountered by local low-income people.

Off-campus study is quite popular, and by graduation about half of each class has spent at least one semester studying away from Oberlin. Nearly two dozen programs are available in countries such as Ireland, England, France, China, Kenya, Liberia, Nigeria, Sierra Leone, Japan, Costa Rica, Spain, India, and Scotland. The Mystic Seaport program, a wilderness program, and an urban planning and historic preserva-tion program with Columbia university are among other options.

For members of the Oberlin Student Cooperative Association (OSCA), coopera-tive houses and dining rooms are as much a statement of political conviction as they are place to live and eat. OSCA operates four room-and-board co-ops, and three board-only co-ops on campus. One co-op is kosher, and one is vegetarian. OSCA, a business with a $1 million operating budget, is operated almost exclusively by stu-dents. Members emphasize the democratic nature of decision making in each co-op and in the organization as a whole. On the average, co-op members devote five hours per week to work in the co-op. Working together also saves students money: in 1991-1992 the board fee charged by co-ops was 35% less than that charged in College din-ing halls, and the fee for a double room was 16% less. Co-ops purchase food from local family farms which to quote a student "is more ecologically conscious, healthier, and indicative of a more beneficial social theory." Co-opers also send work crews every week to help in harvesting on the farms.

Oberlin has more than 100 extra-curricular organizations. some of the most popu-lar are the various community service, environmental, human rights, multi-cultural and Lesbian/Gay/Bi-sexual groups.

Oberlin's Experimental College is a student-run organization which sponsors courses (for limited academic credit) taught by members of the community - faculty, students, administrators, townspeople. Each year a very heterogeneous list of subjects is offered including crafts, special interests, community service, and academic subjects not found in the regular curriculum.

MAKING A DIFFERENCE STUDIES

Environmental Studies

Environment and Society
American Environmental History
Environmental Education Practicum
Environmental Economics
Organic Agriculture
Environment, Current Destitution, Future Generations and Moral Responsibility

American Environmental Policy
Ecology and the Environment
Energy Technology
Colloquium on Sustainable Agriculture
Conservation Biology

- **Oberlin and the Biosphere** A seminar that will examine food, energy, water and materials flows, and waste management on the Oberlin campus; what enters and what leaves the campus community. Attention will be given to mines, wells, forest, farms, feedlots, dumps, smokestacks, outfall pipes, and to alternative technologies, and practices. Students participate in a joint research project.

Black Studies

Practicum in Black Journalism
Education in the Black Community
African-American Drama
Pan-African Political Perspective
African-American Women's History

West African Dance Forms in Diaspora
Modern African Literature
Traditional African Cosmology
Cinema and Society: Racial Stereotyping
Langston Hughes and the Black Aesthetic

Women's Studies

The Challenge of Gender and Race
Experiences of Religious Women
Issues in Language and Sexuality
Gender, Race and Rhetoric of Science
The Emergence of Feminist Thought
Feminist Theory and Challenge of Third World Feminisms

Turning Points in Women's History
Nature and Statue of Women
Paid & Unpaid Work: Sexual Division of Labor
Power and Marginality: Women & Develop't
Women in the Transition from Socialism

Sociology

Community and Inequality
Urban Sociology
Gender Stratification
Race and Ethnic Relations
The City and Social Policy

Youth Subcultures, Movements & Politics
Revolution and Reform in Latin America
Sociology of the Black Community
State, Society & Social Change: Latin America
Social Change in Contemporary Societies

Religion

Issues in Medical Ethics
Themes in Christian Ethics
Christian Social and Political Thought
Zen Buddhism
Mysticism in the West
Christian Utopias and Communitarian Movements

Islamic Spirituality and Mysticism
History of African-American Relig. Experience
Religion and the Experience of Women
Taoism
Selected Topics in Early Judaism

History

Latinos in the U.S.
Roots of Feminist Analysis
Nourish or Punish? Ideologies of Poverty in 18th and 19th Century England
Caribbean History: Slaves and Slavery in the New World
Peasant Movements and the Agrarian Condition in Latin America

Race, Class and Gender in the Southwest
History of Vietnam

Economics

Poverty and Affluence
Labor Economics
Economic Development in Latin America
Economics of Discrimination

Public Sector Economics: Health Care Policy
Environmental Economics
Environmental & Resource Economics
Econ. of Land, Location & the Environment

• **Introduction to Political Economy**   Economic problems of unemployment, inflation, the distribution of income & wealth, and the allocation of resources. The basic tools of analysis for studying these problems are developed and the role of public policy in securing economic objectives is explored.

Politics

Political Change in America
Government and Politics of Africa
Public Policy in America
Emergence of Feminist Thought
Political Economy of Women in Late Industrializing States

Federal Courts and the Environment
Urban Politics
Third World Political Economics
Nuclear Weapons and Arms Control

Law & Society

Philosophy and Values
Christian Social & Political Thought
Economics, Ethics and Values
Equal Protection of the Law
Moral Problems in Relig. Perspective

Social & Political Philosophy
Deviance, Discord and Dismay
Reproductive Biology in the 80's
Individual Responsibility
Turning Points: American Women's History

Latin American Studies

Folklore and Culture of Latin America
Dirty Wars and Democracy
Hispanics in American Politics
Revolution and Reform in Latin Amer.
Latin American History: Conquest and Colonialization

Economic Development in Latin America
State, Society and Social Change
Int'l Political Economy / North-South Relations
Female and Male in Latin American History

Anthropology

Native American Literature
Immigration and Ethnicity in US
Immigration and Ethnicity in Israel
Ancient Civilizations of New World

Engendering the Past
Ideology, Power and Prehistory
Jewish Society and Culture in Middle East
Anthropology of Sub-Saharan Africa

Third World Studies

East Asian Studies

Student Body: 10% state, 56% women, 44 % men, 23% minority, 6% int'l
1994-95 costs: $24,570   Apply By 1/15
Editors note: Oberlin's viewbook and catalog were both printed on recycled
paper with a minimum of 10% post-consumer waste. Their viewbook was also
printed using environmentally safe, vegetable-based ink.

• Lacto-ovo Vegetarian Meals   • Internships   • Study Abroad   • Individualized Majors
• Recycling policies in effect

Use form in back to contact: Debra Chermonte
Director of Admissions
Oberlin College   Oberlin, OH 44074
(216) 775-8411
1 (800) 622-OBIE

OHIO WESLEYAN UNIVERSITY

1,800 Students   Delaware, Ohio   Very Selective

Ohio Wesleyan is a dynamic liberal arts university that seeks to prepare students for informed, ethical, productive and satisfying lives in the world community. The University strives to maintain an environment that both challenges and supports: that encourages individuals while it respects diverse opinion, that prizes excellence and applauds effort, that promotes personal growth and demands social responsibility, and that links today's learning with tomorrow's possibilities. The goal of Ohio Wesleyan is to prepare young men and women to know what they believe and why they believe it, where they stand and why they stand there. Says one OWU professor: "The purpose of college is to figure out who you are, and how you can merge your personal and career goals as a caring citizen."

"I have been deeply impresses with the quality of education that takes place at Ohio Wesleyan: This is teaching and learning at its best." says the University's new president, Dr. Thomas Courtice. "It is especially exciting to find this kind of academic excellence in an environment where students, faculty and staff all have a vested interest in contributing to the life of the college. Everyone at Ohio Wesleyan is eager to help address problems and develop solutions."

Since its founding in 1842, Ohio Wesleyan has been a leader in values-centered education, a place where public service and community leadership are the natural outcomes of an outstanding academic experience. At the core of the academic program are the professors: distinguished scholars, accomplished teachers, and dedicated mentors. They are accessible and approachable, and they have a profound impact on the lives of their students. Philosophy Professor Murchland states "Students worry a lot about jobs and how to make money. These are valid concerns. But a real problem in our society is not so much how to make money as how to spend it wisely. Values, decisions, freedom—that's what liberal education is all about."

The most distinctive aspect of an Ohio Wesleyan education is the way it links liberal arts learning with the civic arts of citizenship. The academic program and co-curricular life work together, fostering among students an awareness of their role as responsible citizens of society. Ohio Wesleyan's "National Colloquium" best embodies the college's commitment to citizenship education and value-centered learning. "NC," as the Colloquium is called, involves the entire community in a semester-long examination of an important public issue. Through seminars, guest lectures, exhibits, performances and related courses, NC students wrestle with the multiple public dimensions of complex social issues. Past NC topics include racism, life in the nuclear age, population and the environment, and ethics and public policy. For1994-95 NC will join the national health care debate, with the topic "Our Bodies, Our Selves: Perspectives on Health and Illness."

Ohio Wesleyan's unusually broad curriculum blends traditional classroom learning with hands-on experience through research, independent study, internships, and off-campus experience. The University's 22 academic departments and four interdepartmental programs offer a total of 65 majors; four combined-degree (3/2) programs;

and pre-professional programs in art therapy, dentistry, law medicine, music therapy, public administration and veterinary medicine. Students may also design their own majors. The Center for Economics and Business and the Arneson Institute for Practical Politics further enrich academic life with seminars, guest speakers and special events such as the quadrennial Mock Political Convention.

Involvement is the theme of co-curricular life. From student political groups and media operations to athletics and intramurals, from the Environment and Wildlife Club to Amnesty International, from "improv" theater and modern dance to social organizations and religious groups, the campus hums with activity.

Public service is an Ohio Wesleyan tradition. Once known as "the West Point of Missions" because of the number of alumni in missionary service overseas, the University today continues its commitment to volunteerism as a key component of undergraduate learning. Each year, nearly 90 percent of the student body participates in some form of community service. "Leadership for Tomorrow," a seven-week series of workshops, helps students develop and refine leadership skills in organizational and personal areas of their lives.

Through participation in Habitat for Humanity, or a mentoring program with area adolescents, or any of a huge variety of service projects, students try to "leave the woodpile a little higher than we found it." Most years, some students spend spring break working in health clinics in the Dominican Republic, learning about Third World poverty, neocolonial economics and health delivery systems. During the early years of the Peace Corps, Ohio Wesleyan sent more graduates per capita than any other college or university in the country. Recently Ohio Wesleyan was one of only 16 organizations in the country (and the only undergraduate liberal arts college) selected to host a Summer of Service project, the first step in the Clinton administration's National Service Program. Helping others and giving time and energy back to the community is very much a part of the OWU character.

Diversity characterizes the student body, too: 1,800 students from 45 states and 50 countries. Fully 15.5 percent of the students are either U.S. minorities or foreign students. This multicultural presence is a source of enrichment for all members of the community. OWU also participates in the Black Colleges Exchange with historically important, predominantly black Spelman College and Morehouse College in Georgia.

Cross cultural understanding is further enhanced in the residential area. Among our eight "small living units" are the House of Black Culture, the Women's House, International House, Peace and Justice House and the House of Spirituality.

However students choose to use their years at Ohio Wesleyan, they leave the college with heightened awareness of important world issues and a commitment to share with the world their skills, their insights, and their value-centered concern for others. Observes President Courtice, "Few other institutions so effectively combine quality, in their programs and people, with such a strong sense of community and commitment."

MAKING A DIFFERENCE STUDIES

Environmental Studies

Ecology and the Future of Man
Ornithology
Environmental Alteration
Economic Geography
The World's Cities
Animal Ecology

Plant Communities and Ecosystems
Environmental Chemistry
Biology and Tropical Nations
Energy Resources
Human Ecology
Marine Biology

- **Island Biology** Characteristics of islands, and analysis of why island organisms provide superior examples for the study of evolutionary, ecological, and behavioral phenomena. This course includes a required trip to the Galapagos Islands.

- Faculty Bio **Edward Burtt** Zoology Professor Jed Burtt's knowledge of birds is nearly matched by his commitment to recycling. Dr. Burtt and his family recently were named the most environmentally aware household in the county. He is an active environmentalist, a widely published zoologist, and a research ornithologist. He regularly attracts large enrollments in his ornithology class, inspiring science and non-science majors alike to attend pre-dawn bird-watching labs.

Botany - Microbiology

Bacterial Physiology
Medical Microbiology
Genetics
Cytogenetics
Molecular Biology of Viruses

Biodiversity of Flowering Plants
Biology of the Fungi
Cell and Molecular Biology
Plant Physiology
Immunology

- Faculty Bio **Gerald Goldstein** (Microbiology) Because so few colleges teach virology (the study of viruses) to undergraduates, and even fewer teach it with a lab, Jerry Goldstein decided to write his own laboratory manual. Today, his book is used not only at Ohio Wesleayan, but in graduate-level courses at many other universities. Top OWU students work with Goldstein on research studying herpes simplex, vaccinis and adenovirus. Students also assisted in his landmark work on plasmid DNA isolated from bacteria discovered in intestinal remains of an 11,000 year-old mastodon.

Politics and Government

Civil Rights and Liberties
Judicial Process and Policy-Making
International Politics
Foreign Policies-China, Japan and India
The American Presidency
Political Parties
Public Opinion and Political Behavior

Political Development and Modernization
American Constitutional Law
American and Soviet Foreign Policy
Congress and the Legislative Process
Public Administration
Equality and American Politics
American Political Thought

Psychology

Personality and Adjustment
Abnormal Behavior
Psychology of the Exceptional Child
Adolescent Psychology
Community Psychology

Social and Problem Drinking
Comparative Psychology
Organizational Behavior
Maturity and Age
Learning and Motivation

- **Child Psychology** The psychological and physiological development of the child from conception to 12 years. Effects of parents, school, and community practices on emotion, social and intellectual aspects of child behavior. Opportunities for direct observation of pre-school children.

Sociology/Anthropology

Social Problems
Race and Ethnicity
Peoples and Cultures of Japan and Asia
Health and Illness
The Family
Population Problems
Social Inequality

Peoples and Cultures of Africa
Peoples and Cultures of the Pacific
Science and Society
Gender in Cross-Cultural Perspective
Urban Society
Magic, Witchcraft and Religion
Cultural and Social Change

- Faculty Bio **Mary Howard** (Sociology/Anthropology and Women's Studies) Before joining the faculty in 1985, Dr. Howard spent 16 years as a counselor in the human services field. A scholar specializing in medical anthropology, her research has taken her into Amish communities, inner city shelters, and South African homes. For several years, she has coordinated OWU's Caribbean Seminar, which includes taking students to the Dominican Republic as volunteers in a health clinic for spring break.

Economics

National Income and Business Cycles
Comparative Urban Economics
Economic Development
Industrial Organization
Public Finance

Economic History
International Economics
Labor Economics and Problems
Organizational Theory
Business Ethics

Women's Studies

Feminist Literary Theory
Women in Literature
Women in American History
Psychology of Women
Women in Antiquity

History of Feminism
Labor Economics and Problems
Philosophy and Feminism
Human Sexuality
Equality and American Politics

- **Sociology of Feminism** The diverse range of contemporary feminist social theories will be covered, including: Liberal Feminism, Radical Feminism, Socialist Feminism, Third World Feminism, and Lesbian Feminism. Topics such as (under) paid and unpaid labor, rape and violence against women, sexuality, women in the arts, the women's self-help movement.

Urban Studies

A multidisciplinary program dealing with the character and evolution of complex urban systems, especially the city system of the USA. Introduces students to urban problem-solving, urban planning, and public policy formation.

Public Administration
Economic Geography
Contemporary Amer. Landscape Problems
Urban Society

Comparative Urban Economics
The World's Cities
Technology and Society
Judicial Process and Policy Making

- **Human Values & the Urban Process** An interdisciplinary orientation to the challenges of cities from a liberal arts perspective. Topics include urban structure, history, land use, planning, imageability, and future alternatives as they reflect human values.

Student Body: 49% men, 51% women, 8% students of color, 8% int'l students.
1994-95 costs: $22,382   Apply by 3/1
• Internships   • Study Abroad   • Individualized Majors   • Part-Time Degree Program

Use form in back to contact: Director of Admissions
Ohio Wesleyan University   Delaware, OH 43015
(800) 862-0612 (in Ohio)   (800) 922-8953 (outside Ohio)

PENN STATE UNIVERSITY

59,700 undergraduates at 17 campuses   Rural Central PA.   Very Selective

Penn State, founded in 1855, designated Pennsylvania's land-grant university in 1863, was irrevocably dedicated to a threefold mission of teaching, research and public service. In the years since, Penn State has prepared nearly 400,000 talented men and women to work for a better world.

Even though the idea of the land-grant university—higher education in service to the public good—dates to Abraham Lincoln's time, Penn State and its sister institutions across the nation are constantly finding new ways to make land-grant ideals relevant in a constantly changing world. At Penn State, this idealism, rooted in practicality and the wisdom of experience, remains a great attraction to today's students. More than 33,000 prospective freshmen seek admission annually, and the University receives more unsolicited SAT scores from prospective students than any other college or university east of California.

One reason for this popularity is that teaching has remained central to the University's mission. The University offers studies in about 160 baccalaureate fields, in addition to studies in 150 graduate fields.

Penn State's enrollment makes it one of America's 10 largest universities, but it was one of seventeen public institutions cited as attractive alternates to Ivy League schools for academic quality and ambience in Richard Moll's *Public Ivys*. For 1992-93, nine Penn State students received Fulbright awards, which was third-highest in the Big Ten and 15th nationally.

The quality of the 4,100 full-time faculty is quite high, as well, ranking 4th in the nation for winning prestigious Guggenheim fellowships (91-'92), and seventh in the number of faculty Fulbright awards. Twenty faculty are members of the National Academies of Sciences, Engineering or Medicine, and 47 serve on various committees of the academies. Faculty also edit or co-edit 130 scholarly and professional journals.

Within the larger University community, moreover, numerous programs address the specific interests and concerns of a diverse and questioning student body. The following is intended merely to sample some of the programs and courses available, and is by no means comprehensive.

The University Scholars Program offers unusually flexible and rigorous courses of study for students at all Penn State locations and in all majors. It is designed to challenge, enrich and broaden their general education, and to deepen their preparation for graduate study or a profession. The students say that they have all the benefits of a small, highly selective, private college, but still have the resources of a major research university.

The program's foundation includes a belief that those with special talents have special obligations to others. The scholars program offers seminars and workshops on topics of service and leadership, travel grants, and provides support for exemplary student-initiated projects that enhance various human communities and/or the moral ecology in general. In addition, the scholars may take advantage of summer and service/learning programs that carry academic credit. These activities offer experiences vice/learning programs that carry academic credit. These activities offer experiences in various cultures around the world to students who are, at the same time, making a real contribution to local communities. These experiences may be international work camps or specific needs, such as helping a Mexican village build a basketball court at a community center, or projects organized in consultation with Native American organizations.

Penn State students have been encouraged to think globally through the University's long history of international activities, beginning with a "Penn State-in-China" agricultural assistance program in 1911. It has sanctioned study abroad programs for students since 1908, and is committed to encouraging international cooperation and understanding through scholarship. Nearly 600 Penn State students enroll each year in some forty Education Abroad programs in Europe, the Middle East, Africa, Australia, Latin America, and Asia.

Beginning with the single Penn State-in-China program, the College of Agricultural Sciences is now involved in teaching and programs in such far-flung locations as Egypt, Kenya, Poland, Swaziland, and Ukraine.

Students also may enroll in INTAG, an interdisciplinary minor for undergraduates in international agriculture. They gain an awareness and appreciation for the interrelationships and interdependence of the nations of the world, find out what resources are available to solve international agricultural problems, study the impact of technology transfer across cultures, acquire skills in international development work, and broaden their understanding of agricultural issues at home and abroad.
Environmental education

Environmental education is integrated into a number of college offerings, but one of the most visible is the Shaver's Creek Environmental Center. Located in the 750-acre Stone Valley Recreation Area, Shaver's Creek offers environmental studies and an interpretation laboratory. The center promotes positive attitudes about the Earth; provides opportunities for experiential learning and research; and encourages individual and group development. It is the only center that holds both federal and state licenses to use birds of prey in its public education programs, and is one of the few raptor rehabilitation centers with both federal and state licenses.

One of every 50 engineers in the United States holds a bachelor's degree from Penn State. Engineering education, one of Penn State's traditional strengths, is also more diverse than one might assume. For instance, the Leonhard Center for Enhancement of Engineering Education aims to overhaul engineering education through improvement of the quality and relevancy of the undergraduate experience. The Engineering Coalition of Schools for Excellence in Education and Leadership, consisting of Penn State and six other engineering universities, aims to dramatically improve the effectiveness of undergraduate engineering education, and to significantly increase the number of women and underrepresented minority graduates of these institutions. Minority Engineering Program, recruits and works to retain underrepresented minority students. Women in Engineering Program aids in recruiting and retaining women in engineering programs at Penn State, and assists in creating a more positive environment for women students. Penn State is in the top ten Universities in graduating women engineers.

MAKING A DIFFERENCE STUDIES

Environmental Resource Management
Resource Systems Analysis
Ecotoxicology
Pollutant Impacts on Plants
Water Quality Chemistry
Pollutant Impacts on Animals

Legal Aspects of Resource Management
Case Studies in Ecosystem Management
Economic Impacts of Environmental Pollution
Pollutant Impacts on Aquatic Systems
Environmental Resource Mgm't Orientation

Fuel Science
Combustion Engineering
Chemistry of Fuels
Principles of Chemical Engineering
Elements of Mineral Processing
Fuel Science Laboratory
Mining and Our Environment

Energy and Fuels
Air Pollutants From Combustion Sources
Political Economy of Energy & Environment
Fuel Technology
Coal Preparation
Materials in Today's World

Civil Engineering
Water Pollution Control
River & Waterways Engineering
Solid Waste Management
Environmental Microbiology Lab
Industrial Hazardous & Residual Waste Management

Soils Engineering
Water Quality Management
Environmental Sanitation
Mgm't of Water Pollution Control Processes

Human Development & Family Studies
Communities and Families
Family Development
Infant and Child Development
Biocultural Studies of Family Organization
Policy and Administration
Personal and Interpersonal Skills

The Helping Relationship
Observation with Pre-School Children
Adolescent Development
Policy and Planning for Human Development
Developmental Transition to Adulthood
Adult-Child Relationships

Health Policy & Administration
Health Services Organization
Health Services Policy Issues
Health Systems Management
Principles of Public Health Administration
Field Experience in Health Planning

Intro to Environmental Health
Health Care & Medical Needs
Health Planning Methods
Population and Policy Issues
Comparative Health Systems

Community Studies
Community Systems
Social and Behavioral Change
Environment, Energy & Society
Environment-Behavior Systems
Issues in Community Physical Design
Power, Conflict and Community Decision Making

Youth and Societies
Housing Problems & Policies
Evaluation of Community Service Programs
Comparative Community Development
Planning of Community Social Services

Educational Theory and Policy
Education in American Society
Global Education
Education and Status of Women
Ethnic Minorities and Schools in U.S.
Intro to Philosophy of Education

Introduction to Comparative Education
Education in Socialist Societies
Education in Latin America and Caribbean
Anthropology of Education
Education in Africa

Labor and Industrial Relations

Industrial Relations

Practice of Collective Bargaining

History of the American Worker

Collective Bargaining Trends

History of American Organized Labor

Employment Relationship: Law and Policy

Women, Minorities and Employment

Labor-Management Relations

Occupational Health: Policy and Practice

Industrial Psychology

Sociology with track in Rural Sociology

Social Change in Rural America

Rural Community Services

Social Movements

Poverty Analysis: People & Programs

Wilderness, Technology & Society

Families in Rural Society

Race & Ethnic Relations

Intro to Community Information Systems

Energy & Modern Society

Gender, Occupations & Professions

Economics

Black American Economic Development

Public Finance

Environmental Economics

Economic Demography

Current Economic Issues

Labor Economics

Economics of Public Expenditures

Health Economics

Urban Economics

Economics of Discrimination

Public Service

Public Finance

Regional Economics

Urban Geography

Bureaucracy and Public Policy

Community Organization

Economics of Public Expenditures

Housing Problems and Policies

Planning and Public Policy

Public Management Technology

Urban Sociology

Medical Anthropology

Intro Biological Anthropology

Biomedical Anthropology

Intro to Health Services Organizations

Physiology

Biocultural Evolution

Physical Growth and Development

Evolution of Sexuality

Principles of Epidemiology

Principles of Public Health Administration

Cultural Anthropology

Architectural Engineering

Solar Energy Building System Design

Environmental Systems in Building

Solar Passive Design & Energy Conservation.

Soils Engineering

Advanced Heating, Ventilating and Air Conditioning

**Enviro Education Teacher Certificate   Landscape Architecture   Forestry
Agronomy   Outdoor Recreation & Environmental Interpretation
Agricultural Engineering   Wildlife & Fisheries Science   Health Education
Rehabilitation Services Education   Science, Technology & Society**

Student Body: 82% state, 44% women, 56% men, 9% minority
1994-95 costs: Residents $7862 Nonresidents $11,648   Rolling Admissions
• Field Studies   • Internships   • Study Abroad   • Individualized Majors

Use form in back to contact: Undergraduate Admissions Office
201 Shields Building   Penn State University   University Park, PA 16802-1294
(814) 865-5471

PITZER COLLEGE

750 Students   Claremont, California   Highly Selective

Founded in 1963, Pitzer is a coeducational liberal arts college with a progressive educational philosophy. Enrolling approximately 750 men and women, Pitzer College is part of a uniquely stimulating higher education environment consisting of five schools known collectively as the Claremont Colleges. Together, these colleges bring a vast range of courses and facilities to Pitzer students. Indeed, students on this campus may have the best of two worlds: enjoying, on the one hand, a level of resources usually associated with large universities and, on the other hand, the close student-faculty relationships found within small, human-scale colleges.

Pitzer College offers no short cuts to intellectual discovery, no guarantees as to the kind of person you'll be when you graduate. It does, however, offer a setting rich in possibilities, and if Pitzer graduates are more creative, more independent of spirit, and more willing to seek new answers, then it could be that the opportunities unique to Pitzer helped to make them this way. Because of Pitzer's strengths in the social and behavioral sciences we tend to attract a student body that concerns itself with the critical social and political issues facing our world. Most students arrive at Pitzer already committed to various social or political issues. Once at the college, they're encouraged to develop these interests to a greater degree; to take them further and test them harder. But mostly, the ideals that bring people to Pitzer continue to guide them after graduation. A Pitzer graduate who becomes a lawyer is as likely to use those skills in the public defender's office as in a corporate law firm. The graduate who goes on to earn an M.B.A. may opt not to work on Wall Street, choosing instead to help run a foundation raising money to fight a deadly disease.

Pitzer presents a unique opportunity for self-exploration and for exploration of the world around us and our involvement in that world. The College believes that students should take an active part in formulating their individualized plans of study, bringing a spirit of inquiry and adventure to the process of academic planning. Rather than enforcing traditional requirements, Pitzer provides the following guidelines to students and faculty advisors in order that students will fulfill the College's educational goals:

- Breadth of Knowledge - By exploring broadly the programs in humanities and fine arts, natural sciences and mathematics, social and behavioral sciences, students develop an understanding of the nature of the human experience - its complexity, its diversity of expression, its continuities and discontinuities over space and time, and those conditions which limit and liberate it.
- Understanding in Depth - Through the study of a particular subject matter in depth, students experience the kind of mastery which makes informed, independent judgment possible.
- Critical Thinking, Formal Analysis, and Effective Expression - Through juxtaposing and evaluating the ideas of others, and through participation in various styles of research, Pitzer students develop their capacities for critical judgment. Through exploration of mathematical and other formal systems, students acquire the ability to think in abstract, symbolic ways. Through written and oral communication, students acquire the ability to express their ideas effectively.

- Interdisciplinary Perspective - Through bringing together the perspectives of several disciplines, students gain an understanding of the powers and limits of each discipline and of the kind of contribution each can make to an exploration of the significant issues. Pitzer wants its students to learn the differences and the connections between different disciplines, as well as the ability to look at a situation from different perspectives.
- Intercultural Understanding - Through learning about their own culture and placing it in comparative perspective, students come both to appreciate other cultures and to recognize the ways that their own thinking and actions are influenced by the culture in which they live.
- Concern with the Social Consequences and Ethical Implications of Knowledge and Action - Through examining the social consequences and ethical implications of the issues they explore, students learn to evaluate the effects of individual actions and social policies and to take responsibility for making the world in which we live a better place.

Because of the emphasis on classroom teaching and a student faculty ratio of 10 to1, students and teachers are colleagues in the educational process; faculty do not draw a hierarchical distinction between themselves and the students. The average class size is 18 students and, to facilitate discussion, is often taught seminar - rather than lecture-style.

Pitzer has developed a variety of programs which offer opportunities to specially qualified groups of students as well as all students who participate in special courses, seminars, and programs beyond the regular course offerings. Among these are the New Resources program, designed for the special needs of the traditionally post-college-age students and PACE, designed to provide intensive English language training for international students.

Many students take advantage of Pitzer's interdisciplinary programs and courses in order to broaden their understanding of interpretations of the human experience. Interdisciplinary seminars include the New Resources Seminar: Exploring Uncommon Social Worlds, Pitzer and Energy Use (including an energy audit) and the Politics of Race. Students may take special programs and clusters in International/Intercultural Studies; Social Responsibility Studies; Critical Studies in Science and Technology; The Study of Education, and The Third World.

Internships are a popular way to apply theories to practical experience, and many Pitzer students have begun fulfilling careers through the internship program. Internships affirm Pitzer's commitment to connecting knowledge and action, and provide opportunities to link students to social issues in Los Angeles communities and thereby develop feelings of social responsibility. Independent study allows students to create a curriculum that meets their individual needs and goals. Through this program, students work individually with faculty to create a course and to work through the materials. External programs in over 150 locations throughout the U.S.A. and abroad have become a part of the curriculum for the majority of Pitzer students. With programs offered in New York, Spain, Costa Rica, Indonesia, Kenya, Cameroon, Fiji Nepal and Zimbabwe, Pitzer's External Studies program goes far beyond traditional programs. Students have opportunities for intensive language study, internships, independent research, and significant interaction with peoples of other cultures.

MAKING A DIFFERENCE STUDIES

Environmental Studies

Environmental Studies can provide an integrated, unifying perspective on life, as well as a program for radical change.

Conservation Ecology and Management
Environmental Ethics
Population and Society
Natural Resource Management
Water Policy: Concepts and Technology
Technology and People

Constructing Nature
Women & Natural Environment in US History
Ecological Anthropology
Studies in Land Restoration
Marine Ecology
Energy Economics and Policy

- **Consciousness, Environment & Self: Multicultural Perspectives** How perception of the natural environment, self and society result in different ways of knowing the world. The notion of "consciousness" will be explored as reflected in diverse spiritual, social, and political forms and practices. How stereotypical "western" and "eastern" perspectives differ, but also coalesce in the context of the global paradigm.

Freshman Seminars

Rites of Passage
The Lotus or the Robot

Nationalism & Ethnicity in the New Europe

The 1992 Presidential Elections in Historical Context: 1992=1932? Germany or U.S.A.?

American Studies

Native American Voices
Cars and Culture
Politics of Ecology
African American History
Political Corruption
Women at Work

Native Americans and Their Environments
Chicano Literature
Politics of Water
Slavery and Freedom in the New World
Social Responsibility and Corporations
Urban Ethnic Movements

Asian Studies

Women and Religion in Asia
Introduction to Nepal
Chinese Revolution
Eastern Religious Traditions

Advanced Topics in Himalayan Studies
Asian Traditions
The Vietnam War
Cults: Wisdom of East in West

Tradition and Experience in Hinduism and Buddhism

Black Studies

Black American Literature
Black Feminist Criticism
Slavery & Black and Female in USA
African and Caribbean Literature

Black USA Women Fiction Writers
Politics of Race
Blacks in American Politics
History of Africa

Industrialization and Social Change in Southern Africa

Chicano Studies

Chicano Literature
U.S. Immigration Policy
Latina Feminist Traditions
Chicanos in the American Southwest
Chicano Ethnic Movements

Regional Dances of Mexico
Latino Politics in the 90's
Contemporary Chicano Narrative
Educational Psychology of the Chicano
Latinos and Politics of Religion

Science, Technology and Society
Ethical Issues in Science and Engineering
Environment and Resource Economics
Politics of Ecology
Chemicals in the Environment
Confrontations and Encounters: Nature and Western Society

Science in the Ancient World
Discovery, Innovation and Risk: Energy
Gender and Science
"Race" & Social Stratification in the Americas

Film and Video Studies
Film and video as media for creativity, expression, social responsibility and multicultural understanding. Production courses stress independent fiction and documentary film/video. Links art, anthropology, sociology, political studies, world literature, and women's studies.
Ethnographic Images
Sociology of Communication
Modern Polish Literature & Film
Vietnam: Myths & Realities

Media and Politics in the Third World
Modern Cuban Literature & Film
Third World Cinema
Film Studies: Gender and Sexuality

Video History/Theory & Criticism: Race, Class, Gender & Sex in TV, Independent Video

Gender and Feminist Studies
Focuses on the relations of power which have produced gender inequality, analyzing it as a human construction subject to change, rather than an innate, ordained condition. Challenges conventional concepts and analysis and encourages formulation of new paradigms of teaching, learning, and research that reflect heterogeneity of women's experience.
Politics of Gender: Humanities
Women and Nature
Women in the Third World
Women and Language
Visions of the Divine Feminine

Politics of Gender: Science and Technology
Women and Education
Women and Development
Women's Work in Early Modern Society
Violence in Intimate Relations

Organizational Studies
Politics and Public Administration
Economy and Society
Women at Work
Public Choice
Social Responsibility and the Corporation

Technology and People
Sociology of Health and Medicine
Power and Participation in America
Negotiating Conflict
Resource Policy Analysis

Political Economy
Race, Class and Power
Water Policy
International Political Economy
Practice of Democracy
Urban Politics
Social Indicators and Public Policy

Agricultural Development in the Third World
State and Development in Third World
Third World in Global Economy
Political Psychology
American Indian Policy
Environmental Ethics

Chemical Dependencies: Policy Issues and Perspectives

Student Body: 43% state, 52% women, 48% men, 38% minority, 7% int'l.
Faculty: 55% Male, 45% Female, 22% Minority
1994-95 Costs: $25,135   Apply By: 2/1   Average students in first year classroom: 15
Full recycling and energy conservation programs in effect since founding of college in 1963
• Study Abroad   • Exclusive Seminar Format   • Individualized Majors
• Team Teaching   • Core/Multidisciplinary Classes   • Vegetarian Meals

Use form in back to contact: Office of Admission
Pitzer College   Claremont, CA 91711
(909) 621-8129

PRESCOTT COLLEGE

800 Students   Prescott, Arizona   Moderately Selective

It is the mission of Prescott College to educate students of diverse ages and backgrounds to understand, thrive in, and enhance our world community and environment. Reality and intelligence are culturally relative. Prescott College does not hold any one world view to be correct or absolute and strives not to use one culture's criteria to judge another. Prescott therefore accepts the values of human wisdom embodied in all world views and in all languages.

Prescott College regards learning as a continuing process and strive to provide an education that will enable students to live productive lives while achieving a balance between self-fulfillment and service to others. Students are encouraged to think critically with a sensitivity to the human community and the ethics of the biosphere.

A liberal arts college with a very strong environmental component, the broad academic program utilizes classroom work, independent studies, library research, and field studies. Students are expected to demonstrate competence in individually designed study programs and possess two breadths of knowledge beyond their major areas of study. Prescott's educational philosophy stresses experiential learning and self-direction within an interdisciplinary curriculum. Programs integrate philosophy, theory, and practice so that students synthesize knowledge and skills to confront important value issues and make personal commitments.

In addition, the College expects its graduates to demonstrate integration of the practical and theoretical aspects of human existence; integration of the spiritual, emotional and intellectual aspects of the human personality; sensitivity to and understanding of one's own and other cultures; commitment to responsible participation in the natural environment and human community. To this end, the College offers programs in the areas of Human Development, Environmental Studies, Outdoor Education and Leadership, Cultural and Regional Studies, and Humanities.

Prescott College's programs and process are individualized in ways that reward the student personally and intellectually. Since learning takes place in different ways for different people, education at the College is often self-directed. Prescott College wants its students to be problem solvers by the time they graduate; therefore, students are introduced to real, often original problems with all their accompanying complexity and frustration. The College also wants its students to know how to adapt in a changing world.

Beginning with a 21 day Wilderness Orientation in areas such as the Grand Canyon and central Arizona, students are introduced to a variety of physical, social and cultural conditions in which they learn the process of adaptation. Upon their return they are assigned an advisor. The relationship with the advisor becomes an integral part of the educational process in which learning is achieved through personal exchange, sharing, and commitment.

The first year is a period of foundation building. Beginning students usually participate in introductory classes or structured field projects, working closely with faculty members and advisors. Small classes promote participation and allow for flexibility to meet individual interests and needs.

As students demonstrate their ability to assume increased responsibilities, they pursue a broader range of learning experiences, emphasis is placed on internships, independent studies and other off-campus projects. Students may work with faculty in apprentice relationships, often serving as assistant teachers, co-researchers and expedition leaders.

Many of the courses at Prescott College have strong field components, and some are conducted entirely in the field. Apprenticeships and internships are encouraged. Students may live and study in cultural contexts outside their normal experience. Three one-month blocks allow for intense immersion in one course, generally entirely in the field, whether it be the back country of Baja California, the alpine meadows of Wyoming, or a local social service clinic.

What forms of education help us become impassioned learners, sensitive listeners, practical idealists, entrepreneurial leaders - all the character traits that yield successful lives and successful societies? Here are a few:

- Small classes that students participate in designing, in which teachers continually challenge students to articulate their beliefs in speech and writing.
- Independent studies and projects working with a supportive advisor to plan, accomplish, and evaluate a significant endeavor
- An interdisciplinary approach to learning where students are challenged to construct complex understandings of real life situations, rather than simplistic, monolithic, rote understandings
- Experiential, adventurous learning in the real world in which students also learn responsibility, appropriate risk-taking, group leadership, and collaborative skills.

Examples of independent studies completed by Prescott students include: Ethnographic Field Study in Mexico; Deep Ecology Through Literature Native Alaskan Cultural Studies; Multicultural Education; and Developing Sustainable Communities. Internships by students have included work with Woodswomen in Minnesota doing logistics training; working with the Arizona Nature Conservancy performing restoration ecology and conservation; working with the Caribbean Conservation Corps in Costa Rica; and doing mountain search and rescue in Denali National Park, Alaska.

Educators have long believed that understanding is best achieved by relating ideas to the environment at hand. Prescott College utilizes the southwestern U.S., Mexico and Latin America as a living classroom. The proximity to the Mexican border provides access to the crucial interactions between First and Third World politics, economics, and environmental and social issues. Prescott College also owns a residence and property in Bahia Kino a coastal fishing village in Kino Bay, Mexico which sits on the edge of one of the world's richest marine environments and one of its most biologically diverse deserts.

In October of 1988, Prescott College established the Center for Indian Bilingual Teacher Education (CIBTE) to deliver the Adult Degree Program to teacher aides with two years of college and who are living on the Indian Nations throughout the Southwest.

MAKING A DIFFERENCE STUDIES

Environmental Studies   Tracks in Environmental Education and Interpretation, Natural History, Human Ecology and Environmental Conservation

Conservation in America	Conservation Biology
Environmental Ethics	Coastal Ecology of the Gulf of California
Population, Resources & Pollution	Consequences of Technological Change
Earth Ethics	Colorado Plateau: Nat. Hist.& Conservation
Wetland Ecology and Management	Weather and Climate

- **Natural History of the Southwest** An introduction to the diversity of the Southwest. Includes weekly field trips of one-half to three days. Principles of communities and ecosystems, geographical ecology, adaptation, and behavior. How landscape and climate interact to produce major patterns of vegetation in Arizona, and how animals respond to these patterns. Identify dominant woody plants typical of formations ranging from Sonoran Desert scrub to montane evergreen forests. Animal distribution and adaptation through indicator species of each formation studied

- Faculty Bio **Mark Riegner** (B.S. Environmental Studies, SUNY Brockport, Ph.D. Ecology and Evolution SUNY Stony Brook) Prior to teaching at Prescott, Mark taught ecology and related courses at Emerson College, a small interdisciplinary college in England whose students originate from over twenty countries. He has taught biological and field-oriented courses at alternative high schools in both England and the US. "By approaching nature with an open-minded attitude and by learning to recognize and formulate our own individual questions, we begin to develop the necessary tools to guide us through life."

Outdoor Action

Experiential Education, Theory & Practice	Kayaking, Basic Whitewater
Cave Ecology and Exploration	Basic Rock climbing
Outdoor Program Administration	Wilderness Leadership
Wilderness Emergency Care	Avalanche Forecasting & Backcountry Skiing
Aboriginal Living Skills	Outdoor Education and Recreation

Cultural and Regional Studies

By studying the delicate interaction of human needs, cultural traditions, economic, political and social forces, and diverse fragile environments, students in this program have the opportunity to investigate complex regions in depth from an interdisciplinary outlook. Areas of concentration of recent graduates include Natural History of the Southwest, Cross-Cultural Education, and Arid Lands Documentation

American Indian Spirituality	Cultural Perspectives on Ecological Design
Environmental Economics	Solar Energy Principles and Systems
Community Planning	Principles of Organic Agriculture
Energy Conservation: Issues & Techniques	Nature of Environmentalism & Social Activism
European Environmental Movements and Green Politics in Germany	

- **Community and Regional Planning for a Sustainable Society**   Problems and prospects for, ecologically sustainable development in both theory and practice. History and present global status of the concepts of ecological sustainablilty and sustainable development. Practice will entail learning current concepts (e.g. bioregionalism or watershed management) and methods (e.g. land suitability) of community and regional land-use in both urban and rural developments. Development of theoretical knowledge and general planning skills necessary to assist people in rural regions.

Humanities

In the context of our increasingly interconnected planet, one of the great challenges of today is to find a way to touch that depth or shared innermost core of the person, while at the same time celebrating our unique differences. In today's world, with its potential for both global unity and annihilation, an active participation in the Humanities and the wisdom they impart is of great value. In the history of civilizations we focus on new social perspectives and religious studies with an emphasis on global spirituality.

Roots of Civilization: The 20th Century
Contemporary Social Problems
Theater, Politics, and Social Change
Literature of the Grand Canyon
Philosophy: Themes and Questions
Lifestyle Choices: Economic Values and the Environment
Third World Development: Theory & Practice
Contemporary Photographic Perspectives
Changing World Order
History and Philosophy of Science
New Religious Paradigms

Human Development: Tracks in Counseling, Psychology, and Human Development

This program believes in human potential and service. The courses offered are dynamic and participatory, emphasizing the development of a deeper understanding of ourselves within a rapidly changing world context. This includes the exploration of personal history and process, contemporary and traditional theories of human development, and more advanced application and practice. We emphasize the development of the collective self, in which "self" has both a cultural and global context. We offer the opportunity to learn the fundamentals of traditional psychology, develop counseling skills, study and practice evolutionary processes, and explore beyond traditional conceptions of human development.

Family Systems
Addiction and Co-dependency
Ecofeminism
Nature of Human Consciousness
Stress Management
Educational Psychology
Psychology for Social Change
Interpersonal Communication
Taoist Studies - Chi Kung in Nature
Group Processes for Wilderness Leaders
Therapeutic Use of Wilderness Experience
Theory and Practice of Bodywork
Women's Lives: A Cross-Cultural View
Men's Studies

- Faculty Bio **Wayne Regina** (B.A. Psychology, SUNY Stony Brook, M.A. Marriage and Family Therapy, US Int'l University, Psy.D. Psychology, USIU) Wayne taught and administered at US International University for ten years, as well as designed curriculum and supervised graduate student training. His specialties include applying systems theory to family and social systems; life stage development and transitions; and integrating psychology, systems, and spirituality. He is a licensed psychologist with over ten years experience in treating individuals and families in transition.

Adult Degree Program

This program enables working adults to complete the last two years of their B.A. degree in their own communities on their own schedules. The Adult Degree Program has an office at the main campus in Prescott and one in Tucson, serving students in southern Arizona.

Student Body: 10% state, 40% women, 60% men, 75% transfers, 5% minority
1994-95 Tuition $9,800   No housing   Apply By: 2/1, 9/1
• Adult Degree Program (602-776-7116) • Mentored Studies • Individualized Majors • M.A. Program

Use form in back to contact: RDP Admissions Office
Prescott College   220 Grove Ave.   Prescott, AZ 86301
(602) 776-5180

ROCHESTER INSTITUTE OF TECHNOLOGY

ENVIRONMENTAL MANAGEMENT PROGRAM

10,584 Undergraduates   100 Enviro Mgm't   Rochester, NY.   Moderately Selective

Rochester Institute of Technology's Environmental Management program is for students who want to tackle environmental programs head-on -- students who want to be part of "the solution." At RIT, Environmental Management students prepare for careers where they can directly protect the environment by conserving resources and preventing pollution.

RIT is the leader in preparing versatile environmental managers for a wide variety of environmental projects and programs. Environmental managers are leaders in their organizations, participating in top-level production and design decisions - decisions that affect the way natural and material resources are used.

RIT's Bachelor of Science in Environmental Management is the first comprehensive undergraduate program in the country to prepare professional environmental managers. Additionally, three certificate programs that parallel the BS concentration are available - one in a distance learning format. The interdisciplinary five-year program and its curriculum were developed with faculty from RIT and a board of expert advisors that included environmental professional from government and industry.

As part of a truly interdisciplinary program, RIT's core courses are taught by a faculty of successful environmental professionals. Rather than focusing upon their individual areas of expertise, say hydrology or engineering, RIT's faculty educate students about environmental management from the perspective of their respective disciplines. Students develop in-depth knowledge of environmental science and technology, skills in environmental finance and accounting, environmental policy and law, project management, and communication. Graduates will contend with such issues as reducing corporate waste, incorporating recycling strategies and technologies, and communicating environmental responsibility within the company and to the public.

In the field of environmental management, hands-on training is essential. Through cooperative education, students integrate their classroom study with practical work experience by alternating periods of study with periods of actually working in industry, government, environmental consulting and waste management.

RIT students have applied their studies to coop positions at Eastman Kodak, Bausch & Lomb Corporation, N.Y. State Commission on the Environment, Lawrence Livermore Laboratories, Waste Management of N.Y., High Acres Landfill and Recycling Center, and the Monroe County Division of Environmental Services.

Graduates can expect employment in both public and private sectors. Positions in the public sector would include "environmental planner," and "recycling coordinator" at the local level and "solid waste management technical specialist" at the state level. In industry, positions include "environmental manager," "compliance coordinator," and "waste reduction specialist." In the consulting field, graduates serve both government and industry by providing expertise in developing waste management plans, conducting environmental audits and complying with environmental regulations. Starting salaries for graduates are estimated in the 30's.

MAKING A DIFFERENCE STUDIES

Environmental Management
Principles of Environmental Management
Land Disposal and Treatment
Energy Recovery
Environmental Geology/Lab
Introduction to Public Relations
Writing for the Organization

Environmental Health and Safety
Special and Hazardous Waste
Introduction to Hydrology/Lab
Environmental Regulatory Law 1 & ll
Business, Public Policy and the Environment

- **Environmental Monitoring and Measurement** An in-depth view of environmental monitoring and measurement, giving the student the knowledge to plan, execute and interpret a sampling project. Also covered: techniques for sampling air, soil, surface water and groundwater with an emphasis on landfill construction and monitoring. Students will learn to plan sampling events, determine the number and type of samples needed, collect quality assurance/quality control samples, determine correct sampling techniques, and document sampling.

- **Recycling** A survey of recycling technology and its relationship to the general problem of municipal solid waste management. Explores both the mechanics and the economics of the problem. Topics include the separation and collection of recyclable materials, recycling as a manufacturing process, the development of markets, and public education issues.

- **Waste Reduction** A study of the techniques and strategies being developed and used to reduce the generation of waste in both public and private sectors. Examines methods of reducing waste toxicity and quantity, and of increasing the recyclability of waste materials.

- Faculty Bio: **John Morelli** (B.S. Syracuse University - Environmental Engineering and Public Affairs, M.S. SUNY College of Environmental Science and Forestry - Environmental Resource Engineering.) Mr. Morelli is department chair for Environmental Management at RIT. He is a former senior project manager with the New York State Energy Research and Development Authority. He is also a professional engineer licensed in New York State and has extensive experience in hazardous waste site clean-up.

Environmental Mgm't Student Body: 80% state, 50% women, 50% men
1993-94 Tuition $13,266   Apply By: 2/1

• Coop Study   • Day, Evening and Distance Learning   • Field Studies
• Deaf Student Support

Use form in back to contact: John Morelli, Chair
Department of Environmental Management
Rochester Institute of Technology
George Eastman Building, 31 Lomb Memorial Drive
Rochester, NY 14623-5603
(716) 475-7213
E-mail: JXMCTP@rit.edu

RUDOLF STEINER COLLEGE

250 Students   Fair Oaks, California   Non-Competitive

Rudolf Steiner College strives to provide a creative educational environment for men and women of diverse ages and backgrounds who seek a deeper understanding of the challenges of modern life and wish to develop new capacities as a basis for their life's work, for social service and cultural renewal.

Founded on the spiritual scientific work of Rudolf Steiner, the College has as its mission to provide programs that:

- awaken independent thinking and healthy judgment about the deepest issues of human life
- school powers of perception'
- cultivate and enrich artistic faculties
- strengthen capacities for practical life

The view of the human being as an individuality encompassing body, soul, and spirit is central to the programs of the College, along with emphasis on the cultivation of the inner life as a source of strength, creativity, and initiative. Programs strive to address the students' quest for the knowledge, insight, and moral imagination needed to bring balance and healing to human beings, communities, and the earth itself.

Rudolf Steiner College offers upper division and graduate level courses. Most students are between the ages of 22 and 45 with a few younger and a few older. Most have already earned at least one academic degree. The cosmopolitan community is comprised of students and faculty from many different countries. They have explored some of the world through travel, study, work and many are also raising families. They come seeking to make a difference in the following ways:

Self-Development Through the Arts -- Students seek to make a difference for the world through cultivating the imagination, insight and initiative required for addressing modern problems. The arts are studied as a basis for sensitivity, deepen perception, social awareness and balance of soul.

Waldorf Education -- Making a difference for the next generations. Waldorf education (K-12 curriculum) seeks to cultivate balanced human beings by educating, head, heart and hand in harmonious interplay. People preparing to teach in Waldorf schools study human development based on the assumption that a human being is a spiritual being, curriculum appropriate to different age levels, and several arts. Waldorf education is the fastest growing independent education movement world wide. Upon graduation, teacher placement is 100%, with most getting multiple job offers.

Bio-Dynamic Gardening and Goethean Studies -- Students seek to make a difference for the earth itself. Bio-dynamic gardening seeks to work with rather than against life forces in the growing of plants. Goethean Studies, initiated by scientist/artist Johan von Goethe, cultivates the powers of observation by bringing together outer and inner experiences.

Those who have successfully completed at least two years of general education courses, may enroll in Rudolf Steiner College programs leading to a B.A. in Anthroposophical Studies or Waldorf Education.

MAKING A DIFFERENCE STUDIES

Foundation Year
Foundation Year speaks directly to the quest for deeper understanding of the human being, to a yearning for self-knowledge and higher wisdom of the world. It is a year of studies designed to introduce and explore the insights and endeavors of Rudolf Steiner, as well as a year of cultural enrichment and personal growth. Because the arts kindle imagination and inner growth, artistic coursework forms a significant part of the Foundation Year and all College programs. Evolution of consciousness in history, art and music. Personal biography and life cycles.

Introduction to Waldorf Education
Spiritual Streams in American Literature
Evolution of Consciousness through Art
Movement and Spatial Dynamics
Karma and Reincarnation

Eurythmy (Movement)
Choral Singing
Parsifal: The Quest for the Holy Grail
World Evolution and Spiritual Development
Philosophy of Freedom

- **The Festivals**   The four seasonal Christian festivals (Michaelmas, Christmas, Easter and St. Johnstide) and the Celtic festivals in between: their significance in history and current times. Enriching the experience of the individual and community through drama, music, eurythmy, pageants, and creating a suitable environment. Study and practical experience in festival preparation.

Waldorf Teacher Education Programs
B.A. programs for Early Childhood, Elementary and High School. Weekend / Summer Extension for San Francisco Bay area (3 years part-time), 4 year part-time summer option for current teachers. In the Waldorf kindergarten, the magic and wonder of childhood are protected through an approach that nurtures the young child's healthy development. In 1st - 8th grade, subjects from fairy tales to physiology, music to mathematics, are presented in a living, imaginative way.

Gardening for Kindergarten Teachers
Instrumental Music for Kindergarten
Practical Aspects of Teaching
Teaching Science in the Elementary Grades
Adolescence and High School Teaching
Movement and Games for Class Teachers

Storytelling and Puppetry for the Young Child
Learning and Development of the Young Child
Inner Work of the Waldorf Teacher
Teaching of Geography
Working With Colleagues in a Waldorf School
Child Dev. & Its Relation to Teaching Methods

Arts Program
Integrated studies of visual and performing arts. Eurythmy: an art of movement to speech and music. Speech, singing, new musical instruments. Watercolor painting: veil and wet-method .

Biodynamic Studies
Soil preparation. composting. Bio-dynamic preparations and sprays. Crop rotation. Earthly and cosmic forces in plant growth. Pest management, seed saving.

Goethean Studies
Goethe's theory of knowledge as a path to deepened perception and higher cognition. Botany, color study, meteorology, comparative morphology and study of sacred geometry, Gaia/Sophia and the alchemy of the soul. Exploration of science through various artistic media.

Student Body: 20% international   Faculty: 80% female, 20% male
1994-95 Tuition: $6,600   No housing   Rolling applications
• Part-time, Weekend, and Summer Study   • Vegetarian Lunch Program

Use form in back to contact: Admissions Counselor
Rudolf Steiner College   9200 Fair Oaks Blvd.   Fair Oaks, CA 95628
(916) 961-8727

RUTGERS STATE UNIVERSITY OF NEW JERSEY
COOK COLLEGE

2,800 Undergraduate Students   New Brunswick, N.J.   Moderately Selective

Human impacts on the earth's ecosystems are profound and far-reaching. Cook College is committed to educate students to understand and sustain the integrity of this ecosystem as both specialists within their fields of concentrations and as well-informed citizens. The educational programs of study offered by Cook College apply the natural and social sciences to this dynamic system. The curriculum is designed to achieve the following goals:

• To understand and appreciate the interaction between the natural and social sciences as they relate to the earth's ecosystem, students should master the basic knowledge and approaches of a field of concentration related to the environment, natural resources, food, or agriculture and be introduced to multidisciplinary perspectives that will locate their field and its contributions in this larger context.

• To become autonomous, versatile, and productive people who understand that they are inextricably related to the natural world and other people, students should learn to evaluate issues critically. Mastery of both quantitative and qualitative modes of inquiry develops the ability to deal with the complexity and dynamism of real world issues.

• To understand and appreciate the human impacts on the earth's ecosystem, students will develop an historical, global and multicultural consciousness in order to expand their bases for decision-making.

• To sustain the integrity of our ecosystem, students should develop the ethical sensitivity and the analytical skills to address questions of social responsibility, environmental ethics, moral choices, and social equity.

The objectives in the curriculum design include

• The ability to think critically, to address problems with a variety of mode of inquiry, as well as to recognize and assess ethical problems related to their field, in order to make decisions based upon an understanding of the long- and short-term implications of the various choices. 5 credits course in ethical analysis is required.

• Understanding and evaluating contemporary issues related to science.

• Developing an understanding of the diversity and variability of cultures, individuals and institutions. Students also should understand the complex and changing interplays of biological, cultural, situational and institutional factors as determinants of human behavior. Students must take 6 credits of courses in human diversity.

• Developing an understanding of political and economic systems,students should understand how public policy is implemented and how political and economic systems allocate scarce resources among competing uses.

• Through experience-based education, in the forms of Co-op Education, practica, internships, developing in all students the ability to apply classroom-based learning in applied settings. This offers students the opportunity to develop higher-order thinking skills and to demonstrate a wide range of competencies in their personal, education and professional development.

MAKING A DIFFERENCE STUDIES

College Mission Courses
Elements of Environmental Pollution
Conservation Ecology
Energy and Society
Economic Growth, Man & the Environment

Environmental Issues in the U.S.
Social Responses to Environmental Problems
Systems Thinking and Systems Approach
Human Response to Chem's in Environment

Environmental Planning & Design
Environmental Management
Legal Aspects of Conservation
Land Planning and Utilization
Social Aspects of Environmental Design

Environmental Law
Rural Communities
Legal Foundations of Urban Planning
Planning & Administration

Bioenvironmental Engineering (5 year program)
Elements of Environmental Pollution
Solid Waste Mgm't and Treatment
Conservation Ecology
Land and Water Resources Engineering
Conservation of Natural Resources

Principles of Applied Ecology
Water Resources-Water Quality
Energy Tech and Its Environmental Impact
Environmental Statement & Impact
Land & Water Resources Engineering

International Environmental Studies
Research Methods in Human Ecology
Population, Resources and Environment
Rural Communities
Environmental Teacher Education
International Environmental Policy

Environment & Development
Economics of World Food Problems
Social & Ecol. Aspects of Health & Disease
Rural Development
Economics of Peasant Agriculture

Pollution & Treatment Sciences
Solid Waste Management and Treatment
Soils and Water
Principles of Air Pollution Control
Radioactivity & the Environment

Environmental Pollution in Int'l Perspective
Problems of Polluted Aquatic Environments
Hazardous Wastes
Water Resources-Water Quality

Public Health
Biology and Biomedical Issues
Social Public Policy
Enviro and Public Health/Epidemiology
Health Ethics

Elements of Environmental Pollution
Health Services Policy
Public Health Economics
Financial Aspects of Urban Health

Social Strategies for Environmental Protection Certificate
Behavior & Environmental Quality
Politics of Environmental Issues
Energy Resource Management
Social Action Strategies and Techniques

Environmental Management
Environmental Ideology & Media
Municipal Implementation/Planning Programs
Environmental Sociology

Integrated Pest Mgm't Systems   Forest Resource Management
Fishery Science   Wildlife Science   Water Resources
Environmental Health Science   Environmental Journalism & Mass Media

Student Body: 90% state, 55% men, 45% women, 20% minority
1993-94 costs: Residents Tuition & Fees $9,197   Nonresidents $13,140   Apply By 1/15

Use form in back to contact: Undergraduate Admissions
Rutgers State, Cook College   New Brunswick, NJ 08903
(908) 932-8787

SAINT OLAF

2,993 Students   Northfield, Minnesota   Very Selective

St. Olaf provides an education committed to the liberal arts, rooted in the Christian Gospel, and incorporating a global perspective. In the conviction that life is more than a livelihood, a St. Olaf education focuses on what is ultimately worthwhile and fosters the development of the whole person in mind, body, and spirit.

St. Olaf College strives to be an inclusive community, respecting those of differing backgrounds and beliefs. Through its curriculum, campus life, and off-campus programs, it stimulates student's critical thinking and heightens their moral sensitivity; it encourages them to be seekers of truth, leading lives of unselfish service to others; and it challenges them to be responsible and knowledgeable citizens of the world.

This liberal education cherishes a sense of continuity with the past, finding in the past not rigid, dead paradigms, but the vital wisdom of experience and the recognition of errors we should aspire not to repeat. Alive to change, this education celebrates the venturesome spirit of risk-taking ancestors who sought freedom, and it welcomes all who seek a similar adventure. It finds in this daring spirit of earlier generations the roots of compassion for others of diverse origins.

At St. Olaf, liberal education accepts the intriguing challenge of communication under the conditions symbolized by the destruction of the Tower of Babel, and the confusion of tongues. It accepts the responsibility to listen, study, and speak with all our brothers and sisters of every tongue and race. A cross-cultural component in the core curriculum insures that every St. Olaf student gains some insight into significant aspects of non-western culture or minority cultures of North America.

About 500 students participate in the St. Olaf International Studies Program each year. Typically, they study in Africa, Asia, Europe, Latin America, the Middle East, and the former USSR, with more than half of every graduating class having studied abroad at least once. Options include one month interim courses, semester, and year-long programs. All the programs add a cross-cultural dimension to a liberal arts education and aid in developing a global perspective.

St. Olaf students participate in numerous volunteer services, regularly visiting with juvenile offenders, with the physically and mentally impaired, visiting senior citizens in local hospitals and retirement centers, and as big brothers or sisters.

Study/Service programs provide students with a challenging and independent study abroad experience. The aim is to provide an international experience combining academic study and active participation with nationals in rural and urban settings through local organizations. Programs provide enriched learning experiences through immersion in a local situation (in most cases Third World) and to make a direct contribution to the local community through a service project coordinated by the host institution.

St. Olaf's Paracollege offers an alternative means of earning the B.A. degree. Paracollege students develop individualized plans for their education. Students implement their goals through a variety of educational options, especially tutorials, where they explore topics of their choice with the guidance of a faculty member, and seminars, which are small discussion courses frequently team-taught by professors from different disciplines.

MAKING A DIFFERENCE STUDIES

Environmental Studies
Introduction to Environmental Studies
Canyonlands Geology
Coastal Biology in California
Environmental Ethics
Ecological Principles

American Ecological History
Desert Ecology
Winter Ecology
Water Resources Management
The Land, American History and Culture

Women's Studies
Women's Health
Women in the Visual Arts
Family and Economy
American Feminist Thought
Family & Gender in Cross-Cultural Perspective

Philosophy and Feminism
Dance, Gender and the Church
Women and Judeo-Christian Tradition
Women in America

American Racial and Multicultural Studies
Introduction to ARM Studies
Native-American-White Relations
Race and Class in American Culture
Contemporary Native American Issues

From Wounded Knee to Red Power
Ethnic Music
Black American History
Dance in America

Economics
Energy Economics
Development Economics
Ethical Management
Labor Economics

Environmental Economics
Economics of Health Care
Economics of the Public Sector
Environmental Policies and Regulations

Sociology
Men and Women in American Society
Social Problems and Social Change
Sociology of Global Interdependence
Encountering the "Primitive" Tribal and Peasant Societies
Forging a Latin American Culture: Indians, Conquerors and Revolutionaries

Contemporary Native American. Issues
Race and Class in American Culture
Culture, Conflict and Nonviolence

Latin American/Latino Studies
The U.S. and Peoples of Latin America
Politics of Developing Nations
Problems in Political Development
Modern Mexico

Development Economics
Latin American Literature
Culture and Civilization of Latin America
Progress & Poverty: Modern Latin America

- **Brazil from Colonial to Modern Times** Surveys Brazilian history from its colonial beginnings as a slave-based export colony to its twentieth-century struggle for industrialization and political stability. Race relations, cultural and economic nationalism, the importance of the frontier, military regimes, liberation theology, and the transition to democracy. Relationship between elites and masses, and how popular religious and cultural movements have served both to unite and divide Brazilians.

Family Resources
"The family" as a focus for a discipline in higher education has increased in significance as the well-being of individuals and families has become an area of major national concern,
Family Relationships
Child Development in the Family
Nutrition in the Community
Maternal and Child Nutrition

Lesbian and Gay Issues
Human Sexuality
Family Resource Management
Marriage

Interim (January) Studies

Biomedical Ethics

Economic Justice: Government vs. Market

Women and Work in Africa

Wilderness in American Life

Human Relations in Cross-Cultural Perspective (abroad)

Public Policy and the Family

Liberation Theology

Freudian & Buddhist Psychology

Ethics, Animals & the Environment

Paracollege Seminars:

Planning for the 21st Century

The Legacy of Columbus

Family, Gender and Economy

Feminism and Philosophy

Gender in the 1990's: New Women? New Men?

Saving Wild Places: The American Conservation Movement

Red, Black and White in American Religion

Religion, Theology and Ecology

Economics of Resource Depletion

Global Climate Change

Interdisciplinary Courses

Values

Science, Technology and Values

Peace and Violence

Spain and Latin America from 1491 to 1992

Around the World - The Global Semester

In cooperation with a St. Olaf coordinator at the American University in Cairo, Egypt, and with staff members from Bangalore, India; Taipei, Taiwan; and Kyoto, Japan, St. Olaf students may spend the fall semester and the Interim studying sociocultural developments in the non-western world.

- **India Studies:**After an intensive ten-week orientation term, including language study, participants spend six months in Pune living with Indian families, and enroll at Tilak Maharashtra Vidyapeeth where they continue language instruction and other studies.

- **Biology in South India:** Following a five week study and orientation session in Madras, students do independent study/internships in rural and/or urban health care, agriculture, fishing village, mountain ecology

- **Indonesia:** Students work as teaching assistants in the English Dep't at Nommensen University in Sumatra, and at Satya Wacana Christian University in Java.

- **New Guinea:** Students work with English conversation programs or participate in local church activities such as religious education classes or alcohol abuse prevention. Ten weeks of course work are followed by ample time to visit villages.

Africa and the African Diaspora
Social Work

Hispanic Studies
Philosophy

Student Body: 57% state, 45% men, 55% women, 7% minority, 2% int'l
Faculty: 63% male, 37% female, 11 minority faculty   Avg. students in first year classroom: 21
1994-95 Comprehensive Fee: $18,100   Apply By 3/1
Energy conservation and campus wide recycling policies are in effect at Saint Olaf

• Field Studies • Internships • Third World Study Abroad & Service-Learning
• Team Teaching • Individualized Majors • Evening Classes • Vegetarian Meals

Use form in back to contact: Director of Admissions
St. Olaf College   Northfield, MN 55057-1098
(507) 646-3025

SARAH LAWRENCE COLLEGE

1,200 students   Bronxville, New York   Very Selective

Sarah Lawrence, a small coeducational liberal arts college, holds a unique place in American society: It was the first college to propose that education be shaped to fit the individual; that genuine learning engages both the intellect and the imagination; and, above all, that there must be a sustained, humane commitment to people, their needs and talents. Other innovations include:

- A seminar/conference system where students learn in small, highly interactive classes (few larger than 15 students), and in private tutorials. Its student/faculty ratio is 6:1, one of the lowest in the country
- A system in which each student works with a faculty advisor, or don, to design an individual program of study and through which the advisor provides ongoing guidance
- The use of written evaluations for coursework
- A system in which there are no graduate assistants, instructors, or adjunct lecturers. Each teacher is fully a teacher, available to freshmen as well as upperclassmen.

The College believes the most profound learning takes place when education is linked to the experiences, interests and capacities of the individual student. It endeavors to explore intellectual issues within a framework of humanistic values, to blend intellectual rigor with a passion for human concerns, to approach learning with a sense of meaning and urgency. The College believes an educated person is one who combines skepticism with reverence, and who recognizes an obligation to serve the larger community. Sarah Lawrence is concerned, above all, with endowing students with the efficacy and the will to make a difference in their own lives and in others.

The curriculum is spread over four academic areas: The Humanities, the Creative and Performing Arts, History and the Social Sciences, and the Natural Sciences and Mathematics. The coursework guides students to see connections between academic disciplines and to cross ethnic, economic, social and political boundaries. Sarah Lawrence emphasizes program planning and encourages students to choose courses most meaningful to them. Students are given the time and support to study their interests with intensity and are encouraged to explore the moral and political implications of all areas of study.

Sarah Lawrence was one of the pioneers in incorporating fieldwork into the college curriculum. Many students supplement their education with fieldwork in a variety of settings, such as the NAACP Legal Defense Fund, the Bronx Zoo, the American Civil Liberties Union, and the Landmark Preservation Commission. In the theater and dance programs, students participate in performance and teaching outreach groups that work with small theaters, schools and centers.

The College is among a select group of schools known as the International 50 that graduates a disproportionately high number of students who go to work in international affairs, government or academia. Its curriculum helps prepare students for global citizenship -- to meet the challenges of living and learning in a multicultural world.

MAKING A DIFFERENCE STUDIES

Public Policy
Economics of the Environment
The Meaning of Work
Global Economic Development
Women, Families & Work
Changing Places: Social/Spatial Dimensions of Urbanization

Survival & Scarcity: Resources for the Future
Econ. Policy & the Environment of the Future
Science, Technology & Human Values
Ecological Principles: Science of Environment

Political Science
African Politics
Politics of American Elections
Drugs, Trade, Immigration: U.S.-Mexico Relations in the Late 20th Century
Nuclear Weapons: Selected Explorations of their Impact on Modern Life
Is America a Democracy? Class, Race, Gender, & Political Participation
Politics & History: Conservative, Radical & Liberal

Politics & Government of Latin America
Perspectives on Politics & Society in 20th Cent

Area Studies
Images of India
Islam, Flower in the Desert
Literature of Exile
Asian Religion
Middle East History & Politics
African Identities: Lives in Contemporary Sub-Saharan Africa

Culture & Society: Anthro Perspectives
Chinese & Japanese Literature & History
Tradition & Change in Modern China
Russian History, Literature & Politics
Latin American Literature & Politics

Sociology
Crime & Deviance Theory
Contemporary Urban Lives
Social Movements & Social Change
Colonialism, Imperialism, Liberation: Third World Perspectives

Inequality: Social & Economic Perspectives
Social Theory: Class, Race, Gender & the State
African-Americans & Social Science Research

Psychology
Education: Theory & Practice
Moral Development
Ethnicity, Race & Class: Psychosocial Perspectives
Ways of Knowing: Gender and Cultural Contexts
Deception & Self-Deception: The Place of Facts in a World of Propaganda

Social Development Research Seminar
Social Psychology

Women's Studies
Equality & Gender
Mothers & Daughters in Literature
Daughters of Africa Circa 1992
The Female Vision: Women & Social Change in American History
Veiled Lives: Women & Resistance in the Muslim World
Theories & Methodology of Women's History & Feminism

Psychology of Women
Gender, Sexuality & Kinship
Women in Asian Religions

Student Body: 30% in-state, 70% women, 30% men, 24% minority, 10% international
1994-95 tuition/room/board: $26,258   Apply by February 1
• Fieldwork   • Internships   • Individualized Programs   • Multi-disciplinary Courses
• Seminar/Conference Format   •Study Abroad   • Continuing Education   • Vegetarian Meals

Use form in back to contact Office of Admissions
Sarah Lawrence College, Bronxville, New York 10708
(914) 395-2510

THE SCHOOL FOR FIELD STUDIES

Based in Beverly, Massachusetts

The School for Field Studies provides motivated young people - from secondary schools, colleges and universities nationwide, and from a variety of academic backgrounds - with an action-oriented, experience-based education in environmental issues. At the same time, students are able to make immediate and real contributions toward sustainable management of natural resources. In doing so, we seek to make tomorrow's leaders more environmentally literate, aware and able to recognize the environmental effects of how they choose to live.

Since its inception in 1980, SFS have given more than 5,000 students a unique opportunity to conduct hands-on field studies and research addressing some of the most critical environmental issues facing the world. SFS is the largest private educational institution exclusively offering courses and fieldwork for undergraduates in the increasingly important fields of research management and conservation biology.

In an SFS program, students are face-to-face with the issues. Rainforests don't fit under a microscope. Giraffes don't graze in a test tube. That is why SFS courses don't take place in a classroom. SFS takes students to the best possible laboratories for environmental studies, the actual ecosystems where problems are occurring. This provides dramatic, real-life illustrations of the issues that can only be imagined through lectures and textbooks. SFS provides an educational experience which fully integrates theory and practice.

SFS teams range from 15 students and two faculty on a month-long course to 30 students and three to four faculty for semester programs. As an SFS team member, students are actively involved in all aspects of research and day-to day living. This team approach to learning and problem solving is at the heart of the SFS educational philosophy and it is one of its greatest strengths.

SFS semester programs require successful completion of one college level ecology or biology course. Applicants to semester programs must be at least 18 years of age and should have completed at least one semester at a college or university. Since a 15 week semester is compressed into 13 weeks (by working on weekends among other methods), be prepared for an intensive learning process.

Of course, you will receive college credit. SFS students are registered with Northeastern University in Boston. Credit for SFS participation was accepted or awarded by over 150 colleges and universities during the past year. Financial assistance is available to qualified students based on need and comes in the form of scholarships and/or interest-free loans.

Summer courses are offered at the college introductory. The low student to faculty ratio and interactive teaching approach allows SFS to adjust course pace and content to suit the needs of the team. Summer participants must be at least 16 years of age and have completed the junior year of high school.

SFS operates seven Centers where students can participate in 13-14 week semester programs with a 21 quarter credit courseload. These Centers also offer month-long summer courses in which participants receive 8 quarter credits.

MAKING A DIFFERENCE STUDIES

The Center for Island Management Studies in the Republic of Palau
Semester Program: Island Management Studies

Tropical Ecology & Sustainable Dev.   Directed Research
Principles of Resource Management   Env. Policy and Socioeconomic Values
Summer Program: Management of Island Resources

The Center for Coastal Studies on Vancouver Island, British Columbia
Semester Program: Coastal Resource Management

Coastal Ecology   Directed Research
Principles of Resource Management   Economic & Ethical Issues in Sust. Dev.
Summer Program: Saving the Rainforests of Ho

The Center for Rainforest Studies in Australia.
Semester Program: Tropical Rainforest Management

Rainforest Ecology   Principles Of Forest Management
Ecological Anthropology   Directed Research
Summer Program: Tropical Reforestation (exception: 6 weeks/11 quarter hrs.)

The Center for Marine Resource Studies in the Caribbean
Semester Program: Marine Resource Management

Tropical Marine Ecology   Directed Research
Principles of Forest Management   Ecological Anthropology
Summer Program: Marine Parks Management

The Center for Wildlife Management Studies in Kenya
Semester Program: Wildlife Ecology and Management

Techniques of Wildlife Management   Wildlife Ecology
Enviro Policy & Socioeconomic Values   Directed Research
Summer Program: Community Wildlife Management

The Center for Marine Mammal and Island Biodiversity Studies in Baja Mexico
Semester Program: Marine Mammal Conservation and Island Biodiversity

Marine Mammal Biology   Resource Ecology & Management
Enviro Policy & Socioeconomic Values   Directed Research
Summer Program: Sea Lion Conservation

The Center for Sustainable Development Costa Rica in Costa Rica
Semester Program: Studies in Sustainable Development

Tropical Ecology & Sustainable Devel.   Economic & Ethical Issues in Sust. Devel.
Socio-Political Systems & Sust. Devel.   Directed Research
Summer Program: Alternative Strategies for Preserving Tropical Ecosystems

At SFS satellite sites at environmental "hot spots", you can spend a month examining such critical issues as: •Village Development of Fragile Mountain Ecosystems in Nepal •Conservation Education in Belize •Protecting Birds of Prey in Montana •Ecology of Killer Whales in Puget Sound •Planning Parks for Preservation in Argentina •Ethnobotany: Uses of Plants by Indigenous Peoples in Mexico •Design and Delivery of Appropriate Energy Technologies in Zimbabwe

1994 tuition for semester programs: $10,350 (plus transportation)
Average tuition for summer courses: $2,880(plus transportation)

Use form in back to contact: School for Field Studies
16 Broadway   Beverly, MA 01915-4499
(508) 927-7777

SCHOOL FOR INTERNATIONAL TRAINING
BACHELOR'S PROGRAM IN WORLD ISSUES

110 Students   Brattleboro, VT   Moderately Selective

Senator William Fulbright has commented that the world's problems are not technological, but human. Unless we can obtain the knowledge, experience, and skills required to interact constructively with people from cultures and countries other than our own, the world's future will be bleak. The School for International Training, the accredited college of World Learning, prepares students for careers in international affairs, Third World development, student exchange, and language teaching. In the Bachelor's Program in World Issues, a two-year, upper division program leading to a B.A. in International Studies, students are challenged both to understand international issues and work toward their resolution. The Peace Corps recently designated a track within the Bachelor's Program in World Issues as a Peace Corps Preparatory Program.

Through a unique combination of classroom and experiential learning -- including a seven- to eleven-month internship anywhere in the world -- students develop the ability to rigorously analyze such complex and interrelated issues as poverty, hunger, environmental degradation, over-population, war, racism, and sexism. In the process, students participate in a supportive learning community that collectively shares a common commitment to integrating idealism with pragmatic, well-informed social action.

MAKING A DIFFERENCE STUDIES

Phase 1: On-Campus Study/Tracks in Environment, Development, and Peace
During the first two semesters students take a sequence of courses, seminars, colloquia, and workshops which provide them with a solid intellectual grounding in international issues and practical skills needed to pursue the internship phase of the curriculum.

Development Economics	Design for Sustainability
International Environmental Issues	Intercultural Human Relations
Issues in Peace and Conflict	Conflict Resolution Strategies
Population: Demography and Migration	International Relations
Population: Health and Development	International Communications
Gender and Development	Appropriate Technology
Conservation and Development	Current World Issues
Program Planning and Proposal Writing	Cross-Cultural Service Skills
Methodologies	Media Skills

Language
Students are required to have conversational skills in at least one foreign language. Spanish, French, Russian, Arabic, Japanese, Indonesian, and Chinese are taught on campus. Guided self-instruction is available in a variety of languages, from Bengali to Thai

Phase 2: The Internship
Internships take a variety of forms. Many students meet their requirements through serving as volunteers in organizations related to their course sequence in Phase 1 of the program. Others find paying positions in similar agencies. Some students begin the internship phase

by participating in the fall term of one of the over thirty different College Semester Abroad programs offered by SIT. Others participate in the ORAP/SIT Grassroots Development and NGO Management program in Zimbabwe. Typical internships include training health workers in Honduras, community development work in Indonesia with Save the Children, doing research for a women's group in Italy, working with Amnesty International in Japan, and doing research for the Gandhi Peace Foundation in India.

Phase 3: Synthesis and Evaluation

Students return to campus in April after the internship to complete a two-month examination of the field experience. This analysis begins with a "re-entry seminar" in which returned interns present their experiences and discuss them with fellow students and the faculty. The remainder of the term is devoted to preparing a formal paper and public presentation, written for a professional audience familiar with the topic, which investigates an important area of learning or topic arising from the internship.

All WIP faculty have doctorates in fields as diverse as anthropology, economics, international relations, communications and education, with research and area specializations in Africa, Asia, and Latin America. Yet all have also been practitioners, working as professionals and consultants in community organization, economic development, journalism, appropriate technology, energy conservation, environmental policy, and multi-cultural education. They maintain personal contact networks with numerous organizations in the field, from the International Union for the Conservation of Nature in Geneva to local development organizations in Botswana, which inform their teaching and allow them to assist their student advisees when they are exploring internship options.

Grassroots Development Program

The Organisation of Rural Associations for Progress (ORAP) in Zimbabwe and SIT are combining their respective experiences and resources to help educate a new generation of development workers and leaders from both Africa and the USA. Students learn the competencies needed to mobilize grassroots action for culturally appropriate, sustainable social and economic development and to establish new and more equal relations in South-North development cooperation. The core curriculum addresses complexities of both village-level grassroots development strategies and the management of Non-Governmental Organizations (NGOs) facilitating such development. Students receive a Certificate in Grassroots Development and NGO Management. 24 credits are transferable toward a B.A. degree through SIT's Bachelor's Program in World Issues. African students study academic and professional writing skills with help from U.S. students. U.S. students study Ndebele, Shona, or another southern African language, with tutorial help from the African students.

Introduction to Rural Mobilization	Int'l. Dimensions of Grassroots Development
Development Skills	NGO Management Skills
Internships	Integration Seminar and Project

Student Body: 2% state, 50% women, 50% men
1993 costs: $15,500   Rolling Admissions • Apply early for financial aid
Energy conservation policies and solar water heating systems in place.
• Individualized Majors   • Life Experience Credit

Use form in back to contact: School for International Training
Admissions, Bachelor's Program in World Issues
P.O. Box DSOMD, Brattleboro, VT 05302-0676
(800) 451-4465

SHELDON JACKSON COLLEGE

300 Students   Sitka, Alaska   Moderately Selective

Sheldon Jackson College is for the college student who chooses a decidedly different and bolder path through life. The campus of Sheldon Jackson is located on the western shore of Baranof Island in Southeast Alaska. Encircled by mountains and settled between ancient forests and the Pacific Ocean, it provides a vast wilderness classroom for education and discovery. Within walking distance of campus students can investigate tidelands, walk through old-growth spruce and hemlock forests, observe freshwater estuaries, muck about in muskeg, hike into high alpine meadows or kayak through Sitka Sound paddling past sea lions or humpback whales. Sheldon Jackson's campus is surrounded by 16.8 million acres of the Tongass National Forest, which encompasses the largest temperate rain forest in North America.

Opportunities abound for students to become involved as explorers and caretakers of this precious world resource. The Environmental Awareness Team and Outdoor Recreation Program sponsor a very successful city-wide Spring Expo to celebrate Earth Day, complete with Intertribal Native drumming, an Eskimo blanket toss, sea kayaking, a river traverse, climbing wall session, snorkeling, tree planting and bald eagle release from the Alaska Raptor Rehabilitation Center. A Wilderness Orientation Program allows new students to participate in a ten-day wilderness adventure complete with a seven mile sea kayak, a four mile hike to the crater of Mt. Edgecumbe on nearby Kruzof Island, and a sampling of wild edibles.

While many colleges make commitments to the importance of ethnic diversity and cultural sensitivity in attempting to create a multicultural learning environment, Sheldon Jackson College provides the reality of such a community. Alaska natives and Native Americans currently comprise twenty-eight percent of our student body. Some of these students come from villages in the Alaska "bush" where subsistence hunting, fishing and gathering are essential to survival, while other students celebrate their native heritage within a westernized society. The Annual Gathering of the People celebrates the heritage, culture and current experiences of Alaska's Native Peoples, complete with native dancing and a potluck dinner in which traditional native foods (seal, whale, herring eggs, moose and eskimo ice cream) can be sampled along with more common Lower 48 dishes. This is a college of rich cultural and geographical diversity. Students come from 40 states and several foreign countries. At SJ diversity is something you encounter in the residence hall as well as in the classroom.

Sheldon Jackson believes that it is important for students to explore and develop the spiritual component of their life, and to commit themselves in very practical ways to the application of that understanding in the profession of service. SJ is affiliated with the Presbyterian Church and provides an education in which the exploration of Christian faith and values is nurtured, while challenging students to develop an understanding and sensitivity to other faith traditions as well. The Carpenter Leadership Program provides opportunities for students to volunteer while receiving tuition assistance for their service. All students who receive financial aid will be expected to provide "tuition sweat equity," working on-campus to pay for the partial cost of their education.

MAKING A DIFFERENCE STUDIES

Aquatic Resources Tracks in Aquaculture, Fisheries, Marine Biology
Sheldon Jackson has the only college owned private salmon hatchery in the U.S. Hands-on work experience includes culturing shellfish and algae, taking eggs, and collecting samples

Salmonid Culture
Forest Ecology
Fish Health Management
Mariculture
Ecosystem Analysis
Marine Invertebrate Zoology

Intro to Natural Resources Mgm't & Dev.
Marine Biology
Water/Genetics/Nutrition
Oceanography
Fish Ecology
Micro Economics

- **Fish Husbandry** Hydraulics and hatchery plumbing, fish rearing containers, carrying capacity calculations, programming of fish growth, fish nutrition, fish disease, marking and tagging of fish, and computer applications of fish husbandry.

Natural Resource Management & Development

Surveying and Mapping
Field Studies in Resource Management
Native Perspectives on Resource Mgm't
Natural Resource Policies and Law
Wildlife Ecology and Management

Forest Mensuration
Forest/Range Soil
Photogrammetry
Economic Considerations in Natural Resources

Outdoor Recreation

Intro to Outdoor Recreation
Hiking
Sea Kayaking
Outdoor Leadership
Small Business Management

Outdoor Survival
Public Speaking
Environmental Interpretation
Rock Climbing and Mountaineering
Principles of Outdoor Rec. Planning & Mgm't.

Business Administration

Prepares graduates for making intelligent business decisions based on analytical, moral ,ethical and environmental decisions; making decisions from an international/global perspective; and conducting business in a manner that accommodates different cultural expectations.

General Psychology
Ethic
Personnel and Labor Relations
International Business

Environmental Issues and Business
Business Policy and Organization
Techniques Developing Creativity
Principles of Management

- **Native Issues in Business**   Issues and problems important to Native Americans as they relate to business, society, and the physical environment. An Alaska Native focus will be stressed. Topics include Alaska Native Corporations, cultural and environmental issues, accommodating-integrating native perspectives and cultural sensitivity into business, multiculturalism and the future of Native Americans in business.

Education   Forestry Technology Certificate   Fish Husbandry Certificate

Student Body: 40% state, 48% women, 52% men, 33% minority (21% Alaska Natives), 40% transfer
1994-95 costs: $14,050   Rolling Applications
Average number of students in first year class: 18
• Service-Learning Programs   • Individualized Majors

Use form in back to contact: Director of Admissions
Sheldon Jackson College   801 Lincoln St.   Sitka, AK 99835
(800) 478-4556   (907) 747-5221

SIERRA INSTITUTE
UNIVERSITY OF CALIFORNIA EXTENSION, SANTA CRUZ

At the end of his sophomore year the young John Muir left the University of Wisconsin of what he called the "university of the wilderness". He traveled to the Sierra Nevada mountains in California and began a lifelong adventure in learning directly from nature. It is that first-hand contact with the natural world that Sierra Institute programs seek to provide.

The Sierra Institute offers academic field courses taught entirely in wildlands — students never enter a campus classroom. For up to a full academic quarter, students from around the country join with instructors to form small traveling field schools, backpacking throughout bioregions in the western U.S. and Central and South America.

Program coursework is diverse, interdisciplinary, and always focused on specific places. You can study field ecology and natural history in Utah's canyonlands, California's Sierra Nevada, or the rainforests of Belize and Guatemala. Unlike classes on campus, the plants, animals, and ecosystems of these bioregions are always available to you because you are living among them. If you study environmental ethics and philosophy in the Sierra, you will read John Muir and Gary Snyder while following in their footsteps through the mountains. In the Pacific Northwest you will experience old growth forests, northern spotted owls, clearcuts, and conservation biology while studying public lands management.

Whether studying natural science or nature philosophy, Sierra Institute students all share a common experience —their classroom is alive. There is an immediacy to coursework that enhances and supplements the educational process. Academic and experiential learning combine to create a richness rarely found on campus. The direct knowledge of the rhythms of the natural world that students get through learning outside also fosters a deep sense of place. Accordingly, personal growth is often an important part of the learning experience.

Along with the outdoor classroom, all Sierra Institute programs share several academic and logistical themes. All instructors have advanced degrees and are skilled wilderness leaders with appropriate first aid training. Programs offered by the Sierra Institute are first approved by the Environmental Studies Board at the University of California, Santa Cruz. Courses are generally at the lower-division undergraduate level; there are no prerequisites. The application process can be somewhat competitive depending on how many people apply for a given program by the application deadline.

Group size is limited to 12-13 students. Academic materials (books, papers, journals) are packed into the backcountry by the group. All instruction takes place outdoors, usually on a series of backpack hikes ranging from 4-14 days long. Yet the physical pace is slow, allowing participants to sink into the place and come to know it well. (No prior backpacking experience is necessary.) Groups commonly hike to base camps, conduct classes, take day hikes to explore the area, then move to a new location. Because of the small group size, daily lectures and discussions are usually lively and always intimate. Students use many of the same academic tools that they are familiar with from campus including seminar discussions, field journal assignments, lectures, required readings and papers.

How are academics integrated into the wildlands classroom? Using the Desert Field Studies program (see description under Spring) as an example, a few days on the trail might look like this: A four mile hike to a new base camp might occupy the morning. After camp is set up and lunch is eaten, students pair off along a mile of canyon bottom and search for different species of returning spring birds. They are asked to take notes on diagnostic marks, behavior, and habitat. After a few hours the group gathers to share observations and an overview of the avian community begins to emerge. Field marks, observation techniques, and record keeping are stressed. A paper in the course reader by a contemporary nature writer on canyon birds is assigned for the following day. After dinner as the evening falls, the group visits a nearby Anasazi site for an encounter with prehistory. Later they will be asked to write about the ecological limitations that the Anasazi must have encountered living in the desert.

The following day is devoted to geology. After a short day hike, the group reaches an inspiring classroom on top of the slickrock. It is a perfect place to unravel sandstone, joints and faults, bedding planes, and geologic time. Returning to camp, the afternoon is reserved for catching up on reading and journal assignments and swimming. After supper, everyone gathers by candlelight to share discoveries, ideas, hassles, and sore muscles.

Over the following days as their academic knowledge deepens, students gain insight into desert spring windstorms, heavy packs, and problem solving with a group of peers. Though living and studying outdoors for an entire season, academic and experiential education intermingle. The body is connected to the mind by a backpack full of books, and walking over sandstone.

A Sierra Institute experience may serve as a powerful springboard back into the university and city life that surrounds and increasingly threatens the backcountry. Many students upon returning to campus are inspired to work on the environmental problems facing society. John Muir said, "I went out and found that I was coming home." One recent student remarked that "until Sierra Institute I had thought environmental issues were not worth discussing because they were hopelessly unsolvable. Now I know there exist positive solutions and that change is possible".

University-level wildlands programs work best when they combine critical perspectives with profound personal experience. The Sierra Institute seeks to combine these two and to stimulate an overall ecological literacy in participants. Ecological literacy asks of students to both understand the ecology of their place and work toward sustainable living in school and beyond. In an urban culture that continues to separate itself from its wild roots, we need educational opportunities that reconnect culture with nature. It is just these bonds that Sierra Institute programs foster.

MAKING A DIFFERENCE STUDIES

Sierra Institute field programs vary from year to year. The following is a sample of recent offerings.

SUMMER (application deadline early May)

Mountain Ecology: The High Sierra. This 8-week program explores the ecology and natural history of John Muir's high Sierra. Most of the hiking routes and classrooms are in forests and meadows above 9000 feet in Yosemite and the north-central Sierra. This program was created for students in love with natural history and wild mountains. This program is comprised of three courses: Introduction to Natural Ecosystems, Sierra Nevada Natural History, and Wilderness Education.

Spirit in the Mountains: Idaho Wild. There is a rich relationship between humans, creativity, and nature -- this program explores these key interrelationships while hiking in Idaho's spectacular Sawtooth Mountains. Our methods include the cross cultural analysis of myth and poetry, environmental ethics, and the art of journal writing. We will also focus on the contemporary ecofeminism and deep ecology movements. This program is comprised of two courses: Perspectives on Nature, and Wilderness Education.

Wilderness At Risk. This is a special hands-on field course in conservation biology and ecosystem management in the North Cascades of Washington. Hiking on both sides of the Cascades, you will encounter owls and ancient forests, public lands managers, grassroots activists, and more. The two courses are: Ecosystem Management and Wilderness Education.

Other Sierra Institute summer offerings include studying environmental ethics in the Olympic Mountains, public lands politics in Montana, and natural history and ecology in northern California.

FALL (application deadline mid-July)

Mountains, Canyons, Mesas: Southern Rockies Field Studies (Sept.-Oct., 1994)
From the peaks of the Colorado Rockies to Mesa Verde and the canyons of the Four Corners country, this program explores southwestern field ecology and environmental issues. If you want a broad introduction to the natural history and resource conflicts of this fascinating region, this program is for you. The three courses are: Introduction to Natural Ecosystems, Contemporary Environmental Issues, and Wilderness Education.

Sierra Field Studies: The Mountains of California (Sept.-Oct., 1994). This is our longest running field program and the reason for it's popularity is clear -- Wild California. From the Sierra to the Big Sur coast students follow a fascinating ecological transect of the state. The focus is on introducing students to biodiversity and natural history from the mountains to the sea. The three courses are: Introduction to Natural Ecosystems, Sierra Nevada Natural History, and Wilderness Education.

California Wilderness: Nature Philosophy and Religion (Sept.-Oct., 1994). California's landscapes are diverse —the desert of Death Valley, the High Sierra, the Big Sur coast, and secret ranges in the north. These are the places that help spark our exploration of nature's influence on American philosophy, religion, ethics, and literature. This program affords provocative reflection at the boundary of nature and culture. The three classes are: Perspectives On Nature, American Nature Philosophers, and Wilderness Education.

WINTER (application deadline early November)

Our international winter programs in Central and South America are unique and very popular. Unlike other field programs abroad, you are not be based out of a field station. Instead, you immerse yourself in the natural and cultural landscapes of our neighbors to the south. You travel with the locals on public transportation, live and work with villagers, and backpack in the bush far from any tourist routes.

Rainforest Field Studies: Guatemala and Belize (Jan.-March 1995) The natural history and ecology of Guatemala and Belize are the focuses of this field program. With your instructors you live and work with Maya villagers in the Guatemala highlands, explore the temples and forests of Tikal National Park, visit an agoforestry research station, backpack in Belize's wildest mountains, and camp on a Caribbean coral reef caye. The protection of tropical ecosystems and human cultural adaptations past and present are emphasized in academic work. The three courses are: Evolution and Conservation of Neotropical Diversity, Natural and Cultural History of Central American Rainforests, and Wilderness Education.

Endangered Wildlife: Chile (Jan.-March 1995) Enter into the fascinating world of ecosystem planning and international conservation politics through study of the huemul and it's habitat. The secretive huemul deer serves as Chile's national animal as well as one of the country's most endangered species. You will backpack into several mid-elevation study sites in the Andes and search for remnant huemul populations, meet will Chilean campesinos, foresters, and conservationists, and contribute to ongoing research that seeks to protect Chile's wild places from development. The three courses are: Wildlife Conservation in Chile, Ecosystem Management in Chile, and Wilderness Education.

SPRING (application deadline early January)

Desert Field Studies: The Canyons of Time (April-May 1995) Natural history and nature writing are combined in this program that explores the slickrock country of pinyon pine and juniper, Ed Abbey and Terry Tempest Williams. The combination of ecological observation and exploration of landscape and self through writing is powerful. The field journal from both the naturalist's and nature writer's perspective is emphasized. The three courses are: Natural History of the Colorado Plateau, Introduction to Nature Writing, and Wilderness Education.

Nature and Culture: Cultural Ecology and Environmental Issues (April-May 1995) This program explores the interconnections between human cultures and landscapes from Death Valley to Mount Shasta and wild southern Oregon's Siskyou Mountains. Using interdisciplinary studies from ecology, environmental history, literature, and anthropology, the role of wild nature in shaping people and their world views comes alive. The three courses are: Cultural Ecology, Contemporary Environmental Issues, and Wilderness Education.

Other Sierra Institute spring offerings include Sierra Field Studies: The Mountains of California and California Wilderness: Nature Philosophy and Religion. (See Fall descriptions.)

Student Body 80% state, 7% minority, 60% women,40% men, 3% int'l.
Faculty 55% male 45% female   • Actively seeking minority students
1994-5 costs: $2,000 per quarter includes tuition and personal expenses
• Field Studies   • Team Teaching   • Core/Multidisciplinary Classes   • Vegetarian Meals

Use form in back to contact: Sierra Institute
UC Extension 740 Front St. Box C
Santa Cruz, CA 95060
(408) 427-6618

SOUTHERN ILLINOIS UNIVERSITY

20,500 Undergraduates   Carbondale, Illinois   Moderately Selective

MAKING A DIFFERENCE STUDIES

Geography/Environmental Planning
Geography of Urban Environments
Economics in Geography and Planning
Natural Resources Planning
Environmental Disaster Planning
Environmental Impact Analysis
Intro to Environmental Planning
Water Resource Planning Simulation
Environmental Perception and Planning
Solar and Alternate Energy Planning
Climatic Change- Inevitable & Inadvertent

Agricultural Education - Teacher Certification Grades 9-12
Agricultural Education Programs
Agric. & Forestry Environmental Problems
Environmental Interpretation
Leadership of Youth and Peer Groups
Fundamentals of Environmental Education
Ecology of North American Forests

Forestry: Tracks in Forest Resources Mgm't, Outdoor Recreation Resources Mgm't, and Forest Science
Social Influences on Forestry
Forest Protection Field Studies
Fire in Wildland Management
Forest Management for Wildlife
Forest Land-use Planning
Enviro Impact Assessment in Forestry
Insect, Abiotic and Other Stresses
Forest Ecology Field Studies
Forest Ecosystems
Forest Resources Decision Making
Wildland Watershed Management
Wilderness Management, Policy & Ethics

Mechanical Engineering & Energy Processing
Energy Conversion Systems
Air Quality Lab
Energy Management
Energy Conversion Systems
Air Pollution Control
Hazardous Waste Incineration
Passive Solar Design

Plant & Soil Science: Tracks in Environmental Studies/Landscape Horticulture
Politics and Environmental Policy
General Horticulture
World Crop Production Problems
Soil and Water Conservation
Irrigation Principles and Practices
Landscape Plant Materials
Admin. of Enviro Quality &Natural Resources
Soil Science
Crop Pest Control
Fertilizers and Soil Fertility
Animal Waste Management
Plant and Soil Evaluations

Plant Biology
Plant Diversity
Introduction to Forest Pathology
Grassland Ecology
Wetland Plant Ecology
Natural Areas and Rare and Endangered Species
Elements of Plant Systematics
Field Mycology
Forest Ecology and Reclamation
Field Studies in Latin America

Anthropology
Educational Anthropology
Indians of the Americas
Slavery and the Black Diaspora
Separate Realities
Ecological Anthropology
Anthropology of Sexual Behavior
Native American Art and Culture
Economic Anthropology
Anthropology of Law
Anthropology of Religion

Black Studies
The Third World: The African Model
Black American Social Problems
Black Theater Workshop
Sociological Effects on Black Education
Investigative Procedures & Techniques for the Affirmative Action Officer

Social Change in Africa
Law and Civil Liberties
Black Political Socialization
Leaders of the Black World

Political Science
Politics and Public Policy
Civil Liberties and Civil Rights
Intro to Public Administrations
Field Research in Public Policy
Political Violence
Interest Group Politics

Politics and Environmental Policy
Political Socialization
Problems in American Public Policy
Admin. of Enviro Quality & Natural Resources
Women & the American Political Process
Public Financial Administration

Philosophy
Ethical Theories
Philosophical Foundations of Ecology
Oriental Philosophies
Philosophy of History
Philosophy of Mind

Science & Technology in Western Societies
Philosophy of Education
Philosophical Perspectives on Women
The Biomedical Revolution and Ethics
Philosophy of Religion

Economics
Poverty and the Economy
Labor Problems
Intro to Economic Development
Regional and Urban Economics
Health Economics

Contemporary Economic Problems
Collective Bargaining & Dispute Settlement
Economics of the Environment
Latin American Economic Development
Land Resource Economics

Health Education/Health Ed. Teaching Credential
Evaluation in Health Education
Consumer Health
Drug Education
Health Issues in Aging
Community Health Admin. in U.S.

Intro to Community Health
Death Education
Emergency Med. Technician in Wilderness
Women's Health
International Health

Physical Therapy Assistant
Physical Therapy Orientation
Therapeutic Exercise
Physical Therapy Assistant Practicum
Physical Therapy Science

Physical Rehabilitative Techniques
Massage
Clinical Internship
Pathology

Social Work   Womens' Studies
Teacher Certification in Geography (essentially Environmental Studies)

Student Body: 75% state, 41% women, 59% men, 13% minority, 10% int'l.
1994-95 costs: Residents $6340   Non-residents $10,990   Rolling Admissions
• Field Studies • Internships • Study Abroad
• Individualized Majors • Co-op Education

Use form in back to contact:Director of Admissions
Southern Illinois University at Carbondale   Carbondale, IL 62901
(618) 536-4405

STATE UNIVERSITY OF NEW YORK
COLLEGE OF ENVIRONMENTAL SCIENCE & FORESTRY

1,200 Undergraduate Students   Syracuse, New York   Very Selective

When the rest of the country celebrated the first Earth Day in 1970 it finally caught up with the College of Environmental Science and Forestry. Since 1911 when the College first opened its doors, ESF began preparing scientists, resource managers, and engineers to nurture the home planet, and to teach scientific principles and applications that would maintain and improve forest lands and support the wise use of natural resources. Today, ESF leads in the discovery of new knowledge and the use of new tools to deal with continuing, current, and future environmental challenges. Students in all programs at SUNY-ESF gain a coherent understanding of their natural environment and learn ways to improve its health and productivity. All students share an interest in the environment and science, design or engineering required to conserve resources and enhance the health of the Earth. SUNY-ESF has prepared people to sustain and improve the environment for almost a century.

ESF's mission is to be a world leader in instruction, research, and public service related to: understanding the structure and function of the world's ecosystems; developing, managing, and use of renewable natural resources; improving outdoor environments ranging from wilderness to managed forests to urban landscapes; and maintaining and enhancing biological diversity, environmental quality, and resource options.

As the 21st century looms and society becomes increasingly concerned about the environment, members of the ESF family have timing in their favor. The future of the world may be determined by those who have broad foresight and a balance of judgment in applying, scientific, technical, and sociological knowledge to guide environmental and human forces. Modern society with its compelling demands from industry and government needs people who think objectively and constructively, and act creatively and responsibly. Faculty and students are committed to resolving immediate environmental hazards, learning how to avoid future problems, and offering policy alternatives that will protect the environment and meet the needs of a global society.

Academic programs at ESF share a foundation of rigorous science and dedication to wise use of natural resources. The faculty's cutting-edge research becomes part of the classroom experience, and the classroom merges with the world beyond the campus. Paper science students at ESF earn real-world experience and paychecks through required summer work at leading paper companies.

Students participate in hands-on and laboratory work at the main campus and on the 25,000 acres of ESF campus outside Syracuse. The College's largest regional campus at Newcomb is located on the 15,000-acre Huntington Wildlife Forest. Faculty, undergraduates, and visiting scientists use the facility for general research and work related to forest management. The Wanakena campus is the site of the College's Forestry Technology Program. The summer session in field forestry, required of environmental and resource management majors and the dual option in environmental and forest biology and resource management, takes place at Wanakena. All locations are equipped with the latest technology.

MAKING A DIFFERENCE STUDIES

Dual Program in Environmental & Forest Biology and Resources Mmg't
Plant Ecology
Diversity of Plants
Wildlife Conservation
Principles of Animal Behavior
Ecology of Freshwaters

Ecology of Adirondack Fishes
Ecological Biogeochemistry
Principles of Forest Entomology
Wildlife Habitats and Populations
Wildlife Ecology & Management Practicum

Environmental Studies
Environmental Geology
Intro to Environmental Impact Analysis
Natural Processes in Planning & Design
American Landscape History
Environmental Studies Internship

Environmental Communication
Decision Modeling for Environmental Mgm't
Government and the Environment
Social Processes and the Environment
Technologies: Water & Wastewater Treatment

Landscape Architecture
Intro to Landscape Arch. & Planning
Site Research & Analysis
Plant Materials
Comprehensive Land Planning
Community Land Planning Workshop

Fundamentals of City & Regional Planning
Natural Processes in Planning & Design
Selected Readings in Enviro Studies
Professional Practice in Landscape Arch.
Negotiating Environmental Disputes

Forest Technology and Resource Management
Forest Ecology
Timber Harvesting
Soil and Water Measurements
Forest Influences
Soils
Forest and Resource Economics

Personnel Management
Elements of Wildlife Ecology
Structure and Growth of Trees
Silviculture
Forest Protection
Natural Resource & Environmental Policy

Forest Engineering
Water Pollution Engineering
Harvest Systems Analysis
Soil Mechanics and Foundations

Resource Policy and Management
Air Pollution Engineering
Forest Engineering Planning and Design

Forest Technology (Ranger School) AAS Degree
Forest Entomology
Forest Roads
Fire Management
Structure & Growth of Trees
Computer Applications

Aerial Photogrammetry
Forest Pathology
Personnel Management
Forest Recreation
Elements of Wildlife Ecology

Accelerated five-year BS/MS track in Plant Biotechnology, Environmental Science, Resources Management (Forestry), and a master's degree in landscape architecture.

Student body: 81% state, 60% men, 40% women, 4% minority
1994-95 Tuition: Residents $2,936 Non-residents $6,836   Rolling Admissions
• Dining, housing, and medical services are available at nearby Syracuse University

Use form in back to contact: Director of Admissions
SUNY College of Environmental Science and Forestry
1 Forestry Drive   Syracuse, NY 13210-2779
(315) 470-6600
800-777-7 ESF

STERLING COLLEGE

90 Students   Craftsbury Common, Vermont   Moderately Selective

Sterling is the smallest coeducational, accredited, degree-granting college in the United States. Sterling has won national attention for its programs, which blends environmental studies, hands-on skills work, productive work, and outdoor group initiatives into one integrated learning experience.

At the core of all Sterling programs is a concern for the relationship between individuals and the environment. Modern society must rebuild that relationship in a life-sustaining way -- and neither technicians nor idealists can do this on their own.

Sterling's subject matter is the environment, the outdoor world and our natural resources. Sterling approaches this in a broad way, working to build understanding about each person's biological, ethical, cultural, and social relationship with the land and resources that sustain us all. Sterling thinks this understanding is critical to living productively as a whole human being, in a society that urgently needs people who can make a difference.

Sterling College's distinctive approach to education can be described as an equal-sided triangle. Its three parts -- each of them indispensable to the whole - are academic studies focusing on natural resources; Bounder, a philosophy of life and problem solving built initially through an intensive program of outdoor challenges and group initiatives; and the application of ideas and concepts through work on the farm and woodlot during the first year of studies, and at off-campus work placements during the second year. Though none of these is a unique approach, Sterling connects all three in an original way for an education that is compelling, motivating, and intellectually engaging.

For those who wish to use the outdoors as a learning laboratory, Sterling offers an ideal education. For students who hope to make the critical first year of college a rich and activating experience, Sterling's Grassroots Year in Vermont is designed to do just that. For students interested in earning an Associate's of Arts degree with unusually broad applications, Sterling's Resource Management Program builds on the Grassroots Year for an integrated, powerful education through coursework alternating with off-campus work placements throughout the U.S.

This curriculum design moves students back and forth between the conceptual presentation of materials, and the concrete experiences such as raising a farm animal, participating in a logging operation, or keeping a wildlife observation journal, that demand interpretation and application. Students are also required to participate in non-credit community work programs.

For more than two decades, Sterling has been a leader in experiential, hands-on education. Sterling is more than sitting and listening in class. Its mission is to help students become problem-solvers, confident and effective -- people who make a difference, no matter what they choose to do.

MAKING A DIFFERENCE STUDIES

Grassroots Year In Vermont (first year of studies)

Resource Issues
Conservation Skills
Literature of Rural Experience
Agricultural Techniques
Intro to Fish and Wildlife Management
Vertebrate Natural History
Farm Workshop
Humans in the Environment: Value & Resource Use

Fundamentals of Ecology
Farm and Forest Workshop
Draft Horse Management
Triumphs of the Human Spirit
Plant and Soil Science
Recreation Management: Canoe Tripping
Wood Harvesting

- **Bounder:** Challenge activities to promote group problem solving and individual initiative. Preparation for winter expedition; ropes and initiatives course; fires and shelters; winter camping techniques; prevention of frostbite and hypothermia; map and compass. Expedition (four day trip), winter camping (three day trip). Also, basic flat and whitewater canoeing, rock climbing, and orienteering.

- Faculty Bio **Charles Coghill Ph.D.** (University of Toronto) An ecologist with increasing interest in the impact of prior land use on current ecological systems; teaches the Geography and History of Land Use.

Resource Management Program (second year of studies leading to A.A.)

Writing and Communication
Land Use Planning
Introduction to Forestry
Resource Economics
Geology
Internship

Management and Leadership Fundamentals
Geography and History of Land Use
Intro to Education and Learning Theory
Agricultural Techniques
Group Dynamics
Independent Study

- **Resource Management** A study of the manipulation of resources to meet specific objectives. The course investigates the relationships among resources and the short and long term effects of manipulation with focus on water, soil, fisheries, forage, forestry and wildlife resources. Built into this investigation is exploration of methodologies of management.

- Faculty Bio **Farley Brown M.S.** (Natural Resource Planning, U of Vermont) A land-use planner with a strong emphasis on promoting public involvement with environmental planning, Farley teaches Introduction to Land Use Planning.

Short Term Programs For Adults

Outdoor Leadership (for grades 8-12)
Forest Management for Landowners

Wildbranch Writers Workshop
Canoe Building

Student Body: 55% men, 45% women
10 male faculty 6 female faculty
1994-95 costs: $17,999 (tuition , room and board)   Rolling Admissions

Use form in back to contact: Admissions Office
Sterling College   Craftsbury Common, VT 05287
(802) 586-7711
1 (800) 648-3591

TUFTS UNIVERSITY

4,700 Undergraduate Students   Medford, Mass.   Most Selective

Tufts is a community of scholars committed to change - leaders in the research and policy planning that is allowing citizens of the world to maintain peace, prevent famine, promote responsible development, and manage the environment.

Discover an education that changes to meet the challenges of a fast-evolving, multicultural, international, and technologically based world. Firmly rooted in the foundation of scholarly excellence, the curriculum at Tufts has been developed to meet the needs of today's world.

The mission of the university is to educate citizens of the world who will treat the problems of society with insight and compassion and who will possess the intellectual tools needed to make a difference.

At Tufts, the learning process is influenced by innovative programs developed and supported by faculty and students:

- A global classroom project that twice each year incorporates a satellite-linked, interactive televised class between students at Tufts and students at a university in Moscow.

- EPIIC, Education for Public Inquiry and International Citizenship, a program that involves students in an intensive, semester-long seminar followed by a weekend symposium. The symposia, planned and administered by students, features top international experts. Topics such as international terrorism, the militarization of the Third World, and secrecy and U.S. foreign policy have been the focus of past programs. This year students studied "The Environment and International Security."

- World Civilizations, a program that has revolutionized the teaching of world history by following concepts such as calendars, time, and memory across Eastern and Western civilizations. The program's goal is to instill all Tufts students with a fundamental process for investigating world history as well as exposing them to certain basic texts that represent numerous cultures.

- Issues involving the environment are a part of all facets of the Tufts experience. The university has named the nation's only dean of environmental programs to organize Tufts' many resources into comprehensive programs of teaching and research, which include thirteen environmental degrees and numerous environmental interdisciplinary concentrations.

"We hope that students use the university's pioneering and socially-conscious spirit as a model for their own life paths' says Tufts President Jean Mayer. "And while Tufts is dedicated to social issues, it has never relinquished its commitment to the most primary function of higher education - teaching students how to think."

MAKING A DIFFERENCE STUDIES

Energy & the Environment
History of Modern Architecture
Ecology
Hydrology/Water Resource Engineering
Technology as Culture
America in the Nuclear Age

Environmental Biology and Conservation
Environmental Toxicology
Energy and Society
Environmental Politics
Physics for Humanists

Environmental Health Program
Environmental Biology & Conservation
Introduction to Community Health
Environmental Law
Public Health
Exposure Assessment

Environmental Systems Engineering
Wastewater Plant Design
Hazardous Materials Safety
Fate &Transport of Enviro Contaminants
Public Administration

Community Health Program
Principles of Epidemiology
Cancer
Health and the Law
Challenge of World Hunger
Sexuality, Disease and Difference
Contemporary Issues in Health Policy

Intro to Hazardous Materials Management
Occupational and Environmental Health
Addiction
Famine
Human Health and Risk Assessment
Domestic Violence

Peace and Justice Studies
Toward A Just World Order
Internship on Social Change
Contemporary Legal Problems of U.N.
Unions and Collective Bargaining
Racism and Social Inequality

Sociology of War and Peace
Peace, Justice and Global Change
United States and Vietnam
Sex and Gender in Society
Power and Politics in America

American Studies Program
Intro to Hispanic Folklore of the SW
Topics in American Indian Studies
Philanthropy and Community
Diversity in America
Social Policy for Children and Families
Theories of Sexual Inequality

Asian-American Literature
Mothering America
Political Economy, Ethics & the Environment
Environmental Toxicology
Film and Society
Altruism and Aggression

Architecture / Social Focus
Introduction to the City
Urban and State Politics
Urban Sociology
Land Use and Planning Policy
Environmental Facilities for Children

Public Administration
Cognitive Psychology
Housing Theory
Urban & Environmental Planning & Design
Designing Educational & Therapeutic Enviro's

Child Study
The Child and the Education Process
Personal-Social Development
Language and the New Immigrant
American Sign Language and the Deaf
Social Policy for Children and Families

Developmental Crises
Community Field Placement
Fostering Literacy Development
Child Advocacy Educational Rights
Rights of Children to Social Services

Science, Technology, and Society
Chemistry in Art and Archaeology
Human Heredity
Technology as Culture
America in the Nuclear Age
Science, Magic & Society 1100-1700

Man and Nature
Principles of Systems
Environmental Geology
Biotech in Human Systems Design
Contemporary Biosocial Problems in America

Morality and Society
Sexuality, Disease and Difference
Crime and Delinquency
Philosophy of Law
Theories of Human Nature
Bioethics

Social Deviance in European History
Ethics
Racism and Inequality
Witchcraft and Society
German Expressionism in European Context

Ethnic Groups in America
Ethnic Origins of Fantasy
Native North America
Blues
Asian American Literature
Class, Race and Gender in the History of U.S. Education

Italian-American Cinema
Introduction to Yiddish Culture
Racial and Ethnic Minorities
Diversity in the Americas

World Civilizations Program
Time and Festivals
Memory and Identity in World Cultures
A Sense of Place: From Regional to Global Definitions of Place
A Sense of Place: Cultural Construction of Place

Time and Modernity

International Relations
Topics in International Development
Economics of Food & Nutrition Policy
International Global Human Rights
Cross Cultural Political Analysis
Cold War America

Natural Resources & Environmental Economics
Sociology of War and Peace
Political Economy of World Hunger
Non-governmental Actors in Int'l Relations
African Politics

Economics
State and Local Public Finance
Economics of Health
Economic Development
Labor Economics
Economics of Regulation

Environmental Economics. and Policy
Natural Resources & Environmental Economics
Economics of Food and Nutrition Policy
Topics in Income Distribution
International Trade

Environmental Studies

Women's Studies

Student Body: 30% state, 48% women, 52% men, 14% minority
1994-95 Comprehensive Costs: $27,700   Apply By: 1/ 1
• Internships   • Handicapped Programs and Accessibility   • Study Abroad
•"Environmental" Housing   • Individualized Majors   • Mystic Seaport Semester

Use form in back to contact: Office of Admissions
Tufts University   Medford, Mass 02155-7057
(617) 628-5000

UNITY COLLEGE

475 Students   Unity, Maine   Moderately Selective

"We can never have enough of nature"

Henry David Thoreau

Unity College recognizes that we are custodians of a fragile planet. The College intends to graduate individuals with firm values, a sense of purpose, and an appreciation of the web of life. Unity graduates are professionally effective and environmentally responsive, recognizing their responsibilities as passengers on this fragile planet. They understand that as global citizens, they must assume a leadership role in the stewardship of the earth.

Unity College exists for the student whose love of the outdoors is reflected in career choices. Unity College students typically place a premium on jobs that do not require sitting behind a desk, thus Unity College combines academic rigor with equally demanding field experience. Education at Unity can be the first step to a position with a state park, wildlife refuge, nature education center, or wilderness recreation organization.

Unity students come from diverse backgrounds, but they share a spirit of independence and a love of nature. They are individuals who welcome the opportunity to participate actively in their own education and in life in a small college community.

To succeed at Unity College, students must bring with them a willingness to have their ideas questioned – and possibly changed. Students must be prepared to accept new challenges that expand their limits. Climbing an ice-covered mountain demands courage and commitment. Waking up at 4 am. to go out in the field and conduct a small mammal survey requires determination.

Students learn from the core curriculum of liberal arts courses how to communicate, to reason, to think critically, to analyze and solve problems. In technical courses, the specific knowledge and skills needed to enter the job market are developed. Through the cooperative education program, students are able to apply in a professional setting what they have learned in the classroom. Students also have the opportunity to explore new interests and test leadership abilities by participating in a wide range of extracurricular activities.

Unity College has a special location. The mountains, lakes, and rocky coast of Maine offer innumerable opportunities to camp, hunt, hike, canoe, and fish. At Unity, students experience the personal growth that comes from awareness of the connections linking human beings with the natural environment. Nearby habitats as diverse as the ocean, mountains, freshwater wetlands, and lakes provide the opportunity for hands-on study of a variety of ecological systems.

The Learning Resource Center provides all students in need of academic improvement the support services necessary to succeed. The Learning Resource Center offers courses, tutoring, study skills workshops, and personal counseling. A learning disabilities specialist works with students who have specific cognitive disabilities that interfere with learning.

Students who demonstrate academic excellence are eligible to take part in Unity College's Mentor Program which provides an enriched educational experience. The program allows the student to work closely with a faculty member on projects such as research, teaching, or round table discussions.

Most Unity students gain work experience in their major field as part of their education. Students may choose credit-bearing internships, cooperative education work experiences, or summer employment to supplement classroom learning. Positions with state and federal agencies, business, or nonprofit organizations enable students to apply academic knowledge to real working situations. Typical internships by students participating in the Washington Semester have included work with the Environmental Defense Fund, the American Rivers Conservation Council, and the U.S. Environmental Protection Agency. Other internships have included Hurricane Island Outward Bound, Connecticut Audubon Society, Volunteers for Peace, and numerous nature centers and summer camps.

Unity College is the home of the college Conservation Corps of Maine, a partnership between the Maine Department of Conservation and the College. Students enrolled in the 14-month program complete two semesters of college coursework while providing 20 hours per week of conservation-related community service in the Unity area. During the summer, corpsmembers work full-time on conservation projects for state parks, public lands, and non-profit organizations statewide. Through participation in the program, students acquire education and training in conservation work, and develop leadership skills.

Unity students have a long history of participating in community service activities. The college is beginning to formalize its community service program by incorporating service-learning into its programs for first-year students and offering "learning to serve" programming for all students. Through these activities, the college builds closer ties to the community and fosters a tradition of service among the students, faculty and staff.

Unity's campus has a sense of open space that reflects the value Unity College places on the outdoors. Until the mid-1960's, the land was occupied by a farm. Today, the 185-acre campus still retains an agrarian feel, in the warm months cows graze adjacent to the residence halls. Over 100 acres of campus land have been designated a tree farm used for educational and recreational purposes. In addition to its campus property, Unity owns more than 320 acres of land including frontage on Lake Winnecook, a Wetlands Research Area, and a 200-acre tree farm with a working sawmill.

Equally important to many Unity students, is the school's proximity to outdoor recreation areas. Hiking, backpacking, rock climbing, canoeing, sea kayaking, and cross-country and downhill skiing are all popular activities for Unity students.

Unity College recently acquired the old solar energy panels which used to adorn the White House under the Carter Administration. The panels have been installed at Unity as part of its continuing efforts as an environmentally conscious institution.

MAKING A DIFFERENCE STUDIES

Environmental Policy

Environmental Pollution
Environmental Law
Natural Resource Policy
Technical Writing
Soil Science

Land & Water Law
Geology of Environmental Problems
Freshwater Ecology/Limnology
Social Problems
State & Local Government

Arboriculture

This program offers an understanding of how trees live and grow and interact with the living and non-living segments of their environment. Based on an understanding of the tree and how it grows in its natural environment, the environment of the park, backyard, and street are studied and contrasted. The concept of the "urban forest" is emphasized.

Supervisory Management
Landscape Fundamentals
Forest Tree Diseases & Insects
Weather & Climate
Population Ecology

General Ecology
Urban Forest Management
Arboriculture
Conservation History
Forest Practices Safety & Licensing

Aquaculture

Aquaculture is the science and practice of culturing aquatic organisms for providing food and pharmaceutical products or for supporting commercial and sport fishing.

International Aquaculture
Applied Fish Physiology
Freshwater and Marine Fishes
Ichthyology
General Genetics

Fish Disease/Pathology
Fish Disease/Diagnostic Techniques
Anatomy of Fish
Freshwater Ecology/Limnology
Microbiology

Fisheries

Biology
Freshwater Ecology/Limnology
General Genetics
Freshwater and Marine Fishes
Natural Resource Policy

Marine Biology
Ichthyology
Geology of Environmental Problems
Fisheries Science & Techniques
Population Ecology

Pre-Law

In consultation with law schools, this program has been designed with particular attention to the needs of students who wish to enter the field of environmental law.

Ethics
World Politics
Issues in American Indian Studies
Introduction to Sociology
Social Problems

American Government
Natural Resource Policy
Group Process
Social and Political Philosophy
Introduction to Criminal Justice

- **Environmental Politics** This course covers the political aspects of an environmental issue, policy-making process, and assessment of political impact of various parties to an issue. There will be extensive field experience.

Outdoor Recreation Leadership

Wilderness First Responder
Leadership
Group Process
Cross Country Skiing
Adventure Ropes Course

Wilderness Skills & Techniques
Program Planning
Environmental Education:Methods & Materials
Canoeing
Mountaineering

Conservation Law Enforcement

Introduction to Criminal Justice
Courtroom Procedures
Forest Fire Prevention & Control
Geology of Environmental Problems
Environmental Law

Conservation Law Enforcement
Firearms Training
North American Wildlife
Interpersonal Relations
Freshwater & Marine Fishes

- **Wildlife Law Enforcement** Examines the career qualifications of the modern-day conservation officer. Brief introduction. to conservation law history and levels of governmental jurisdiction, types of wildlife violations, search and seizure procedures, arrest tactics, evidence compilation, and court-room presentation. Laws governing use of boats & snowmobiles.

Environmental Education (note - not a teaching credential)

Introduction to Outdoor Recreation
Conservation History
Environmental Ed: Methods & Materials
Group Process
Freshwater & Marine Fishes

Art Media Techniques
Ice Climbing
Instruction Practices & Curriculum. Dev.
Sea Kayaking
Geology for the Naturalist

Ecology

We study the three major ecosystem types: terrestrial, freshwater, and marine. Courses stress the differences and similarities between the ecology of individual organisms or species, and the ecology of populations, communities and ecosystems.

General Ecology
Dendrology
Population Ecology
Ornithology
Political Economy of Environmental Issues

Marine Biology
Freshwater Ecology/Limnology
Forest Ecology
Environmental Plant Physiology
North American Indians

Land Use Planning

A given piece of land may have competing values: residential development, production of food or forest products, provision for recreation or wildlife habitat.

Cultural Anthropology
Introduction to Land Use Planning
Land Use Planning Studio
Ethics
Land and Water Law

Geography
Cartography
Natural Resource Policy
Environmental Law
Environmental Pollution

Park Management

Forest Mgm't Technology A.A.S.

Student Body: 30% state, 34% female, 66% male, 2% minority
1994-95 costs: Residents $13,500 Non-residents $14,300 *Guaranteed 4 years
Rolling Admissions
• Recycling and energy conservation policies in force.
• Internships • Co-op Education • Individualized Majors • Vegetarian Meals

Use form in back to contact: Dean of Admissions
Unity College   Unity, ME 04988
(207) 948-3131

UNIVERSITY OF ALABAMA

17,000 Undergraduates   Tuscaloosa, Alabama   Moderately Selective

MAKING A DIFFERENCE STUDIES

Marine Science
Most courses are taught during the summer session at Dauphin Island, Alabama

Ocean Science
Marine Geology
Coastal Climatology
Marsh Ecology
Coastal & Environmental Law
Coastal Ornithology

Coastal Geomorphology
Marine Biology
Marine Botany
Coastal Zone Management
Marine Ecology
Marine Biology for Teachers

Biological Sciences

Poisonous and Medicinal Plants
Field Ornithology
Economic Botany
Limnology (Freshwater Environments)
Ecology of Aquatic Plants & Wetland Ecosystems

Biology of the Lower Plants
Insects and Public Health
Biology, Environment, and Resource Develp't
Tropical Field Studies

Geology

Environmental Geology
Structural Geology
Volcanology
Coastal Plain Geology
Fluvial Systems
Field Geology

Rocks and Minerals
Ground Water Geology
Coal Geology
Introduction to Geophysics
Geostatistics
Mineralogy

Geography: Tracks in Physical Geography and Natural Resources; Urban, Economic and Planning; Regional and Human Geography; Geographic Technique

Geography of the National Parks
Natural Hazards
Soil Science
Political Geography
Community Facilities Planning
Regional Planning and Analysis

Natural Resources & Environmental Planning
Cultural Geography
Urban Geography
Urban Planning and Analysis
Land Use Planning
Forest Ecology

Special Education: Tracks in Orthopedically Handicapped & Other Health Impaired (OHOHI); Early Childhood Ed. for the Handicapped; Hearing Impaired; Learning Disabilities; Emotional Conflict; Mental Retardation; Speech Pathology

Introduction to Special Education
Education of the Hearing Impaired
Introduction to Learning Disabilities
Adapted Teaching
Behavior Management

Instructional Sign Language
Introduction to Communicative Disorders
Emotional Conflict Classroom Methods
Cerebral Palsy Institute
Dev'l Perspectives of Preschool Handicapped

Working With Families With Exceptional Children
Educational Processes for Children & Youth with OHOHI

Nursing

The College values humanistic ideals and believes that the unique experiences of life influence or assist humans to develop as individuals equipped with the capacity to love, value, care, nurture, learn, and creatively solve problems.

International Healthcare
Healthcare of Women
Creative Problem Solving in Nursing
Pain: Holistic Approach to Management
Legal and Ethical Issues in Healthcare
Mental Health Nursing
Family Planning

Abusive Behavior in Families
Cultural Diversity--Impact on Healthcare
Death and Dying: A Personal Perspective
Folklore Health Practices
AIDS: A Caring Response
Community Gerontology
High-Risk Childbearing

Community Health Sciences

Basic Life Support Treatment Modalities
Paramedic Emergency Medical Training
Family Health
Practicum in Emergency Medical Care
The Aging Process

Basic Emergency Medical Technician
Paramedic Clinical
Issues in Contemporary
Intermediate Emergency Medical Technician
Family Health

Health Education

Total Wellness
Personal Health
Community Health
Health Instruction
Design and Evaluation of Health Promotion Programs
Current Issues in Health -- Consumer and Environmental

Introduction to Health Education
First Aid, Safety, and CPR
School Health Programs
Drug Awareness Education

Human Development and Family Studies

Child Devel: Infancy and Toddlerhood
Child Development: School Age
HDFS Internship
Human Development
Conceptual & Creative Experiences for Young Children

Hospitalized Children and Youth
Administering Children's Centers & Programs
Parent and Family Development
Intimate Relationships

Law, Public Policy and Society

American Legal History
Mass Communication Ethics
Power, Public Policy and Technology
Alcohol and Drug Use in America
Environmental Sociology

Consumer Protection
Juvenile Delinquent Behavior
Natural Resources Policy
Law and Society
Modern American Capitalism

"New College" Program

Public Leadership
Science and Technology
Civic Effectiveness
Creativity

Civic Awareness
Social Change
The Population Explosion: Myths & Realities
Human Futures

Civil Engineering

Women's Studies

Student Body: 65% state, 50% women, 50% men, 12% minority,
1994-95 Tuition, Room & Board: Residents $5,810   Non-residents $9,195   Apply By 8/1

Use form in back to contact: Office of Admission Services
University of Alabama   Box 870132   Tuscaloosa, AL 35487
(205) 348-5666 or 1 (800) 933-2262

UNIVERSITY OF ALASKA, FAIRBANKS

3,900 Undergraduates   Fairbanks, Alaska   Moderately Selective

MAKING A DIFFERENCE STUDIES

Natural Resources Mgm't Tracks in Forestry; Plant, Animal & Soil Sciences; Resources

Forest Protection
Introduction to Conservation Biology
Introduction to Watershed Management
Alaskan Environmental Education
Environmental Policies
Ecological Anthropology
Silviculture

Natural Resource Legislation and Policy
Environmental Ethics and Actions
Natural Resources Conservation and Policy
Outdoor Recreation Planning
Cold Lands
Soil Conservation
Internship

Fisheries   **Fisheries Management Option**

The location of UAF is advantageous for the study of interior Alaska aquatic habitats. A number of subartic streams and lakes are within easy reach.

Natural Resources Policies
Geography of Alaska
Magazine Article Writing
Wildlife Management Techniques
Alaska Native Politics

Natural Resources Legislation
Man and Nature
Congress and Public Policy
Wildlife Management--Forest & Tundra
Personnel Management

Wildlife Management

Survey of Wildlife Science
Wildlife Policy and Administration
Wildlife Internships
Wildlife Diseases
Biotelemetry

Wildlife Management Principles
Grazing Ecology
Waterfowl & Wetlands Ecology & Mgm't
Nutrition & Physiological Ecology of Wildlife
Wildlife Populations and their Management

Human Services

Prepares students to function as counselors and social service workers in rural areas. Program is interdisciplinary in its approach, cross-cultural in its content, and rural in its orientation.

Rural Sociology
American Minority Groups
Crisis Intervention
Foundations of Counseling
Sociology of Later Life
Helping Role in Child Abuse & Neglect

Cross Cultural Psychology
Human Behavior in the Artic
Dev. Psych in Cross Cultural Perspectives
Alcoholism:Treatment and Prevention
Community Organization & Dev. Strategies
Group Counseling

Human Service Technology A.A.

Provides training needed for entry level employment in public, private and volunteer human services agencies.

Introduction to Human Service
Cultural Diversity and Human Service
Crisis and Grief Counseling
Family in Cross Cultural Perspective
Ethics in Human Service

Personal Awareness and Growth
Introduction to Addictive Processes
Substance Abuse Counseling
Human Services Practicum
Group Dynamics & Therapeutic Activities

Northern Studies

Perspectives on the North
Visual Images of the North
International Relations of the North
Images of the North
Comparative Government & Politics in the Circumpolar North
Northern Indigenous Peoples & Contemporary Issues

Justice & Social Control in Circumpolar North
Geography of Northern Development
Human Adaptation to Circumpolar North
Researching & Writing Public Northern History

Eskimo Studies: Inupiaq Eskimo or Yupik Eskimo

Inupiaq or Yupik Languages
Native Cultures of Alaska
Peoples of Southwest Alaska
Alaska Native Politics
Inupiaq and Yup'ik People

Eskimo Aleut Languages
Native Alaskan Music
Language and Literacy Development
Historical Linguistics

Rural Development Tracks in Land; Renewable Resources; Local Gov't Administration; Community Research and Documentation; Community Organization and Service

Community Development in the North
Rural Alaska Land Issues
Resource Mgm't Research Techniques
Tribal People and Development
Cultural Impact Analysis
Narrative Art of Alaska Native Peoples
Knowledge of Native Elders
Community Research Techniques

Issues in Alaskan Maritime Development
Perspectives on Subsistence in Alaska
Rural Development in Global Perspective
Community Development Strategies
Women and Development
Economics of Rural Alaska
Rural Social Work
Natural Resource Economics

Education

Alaska Native Education
Orientation to Teaching in Rural Alaska
Marine Education
Cultural Aspects of Language Acquisition
Foundations of Literacy Development

Alaskan Environmental Education
Reading Strategies/ Multicultural Classrooms
Communication in Cross-Cultural Classrooms
Community as an Educational Resource
Microcomputer Application in the Classroom

Fire Science A.A.S. Municipal and Wildlands Fire Control

Wildland Fire Control
Hazardous Materials
Air Operations and Safety
Fire Company Organization and Mgm't
Wildland Fire Business Management
Wildland Fire Prevention, Enforcement and Investigation

Emergency Medical Technician Training
Prescribed Burning & Fuels Management
Wildland Fire Behavior
Fire Research and Development
Emergency Trauma Training

Women's Studies   Forestry-- 3/2 Program with Northern Arizona U.
Social Work   Community Health Aide   Geology

Student body: 89% State, 58% female, 42% male, 14% Alaska Native, 7% other minorities
1994-95 Costs: Residents $6,080   Non-residents $9,916   Apply By 8/1
• Prior Learning Credit   • Weekend & Evening Classes   • Independent Learning
• Third World and Northern Countries Study Abroad

Use form in back to contact: Office of Admissions and Records
University of Alaska, Fairbanks   Fairbanks, Alaska 99775-0060
(907) 474-7821

UNIVERSITY OF CALIFORNIA AT DAVIS

17,5000 Undergraduates   Davis, California   Very Selective

MAKING A DIFFERENCE STUDIES

Civil and Environmental Engineering / Transportation Planning
Transportation planning blends knowledge of the basic concepts of engineering, economics, and planning in the development of policies, programs, and projects.

Construction Principles
Intro to Transportation Planning
Transportation System Design
Energy Policy
Environmental Planning

Intro to Air Pollution
Transportation System Operations
Energy & Enviro. Aspects of Transportation
Methods of Environmental Policy Evaluation
Public Mechanisms for Controlling Land Use

Agricultural Systems and Environment / Sustainable Production Systems
Agricultural Systems and Environment
International Agriculture Development
Forage Crop Ecology
Introduction to Biological Control
Microclimate of Agricultural Systems

Environmental Horticulture
Cereal Crops of the World
Greenhouse and Nursery Crop Production
Ecology and Economics
Conservation of Plant Genetic Sources

Atmospheric Sciences
Introduction to Air Pollution
Atmospheric Dynamics
Boundary Layer Meteorology
Severe and Unusual Weather

Weather Analysis and Forecasting
Computer Methods in Meteorology
Issues in Atmospheric Science
Radiation and Satellite Meteorology

Avian (Bird) Sciences
Intro to Poultry Science
Captive Raptor Management
Fertility and Hatchability
Nutrition of Birds

Birds, Humans, and the Environment
Raptor Migration and Population Fluctuations
Patterns in Avian Biology
Raptor Biology

- **Management of Companion Birds** Captive propagation of birds, including trade and smuggling. Emphasis on parrots and role of captive propagation in conservation.

Environmental Toxicology
Toxicants in the Environment
Food Toxicology
Health Risk Assessments of Toxicants
Principles of Environmental Toxicology

Biological Effects of Toxicants
Air Pollutants and Inhalation Toxicology
Legal Aspects of Enviro Toxicology
Chromatography for analytical Toxicology

Agricultural and Environmental Education   Comparative Literature
Chicana/o Studies   War and Peace   Women's Studies   Entomology
Environmental Studies   Environmental and Resource Sciences

1994-95 Estimated Tuition, Rm. & Board: Residents $10,052   Non-residents $13,412   Apply By 11/30

Use form in back to contact: Office of Undergraduate Admissions
175 Mrak Hall   University of CA   Davis,CA 95616
(916) 752-2971

UNIVERSITY OF CALIFORNIA AT SANTA CRUZ

9,000 Undergraduates   Santa Cruz, CA   Very Selective

MAKING A DIFFERENCE STUDIES

Environmental Studies Tracks in Sustainable Agriculture and Agroecology; Policy, Planning and Public Values; and Natural History and Wildland Conservation

Culture and Environment	Population, Community & Ecosystem Ecology
Natural History of Mammals	Natural History of Birds
Capitalism and Nature	Ecodevelopment
Integrated Pest Management	Principles of Sustainable Agriculture
Environmental Assessment	Environment, Culture and Perception
Conservation Practicum	National Environmental Policy
Energy Resource Assessment and Policy	Watershed Systems Restoration

Political Economy of Sustainable Agriculture in Latin America

Biology Tracks in Marine Biology; Ecology, Evolution and Behavior; Plant Sciences

Kelp Forest Ecology	Intertidal Organisms
Biogeography	Biology of Marine Mammals
Biological Oceanography	Systematic Botany of Flowering Plants
Marine Botany	Infectious Diseases
AIDS: Perspectives on an Epidemic	Biology of Cancer

Community Studies

For students actively committed to social change. Six-month field study or internship.

Social Documentation	Chicanos and Social Change
California: Edge of America	Mass Media and Community Alternatives
Introduction to the AIDS Epidemic	U.S. Regions & the Global Economy
Global Political Economy	Political Economy of U.S. Agriculture
U.S. - Mexico Border Region	Health, Gender and Race

Social Psychology

Health Psychology	Chicano Psychology
Social Psychology of Sex and Gender	Intergroup Relations
Social Psychology of Bilingualism	Social Influences
The Social Context	Psychology and Law
Gender and Power	Organizational Psychology

Sociology/Institutional Analysis

Key Issues in Race and Ethnic Analysis	Family and Society
Development, Inequality, and Ecology	Sociology of Health and Medicine
Communication and Mass Media	Sociology of Education
Drugs in Society	Sociology of Environmental Politics

Sociology of Jury: Racial Disenfranchisement in the Jury and Jury Selection System

Student Body: 91% state, 56% women, 44% men, 32% minority
• The agroecology program maintains a a 25 acre organic garden
1994-95 Estimated Costs: Residents $9,453   Non-residents $16,657   Apply By: 11/30

Use form in back to contact: Dean of Admissions
University of CA, Santa Cruz   Santa Cruz, CA 95064
(408) 459-4008

UNIVERSITY OF COLORADO, BOULDER

25,150 students   Boulder, Colorado   Moderately Selective

As the flagship institution of the four-campus University of Colorado system, CU-Boulder has a long tradition of teaching environmental and social responsibility to students. the campus has an international reputation for environmental education and research programs, which can be pursued through several avenues.

Environmental studies, for example -- a bachelor's degree program in place for more than 40 years - features a comprehensive curricula in the basic sciences, economics, ethics, and policy that prepares students to make a difference in the real world. its two academic tracks -- one in environmental sciences, one in society and policy -- allows undergraduates to specialize in areas ranging from environmental and natural resources to decision-making, planning, and public policy.

The University also offers a unique environmental studies program for undergraduates that offers course work and seminars within a residence hall setting. Basic chemistry and biology classes are offered in sections containing as few as 20 students, providing a small-college atmosphere and personal contact with top-flight faculty.

All of the environmental programs on campus are buoyed by outstanding faculty members, some of whom are affiliated with internationally known campus institutes like the Cooperative Institute for Research in Environmental Science and the Institute of Artic and Alpine Research. The Mountain Research Station, located about 45 minutes from campus, features a long-term ecological study site, and hosts students and faculty from around the world.

The long tradition of volunteer service on campus is underscored by CU-Boulder ranking second in the nation in the number of volunteers recruited by the Peace Corps. A total of 253 students have gone on to Peace Corps service over the past six years, helping people in developing countries to help themselves.

The Center for Studies of Ethnicity and Race in America is one of only four academic programs in the nation to study issues of ethnicity and race. CSERA promotes interdisciplinary research and teaching in Afro-American, American Indian, Asian American and Chicano studies, and cross cultural and comparative race and ethnic studies. The primary focus is on people of color and indigenous peoples of the US, but it also considers important the study of race and ethnic issues in terms of global interaction.

MAKING A DIFFERENCE STUDIES

Environmental Conservation

Principles of Ecology
The Environment and Public Policy
Forest Geography: Principles & Dynamics
Environments and Peoples

Conservation Practice
Remote Sensing of the Environment
Water Resource & Management of Western US
Energy in a Technical Society

Biology: Environmental, Population and Organismic

Environmental Issues and Biology
Conservation Biology for Nonscientists
Artic and Alpine Ecology
Ecosystem Ecology
Ecological Perspectives on Global Change

Principles of Ecology
Global Ecology
Limnology (Water Ecology)
Medical Ecology & Environmental Health
Topics in Montane Ecology

Geography

World Geographic Problems

Conservation Thought

World Agriculture

Nature and Properties of Soils

Mountain Geography

Natural Hazards

Migration, Urbanization and Development

Water Resources & Mgm't of Western US

Urban Geography

Geoecology of Alpine and Artic Regions

International Affairs

Political Geography

International Conflict in a Nuclear Age

Alternative World Futures

International Economics and Policy

Cross-Cultural Aspects of Socioeconomic Development

American Foreign Policy

International Relations

Power: Anthropology of Politics

Comparative Politics: Dev. Political Systems

Sociology Tracks in Population & Health Issues/Health & Medicine/Social Conflict/ Sex and Gender

Sociology of Gender, Health and Aging

Population Control and Family Planning

Men and Masculinity

Nonviolence & Ethics of Social Action

Folk Medicine and Psychiatry in Mexican/Chicano Communities

Women, Development and Fertility

Sex, Gender and Society

Social Issues in Mental Health

Sociology of Natural and Social Environments

Anthropology

Hopi & Navajo, Cultures in Conflict

The Maya

North American Indian Acculturation

Medical Anthropology

Amazonian Tribal Peoples

Ethnography of Mexico & Central America

Analyzing Exotic Languages

Urban Anthropology

Chicano Studies

The Mexican Revolution

The Contemporary Mexican American

Chicano Poetry

Barrio Issues

Hispanic & Native American Culture of SW

Latinos and the American Political System

Folklore, Mysticism & Myth of Hispanic SW

History of the Chicano in Amer. Labor Mvm't

International and National Voluntary Service Training Certificate

Program in global development, human ecology and social justice. Financial aid in return for 1-2 years of community, nat'l or int'l humanitarian service. 6 weeks of travel to a foreign country.

Democratic & Nonviolent Social Mvmts

Global Human Ecology

Facilitating Peaceful Community Change

Global Development

Kinesiology

Scholarly understanding of the multidimensional aspects of human movement and performance.

Introduction to Kinesiology

Modality Usages in Sport Medicine

Nutrition and Physical Performance

Exercise Physiology

Human Development & Movement Behavior

Disabilities and Motor Development

Theory and Practical Applications of Resistance Exercise and Conditioning Programs

Peace & Conflict Studies   Philosophy   Women's Studies   Sociology

Student Body: 67% state, 48% women, 52% men, 13% minority,
1993-94 Costs: Residents $6,410   Non-residents $15,916   Apply By 2/15

Use form in back to contact: Office of Admissions
CPO 30   University of Colorado at Boulder   Boulder, CO 80309-0030
(303) 492-6301

UNIVERSITY OF HAWAII AT MANOA

13,000 Undergraduates   Honolulu, Hawaii   Moderately Selective

MAKING A DIFFERENCE STUDIES

Botany
Plants and Pollution
Plants in the Hawaiian Environment
Ethnobotany
Natural History of Hawaiian Islands
Hawaiian Ethnobotany

Resource Mgm't & Conservation in Hawaii
Ecology of Hawaiian Coastal Algae
Inside Tropical Rainforests
Vegetation Ecology
Plant Evolutionary Diversity

General Science Enviro. Science; Island Environments; History & Nature of Science
Intro to Science: Hawaiian Environments
Technology and Ecology Forum
Endangered Species
Man and Energy in the Island Ecosystem
Natural Science as a Human Activity

Women and Genetics in Society
Environmental Issues
The Atoll
Human Role in Environmental Change
Island Ecosystems

Geography: Tracks in Enviro. Studies and Policies; Resource Systems; Population, Urbanization & Regional Dev.; Cartography, Remote Sensing & Computer Applications
Resource Management in Asia-Pacific
Ecological Concepts and Planning
Tropical Agrarian Systems
Plants, People and Ecosystems
Conservation and Resource Management

Planning in Developing Countries of Asia
Atmospheric Pollution
Environment and Culture
Hazard and Human Decision
Energy Resources

American Studies
Diversity in American Life
Filipino Americans
American Environments: Survey
Nonethnic Minorities
Race and Racism in America

Japanese-American Experience
Contemporary Hawaiian Issues
Television in American Life
American Ideas of Nature
Native America: Hawaiians & White Conflict

Anthropology
Technology and Culture
Pacific Island Cultures
Ecological Anthropology
Polynesian Cultures
Pre-European Hawaii

Aggression, War and Peace
Ethnographic Field Techniques
Medical Anthropology
Micronesian Cultures
Melanesian Cultures

Agronomy and Soil Sciences
Our department is one of only a few in the nation with a special commitment to linkages with the developing world, and the only one fully dedicated to crops and soils of the tropics.

**Civil Engineering   Hawaiian Studies   Entomology   Pacific Island Studies
Social Work   Peace Studies   Women's Studies**

Student Body: 90% state, 54% women, 46% men, 58% Asian-American, 7% Native American, 1994-95 Tuition: Residents $1,556   Non-Residents $4,556   Apply By: 6/15

Use form in back to contact: Director of Admissions
University of Hawaii at Manoa   Honolulu, HI 96822
(808) 956-8975

UNIVERSITY OF MAINE

10,000 Undergraduates   Orono, Maine   Moderately Selective

MAKING A DIFFERENCE STUDIES

Forest Biology—Five year Program

Forest Resources   Forest Surveying & Mapping
Forest Ecology   Silviculture
Forest Protection   Forest Resources Policy
Conservation Biology   Artificial Regeneration
Tropical Deforestation   Wildlife Conservation
Forest Wildlife Management   International Conservation

- **Sustainable Tropical Forestry** An exploration of strategies for producing and extracting products from tropical forests in sustainable ways which will provide maximum employment for indigenous people and cause the least environmental harm.

Bio-Resource Engineering

Intro to Bio-Resource Engineering   Water Supply and Waste Management
Energy and Society   Engineering for Sustainable Agriculture
Energy Efficient Housing   Soil and Water Resources Engineering
Irrigation and Water Supply Design   Plant Science
Coastal Engineering   Aquatic Food Webs

- **Metals and Society** Metals technology in society, past and present, including the scope of our metallic resources, mining and concentration methods, extraction, refining, and fabrication. Covers environmental effects and recycling.

Geography/Rural Resource Management

Geography of Maine   Geography of Canada and U.S.
Sociology of Rural Life   Soil and Water Conservation
Contemporary Rural Problems   Resource Economics
Land Use Planning   Government Policies Affecting Rural America
Resource Economics   Natural Resource Economics and Policy
The Individual and the Community   Forest Recreation Planning

Geography/Human Use of Earth

Intro to Ecology   Cultural Geography
Soil and Water Conservation   Environmental History of Europe
Land Use Planning   History of Treatment of American Environment
Landscape Design Problems   Forest Watershed Management
Interaction Between Humans and Their Environment

Natural Resources Tracks in Resource & Environmental Economics, Marine
Sciences; Soil and Water,Environmental Entomology; Waste Management

Natural Resource Economics and Policy   Resource Economics
Public Finance and Fiscal Policy   Forest Economics
Public Management   Introduction to Public Policy
Marine Fisheries Management   Microeconomics
Marine Mariculture   Shellfisheries Biology
Aquatic Food Webs   Fundamentals of Environmental Engineering
Urban Policy and Management   Algae Growth and Seaweed Mariculture

Sustainable Agriculture

Integrated ecologically sound strategies, how to build soil tilth and fertility through rotations, multiple cropping, nutrient recycling, protection of water quality and human health.

Insect Pest Management
Soil Organic Matter and Fertility
Engineering for a Sustainable Agriculture
Agricultural Ecology
Agricultural Pest Ecology
Sustainable Animal Production

Pest-Plant Interactions
Plant Science
Ecology
Pesticides and the Environment
Principles and Practices of Sustainable Agric.

Public Administration

Foundations of Public Administration
Health Care and Human Services
Human Resource Management
Medical Anthropology
Ethical Issues in Health Care
Environmental Engineering

Critical Analysis in Public Administration.
Urban Politics
Topics in City and Town Management
Industrial Workers in America
Sociology of Mental Illness
Public Organization and Management

Recreation & Park Management/Interpretation Concentration

Conservation Biology
Environmental Interpretation
Wilderness and Wild River Management
Field Ornithology
Geology of Maine

Aspects of the Natural Environment
Visitor Behavior and Management
Field Natural History of Maine
Social Problems
Introduction to Forest Resources

Peace Studies

The U.S. and Vietnam: A History
Islamic Fundamentalism
Hunger as an Issues in Social Welfare
U.S. Foreign Policy
Religion and Politics
Hunger in U.S. and the World
Tropical Deforestation Seminar
Wealth, Power and Prestige
Perspectives on Women
World Food Demand, Population and World Food Supply

Latin America: Reform and Revolution
African Politics
Nuclear War
Sustainable Agriculture
Violence in the Family
Economic Development
Race and Culture Conflict
International Conservation
Education for Intercultural Understanding

- **Humanistic Economics** Body of economic thought that explicitly values human dignity and ecological sustainability. Socio-economic institutions and modern economic doctrines will be re-examined in light of these two basic values. Wage systems; economic cooperatives; international economic order; economic. rationality and efficiency; economic imperialism; sustainable development and Third World poverty.

Land Use Planning
Women's Studies

Natural History & Ecology
Forest Engineering

Student Body: 81% state, 47% women, 53% men, 4% students of color
1994-95 estimated costs: Residents $7,958   Non-residents $14,352   Apply By 2/1

Use form in back to contact: Admissions Office
University of Maine   Orono, ME 04469-5713
(207) 581-1561

UNIVERSITY OF MINNESOTA

COLLEGE OF NATURAL RESOURCES

28,000 Undergraduates   Minneapolis, Minnesota   Moderately Selective

MAKING A DIFFERENCE STUDIES

Fisheries and Wildlife

Fisheries and Wildlife Techniques
Important Plants in F & W Habitats
Ecology of Fishes
Writing in your Profession
Avian Conservation
Environmental Policy

Ecosystems: Form & Function
Fisheries and Wildlife Management
Wildlife: Ecology, Values and Human Impact
Natural Resource Inventory
Water Quality in Natural Resource Mgm't
Pollution Impacts on Aquatic Systems

- **Ethics and Values in Resource Management**   Various aesthetic, economic, and ecological values of wildlife and fisheries resources. Process and ethics of resource management, and such controversies as sport, subsistence, and native peoples' harvest rights and genetic engineering.

Paper Science & Engineering

Bio & Enviro Science of Pulp & Paper
Pulp and Paper Operations
Analysis of Production Systems
Role of Renewable Natural Resources in Developing Countries

Analysis and Design of Wastewater Systems
Analysis and Design of Water Supply Systems
Surface & Colloid Chemistry of Papermaking

Forest Products   Tracks in Marketing and Production Management

Forest Products Marketing
Buyer Behavior and Marketing Analysis
Public Relations
Quality Control & Reliability
Analysis of Production Systems

Public Speaking
Wood Drying and Preservation
Natural Resource Policy and Administration
Industrial Safety
Renewable Nat. Res. in Developing Countries

Forest Resources

Forest Resources Orientation
Minnesota Plants
Field Forest Measurements
Forest Recreation Planning
Soil-Site Relationships

Elements of Surveying
Northern Forest Ecosystems
Forest Ecology
Techniques of Forest Wildlife Mgm't
Forest Economics & Planning

Forest Resources - Hydrology Emphasis

Water Resources Engineering
Water Quality in Natural Resource Mgm't
Range Management
Soil Physics
Forest Soils

Watershed Engineering
Water Quality Engineering
Groundwater Geology
Microclimatology
Advanced Forest Hydrology

Forest Resources: Soils Emphasis

The Soil Resource
Forest Soils
Intro Tree Physiology & Genetics
Glacial Geology
Field Study of Soils for Environmental Assessment

Soil Fertility
Forest Entomology
Soil Biology
Interpretation of Land Resources

Forest Resources Management & Administration Emphasis
Introduction to Planning
Legal Environment of Public Affairs
Business and Society
Human Relations and Applied Organization Theory
Natural Resource Management: Political and Administrative Processes

Quantitative Techniques in Forest Mgm't
American Bureaucracy
Psychology in Management

Forest Harvesting
Forest Fire Management
Low Volume Forest Roads
Engineering Economics
Natural Resources Inventory

Forest Economics and Planning
Topics in Forest Industries Management
Range Management
Forest Ecology

Silviculture / Forest Biology
Forest Entomology
Forest Soils
Forestry Applications of Microcomputers
Remote Sensing of Natural Resources

Forest Pathology
Ecological Plant Geography
Ecology of Plant Communities
Soil Biology

Natural Resources and Environmental Studies: Core Curriculum
Intro to Meteorology
Problem Solving in Natural Resources
Intro to Fisheries and Wildlife
Hydrology and Water Quality
Technology and Western Civilization

Forest Hydrology
Experience and Training in Field Setting
Resource Dev. & Environmental Economics
The Soil Resource
Anthropology of Resource Management

Resources and Environmental Protection
Land Economics
Pollution Impacts on Aquatic Systems
Organic and Pesticidal Residues
Environmental Policy

Resource and Environmental Economics
Assessing the Ecological Effects of Pollution
Intro to Hazardous Waste Management
Ecology & Mgm't of Fish & Wildlife Habitats

Environmental Issues and Planning
Economic Dev. of American Agriculture
Energy Research Use
Recreation Land Policy
Politics, Planning and Decision Making
Politics of the Regulatory Process

Resource Dev. & Environmental Economics
Assessing the Ecological Effects of Pollution
Environmental Policy
Management of Recreational Lands
Impact Assessment and Enviro Mediation

Urban Forestry
Urban Forest Management
Insect Pest Management
Nursery Management & Production
Plant Propagation
Forest Genetics

Forest Economics and Planning
Farm and Small Woodlands Forestry
Herbaceous Plant Materials
Landscape Management
Strategy and Tactics in Project Planning

Waste Management
Soil Resources

Water Resources
Resource Assessment

UM Student Body: 88% state, 50% women, 50% men, 9% minority
1994-95 Estimated costs: Residents $5,563 Non-residents $9709   Rolling Admissions
• Field Studies   • Internships   • Co-op Work Study   • Independent Study

Use form in back to contact: Office of Admissions
University of Minnesota   Minneapolis, MN 55455
(612) 625-2006

UNIVERSITY OF NEW MEXICO

20,000 Undergraduates   Albuquerque, New Mexico   Moderately Selective

MAKING A DIFFERENCE STUDIES

Geography
Economic Geography
Human Geography
Urban environment
Problems in Arid Lands
Latin American Development
Biogeography

Survey of Environmental Issues
Water in Environmental Systems
Land Use Practice and Planning
World Food Systems
Environmental Conservation
Nature and Culture in America

Sign Language
Introduction to Signed Language
American Sign Language
Interpreting
Dynamics for Interpreters
Signed Language Linguistics

Orientation to Deafness
Manually Coded English
Fingerspelling
Language & Culture in the Deaf Community
Practicum in Sign Language Interpreting

Economics
The Environmental Problem
The Economic Status of Women
Economics of Poverty
American Indian Economic Development
Labor and Public Policy
Natural Resources

Radical vs. Conservative Economics
Economics of Labor Relations
Economics of Health
Urban Economics
Energy Policy & Administration
Environmental Economics

Community and Regional Planning
Intro to Environmental Problems
Environmental Evaluation
The Housing Process
Community and Regional Planning
Planning Process and Issues of Native American Reservations

Community Planning: Concepts & Methods
Land Development Economics
Cultural Aspects of Community Development
Community Growth and Land Use Planning

American Studies
Myths and Rituals of American Life
Southwest Indian Communities
Schools in Crisis
Blacks in the US West
Technology and Society

The Black Experience in the US
Ecology in American Thought
Women and Nature
La Mujer Chicana
Women's Experience in the US

Mechanical Engineering
Energy Utilization and Conversion
Solar Thermal Energy System Design

Solar Thermal Energy System Components
Entrepreneurial Engineering

Native American Studies   **African-American Studies**   **Chicano Studies**
Aging Studies   **Women's Studies**   **Peace Studies**

Student Body: 88% state, 51% women, 49% men, 33% minority
1994-95 Tuition: Residents $1,884   Non-residents $7,114 Rm & Board $4,000   Apply By: 7/20

Use form in back to contact: Director of Admissions
University of New Mexico   Albuquerque, NM 87131
(505) 277-2446

UNIVERSITY OF NORTH DAKOTA

10,650 Undergraduates   Grand Forks, North Dakota   Noncompetitive

MAKING A DIFFERENCE STUDIES

Environmental Geology & Technology
View of the Earth and Planets
Moral Questions and the Professions
Wildlife Conservation
Fisheries Management
Promotional Methods
Air Pollution
Hydraulic Engineering

Tracks in Enviro Studies & Water Resources
Natural History of the Northern Plains
General Ecology
Aquatic Ecology
Fundamentals of Public Speaking
Economics of Natural Res.& the Environment
Natural Science and Culture of the Plains
Subsurface Disposal of Liquid Waste

Meteorological Studies
Air Pollution Meteorology
Meteorology Instrumentation
Computer Concepts in Meteorology
Co-operative Education

Meteorology
Dynamic Meteorology
High Altitude Meteorology
Cloud Physics

Social Work
Social Policy Analysis
Culture, Illness & Health
Contemporary Issues in Rehabilitation
Social Welfare
Black American Writers

Social Work in a Modern Society
History of Three Affiliated Tribes
Culture Area Studies
Social Inequality
Introduction to Indian Studies

Social Work: Chemical Use/Abuse Awareness
Drugs: Addiction Dynamics
Drugs and Society
Contemporary American Indian Issues
Social Problems

Drugs Subject to abuse
Principles of Drug Action
Dynamics of Addiction
Development and Education of Adolescents

Indian Studies
UND serves reservation communities, especially in educational & human service programs.
North American Indians
Indian Sign Language
Intro Survey of Chippewa History
Contemporary Plains Indian Culture
Primitive Technology
History of Federal Indian Law and Policy

Contemporary American Indian Issues
American Indian Languages
History of the Western Sioux
Urban Indian Studies
Native American Arts and Crafts
Cultural Uses of Plants by Regional Indians

Fisheries & Wildlife Biology
Public Administration

Gerontology
Peace Studies

Student Body: 90% state, 4% minority, 46% women, 54% men
1994-95 Costs: Residents $5,158   Non-residents $8,682   Apply By: 7/1
• Note: UND Energy and Environmental Research Center conducts research on
geothermal resources, solar,wind, biomass and oxygenated fuels. Topics include energy
policy, air-emissions control technologies, and mined-land reclamation.

Use form in back to contact: Enrollment Services Office
University of North Dakota   Grand Forks, ND 58202-8135
(701) 777-4463

UNIVERSITY OF OREGON

14,000 Undergraduates   Eugene, Oregon   Moderately Selective

The University of Oregon is recognized nationally and internationally as a research university committed to liberal arts and sciences education as well as professional preparation. The liberal arts serve as the core of our university. Regardless of your major, you'll have the chance to explore a wide range of ideas and concepts. Open discussion, experimentation, questioning, and sharing information are what UO values. If you're curious, you will like it here.

As a UO student, you can choose a course of study from more than 90 comprehensive programs, including professional schools of architecture, business, education, journalism, law, and music. UO has developed innovative programs to ensure that its undergraduates have access to seminars, discussion groups, and other small-class settings that encourage direct interaction with some of our finest teachers and researchers.

Freshman Interest Groups provide academically based social groups by placing participating freshmen in small-class settings and seminars with students who have similar interests or majors. Freshman seminars are small, discussion oriented classes that put some of our most respected professors in touch with our newest students.

UO's more than 300,000 graduates include leaders in business, economics, publishing, government, education, science, and the arts -- including two Nobel Prize winners, a Pulitzer Prize-winning author, six U.S. senators, eleven U.S. representatives, and six Oregon governors.

The sharing of knowledge and the love of learning do not stop at the borders of the campus. Public service is also important to the university. Members of the UO faculty share their experience and knowledge in numerous community activities. Students work as interns in a wide variety of education programs in the community and volunteer their help in service activities.

The University's Solar Energy Center emphasizes a regional approach to research in the utilization of the sun's radiant energy for heating water; for the lighting, heating, and cooling of buildings; and for the generation of electricity. Current work includes the development of passive solar design information in solar heating, passive cooling, and daylighting. The center sponsors frequent seminars attended by university and community people involved in various aspects of solar energy use.

UO off-campus facilities include Pine Mountain Observatory and the Oregon Institute of Marine Biology, situated on 107 acres of coastal property along Coos Bay. The many different marine environments in that area provide an ideal location for the study of marine organisms. The institute offers summer and fall programs, and an interdisciplinary courses including marine ecology, marine mammals and birds, algae, and biological oceanography.

We're located in a city known for its individuality. Eugene combines the relaxed amenities of a small town with the cultural offerings of a much larger city. The Pacific Northwest offers a world of recreational activities: watch migrating whales or spectacular sunsets from rocky cliffs, or charge downhill through a flurry of light powder at the Mt. Bachelor ski area.

226

MAKING A DIFFERENCE STUDIES

Environmental Studies
This interdisciplinary minor investigates the relations of humans and their environment.

American Environmental History
Environmental Alteration
Marine Field Studies
Population Ecology
The Natural Environment
Marine field Studies

Earth Resources and the Environment
Freshwater Ecology
Natural Resource Policy
Solar Energy
World Value Systems
Environmental Alternation

Architecture
This five-year program addresses design technology; social and behavioral factors in design; housing in society; and light and color in the environment.

Architectural Form and Urban Quality
Environmental Control Systems
Light and Color in the Environment
Seismic Study
Spatial Composition and Dynamics

Daylighting
Housing in Society
Preservation and Restoration Technology
Solar Heating
Settlement Patterns: Japanese Vernacular

- **Passive Cooling** Passive or natural cooling for buildings emphasizing design implications. Theory, application, and special problems in ventilation, and storage mass, radiation, evaporation, earth contact, and shading.

Landscape Architecture - Five year program
This environmental profession is concerned with design, planning, and management of landscapes. It includes landscape architecture technology; plant materials; landscape analysis and planning; history, and literature. The goal is to produce visually literate and environmentally responsible citizens capable of playing a central professional role in the evolving landscape.

Environmental Alteration
Landscape Preservation
Natural Resource Policy
Plants
The Garden

Hydrology and Water Resources
National Parks
Planting Design Theory
Site Planning and Design
Urban Farm

Planning, Public Policy and Management Tracks in Planning & Community Dev., Public Policy and Mgm't, Resource Development & Enviro Mgm't, or Social Policy Dev.
How government and other public institutions adapt to and manage change to meet societal needs. Options for study and work in Marshall Islands, Micronesia, and Republic of Palau.

Communities and Regional Development
Contemporary Housing Issues
Forces that Shape the Urban Environment
Natural Resource Policy
Topics in Natural Resource Planning
Policy Development and Evaluation

Community Planning Workshop
Environmental Health Planning
Managing Nonprofit Organizations
Neighborhood and Community Revitalization
Women in Planning and Public Policy
Socioeconomic Development

Peace Studies

American Radicalism
Crisis in Central America
Irenology: The Study of Peace
Population and Global Resource

Conflict and Negotiation
Current Issues in Peacemaking
Nonviolence and Peacemaking
Sustainable Develp't: Women & Peace Politics

International Studies

International relations, regional cultures and area studies, and global perspectives and issues. The UO has particular strengths in the study of New Europe, Russian and Eastern European studies, Asian and Pacific studies, Southeast Asian studies, and Latin American studies.

Aid to Developing Countries
International Protection of Human Rights
Population and Global Resources
Global Ecology
World Value Systems

Environmental Planning
Introduction to World Value Systems
Rich & Poor Nations: Conflict &Cooperation
Ethnology of Hunters and Gatherers
Women and Development in Third World

- **Int'l Community Development** Village communities and their development. Critical skills for effective community develop't work. Values & alternative develop'nt strategies.

Outdoor Pursuits Leadership:

Backpacking Preparation
Cross Country Skiing
Mountain Rescue Techniques
Rock Climbing
Principles of Outdoor Leadership

Canyoneering
First Aid
River Rescue Techniques
Snow Camping Preparation
Principles of Outdoor Education

Women's Studies

History of Women in the U S
Women's Issues in Aging
Philosophy and Feminism
Sociology of Social Welfare
Sociology of Women

Women in Chinese Literature
History and Development of Feminist Theory
Women and Their Art
Women, Minorities and the Media
Educational History of American Women

Political Science

Public Policy and Citizen Action
Women and Politics
Public Policy and Administration
Environmental Politics
Politics of Multi-Ethnic Societies

Political Power, Influence and Control
Mass Media and American Politics
Ocean Politics
International Protection of Human Rights
Inequality and Public Policy

The International College

This program is for students interested in global issues, requiring classes which have an international focus. It is both an academic and residential program. The student body, half of whom are international students, take classes together and also live together. The college is designed to accommodate students in any major, including professional schools and the sciences.

Study Abroad: Australia, China, Czechoslovakia, Denmark, Ecuador, England, Finland, France, Germany, Hungary, Indonesia, Israel, Italy, Japan, Korea, Mexico, Netherlands, Norway, Poland, Russia, Scotland, Spain, Sweden, Thailand, and Vietnam.

Journalism   Women's Studies   Burmese, Thai, Indonesian Languages

Student Body: 64% state, 51% women, 49% men, 10% int'l, 10% students of color
1994-95 Estimated Tuition: Residents : $3,100   Nonresident: $10,600   Housing: $3,800
Apply by 3/1   Avg. students in first year class: 33
- Internships   • Co-op Work Study   • Individualized Majors
- Single Parent Programs   • Core/Multidisciplinary Classes   • Vegetarian Meals

For more information contact: Office of Admissions
1217 University of Oregon   Eugene, OR 97403-1217
(503) 346-3201

UNIVERSITY OF VERMONT

8,000 Undergraduates   Burlington, Vermont   Moderately Selective

MAKING A DIFFERENCE STUDIES

Agroecology (Sustainable Agriculture)

Requires a 12 week internship at an approved farm practicing sustainable agriculture.

Agriculture & Resource Economics	Agriculture in the Third World
Alternatives for Vermont Agriculture	Energy Alternatives
Integrated Forest Protection	Livestock Production
Biosphere (Gaia) Ecology	Soil Erosion & Conservation
Insect Pest Management	Environmental Economics
Biological Control of Pest Insects	Environmental Soils
Agroecology	Composting
Farming Internship	Ecological Vegetable Production

- Faculty Bio **William Murphy** (Ph.D. in Agronomy, U of Wisconsin) Bill Murphy grew up on a Wisconsin dairy farm. As a Peace Corps volunteer in Chile, and having done both graduate research and United Nations work in Brazil, he has experience with many agricultural systems.

Agricultural & Resource Economics Tracks in International Dev.; Rural Economy

Comparative Economic Systems	World Food, Population & Development
Agriculture in Economic Development	World Food Problems & Policies
Agriculture, Planning & Project Dev.	Anthropology of Third World Development
World Natural Environments	Intro to Economic Geography
Intro to Urban & Regional Planning	Community Organization & Development
Rural Planning	Natural Resources Evaluation
Public Policy Analysis	Resource Economics
Land Economics Issues	Rural Communities in Modern Society

Natural Resources Tracks in Enviro Studies-Natural Resources; Aquatic Resources; Integrated Natural Resources; Terrestrial Ecology; Forest Biology; Forest Mgm't; Public Outdoor Recreation; Urban Forestry; Wildlife Biology & Fisheries Biology

Draws from the traditional disciplines, and provides a contemporary holistic framework that complements traditional natural resources curricula.

The American Wilderness	Forest Ecology
Water as a Natural Resource	Environmental Policy
Int'l Problems in Natural Resource Mgm't.	Assessing Environmental Impact
Principles of Wildlife Management	Ecological Aspects of Nat. Res. Conservation
Race & Culture in Natural Resources	Natural Resource Measurements & Mapping
Environmental Aesthetics & Planning	Landscape Ecology
Wilderness & Wilderness Management	Natural Resource. Biostatistics
Toxic & Hazardous Substances in Surface Waters	
Effect of Human Activities on the Lake Champlain Ecosystem	

Forestry Tracks in Urban Forestry & Landscape Horticulture

North American Trees	Principles of Agriculture Resource Economics
Woody Landscape Plants	Soil Fertility & Management
Forestry	Landscape Design
Forest Entomology	Garden Flowers & Indoor Plants
Urban Forestry	

Environmental Studies

Intro to Environmental Studies
Environmental Theory
Environmental Practicum
Environmental Policy
Environmental Education

International Environmental Studies
Environmental Ethics
Environmental Economics
Environmental Law
Research Methods

Wildlife and Fisheries Biology

Wildlife Conservation
Fisheries Biology
Florida Ecology Field Trip
Uplands Wildlife Ecology
Wildlife and Fisheries Practium

Ornithology
Wildlife Habitat & Population Measurements
Wetlands Ecology & Marsh Management
Marine Ecology
Principles of Wildlife Management

Women's Studies

Images of the Goddess
Women & Public Policy in Vermont
Feminist Theory
Women, Society & Culture
History of Women in US

Women & Society
Studies in Gender & Religion
Women in Develop't: Third World Countries
Psychology of Women
Women in the U.S. Economy

Sociology

Social Movements & Collective Behavior
Race & Ethnicity in Canada & U.S.
Population, Environment & Society
Aging & Ethical Issues
Affluence & Poverty in Modern Society

Race Relations in the US
Drugs & Society
Minority Groups
Sex, Marriage, Family
Alienation in Modern Society

Early Childhood and Human Development

Intro to Early Childhood & Human Dev.
Public Policy and Programs for Elders
Infancy
The Emerging Family
Adolescent Development

Contemporary Issues in Parenting
Family Ecosystems
Personal & Family Development in Later Life
Human Relationships and Sexuality
Creative Curriculum Activities

Communication Science and Disorders

Voice and Articulation
Disorders of Language
Current Research in Language Acquisition
Audiological Assessment
Measurement & Mgm't of Communication Disorders
Auditory Habilitation of Hearing Impaired Children

Fundamentals of Hearing
Disorders of Speech
Physiological Phonetics

Social Work   Teaching Credential in Enviro Studies (7-12)

Student Body: 50% state, 6% minority, 54% women, 46% men, 1% int'l
1994-95 costs: Residents $11,768 Nonresidents $21,070   Apply By 2/1

• Field Studies • Internships • Study Abroad • Individualized majors

Use form in back to contact: Director of Admissions
University of Vermont   Burlington, VT 05405
(802) 656-3370

UNIVERSITY OF WASHINGTON
COLLEGE OF FOREST RESOURCES
150 Students (CFR)   Seattle, Washington   Moderately Selective

MAKING A DIFFERENCE STUDIES

Urban Forestry
Role of plants and ecosystems in urban environments; role of people in mgm't of urban forests.

Landscape Plant Recognition	Curatorial Practices in Public Gardens
Landscape Plant Selection	Landscape Plant Management
Computers in Enviro Design & Planning	Urban Plant Protection
Public Outreach in Urban Horticulture	Wetland Ecology & Management
Site Planning	Ecological Concepts & Urban Ecosystems

Forest Resources Management

Forest Transportation	Forest Ecosystems
Forest Stand Dynamics	Intro to Forest Resources Management
Wildlife Biology & Conservation	Forest Protection
Forest Management & Economics	Environmental Impact and Assessment
Forest Planning & Project Management	Management of Wildland Recreation

Conservation of Wildland Resources

Introduction to Wildland Conservation	Wildlife Biology and Conservation
Forest Resources	Social Functions of Forest Ecosystems
Dendrology and Autecology	Physical Aspects of the Forest Environment
Forest Policy and Law	Wilderness Preservation and Management
Economics of Forest Use	Natural Resources Utilization & Public Policy

- **Global Change & Forest Biology** Ecological & Biological effects of atmospheric pollutants, acid precipitation, and climate change on forest trees and ecosystems. Potential climate changes are compared to current and historical climates.

Wildlife Science

Wildlife Field Techniques	Biology and Conservation of Birds
Wildlife Biology and Conservation	Range and Wildlife Habitat
Wildlife Seminar	Human Culture and Wildlife Conservation
Social Functions of Forest Ecosystems	Quant've Assessment of Wildlife Populations

Forest Products & Engineering
Forest engineers evaluate engineering, economic, biological, environmental, and social aspects of forest multiple use mgm't, as affected by access, harvest, transportation, and timber use.

Forest Surveying and Transportation	Timber Harvesting Management
Creativity and Innovation	Introduction to Soil Mechanics
Snow Hydrology	Wildland Hydrology
Forest Harvesting	Microclimatology
Hillslope Stability and Land Use	Hillslope Hydrology

Student Body: 90% state, 48% women, 52% men, 23% minority
1994-95 costs: Residents: $7,851   Non-residents: $13,143   Apply By 2/1

- Note: Forestry Dep't indicates there is a lot of room in forestry programs, and very small classes

Use form in back to contact: Director of Admissions
College of Forest Resources   University of Washington   Seattle, WA 98195
(206) 543-9686

UNIVERSITY OF WISCONSIN, STEVENS POINT
COLLEGE OF NATURAL RESOURCES

1,500 CNR Students   Stevens Point, Wisconsin   Moderately Selective

The College of Natural Resources (CNR) is widely regarded as the leading undergraduate program in natural resources in the United States. It began in 1946 with the nation's first conservation education major. The conservation education program provided a broad background in natural resources management, ethics and philosophy for high school teachers. In 1970, the College was formally established and is now the largest undergraduate program in North America, with over 60 faculty and staff, 1600 undergraduates and 70 graduate students. The strength of the program is the interdisciplinary education of our students. All students take coursework in forestry, wildlife, water resources and soils before focusing on their major.

Graduates of the CNR are in great demand. Our students have many job offers and overall, 80 -100% either go to graduate school or find jobs in their fields.

All of CNR's faculty are committed to undergraduate education with over one fourth receiving the coveted excellence in teaching recognition at UW Stevens Point.

UWSP is located on the north edge of Sevens Point in Portage County, the geographic center of Wisconsin. Portage County is located within an ecological "tension zone" that separates northern plant and animal communities from those in the south. As a result, the county has a rich diversity of flora and fauna. A general inventory of the county includes: 160,000 aces of forest land, 32,000 acres of wetlands, 31,000 acres of public lands within a 20 mile radius of campus, 64 streams and 135 lakes.

Students at CNR are are involved. The CNR has 16 student professional organizations with over 650 active members. Student organization members gain skills and experience in leadership development, communications, public relations and practical application of their knowledge. Over 150 students held paying internship positions in 1992, earning in excess of $300,000, with 56 state, federal and private agencies throughout the United States.

The CNR emphasizes field experience in all curricula. The College operates three field stations. Treehaven is a 1,200 acre field station near Tomahawk, Wisconsin that serves as a year round conference center as well as a base for our summer camp and short courses. All CNR students participate in a six week summer camp field experience at Treehaven or attend a similar program in Europe. The Central Wisconsin Environmental Station (CWES) is a 500 acre facility on Sunset Lake, 17 miles east of Stevens Point. CWES is a year-round conference and education center. The Schmeeckle Reserve is a 200 acre nature preserve, adjacent to the UWSP campus, that provides a field laboratory for many UWSP classes as well as an extension of the city park program.

CNR international programs allow students to gain a global perspective on resource management. The three international programs coordinated by the CNR are: the European Environmental Studies program in Poland and Germany for 6 weeks; a semester abroad in Australia, New Zealand & the Fiji Islands; and an interim trip to study rain forest ecology in Costa Rica for 3 weeks.

MAKING A DIFFERENCE STUDIES

Wildlife
Wildlife Ecology
Wildlife and Society: Contemporary Issues
Wildlife Diseases
Wildlife Population Dynamics
Human Dimensions of Wildlife and Fisheries Management

Wildlife Forum
Principles of Captive Wildlife Management
Management of Wildlife Habitat
Nonconsumptive Uses of Wildlife

International Resource Management
International Resources Management
Processes of Sociocultural Change
Peoples of Central & South America
World Populations & Resources
United Nations At Work

Internship
International Economics
Latin American Development
Introduction to Environmental Study
Environmental Psychology

Resource Management (Conservation) Secondary Teaching Certification
Foundations of Enviro Education
Environmental Policy
American Environmental History

Resource Economics
Population Problems
Environmental Degradation: World Survey

Environmental Education Elementary & Middle School
Intro to Enviro Study & Enviro Education
Environmental Field Studies
General Ecology

Environmental Field Studies
Environmental Ethics
Physical Environment Under Stress

Captive Wildlife Management
Animal Physiology
Wildlife Diseases
Animal Behavior
Museum Methods

Principles of Captive Wildlife Management
Techniques of Captive Wildlife Management
Wildlife Economics
Animal Parasitology

Environmental Communication
Natural Resources and Public Relations
Interpretive Publications
Planning for Interpretation
Interpersonal Communication
Film Laboratory

Interpretive Signs, Trails and Waysides
Interpretation for Visitor Centers
Oral Interpretation Methods
Basic Broadcasting Laboratory
Local Production of Media

Natural Resources Tracks in Enviro Education & Interpretation; Land Use Planning; Youth Programming & Camp Mgm't; General Resource Mgm't
Environmental Interpretation Practicum
International Resource Mgm't
Integrated Resources Management
Environmental Law Enforcement
Park Interpretation

Citizen Action in Environmental Education
Resource Economics
Environmental Issues Investigation
Natural Resource and Public Relations
Soil Conservation & Watershed Inventory

Urban Forestry Mgm't   **Soil Science**   **Aquatic Toxicology**

Groundwater Mgm't   **Water Chemistry**   **Fisheries**

1994-95 Estimated costs: Residents $5,168 Non-residents $9644   Rolling Admissions

Use form in back to contact: College Of Natural Resources
University Of Wisconsin - Stevens Point   Stevens Point, WI 54481
(715) 346-2441

WARREN WILSON COLLEGE

500 Students   Asheville, North Carolina   Moderately Selective

Warren Wilson College is located on a beautiful 1100 care campus in a mountain valley that the Native Americans called "Swannanoa -- "Land of Beauty." It is a setting that throughout history has inspired community, creativity, learning and a sense of harmony with the environment. The mission of Warren Wilson College is to provide a liberal arts education combining study, participation in a campus wide work program, and required community service in a setting that promotes wisdom and understanding, spiritual growth, and contribution to the common good. Each component of this triad plays an important role in the education of a whole person.

The college invites to its educational community individuals who are dedicated to personal and social transformation and to stewardship of the natural environment. The core curriculum emphasizes how we learn and explores various "ways of knowing" in which humans have created or found meaning. A required freshman seminar such as "Thinking Globally, Acting Locally"; "Cosmologies; War in the Modern World"; and "Centering on the Creative Self" allows new students to explore various fields of study. The four-term calendar (students normally take two or three courses per term) allows concentration in a few subjects at a time. Classes are small (average class size of 11) and there are ample opportunities for independent tutorials.

Students have been the core work force for the college since its founding 100 years ago. Each student works 15 hours each week on one of 70 work crews that help run the campus, and the work compensates for approximately $2,040 toward school costs. The work crews give students experiential learning opportunities in their field of study: pre-vet students feed and medicate the pigs and cattle on the 300 acre college farm; education majors assist at the Early Learning Center where low-income families enroll their children in a Head Start nursery school, while others might provide support to the English Department or work in the campus computer center.

The work crew is not the only commitment Warren Wilson students make. Each student is also responsible for giving a minimum of 20 community service hours each year in the Asheville community, their home town, or in another country. The college believes that service to society enables students to make a difference in the world, understand the needs of others, and develops a moral perspective that benefits humankind. Examples of service projects include working at homeless shelters, rape-crisis centers, building homes with Habitat for Humanity, serving as Big Brothers and Sisters at juvenile jails, establishing tree plantations in Nicaragua, building one-room school houses in Indian villages, and developing water collection systems in Kenya.

Warren Wilson's student body comes from 40 different states and 30 different countries. Because the college is a small community of 500 students, it is a natural environment for students and staff to learn about different cultures whether, it be a different part of the United States or an entirely different nation. Ninety percent of Warren Wilson students and seventy-five percent of the faculty and staff live on campus. Because students and staff live, work, and serve together, there is a strong sense of coherence and membership in the campus community.

The college is the perfect size for both students and staff to be involved and challenged with community leadership roles. The staff meets bi-weekly for a staff forum where issues, goals, and ideas are communicated and acted upon. The student government also plays an important role in the college's short and long term plans. They meet each week to discuss student concerns, plan events, communicate ideas and concerns to the administration, and make policy recommendations.

Community members meet often to address issues on sexism, diversity, the state of the world, peace issues, and other current local and global issues. The administrators are supportive of the community when communicating their feelings, reactions, and opinions. Students and staff are particularly sensitive to environmental issues. For more than ten years Warren Wilson has been recycling on campus. Students work crews are responsible for all aspects of the program, which includes five drop-off sites in communities east of Asheville, as well as curbside pickup for campus buildings and residences. The College also sponsors an annual clean-up of the Swannanoa River, which runs through the campus, and carefully maintains its 700 acre forest, 25 miles of hiking trail, and a Class 11 whitewater course. Additionally, students and faculty have participated for more than twenty years in an excavation of a pre-historic Indian village located on the campus.

Warren Wilson College is currently cultivating an exciting new partnership wit the North Carolina Outward Bound program. A new, and already very popular major program in Outdoor Leadership has just been instituted. The partnership with Outward Bound, the new major, and the Discovery Through Wilderness program have been received with great enthusiasm from the greater Warren Wilson community.

In 1994 Warren Wilson was one of just ten colleges nationwide to have received a grant from the Council of Independent Colleges to incorporate it's community service program into a for-credit service learning program.

Taking advantage of the special heritage of its Southern Appalachian location, Warren Wilson offers a program of Appalachian music, including instruction in the more common instruments used in the genre. Students and staff join together to create an Appalachian String Band which performs for campus activities.

Warren Wilson affirms a commitment to spiritual growth and social responsibility by emphasizing the practical application of Christian convictions, while respecting other religious faiths and secular perspectives. Will McDowell, a current student, reflects: "Since I've been at Warren Wilson I've found with a little self-initiative there are no wall, only opportunities. Having served on committees, played intercollegiate sports, worked hundreds of hours and experienced close relationships with students, staff, and faculty, I've discovered that my view is only one of 600, making this community a whole."

On weekends, students stay on campus to enjoy a play, performance or music, see an art exhibit, go to dances, or create their own entertainment. The Outing Club, the largest club on campus, sponsors scheduled outdoor recreation trips each weekend with activities such as hiking, canoeing and rafting, rock climbing, mountain climbing, horse-back riding, cross-country skiing, and caving. The college's location just outside Asheville in the world famous Smokey Mountains provide many fascinating opportunities for students.

MAKING A DIFFERENCE STUDIES

Environmental Studies: Tracks in Environmental Analysis; Enviro Education; Enviro Policy; Forest Resource Conservation; Plant Biology & Horticulture; Wildlife Biology.

Horticulture	Conservation of Natural Resources
Forest Biology	Aquatic Ecology and Water Pollution
Community and Regional Studies	Environmental Issues for the 90's
Wilderness: Past and Prospects	Introduction to Environmental Education
Environmental Impact Assessment	Environmental Policy
Thinking Globally, Acting Locally	Wildlife Management

Methods and Materials in Environmental Education

- **Discovery Through Wilderness**   Students in their junior year may register for this interdisciplinary learning experience that involves extensive study of a geographical area which is largely wilderness. The course challenges participants to explore their personal limits and to integrate knowledge from several academic disciplines. In the classroom, students study the history, geology, politics, culture, ecology, and the resources of the region. The class then travels to the region for a month of camping and backpacking. Past trips have visited New England, Atlantic Canada, the Pacific Northwest, and Caribbean islands.

- Faculty Bio   **Dr. Mark V. Brenner** (B.S.U of Wisconsin - Stevens Point, M.S. and Ph.D. U of Washington) is the chair of Environmental Studies Department. Mark's specialty is aquatic ecology and the ecological effects of pollution. He has assisted a number of students in doing research projects related to aquatic ecology and pollution. Currently Mark is working with waste recycling research, composting techniques, and waste from aqua-culture. He feels that most waste is just resources out-of-place. For fun Mark plays on Warren Wilson's club volleyball team and he also leads the Discovery Through Wilderness - Pacific Northwest trip.

Biology

Field Natural History	Ecology
Field Ornithology	Animal Behavior
Evolution	Immunology and Infectious Disease
Plant Morphology	Special Topics in Biology

Peace Studies

Introduction to Peace & Conflict Studies	Special Topics in Peace Studies
Lifestyles of Nonviolence	Politics of Peace
Resolving Conflict: Global and Local	Current Issues of Peace and Justice: America

Social Work

The Aged: Issues and Interventions	Substance Abuse: Issues and Interventions
Social Welfare as a Social Institution	Human Behavior in the Social Environment
Micro-Practice: Individuals	Micro-Practice: Groups and Families
Field Instruction	Social Work in the International Community

Macro-Practice: Communities, Organizations, and Policy Development

- Faculty Bio **Dr. Deanna Morrow** (B.A. Catawba College; MAEd. Western Carolina U: MSW U of Georgia, Ph.D. North Carolina State) is a professor in the Social Work Department and is Director of the Social Work Program. Deanna's primary focus is teaching WWC students, but she also has a private counseling practice in the Asheville community. She volunteers with local community agencies as either a facilitator or board member. Deanna's special passions are jogging and hiking.

Intercultural Studies
Studies in this interdisciplinary field provide a foundation for further study and work in private or government international agencies, conflict resolution, and global development.

Economic Development	The Holocaust
Mahatma Gandhi	Worlds of Change
Human Behavior in Social Environment	Latin American Civilization
Global Issues	Social Work in the International Community
Intercultural Communication	Development Agencies at Home & Abroad
Poverty and the American City	Cross Cultural Field Study

- **International Development Practicum**   This course involves participation in a work-study service overseas field project of the international development program. Emphasizes providing a useful service to a local community program through use of appropriate skills.

History and Political Science

The Holocaust	Latin American Civilization
Civil War and Reconstruction	History of Black Experience in America.
Poverty and the American City	Politics of Developing States

American Immigrant Experience Thru Ethnic Literature
Mahatma Gandhi: Experiments With the Truth

Religion

Social Ethics in Story Theology	Eastern Religions
Religious America: Four Distinct Paths	Christ and Contemporary Culture

Heaven on Earth: Religious Lifestyles in 19th Century America

- **The Sacred/Secular Search** This course explores fundamental questions concerning the nature of religion. Eastern and Western religions, and innovative as well as traditional examples of religious practice are examined. Particular attention is paid to the relationship between "religious" and "secular" claims upon one's time and energy; diverse rivals for our "ultimate concern" are studied, whether or not they bear overt religious labels.

Appalachian Studies

Introduction to Appalachian Studies	Folk Tales and Storytelling
Appalachian Folk Arts	Appalachian Folk Medicine
Archaeological Field School	Native Americans of the Southeast
Southern Appalachian Term	

Outdoor Leadership	**Human Studies (Social Sciences)**
Philosophy	**Psychology**

3/2 Pre-forestry co-operative program with Duke University

Student Body: 33% state, 54% women, 46% men, 5% minority, 9% int'l, 22% transfer
1994-95 Comprehensive fees: $11,577 (after deduction for work)   Apply By 3/15

- Individualized Majors • Service-Learning Programs • Core/Multidisciplinary Classes
- Required Community Service • Work Program • Vegetarian & Vegan Meals

Use coupon in back to contact: Office of Admissions
Warren Wilson College
P.O. Box 9000   Asheville, NC 28815
(704) 298-3325   (800) 934-3536

WASHINGTON STATE UNIVERSITY

19,000 Students at four campuses   Pullman, Washington   Moderately Selective

Founded by the Legislature in 1890 as the state's land-grant university, Washington Sate University is today a four-campus university with a growing national reputation. WSU offers a liberal arts education balanced with practical instruction in professional and technical fields. Quality teaching and a special student experience in and out of the classroom are hallmarks of a WSU education.

The University includes the historic home campus in Pullman, a pleasant college town of 24,000 in the agriculturally rich Palouse region of southeast Washington, and three new campuses in Spokane, the Tri-Cities and Vancouver.

WSU has a number of unique programs that prepare students to make a difference in society. For example, the university offers:

- the nation's most comprehensive educational program in pollution prevention. Students learn to assess business and industrial practices to identify ways to keep pollution from occurring.
- a speech and hearing program aimed at training native American students to work with their own people,who have communication disorders at 5 to 15 times more often than the general population.
- sustainable agriculture and integrated pest management
- the Extended Degree Program, using various teaching technologies, that allows Washington residents in the rural areas of 16 counties to take junior and senior year courses to complete a bachelor's degree in social sciences.

In 1993, Money Magazine ranked WSU and just 14 other western universities as "Best Buys" for a college education. Among the other campuses named were UCLA, Cal Berkeley, and Stanford. At the same time, Money named WSU's Honors Program as one of the best eight at public universities in America, out of more than 435 such programs nationwide. The top honors programs offer "Ivy League quality at state school prices," the Money article said. Highly regarded academic programs include the famous Edward R. Murrow School of Communications with one of the country's top broadcasting programs; the biological sciences, especially biochemistry; the College of Veterinary Medicine, known for a commitment to animal well being; and sociology.

One of the state's two public research universities, WSU is known for teaching and research that makes a difference in people's lives, and the state's industries and professions. Current studies range from cancer prevention to analog-digital computer chips, disease-resistant crops to qualities of successful marriages, education reform to animal health. WSU faculty work in an array of developing countries on agricultural, animal health and educational projects to improve the quality of life.

International elements can be seen in many of WSU's academic programs. They are part of a comprehensive effort to increase student understanding of diverse cultures, economies, political systems and environments. A pair of world civilization courses, required for undergraduates students, is at the heart of WSU's nationally recognized core curriculum. WSU is one of the top universities in funding from the Agency for International Development.

MAKING A DIFFERENCE STUDIES

Environmental Science and Regional Planning
Environmental Science majors can specialize in agricultural ecology, human or cultural ecology, environmental education, environmental quality control, hazardous waste mgm't, natural resource mgm't systems, or resource mgm't. Regional planning majors specialize in natural & physical resources, planning, transportation & local government planning.

Topics in Radiation Safety
Environmental Impact Statement Analysis
Environmental Ethics
Environmental Policy
Environment and Human Life

Natural Resource Policy & Administration
Hazardous Waste Management
Human Issues in International Development
Economic Development&Underdevelopment
Advanced Resource Economics

Natural Resource Sciences
Intro to Natural Resources Mgm't
Conservation of Renewable Resources
Natural Resources and Society
Natural Resources Planning
Animal Population Dynamics

Forest and Range Plant Resources
Forest Biology
Wildlife Field Studies
Issues and Ethics in Natural Resources
Natural Resources Policy & Administration

- **Low Volume Forest Roads**   Road classification; design of forest roads, construction techniques, environmental considerations. Three days of field trips.

Bio-Agricultural Engineering -- Five Year Program
Conservation Engineering
Irrigation Engineering
Agricultural Processing and Environment
Drainage System Design

Global Agricultural Engineering
Soil and Water Engineering
Hydrology
Irrigation Water Requirement

Soil Resources and Land Use
Land use planning, soil conservation and sustainable agriculture.

Soil Conservation
Botany
Remote Sensing:Terrain Evaluation
General Ecology
Soil Microbial Ecology

World Agricultural Systems
Soil & Water Conservation and Management
Soil Analysis
Forestry Application /Airphoto Interpretation
Soil-Plant Relationships in Mineral Nutrition

Entomology   Integrated Pest Management
A multidisciplinary course of study sponsored by the Dep'ts of Crop and Soil Sciences, Entomology, Horticulture and Landscape Architecture and Plant Pathology. Holistic perspective and ecological understanding of the philosophy, principles, and practices of pest mgm't.

Pest Management Internship
Insects and People
Toxicology of Pesticides
Urban Entomology
Pest Mgm't in a Quality Environment
Pesticides and the Environment

Urban Entomology
Beekeeping
Photography for Entomologists
Insect Ecology
Systems of Integrated Pest Management
Biological Control: Arthropod Pests & Weeds

Landscape Architecture
The Built Environment
Landscape Architecture History
Principles of Planning
Remote Sensing of Soils
Plant Community Ecology

Plant Materials
Landscape Architecture Design
Land Inventory
Regional Landscape Inventory and Analysis
Computer Graphics

Civil and Environmental Engineering (Five year program)

Air Pollution Control Engineering
Soil Dynamics
Atmospheric Dynamics
Ethics and Professionalism
Environmental Geology
Hazardous Waste Treatment
Instrumental Analysis of Environmental Contaminants

Industrial Waste Problems
Water Resources Planning
Solid Waste Management and Design
Water and Wastewater Treatment
Fisheries Engineering
Environmental Engineering Unit Operations

History

History of Medicine
Native Peoples of Canada
History of Cuba & the Caribbean
History of Women in American West
Intro to South Asian Culture

North American Indian History
History of the Pacific Northwest
Politics of Developing Nations
Gandhi & 20th Century India
Cultural History in Latin America

Political Science

Comparative Public Policy
Human Issues in Int'l Development
Political Parties and Pressure Groups
Public Budgeting
Latin American Governments
Public Administration & Program Development in Developing Countries

Politics of Postindustrialized Nations
Civil Liberties
Gender and Politics
Canadian Political System
Politics of the Third World

Native American Studies

An interdisciplinary program intended to prepare the students to live knowledgeably and constructively in a pluralistic society in which the land was illegally appropriated from the first Americans.

Native Music of North America
Native American Literature
Indians of the Northwest
Native Peoples of North America
Inter-American Native Communities of North America

Native Peoples of Canada
American Before Columbus
Indians of the Southwest
Contemporary Native Peoples of the Americas

Child/Consumer/Family Studies

Patterns of Chicano Families
Family Housing Decisions
Families in Crises
Perspectives on Aging
Management Experiences With Families

Guidance of Young Children
The Child and Family in Poverty
Women in Management
Curriculum for Young Children's Programs
Adolescent and Early Adult Development

Asian American Studies   **Peace Studies**
Chicano Studies   **Women's Studies**   **Geology**
Natural Resources Mgm't: Tracks in Wildlife; Range; Forestry; Wildland Recreation

Student Body: 77% state, 47% women, 53% men, 9% minority, 8% int'l.
1994-95 Costs: Residents $6,707 Non resident $11,999   Apply by: 5/1
• Co-op Education   • Internships   • Study Abroad   • Service-Learning
• Nonresident Degree Program   • Vegetarian Meals

Use form in back to contact: Director of Admissions
Washington State University   Pullman, WA 99164
(509) 335-5586

WELLESLEY

2300 Women Students   Wellesley, Mass.   Most Selective

Wellesley College is an independent, residential, liberal arts college for women with an enrollment of 2340 students. Since opening its doors in 1875, Wellesley has been a community of scholars rich in cultural, religious and ethnic differences. Wellesley is a college for the serious student, one who has high aspirations. Understanding, respecting and learning from one another's heritage enriches the Wellesley student's experience. The Wellesley education is founded on the conviction that women can do anything. As a Wellesley senior put it, "To celebrate our diversity, to learn from our difference; that is the Wellesley legacy."

Wellesley has distinguished itself as a community where-re faculty and students feel a collegial link often lacking in larger institutions. The College's student-faculty ratio of 10 to 1 enables students to participate in research, in the preparation of professional papers and in similar academic experiences normally reserved for graduate students at other colleges. Wellesley's diversity is reflected strongly in the curriculum. Students may choose from more than 125 courses that fulfill the multicultural distribution requirement introduced by the College in 1990. The emphasis on concentrated, small-group learning, even in the first and second years maximizes student involvement and faculty attention. The enduring strength of a Wellesley education resides in the expansive foundation it establishes, the critical skills it

One of things that Wellesley can provide is an active community of role models, people who have met the challenges that are particular to women, Part of what draws and keeps the Wellesley community together is a graceful blend of tradition and contemporary life which characterizes the College in every aspect from academics to architecture. In addition to offering a strong liberal arts foundation, the College helps prepare women to succeed in an increasingly global society. Opportunities for career exploration are offered through the Shadow Program, volunteer/community service experiences and over 1,500 internship listings.

The Center for Research on Women was established in 1974. The Center's policy-oriented studies focus on women's education, employment, and family life. Extensive research is conducted on gender equity, curriculum change, childcare, mother/infant bonding, the effects of economic and social policies on women of all races and social classes, and women in the sciences.

At Wellesley, the possibilities are abundant for cultural and intellectual exchange, athletic activities, performance in the arts, political activism, religious observance, social service — and, of course, casual conversation, relaxation and fun. Cultural diversity provides an essential context for knowing oneself and understanding others. Most important of all, though, is the relationship that students develop with themselves at Wellesley. The academic journey they embark upon here allows students to find the very center of themselves, to define themselves in an atmosphere where their ideas are important, where women are significant role models, where each individual's gifts-are revealed and cherished.

MAKING A DIFFERENCE STUDIES

Peace Studies

Anthropology of Law and Justice
Urban Poverty
Politics of the World Food System
Human Rights
Gender, Culture and Political Change

Politics of Race Domination in South Africa
Contemplation and Action
Liberation Theology
European Resistance Movements in WW 11
Technology and Society in Third World

Women's Studies

Feminism and the Environment
Women, Social Policy and the State
The Body Politic
The Virgin Mary

Women's Lives Through Oral History
Asian Women in America
The Politics of Caring
Women in the Civil Rights Movement

Women and the African Quest for Modernization and Liberation

- **Women, Peace & Protest: Cross-Cultural Visions of Women's Actions** Women's participation in the movements of nuclear disarmament, human rights and social and economic justice. Under what circumstances gender becomes a central force in the development of these movements. Why and in what ways have women been central to the European peace movement; how has the involvement of women helped to define the human rights movement in Latin America?

First Year Cluster Program Construction of Self: Gender, Reproduction, Sexuality

Develops a sense of the relationship between materials and methods of different disciplines.
Gender and Genre in the Visual *Arts*   *Psychological* Perspectives on Sex & Gender
Spanish: Sexual and Literary Identity   *Biology* &Technology of Human Reproduction
Sociology :Fertility and Infertility: Importance of Children to Women in America
Women's: The Intersection of Sexuality, Gender and Culture

Political Science

Mass Media in American Democracy
Political Economy of the Welfare State
Gender, Culture, and Political Change
Politics of Health Care
Women, the Family and the State

Political Econ. of Dev. & Underdevelopment
The Military in Politics
Politics of the World Food System
Human Rights
Politics of Minority Groups in US

- **Ethics and Politics** Ethical issues in politics, public policy and the press. Is it permissable to lie? Does it matter who your friends are? Do some purposes justify deception, violence or torture? Proper role of journalists in upholding ethical standards.

Chinese Studies

Diverse Cultures of China
Introduction to Asian Religions
Buddhist Thought and Practice
Images of Women in Chinese Literature
Politics of East-West Relations

The Cultural Revolution in China
Political Economy of E. Asian Development
Democracy Movements in East Asia
China on Film
Tienanmen as History

Student Body: 16% state, 100% women, 33% minority, 6% int'l.
Faculty: 55% female, 45% male, 17% minority   Avg. students in a first year classroom: 20
1994-95 Costs: $24,860   Apply By 1/15
• Internships • Study Abroad • Individualized majors

Use form in back to contact: Director of Admissions
Wellesley College   Wellesley, MA 02181
(617) 235-0320

WESLEYAN UNIVERSITY

2,700 Students   Middletown, Connecticut

Wesleyan has long been known as an institution committed to preparing students with such a diverse education that they are poised to make a difference upon graduation. Sometimes dubbed "diversity university" for its long-standing commitment to a multicultural student body, Wesleyan's students also boast a diversity of ideas, interests, and viewpoints, as well as diverse socio-economic, geographic, and international backgrounds. The interaction of these factors on a small campus, coupled with top-notch academic departments, enables Wesleyan students to understand "the big picture". Wesleyan graduates are involved at all levels of public and private service, education, community organization, and academia.

The Center for Afro-American Studies (CAAS) sponsors a wide range of academic, social, and cultural events open to the entire university community. Established in 1974, the Center's annual roster of events includes a lecture series, jazz concerts, dance performances, art exhibits, a spring film series, and a Fellows Program designed to encourage students and faculty members to meet informally.

The Mansfield Freeman Center for East Asian Studies presents a continuing program of interesting exhibitions, concerts, courses, lectures, and special events. The Center is a place to meet distinguished visitors and faculty and to learn from first-hand observers about current political and cultural events, from the repercussions of Tiananmen Square to contemporary theater and philosophical trends. Majors in East Asian Studies are able to have a concentration on either China or Japan, but the societies and cultures of both countries are treated as an interrelated field of study. Most majors study abroad during their junior year, making it especially important to begin required language and history courses as early as possible.

Science and Technology in the 20th century have had an increasing impact on people's lives and on human societies. Along with this impact has come the realization that social, economic, and political factors in turn orient scientific and technical development. Wesleyan's Science in Society curriculum has been designed to help students explore systematically the interrelations between scientific knowledge, society, and the quality of human life.

Wesleyan's' Earth and Environmental Science department emphasizes field work on the coast and inlands of Connecticut, and is known for the cohesiveness that field experiments help create. Faculty have taken students to Central America, Newfoundland, Montana, Greece, Italy and elsewhere.

Students have been involved in a broad range of internships in hospitals, museums, television stations, architectural firms, publishing companies, and educational institutions. The College Venture Program places students for 3-6 months in positions such as advocate for the homeless, research assistant, and teaching.

All students are encouraged to become involved with the local community and to use the Office of Community Service as a resource for volunteer opportunities. The OCS supports for student-run tutoring programs, and offers mini-grants to students who create programs for local children, and sponsors service projects.

MAKING A DIFFERENCE STUDIES

Earth and Environmental Science
Physical Geology: Our Dynamic Earth
Geology of Connecticut
Coastal and Estuarine Environments
Invertebrate Paleontology
Water Resources

Introductory Oceanography
Environmental Geology Seminar
Principles of Geobiology
Coral Reef Ecology & Geology (in Belize)
Global Change

Science in Society
Philosophy of Science
Sociology of Health and Illness
Policy Implementation
Sociology of Science and Technology
Discourse, Text and Gender: A Feminist Methodology?

History of Scientific Though to 1700
Myths and Paradigms
Cultural Studies of Scientific Knowledge
Public Policy Analysis

Women's Studies
Areas of study include Women and History, Gender in Cross-Cultural Context, Gender
and Society, Gender and Representation, and Science and Gender.
Feminist Ethics
Women in History and Memoir
Domesticity & Gender-Mid 19th Century
Modernity, Gender and War
Psychology of Gender: Cultural and Historical Perspective

The Newest Minority
Feminism in Global Perspective
Women, Health and Technology
Women and Political Power

Government
The Moral Basis of Politics
Unheavenly Cities
Educational Policy
Caring, Rights, and Welfare
Conflict in the Middle East

Urban Politics
Strategies of Political Mobilization
Expert Knowledge & Political Accountability
Comp. Welfare States in Europe & America
Arms Control and Global Security

Afro-American Studies
Interdisciplinary major offers broad knowledge of the life of blacks in US & Caribbean
Education and the Urban Poor
Making the Underclass
Black Politics in Urban America
Toni Morrison
Power and Poverty in Postindustrial Cities

Religions of Afro-American Peoples
Women of Color and Identity
Race, Gender and Ethnicity in America
Other than Black and White
Education and the Urban Poor

East Asian Studies
Introduction to East Asian Music
Traditional China
Taoism: Visionaries and Interpreters
Salvation and Doubt
Japanese Film & Japanese Society

Japanese Literature 1700-1945
Tibetan Buddhism
Twentieth Century Japan
Women in Buddhist Literature
Politics & Political Development in China

Student Body: 10% state, 51% women, 49% men, 27% students of color
1994-95 costs: $25,520   Apply by 1/15
• Co-op Education   • Study Abroad   • Individualized Majors   • Vegetarian Meals

Use form in back to contact: Dean of Admissions
Wesleyan University   Middletown, CT 06457
(203) 347-9411

WESTERN WASHINGTON UNIVERSITY
FAIRHAVEN COLLEGE

330 Students   Bellingham, Washington   Moderately Selective

At Fairhaven, students are challenged to bring what they learn to bear on human concerns and crucial real world problems, to experiment, to discover, and to act. This style of education supports the development of certain values and practical skills: discipline, resourcefulness, initiative, flexibility and adaptability. Fairhaven is committed to curriculum integration: that is, courses are expected to use a gender-conscious and multi-cultural approach to topics, resources and classroom practice. Fairhaven students take, on the average, about half their classes from other departments within WWU. Fairhaven is an experimenting college where innovative teaching methods and varied classroom structures are welcomed. The interdisciplinary curriculum emphasizes relationships between disciplines. Important emerging studies are discussed along with and in relation to traditional knowledge. Vital aspects of Fairhaven are the love of learning and passions for social and cultural renewal.

The Fairhaven Interdisciplinary Concentration provides an opportunity for developing an individually designed major for the B.A. or B.A. in Education degrees. Some concentrations recently completed by Fairhaven college students include: Native Cultures and Nutrition; Spiritual Ecology; Wetlands Assessment and Policy; Studies in Power: Women, Law and Policy.

MAKING A DIFFERENCE STUDIES

The following are areas of concentration, rather than majors.

History, Culture and Society

Television and Media: A Critique
Political Economy and Status of Women
Indian History/Federal Policy
The US in Central America

Sexual Minorities
The Philosophy of Nonviolence
Third World Women & Econ. Development
Origins of Consciousness

Curers, Clients and Culture: Cross-Cultural Perspectives on Health & Illness
Women, Ideas and Change: A History of Feminist Thoughts and Actions

Nature, Science and the Environment

Organic Gardening
Current Environmental Topics
Regional Ecologies

Patterns in Nature
Feminist Science
Frontiers

Human Development, Personal Identity and Socialization

Awareness Through the Body
Death and Dying

Personal Empowerment
Men and Identity

Adult Development in Women: Choices and Conflict

Arts, Self-Expression & Creativity

Inward Journey
American Culture in the Video Age

Dreams, Imagination and Creativity
Art and Society

- **Shamanism: Healers, Visionaries and Dreamers** Cross-cultural comparison of the roles, recruitment, techniques and performances of shamans, those ceremonial practitioners who move in a state of ecstacy between various spiritual realms.

WESTERN WASHINGTON UNIVERSITY
Huxley College of Environmental Studies

As we approach the beginning of the 21st century, it is clear that one of the responsibilities of colleges and universities is to help society become aware of environmental problems and issues. A new synthesis of knowledge is needed that is global in its frame of reference, interdisciplinary in its character and experimental in its work.

Huxley College contends that the more people know about their environment in its interdependent detail, the better they will be able to make decisions relative to a quality of life that depends on the environment. To this end the College teaches and researches, in an interdisciplinary and systematic way, the complex issues and problems of the natural environment and its social overlay. Huxley is a gathering place and focus for those genuinely concerned about environmental well-being of the earth.

Environmental studies at Huxley centers on three academic majors: environmental science, environmental policy and assessment, and environmental education. Studies in these areas allow students to pursue specialization or breadth, to acquire a synthesis of environmental knowledge and to develop skills applicable to careers or further advanced study.

At Huxley, faculty staff and students alike work to create a teaching-learning environment that reflects the ideals and values of personal communication, independent learning, new approaches to education and a sense of community. Students often attend faculty meetings, co-sponsor seminars with faculty members, and work with faculty and staff on decision-making College committees.

Huxley College was created in 1968 to develop programs of environmental studies that reflect a broad view of man in a physical, biological, social and cultural world. Most of Huxley's courses are at the junior and senior levels. Lower-division preparation may be completed at WWU or at another institution. Admission to Huxley is through WWU. Huxley courses and seminars are open to all students at WWU.

Huxley's common requirements consist of five core courses; Huxley seminars; and the choice of a senior thesis, a senior project or an internship. The core courses provide a common background of environmental concepts, knowledge and perspectives. Recent seminars include: Bioregionalism: Cultural Approaches to Environmental Problems; The U.S. High-Level Radioactive Waste Program; and The Media and the Environment. The Senior Project may be a creative or community project such as writing of a children's book on ecology or the establishment of an interpreted nature trail. Recent examples of internships include work with Olympic National Forest, Wolf Hollow Wildlife Rehabilitation Center, Environmental Resource Services, State Legislatures, and National Parks.

The Institute for Environmental Toxicology and Chemistry provides opportunities for research and education of the effects of toxic substances on aquatic and terrestrial species, and the Institute for Watershed Studies provides opportunity and specialized equipment for freshwater and watershed studies. The Leona M. Sundquist Marine Laboratory on Fidalgo Island, within easy traveling distance of the campus, provides facilities for marine students.

MAKING A DIFFERENCE STUDIES

Environmental Studies

Environmental Systems
Human Ecology
Environmental Decision-Making
Current Forest Practices in Washington

Environmental Pollution
Environmental Ethics
Coastal Ecosystems Management
U.S. High-Level Radioactive Waste Program

Bioregionalism: Cultural Approaches to Environmental Problems

Environmental Science

Ecology
Environmental Physiology & Biochemistry
Air Pollution
Water Quality Lab

Introduction to Environmental Toxicology
Energy & Energy Resources
Environmental Impact Assessment
Conservation of Biological Diversity

Environmental Policy and Assessment

Leaders of politico-economic systems, awakening to world-wide dangers as resource depletion, desertification, climate change, population growth, and urban blight and congestion
are beginning to realize that during the coming few decades great political and economic
reforms may have to be made.

Alternative Energy Sources and Systems
Social Impact Assessment
Environmental Impact Assessment
Environmental Risk Management
Conflict Resolution of Current Issues

Modeling Alternative Futures
Environmental Design: Processes & Problems
Effects of Global Climate Change
Comparative & Int'l Environmental Policies
The History of Conservation in America

Outdoor Education and Interpretation

Environmental Education
Environmental Interpretation
Adventure Programming and Leadership
The Writings of American Naturalists

The Environmental Education Curriculum
Outdoor Education
Experiential Learning in Environmental Ed
History of the Concept of Nature

Environmental Studies/Economics

Resource Economics
Economics, The Environment, & Nat. Res.
Environmental Ethics
Environmental Impact Assessment

Environmental Economics
US Environmental Policy
Comparative & Int'l Environmental Policies
Environmental Risk Management

- **Multinational Corporations and Global Ecology** The character, functions and values
  of multinational corporations. Assessment of impacts of such companies on Third
  World economies and environments and the economy of the U.S.

Marine Biology   **Environmental Studies/Journalism**
Mass Communication and Environmental Education Option
B.A. in Education/ Environmental Studies (Elementary)

WWU Student Body: 94% state, 55% women, 45% men, 6% minority
1994-95 costs: Residents $6550   Non-residents $12,268   Apply By: 3/1

Use form in back to contact: Director of Admissions
Western Washington University   Bellingham, WA
(206) 650-3440

YALE UNIVERSITY

5,217 Undergraduates   New Haven, Connecticut   Most Selective

Yale welcomes students who will take advantage of its resources and contribute to its community. The wide range of racial, religious, cultural, and socioeconomic backgrounds within the undergraduate population creates a remarkable exchange of ideas.

In a class of 1,300 students from all over North America and the world, everyone at Yale encounters difference and is challenged in his or her assumptions and beliefs. The student body is also large and diverse enough that all students can find the support they need to develop and articulate their concerns. The subsequent dialogue and exchange has enlightening, and often unexpected, results.

Students at Yale learn about being part of a larger community, and that community extends beyond the campus to include New Haven, a city whose roots the stretch back to the 1600's. More than 50 percent of the student body is involved in volunteer work in the community. Yale students participate in the cultural, recreational and political opportunities the city offers, and many work in local educational and cultural centers, offices, and businesses.

Among major universities Yale is distinctive for the number of courses with comparatively small enrollments. About 85 percent of its 2,000 courses register fewer than twenty-five students. Equally important, the professors at Yale are dedicated to undergraduate teaching. From the most widely respected senior professors to young aspiring scholars, they share their passion and extensive knowledge in classes and in one-on-one conversations during weekly office hours. The quality of the student-faculty relationship at Yale is often cited as one of the College's most important strengths.

Students at Yale are not in competition with one another; every student's course of study is self-selected and unique. Without requiring specific courses, Yale asks that each student take a broad sampling of courses across the humanities, arts, sciences, and social sciences. A course selection period at the beginning of each semester and the Credit/D/Fail option encourage exploration of new subjects and approaches. Yale's extensive array of academic resources and facilities offers undergraduates unparalleled opportunities to explore and learn. With its combination of breadth and depth, a Yale education starts students on a path of learning that lasts throughout their lives.

Yale stays abreast of new philosophies of education and recognizes that, in today's complex world, people need to develop a broad cultural and ethical awareness. Several interdisciplinary majors at Yale respond to these and other issues: International Studies focuses on socioeconomic, environmental, and political changes in our planet; "area studies," such as Latin American Studies, examine the language, literature, and political and social history of major areas; and Ethics, Politics, and Economics examines the institutions, practices, and politics that shape our world. Within many majors there are "tracks" for students interested in special subtopics, such as the new Geology track, Earth, Environment and Resources.

Each of Yale's 5,100 undergraduates belongs to a residential community that offers the close-knit environment of a small school. All incoming students are assigned to one of twelve residential "colleges" before they arrive freshman year.

Because they live together for four years, the members of each college (400 people on average) know one another well and contribute to making each community unique. The residential colleges sponsor numerous academic and extracurricular programs including musical performances, dramatic productions, visiting fellowships and full-credit academic seminars. Yale students interact with faculty in a variety of ways through the colleges: faculty "fellows" participate in the life of the college by advising students, eating meals in the dining hall, and sometimes living in the college. Yale students quickly learn how easy and rewarding it is to approach professors both as people and as scholars. The residential colleges provide a structure that makes Yale unique among its contemporaries. By offering a small community of students and faculty, as well as extracurricular and academic opportunities, the residential colleges create the intimacy of a small school to complement the vast resources of the surrounding university.

Qualifications for admissions to Yale include not only the reasonable well-defined areas of academic achievement and special skills in nonacademic areas, but also the less tangible qualities of capacity for involvement, commitment, and personal growth.

Yale students have a tradition of civic activism. Each semester Dwight Hall coordinates 2,000 undergraduate volunteers, the largest organization of its kind in the country, as students actively address critical social issues such as hunger, homelessness, poverty, concerns of the elderly, and weaknesses in the educational system. Student volunteers work with local children as tutors, big sibs, or group leaders, or they volunteer at agencies involved with the elderly, with environmental or political issues, or with legal assistance and community-organizing efforts. Yale undergraduates over the years have founded many significant community local agencies, many of which have grown into independent institutions. New Haven Halfway House, Community Soup Kitchen, and Columbus House for the Homeless are just a few examples.

A large number of organizations reflect the energy and diversity of the minority communities at Yale. Among the most active are the Black Student Alliance, The Asian American Students Association, Despierta Boricua, an organization for Puerto Rican students, Movimiento Estudiantil Chican de Aztlan, and the Alliance of Native Americans at Yale. Three cultural centers house these and other organizations and provide space for meetings, plays, art exhibits, and parties. These centers foster a sense of cultural identity and educate people in the larger community; they also act as social centers and community bases for students of different ethnic and cultural backgrounds, supplementing the social environment of the larger, pluralistic community.

Yale's diverse and energetic population supports a remarkable variety of extracurricular organizations and activities. More than 200 social, political, cultural, and special interest groups provide forums for students to express opinions about campus, national, and international issues. Many students join organizations that focus on a single issue such as Amnesty International, the Beyond War Project, Coalition for Soviet Jewry, and the Student Environmental coalition.

Student-run club sports provide an important resource, including many activities such as mountain climbing, fishing, kayaking, biking, sailing, skiing, trap and skeet, rugby and ultimate frisbee.

MAKING A DIFFERENCE STUDIES

Ethics, Politics and Economics
Constructive responses to natural and social hazards, allocation of limited social resources (medical care), or morally sensitive political issues (affirmative action), require close knowledge of their political, economic,and social dimensions, and a capacity to think rigorously about the basic questions they raise.

Classics of Ethics, Politics & Economics
Culture and Social Criticism
Enviro. & Development in Third World
Comparative Political-Economic Systems
Welfare Economics, Social Choice and Political Theory

Liberalism and It's Critics
Ethics in International Relations
Gender, Race, and the State in America
The Poltics of Parental Authority

Economics
Labor Econmics
Economics of Developing Countries
The Economics of Population
Int'l Trade, Development & Environment
Economic Problems of Latin America

Health& Social Consequences of Econ. Devlp't
Economics of Natural Resources
Topics in Labor Economics
Corporation & State in 20th Cent. Capitalism
From Plan to Market in Russia & E. Europe

History
War and Society in the U.S.
American Labor in the 20th Century
The Balkan Lands and Peoples
Colonial Latin America
The U.S. in Viet Nam
Excellence & Equity: Competing Goals in American Education

China in Western Minds
The Holocaust in Historical Perspective
Amer. Missionaries & W. African Christianity
New Deal Liberalism and It's Critics
Suburbanization of America: Social History

Literature
Identity & the Landscape in Literature
Science and Literature
Self-Representation and Technology
Art and Ideology
Postcolonial Literatures

Modern French Feminisms
Cultural Perspec tives in Chinese Literature
The Problem of Evil
The Writing of History After the Holocaust
Problems in Cultural Criticism

- **Totalitarian Humanity: Lit & History** Study of ideological-totalitarian regimes of the twentieth century in which intellectuals and artists played a visible role both of support and of defiance. Focus on Soviet terror and the Jewish Holocaust as well as on Yugoslavia. Nationalism, linguistic culture, utopian ideologies, terror and resistance....

Political Science
Multinationals and the State
Ethics in International Relations
Public Opinion
Poltics of National Security and Law
Political Economy of East Asian Newly Industrialized Countries

Intelligence and Covert Operations
Environment & Development in Third World
The U. N. & the Maintenace of Int'l Security
Religion & Politics in Comparative Perspective

Women's Studies   Anthropology   Psychology   Geology & Geophysics

Student Body: 10% state, 48% women, 52% men, 32% minority, 5% int'l
1994-95 costs: $26,3501   Apply By: 12/31
• Individualized Majors • Core/Multidisciplinary Classes • Team Teaching •Vegetarian/Vegan Meals

Use form in back to contact: Office of Undergraduate Admissions
Yale University   POB 1502A   New Haven, CT 06520
(203) 432-1900

Graduation Pledge of Environmental and Social Responsibility

I, _____ pledge to thoroughly
investigate and take into account the
social and environmental consequences of
any job opportunity I consider.

This voluntary graduation oath, first started by students at Humboldt State University, California, is now an offical part of graduation ceremonies at colleges and universities throughout the United States.

BIBLIOGRAPHY AND RESOURCES

Au Sable Institute of Environmental Studies promotes the care and keeping of the whole Creation, through summer and intersession college-level courses and programs in ecology, restoration ecology, conservation biology, field studies, environmental science, environmental ethics and land stewardship. Au Sable operates as a community based on Christian teachings and practice. Surrounded by forest, wetlands, lakes and rivers, participants take courses, gain field experience, and develop practical tools for environmental stewardship. Persons enrolled in the Institute remain students at their home institution. Most enroll through accredited "Participating Colleges," or through colleges and seminaries.
Au Sable Institute   7526 Sunset Trail NE   Mancelona, MI 49659 (818) 567-8888

Campus Daze, Easing the Transition from High School to College George Gibbs
Octameron Press, 1993 (703) 836-5480

California Institute of Integral Studies Primarily a graduate school whose mission is the integration of the intellectual, the spiritual, and the practical spheres of life, CIIS does offer a Bachelor of Arts Completion. program. CIIS is committed to an integral approach to education and encourages multiple ways of learning and knowing, values both cultural diversity and cultural coherence, supports community, commits to world, and offers an innovative curriculum. Their Women's Spirituality M.A. program is the only one in the nation.
CIIS 765 Ashbury St, San Francisco, CA 94117 (415) 753-6100 x 459 or x 460.

Center for Global Education, Augsburg College "Bringing people face to face with others struggling for justice and human dignity." The center was established with a commitment to providing education that expands students' world view and deepens their understanding of issues related to global justice and liberation. Experiential programs in Europe, Southern Africa and Mexico explore "Global Issues and World Churches," "Social Policy and Human Services in Latin America," "Women and Development - Latin American Perspectives," "Int'l Development and Human Rights in Latin America," Sothern African Societies in Transition: The View From Namibia," and "Women and Development: A Southern Africa Perspective."
CGE, Augsburg College   731 21st Ave S. Minneapolis, MN 55454 (612) 330-1159

ECO - The Environmental Careers Organization is a national, non-profit organization, offering paid, short-term environmental positions for senior undergraduates and other entry-level environmental job seekers. They sponsor environmental career conferences, seminars, workshops and advising through their Environmental Career Services. They publish **The New Complete Guide to Environmental Careers** Island Press, 1993, an important resource for environmental job hunting. Contains advice from working professionals, planning you education, breaking in to the profession.

Global Routes is a non-profit organization commited to offering experiences that allow people with different world views to engage eachother in creating a global community. Global Routes designs educational service projects and internships that allow students of all ages to extend themselves by living and working with people in communities throughout the world. Appropriate grassroots community development in Central and Latin America, South and Southeast Asia, Afica, and wlsewhere is at the core of these experiences. While college credit is not offered by GR, students are often able to obtain it through their own schools.
Global Routes   5554 Broadway Oakland, CA 94618   (510) 655-0371

Green Corps, Field School for Environmental Organizing trains college students who have an interest in organizing as a career. Training includes advocacy organizing, case studies of organizing problems, skills and training clinics, working case study, campaign trainings and lectures regarding environmental problems. Green Corps organizers are located in more than 30 cities throughout the US, with offices at many colleges.
Green Corps 1109 Walnut St, 4th fl,Philadelphia, PA 19107 (215) 829-1760

Great Careers: The 4th of July Guide to Careers, Internships and Volunteer Opportunities in the Non-Profit Sector Dean Smith, Editor, Garrett Park Press, 1990

Guide to Careers and Graduate Education in Peace Studies $4.50 from PAWSS, Hampshire College, Amherst, MA 01002 Information on internships, fellowships...

Letting Go: A Parents Guide to Today's College Experience Karen Levin Coburn and Madge Lawrence Treeger, Adler and Adler, 1988 Help for parents of new college students.

Non-Profit Job Finder Details on over 1,000 sources of jobs, internships, and grant opportunities in education, social service, environment, religion, research, fund raising and dozens of other fields. Daniel Lauber Planning/Communications 1992 (708) 366-5200

Student Conservation Association helps colleges students find volunteer positions as professional assistants in national and state parks, national forest and wildlife refuges throughout the U.S. (including Alaska, Hawaii, the Virgin Islands, and Puerto Rico). Students serve for 3-4 months, gain valuable training and field experience while providing needed help for resource managers with budget/staffing constraints. Volunteers are provided with funds to cover travel and food expenses plus free housing. SCA publishes *Earth Work*, a monthly magazine for individuals seeking employment in the conservation community. SCA PO Box 550 Charlestown, NH 03603-0550 (603) 826-4301

Student Pugwash USA is a national, non-profit educational organization providing university and select high school students with a range of programs to prepare them to better understand the social and ethical implications of science and technology. They sponsor biennial international conferences for a week of intensive deliberation. SP has chapters at over 25 colleges and universities, which organize over 100 educational events annually. They publish *New Careers Directory of Jobs and Internships in Technology and Society*, have alternative job fairs, and promote mentor relationships with concerned professionals. Student Pugwash 1638 R St. NW, Ste 32 Washington, D.C. 20009 (800) WOW-A-PUG

Study Abroad, 1992-1994 Describes 4,000 study abroad programs, also offers information on financial aid. $24 UNESCO 1991 To order call (800) 545-2005

Time Out, Taking a Break from School to Travel, Work and Study in the U.S. & Abroad Robert Gilpin, and Caroline Fitzgibbons. Simon and Shuster 1992. Everything high school and college students need to know to plan and enjoy a break from school

Travel Programs in Central America Paul Revier, Ellie Zucker, eds. 1993 San Diego Interfaith Task Force on Central America, POB 3843, La Mesa, CA 91944 Study abroad programs, environmental, human rights, service programs. $8 (619) 698-1150

Western Institute for Social Research WIRS's programs are designed to provide community-involved adults with with learning opportunities, combining academic theory and research with experience-based knowledge to help them develop satisfying careers while providing leadership toward educational innovation and community improvement. Students and faculty are committed to changing today's oppressive patterns of race and gender relations, of wealth and poverty, of extreme power and powerlessness, in peaceful and constructive ways. B.A. and M.A. degree programs. WISR 3220 Sacramento Ave. Berkeley, CA 94702 (510) 655-2830

Whole Work Catalog Resources for career directions, descriptions of hundreds of books on careers from women's to disabled... *free* from New Careers Center (800) 634-9024

STATE BY STATE INDEX

Alabama
University of Alabama at Tuscaloosa
Alaska
SheldonJackson College
University of Alaska at Fairbanks
Arizona
Arizona State University
Prescott College
California
California State Polytech U, Pomona
CA. State U -- Sacramento / San Francisco
Humboldt State University
New College of California - World College Inst.
Pitzer College
Rudolf Steiner Institute
University of CA, Davis
University of CA, Santa Cruz
Colorado
Colorado College
Colorado State University
Naropa Institute
University of Colorado at Boulder
Connecticut
Wesleyan University
Yale College
Florida
New College of University of South Florida
Hawaii
University of Hawaii at Manoa
Illinois
Southern Illinois Univ. at Carbondale
Indiana
Earlham College
Goshen College
Manchester College
Iowa
Grinnell College
Kansas
Bethel College
Kentucky
Berea College
Maine
College of the Atlantic
University of Maine at Orono
Massachusetts
Clark University
Tufts University
Wellesley College
Michigan
Eastern Michigan State
Kalamazoo College
Minnesota
Bemidji State University
Carleton College
St. Olaf College
University of Minnesota at Minneapolis
New Jersey
Rutgers State - Cook College

New Mexico
Armand Hammer United World College
University of New Mexico
New York
Cornell University
Eugene Lang College
Hobart & William Smith College
Iona College
Long Island U --Friends World / Southampton
Rochester Institute of Technology
Sarah Lawrence
State U of NY - Environmental Science & Forestry
North Carolina
Guilford College
Warren Wilson College
North Dakota
University of North Dakota
Ohio
Antioch College
Oberlin College
Ohio Wesleyan University
Oregon
University of Oregon at Eugene
Pennsylvania
Bryn Mawr
California Univ. of Pennsylvania
Juniata College
Penn State University
Rhode Island
Brown University
Vermont
Goddard College
Institute for Social Ecology
Marlboro College
Middlebury College
School for International Training
Sterling College
University of Vermont
Virginia
Eastern Mennonite College
Washington
Bastyr College
The Evergreen State College
University of Washington
Washington State University
Western Washington U - Fairhaven / Huxley
Wisconsin
Beloit
Northland College
University of Wisconsin --Stevens Point

Field Programs
Audubon Expedition Institute
GAIA / Geocommons Program
International Honors Program
School for Field Studies
Sierra Institute

ABOUT THE EDITOR

Miriam Weinstein lives with two of her four children in San Rafael, California. She has an avid interest in education. She studied a great deal about many philosophies of education from elementary level through college for her children, as well as herself. She has been active in environmental and social causes since her teenage years. She is the former director of the Eco Design & Builders Guild, a co-op marketing group she founded in 1991 comprised of ecologically and health minded architects, electricians, builders and natural building consultants, environmental health consultants, suppliers of environmentally safe building materials, landscapers etc. to educate professionals and the public and each other about ecological and healthy building. Ms. Weinstein produced "The Good Home, An Eco/Healthy Building Conference" the "Building For Your Health Conference". Her background is in environmental business and marketing and healthy building materials consulting.

YES, *I WANT TO MAKE A DIFFERENCE*

Please send me more information about your school. I am interested in:

☐ Academic programs in _____
_____

☐ Extracurricular programs in _____
_____

☐ Other _____
_____

☐ Please send me financial aid information
☐ I will be entering _____
☐ I am a transfer student

Name _____
Address _____
City _____ State _____ Zip _____

YES, *I WANT TO MAKE A DIFFERENCE*

Please send me more information about your school. I am interested in:

☐ Academic programs in _____
_____

☐ Extracurricular programs in _____
_____

☐ Other _____
_____

☐ Please send me financial aid information
☐ I will be entering _____
☐ I am a transfer student

Name _____
Address _____
City _____ State _____ Zip _____

YES, I WANT TO MAKE A DIFFERENCE

Please send me more information about your school. I am interested in:

- ☐ Academic programs in _____
  _____
- ☐ Extracurricular programs in _____
  _____
- ☐ Other_____
  _____

- ☐ Please send me financial aid information
- ☐ I will be entering _____
- ☐ I am a transfer student

Name _____
Address _____
City _____ State _____ Zip_____

YES, I WANT TO MAKE A DIFFERENCE

Please send me more information about your school. I am interested in:

- ☐ Academic programs in _____
  _____
- ☐ Extracurricular programs in _____
  _____
- ☐ Other_____
  _____

- ☐ Please send me financial aid information
- ☐ I will be entering _____
- ☐ I am a transfer student

Name _____
Address _____
City _____ State _____ Zip_____

YES, I WANT TO MAKE A DIFFERENCE

Please send me more information about your school. I am interested in:

☐ Academic programs in _____

_____

☐ Extracurricular programs in _____

_____

☐ Other_____

_____

☐ Please send me financial aid information
☐ I will be entering _____
☐ I am a transfer student

Name _____

Address _____

City _____State _____Zip_____

YES, I WANT TO MAKE A DIFFERENCE

Please send me more information about your school. I am interested in:

☐ Academic programs in _____

_____

☐ Extracurricular programs in _____

_____

☐ Other_____

_____

☐ Please send me financial aid information
☐ I will be entering _____
☐ I am a transfer student

Name _____

Address _____

City _____State _____Zip_____

ORDER FORM

❑ Please send me _____ additional copies of
Making A Difference College Guide.

    ❑ I am enclosing a check for $12.95 per copy, plus $2.50 for shipping (add'l copies $1.50 each shipping) plus applicable sales tax for CA. residents.

❑ Please send an order form for **Making A Difference Graduate Guide** as soon as it is available.

    ❑ Please bill my Mastercard/Visa account # _____

Signature_____ Expiration Date_____

Name_____ PO#_____

Address_____

City, State, Zip _____

Please send the person named below information about
❑ Making A Difference College Guide
❑ Making A Difference Graduate Guide

Name_____

Address_____

City, State, Zip _____

Please make checks payable to:
SAGE PRESS
524 San Anselmo Ave. #225
San Anselmo, CA 94960

_____ copies at $12.95 _____
shipping _____
tax for CA. residents _____
total _____